Leif Jerram was born in Woolwich in south-east London in 1971, and lived there until he went to study history at university. After having lived in San Diego, Bremen, Munich, and Paris, he completed his PhD in Manchester—the first industrial city. There he has remained, barring brief stints at Selwyn College, Cambridge, and Keele University. He is currently Senior Lecturer in Urban History in the Department of History at Manchester University. He has published widely in the field of cultural and urban history, including most recently *Germany's Other Modernity: Munich and the Making of Metropolis, 1895–1930* (2007).

Streetlife

The Untold History of Europe's Twentieth Century

LEIF JERRAM

OXFORD
UNIVERSITY PRESS

OXFORD

UNIVERSITY PRESS

Great Clarendon Street, Oxford, OX2 6DP,
United Kingdom

Oxford University Press is a department of the University of Oxford.
It furthers the University's objective of excellence in research, scholarship,
and education by publishing worldwide. Oxford is a registered trade mark of
Oxford University Press in the UK and in certain other countries

British Library Cataloguing in Publication Data

Data available

Library of Congress Cataloging in Publication Data

Data available

ISBN 978-0-19-280707-6 (Hbk.)
ISBN 978-0-19-967116-8 (Pbk.)

Printed in Great Britainby
Clays Ltd., St Ives plc

2 4 6 8 10 9 7 5 3 1

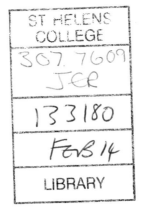

Acknowledgements

It is a cliché, but true nonetheless, that the number of people who built this project with me are too numerous to name, and the ones that don't get named often helped most of all.

But for helping conceive of the project, Katherine Reeve and Richard Evans earn my sincere thanks; Richard has supported me throughout my career. And in helping with the delivery, Matthew Cotton and Luciana O'Flaherty were patient, supportive, tactful, and wise. Peter Fisher helped more than he might realize. Dino Soteriou kept me saner than I otherwise would have been for much of it. My mum has always kept the faith, but with a healthy scepticism; our cities have too many conspicuous citizens whose mums do not. It really makes the difference.

Patient and helpful readers wound me back in from saying unwise things, or wise things (if there are any in here) badly. Many were former students, like James Greenhalgh and Mathew Wintercross; some were friends and family, like Sarah Gaskell, Bruno Auer, and my sister, Georgia; others were colleagues, like Selina Todd and Simon Gunn. Simon, in particular, has never flagged in his enthusiastic support for everything I've ever tried—I am not alone in wishing to offer him thanks. Many of my colleagues would join me. Academics thank too little, and squabble too much. It is a symptom, perhaps, of so little being at stake in so many of our debates. By contrast, Simon is generous to all he meets.

Finally, huge thanks go to my students at the Universities of Manchester and Keele. Their enthusiastic commitment to my courses, and the insightful primary research of their own, taught me so much. For all the times they said, 'Why?' or 'That doesn't add up' or 'What on earth are you talking about?' or 'I don't get it' or 'How do you know?', I thank them. Without them, I wouldn't even try to do the job, let alone be able to.

Leif Jerram
Manchester, 2011

Contents

List of Figures

Introduction

The Untold History of Europe's Twentieth Century

There is a familiar history of the twentieth century—almost comforting in its familiarity, despite its triumphs, drama and tragedy. There is a well-known history of 'great individuals'—Adenauer and Lloyd George, Curie and Pankhurst, Clemenceau and Gorbachev, Stalin and Hitler, Franco and Mussolini. And there is a history of the great movements of nameless individuals, invisibly harnessed to some profound evolving truth: the rise of democracy, of women, of rationalism, of capitalism, of socialism, or of secularization; or the fall of communism, child mortality, or of empires.

But the real drama of history happens where the two worlds collide— where the nameless individual in the crowd meets the great man (or woman). What did the tsar care what the workers of No 6 Shop, Trubochnyi Metal Works in St Petersburg thought? Not much, perhaps. But he would certainly come to care, when they went on strike in 1916 and 1917, destroyed his world, and transformed global politics for our times. As for the people dancing wildly to 'black' jazz in the cellars of wartime Hamburg and Berlin, what did they care about the racial policies of Hitler, Goering, and Heydrich being decided in Berlin in the summer and autumn of 1941? A great deal, it would seem, for dancing to 'black' music in a racist state was a clear rejection of a certain set of ideas—a rejection expressed in the movements of their bodies and the smiles on their faces, but not in the ballot box. We need to tell a different story of a messy continent in a messy century. We have to give up our familiar tidy frameworks and neat narratives. If we want to find the point of encounter, and witness the rendezvous between big and small, we have to start thinking about *where* the twentieth century happened. We have to look at its streetlife.

If we want to find the 'scene of the crime' of the continent's history in the twentieth century, we have to think wisely about where we put our hide, and how we manage the stakeout. The best place to observe the encounter between big and small is the city, and the myriad nooks and crannies, back streets and thoroughfares, clubs and bars, living rooms and factories that made them up. Cities matter, because in the nineteenth century, mankind entered a period of transformation perhaps only equalled in significance by the transformation wrought when, 10,000 years ago, humans stopped wandering and settled down to farm. Beginning in Britain and Belgium in the 1830s, people began to move to cities in their thousands, then their hundreds of thousands, and then their millions. By the end of the nineteenth century, this revolution was starting to transform large chunks of what we call 'the West': the north and east of France; all of Belgium and the Netherlands; northern Italy; the west of the Habsburg Empire in present-day eastern Austria, the Czech Republic, parts of Hungary, and southern Poland; much of Germany; a corridor between St Petersburg and Moscow; chunks of northern Spain; and much of the north-east of the USA. In the following one hundred years, these cities, these islands in rural seas, came to dominate every aspect of human experience in the West, from the ways we think to the ways we love, from the lives of women to the ways we organize our politics, such that by 1970, the village was the exception, and the city the rule. This book tells the story of Europe's twentieth century from the point of view of the street corners, bars, factories, squares and living rooms in which it happened.

The scale and rate of change was enormous, starting first in Britain. A city like Manchester was a modest provincial town in 1800, with a population of about 75,000 souls. But by 1900, it had grown to a mighty conurbation of 2,117,000. Birmingham grew from 71,000 in 1800 to a sprawl of 1,483,000 in 1900—before adding *another* million by 1951. This urban population explosion was not matched in the countryside, and that is just one of the unique features of this revolutionary transformation. While the populations of British cities grew up to thirty-fold, the rural parts of England barely doubled in the same period: Norfolk's population rose from 273,000 in 1801 to 476,000 in 1901.[1]

Britain set the pace for this change, but between 1880 and 1940, large chunks of the rest of Europe began to transform *even more* rapidly. Berlin grew from 826,000 in 1870 to 1.12 million in 1880, to 2 million in 1910, to 4.2 million in 1930. Milan swelled from 322,000 in 1880 to 1.1 million in 1940. Moscow went from 800,000 in 1890 to 2 million in 1930, and 4 million in 1940. The industrial sprawl of the Ruhr valley in western Germany tripled from 196,000 in 1870 to 568,000 in 1900, almost quadrupling to 2.2 million in 1940.[2] By 1900, about 70 per cent of British citizens lived in urban environments, and about 50 per cent of German and French citizens did, so 1900 represents an important tipping point. By 1970, 70 per cent of all Europeans lived in cities. This book, though, focuses on the trend-setters: the transformative core of Europe between Russia in the east and France in the west, Britain in the north and Italy in the south.

But this change from field to street was not just an impersonal demographic process, for which the faceless abstractions of statistics will suffice. The move to the cities, and the population explosion within them, necessitated a profound revolution in the ways that Europeans saw themselves and the world—a revolution we are still living with today. Whereas for thousands of years, Europeans could look to the Torah, the Bible, and the Koran and see their agricultural worlds written there, with rules of morality, political order, economics, and family, the move to the cities made these rule books redundant. New codes, new rule books had to be found, and the new circumstances of life in cities set Europeans on a quest for answers about who they now were, and how they now should live.[3] It was not a deliberate revolution, fomented in the minds of angry men; it was an accidental revolution, a by-product of, say, the quest for cheap cloth, the search for a good night out, or the control of typhoid. The history of the twentieth century was dominated by the questions of who would write the new rule books, and what they would contain.

This transformation of everyday life between the 1890s and the 1970s touched every feature of the continent's history: its politics, its culture, the lives of women, sexual identities, the very fabric of our surroundings, and the assumptions we make about how life should be understood and organized. This book tells the story of that revolution from the perspectives of the places and spaces in which it happened, and the people whose lives we see lived out in them. This focus on the 'crime scene' of history is important, for while I, and all the people I know (academics and 'civilians' alike), are acutely sensitive to where they live and work—and invest huge amounts of time, emotion, and money in arranging their surroundings 'just so'—there is a painful silence about 'where' history has happened in the writings of many historians. This is an obvious paradox—why do people who are so ready to fret about the 'where' of their own lives so often ignore the 'where' of their subjects' lives? Just as any criminal investigation starts with the injunction to all police officers to 'preserve the crime scene', so any historical investigation should look at where it happened for crucial clues about what was happening, how it was happening and why it was happening. We ignore this forensic bonanza at our peril. It is time to put the 'where' into the 'why' of history. 'Where' matters. The physical spaces matter—the layouts of rooms, the relationships of things, the distances between, the temperature, the lines of sight. And the values of a place matter—the ideas it bears, from danger to fun, from sick to healthy, from sacred to profane.

Above all, there is a silence about one of the most crucial *mises en scène* of this revolutionary period in Europe: the city. Some have tried to tell the story of the whole continent.[4] Others have focused on states and nations, offering histories of Britain, Germany or the USSR.[5] Others have focused on great individuals, like Hitler and Stalin, Churchill and Lloyd George, Emmeline Pankhurst and Marie Curie, de Gaulle and Adenauer.[6] There have been outstanding studies of people's everyday lives.[7] And finally, historians often focus on great movements—whether political or social. The 'rise' of women and the working class, and the great sociopolitical movements like capitalism, liberalism, communism, socialism, and fascism all have their histories.[8] It is not my goal to rubbish these historians—without their work, mine could not have been completed. But sometimes, the excellent history in these books happens halfway between 'everywhere' and 'nowhere', and that is not where humans exist. Humans live their lives *somewhere*. *Somewhere* is real, tangible, fixed, located. 'Germany' is not somewhere (its borders have changed with alarming regularity); 'women' are not somewhere, but the office I am sitting in now, writing this, is somewhere. In the words of a leading geographer, 'historians write as if the whole of human history happened on the head of a pin'.[9] He is right; we do. It is time to put the *where* into the *what* and the *why* of this most momentous of human transformations.

This book offers a history of this crucial century that happened *somewhere*: in the streets and factories, cinemas and nightclubs, housing estates and suburbs, offices and living rooms, shops and swimming baths of Europe's booming cities. This book does not seek to imply that cities were the *only* place that the history of Europe happened. The gas chambers of Auschwitz or Treblinka; the great naval battles of the Atlantic or tank battles of Kursk; the corridors of the Kremlin, Whitehall, the Elysée Palace or Bonn; the bourses, offices, exchanges and banking halls; and the army barracks of Spain in the 1930s or Greece in the 1960s, were also places where the destiny of millions have been shaped. About these places this book is largely silent; in some cases, they have their histories already; in others, they remain to be written.

In contrast, *Streetlife* tells five 'stories' of how Europe was transformed in the twentieth century, from the point of view of some of the spaces and places which dominated that transformation, and where the big histories of great individuals and the small histories of 'ordinary' people came together to produce their devastating effect. Chapter 1 explores the century's politics. The power of a Lloyd George does not exist in the issuing of an order in an office in Whitehall, but in its execution in a munitions factory in Manchester—somewhere out there in the real world. We need to turn politics upside down, for every great river is only a sum of its tributaries, be they ever so small. The mighty river does not cause the little brook, but the other way round. It was in the cities that the progressive parties of the twentieth century were formed in the 1890s and 1900s, and it was in cities at the end of the First World War—and not in the trenches—that almost every political system to the east of France collapsed, as communists used the newly formed brigades of industrial workers to topple bourgeois, aristocratic, and monarchical orders. New ideologies, like Italian Fascism and German National Socialism, struggled to make their presence felt in the cities, because they did not have access to the factories, docks, and railways that had provided the bedrock of left-wing politics, but both ideologies had to find ways of penetrating them if they were to succeed in seizing and holding power. And cities always had the potential to destabilize any regime—not just in the 'revolutionary decade' at the 'Great' War's end. In France in 1934, one of Europe's most stable democracies, concerted violence around the Assemblée Nationale brought down the government, and contemporaries expected it to bring down the whole Republic. And it was in the calm suburbs of the post-war settlement that Europeans finally accepted both capitalism *and* socialism. Some 'crime scene investigation' of post-war politics reveals the trivial nature of Parisian violence in 1968—but shows how fragile Soviet domination of Eastern Europe was. Major urban disturbances in Berlin (1953), Warsaw and Budapest (1956), Prague (1968), and the Polish dockyard cities of the Baltic from 1970 until 1989 could have such profoundly destabilizing effects that governments in Moscow might fail, and Communist parties in satellite states be forced into humiliating compromise. And one European city in particular, Berlin, was at the heart of major global geopolitical confrontation from the Airlift in 1948 to the 'revolution' of 1989. It was the spaces of the cities which mattered: the ways factories brought people together in new formations, the layout of streets that made them unpoliceable, struggles to control pubs and bars, the development of suburbs to undermine socialism, the symbolic value of urban settings, and the inability to pacify dockyard disorders. All politics has a 'somewhere', and this book tries to find that place.

Chapter 2 asks what the history of Europe's women might look like from the perspective of the 'streetwalker'. The very fact that that word is so pejorative when used of women speaks volumes about the difficulties women have faced in being able to take hold of urban space, and still retain their 'respectability'. It might seem reactionary to say so, but focusing on the 'where' of women's experiences means recognizing their preoccupation with securing a 'where' of their own—a home as a place where they might transform their lives, perhaps more important than the more 'public' spaces of the street or the workplace. Many women across the century did not aspire primarily to many of the things that we associate today with enhancing women's status, like university education, or achieving senior roles in companies or government. Perhaps surprisingly, many women were at the forefront of campaigns to *prevent* women going to university or taking highly skilled jobs. Outside the home, factories brought women together for the first time in dynamic ways, and crystallized many of the conflicts between working-class women and working-class men that characterized the century. But the idea that all women went to work in factories in the First World War, and then desired to stay there, is not the case. Many women struggled hard to avoid taking up paid work outside the home, so burdensome was their unpaid work within it. We are faced with a paradox: for the last forty years, feminists have argued that women need to get out of the home to succeed. But for the previous eighty or so, most women's goal was not to get out of the home, but to get into one. That is not to say, though, that women were happy to be *confined* to the home: they fought hard in the 1910s, 1920s, 1930s and beyond to force their way into places conventionally barred to them—bars in First World War Vienna, car factories in interwar Birmingham, or rock'n'roll nightclubs in post-war Berlin—and insisted on their right to stay there. It is contentious to say so, but arguably, looking at the 'where' of women's lives suggests there was no 'rise' of women in the twentieth century—at least, not in relative terms. Most women who worked outside the home worked in 'feminine' jobs in service industries throughout the century—the figures changed little. And the humiliation of women with shaven heads in Paris or raped in the hundreds of thousands in Berlin, Warsaw, and Budapest in 1945–6 show how unstable the 'rights' of women have been within living memory (and the rape of women in the former Yugoslavia in the 1990s underlines this). But the achievement of safe, dry, warm housing across Europe, from Moscow to Glasgow to Milan, in the 1950s and 1960s represented a fundamental transformation of women's lives, and did more to liberate women than perhaps any other change.

Chapter 3 explores the way that cities shaped the century's culture. But it does not take the view that culture is a sort of 'medicine', which people should consume for their own benefit. 'Culture' here means the ways that people represented the world to themselves and to each other, the ways they described and understood the world, not the ways that people 'improved their minds'.[10] The unique genius of twentieth-century culture does not lie in the art gallery, the museum, the theatre, or the opera—all urban spaces which revolutionized nineteenth-century culture. Instead, this chapter focuses on seven key places in which Europeans relatively suddenly and relatively quickly chose to produce and consume culture, and thereby revolutionized the ways they related to others and themselves: the chapter moves from the music hall to the cinema, from the football stadium to the dance hall and jazz club, and from the discotheque to the living room. What I am here calling 'culture' is often analysed by historians as 'leisure'—a way to dissipate time—rather than culture—a way to understand the world. Far from just being ways to make time disappear, these places were at the heart of who we have become. When Europeans have loved or mourned, come of age as men, or freed their bodies as women, they have often done so not (just) through great novels or abstract paintings, but through pop songs and in cinemas. What matters is not just the lyrics of pop songs, or the storylines of movies, but the ways those lyrics and storylines were used in people's everyday lives. To understand that, you need to know about the 'where' of the film or the pop song or the football match as much as the 'what'. How these new spaces of culture came about, and transformed the lens through which people viewed the world, is a matter of profound importance. This is not to say that 'high' culture is irrelevant: the gap between 'high' and 'low' culture has often been crossed, and is sometimes barely detectable at all. Great drama, like *Brideshead Revisited* or *Das Boot*, can succeed on television attracting audiences of millions; great music and poetry like *West Side Story* or the *Dreigroschenoper* (*Thre'penny Opera*, by Bertolt Brecht and Kurt Weill) can render the distinctions between 'high' and 'low' redundant. But the music hall transformed the ways we related to our friends on a night out, and thought about performers in ways that still linger: music halls taught us to be still, to turn away from our friends, and to be quiet. The cinema continued that revolution, stealthily promoting silence and stillness in previously restless bodies, and making culture producible only with large amounts of money. The football stadium provided a world of masculine physicality, identity, and debate only paralleled in significance by the world of work or the military—both of which have retreated in the last thirty years, leaving football triumphant. Dance halls segregated young people from their parents in their cultural lives for the first time, creating the 'teenager' as a life phase and identity. Jazz bars shifted the focus of European music from melody to rhythm, challenged imperialist racial hierarchies, and underlined the uncontrollability of city cultures by the authorities. Discos and nightclubs finessed the transformation in people's relationships to their bodies begun in the dance halls. And, finally, living rooms shifted European culture from outside the home to inside the home, first with the radio, and then with the television, which turned families away from facing each other, and organized the geography of the living room in the same way as the geography of the cinema: still, silent people sitting in rows—a totally new model of family interaction.

The fourth chapter shows how urbanization transformed Europeans' sexual identities, the ways that people thought about themselves and their bodies, and the extent to which the state or society might intervene in people's private lives. Up until the end of the nineteenth century, Europeans had slept with all sorts of people in all sorts of ways—homo and hetero, consensual and abusive, legitimate and incestuous. That is not to say that *everyone* experienced sex in this anarchic way: most people around 1900 had relatively concrete preferences for sexual partners, and there were many social conventions which limited people's actions and desires. But the historical record shows a range of sexual activities and identities in the 1890s that make our own age seem very prudish, and blows the idea that the 1960s were an age of sexual liberation right out of the water. In the closing decade of the nineteenth century, in medical consulting rooms, legislatures, bars and backstreets, people started to be defined, and define themselves, more and more in terms of a sexual identity. This effected a revolution in sexuality, bringing it under new forms of control. It transformed people's views of their bodies. And it went to the heart of the relationship between citizen and the state. The histories of heterosexuality and female homosexuality are, at the time of writing, so slim that, to explain this phenomenon, the chapter has had to rely on the evidence surrounding men who had sex with men. This is not intended to be controversial or provocative—it is to do with the accidents of the historical record, and the assumptions of present-day historians on whom I rely. I assume here that 'gay' rights or the dignity and self-hood of 'gay' people is no less and no more than that of any other type of person—Jew, woman, poor, Catholic, old, young. And so gay people will serve as an 'index' and proxy of the freedom of *all* people. For at the turn of the twentieth century, it is clear that homosexuality and effeminacy, and homosexuality and the criminal law, were not things that one would necessarily associate with each other. Masculinity was not based solely on heterosexuality. From the fair grounds, barracks, and cafés of St Petersburg to the shops in London's West End, there was a profound fluidity underpinning the choice of sexual partners for many (not all, but many). Far from being characterized by 'Victorian values', a tour through the parks, bars, and fairgrounds of Europe's *fin de siècle* shows soldiers sleeping with businessmen, coal hauliers dancing with police officers, and diplomats cruising for sex with adolescents. Between the wars in European cities, if we follow the police on their raids or the guidebooks to 'underground' Berlin or London we see the formation of more 'concrete' sexual identities, in two ways. First of all, states became more interested in people's everyday lives, and in regulating them: prosecutions in and across European cities rose quickly in this period—and in 'liberal' London, just as much as Nazi Berlin or Soviet Moscow. We can read in the raids and arrests the inexorable rise of a new sort of interfering state. But individuals themselves also started to view their sex lives not just as what they *did*, but to a growing degree as part of what they fundamentally *were*. This transition of sex from 'doing' to 'being' was important, because on the one hand, it allowed people to organize to acquire 'rights'—but also because it started to exclude people who were not willing to declare (even if only to themselves) that they fundamentally 'were' one thing or another. And if this means the emergence of a 'gay' identity, it also means the emergence of a 'straight' one against which it is defined: it is profoundly intellectually lazy to assume that only gay people have sexuality—straight people have it too (just as white people have an ethnicity, and men have a gender). This process of persecution *and* self-definition spiked in Britain and Germany in the 1950s—above all in Britain—which heightened the persecution of 'non-standard' forms of sexual behaviour to levels never before seen. From the 1960s on, most European cities had a 'scene' that started to diversify within itself, sorting gay people (as other mechanisms were sorting straight people) into 'lifestyles'. This produced a profound spatial liberation, as gay men and women began to 'reclaim' the streets they had lost in the 1930s and 1950s, and straight people began to realize the terrible harm that a restrictive state could bring to anyone. But it also locked people (in this instance, gay people) into quite 'consumerist' ways of defining themselves and their identities—just as straight people were being locked into their own capitalist 'lifestyles', rather than lives.

In a world where most of us would not consider putting up a porch without permission from a planning office, it is hard to grasp just how random late-nineteenth-century cities could be, and how profoundly transformative the idea of planning could seem. The final chapter explores how the very shape, material, and fabric of the city has transformed the way we live—and the very fundamentals of the way we think about the world. Indeed, I argue here that the plan represents the genius of the twentieth century, its guiding spirit and principle. Important attempts had been made to regularize the layout and construction of cities in the nineteenth century—as any visitor to a Berlin

Allee, Parisian sewer, or Manchester terrace of housing can see. But these attempts were focused on three things: the control of disease (which would easily cross over into the dwellings of the rich if they were not controlled); the production of a superficial visible order (the same Continental boulevards of six-storey neo-Renaissance blocks can be found in Vienna, Budapest, Barcelona, Paris, Munich, and Stockholm); and the making of money. This process was revolutionized in the decades either side of 1900: European intellectual life became dominated by the idea of the 'rational plan' to produce a perfect world. In many ways, we have become blinded to the ways our lives are shaped by our physical environment, in the same way that we do not 'notice' oxygen in the air until suddenly we are forced to do without it. In this new way of thinking about the world, environments were thought of not in terms of prevention, but of production: not 'What sort of disease do I want to prevent?', but 'What sort of society, family, and individual do I want to produce?' Starting out in the planning of urban environments, the idea of total knowledge and total planning rapidly expanded to colonize every nook and cranny of human endeavour, such that by 1930, millions of Russian citizens were having their lives transformed by the idea of 'the plan'. This could have huge positive benefits. It meant that by the 1970s, most Europeans had a warm, dry, windproof home, and had little to fear from tuberculosis and typhus—two major killers in the nineteenth century. For the first time in the history of humanity, very poor people might expect to live across more than one room, and might expect never to be cold.

This was a revolution: it separated the sexual and emotional lives of children from their parents, and of children from each other. It gave rise to privacy, and the concept of the 'bedroom' as a special place for solitary reflection—something poor urbanites in the nineteenth century could never have hoped for. Who can estimate the scale and scope of quiet reflection that these spaces have allowed? Rates of incest tumbled, and the pensive, solitary teenager had a space in which to cultivate the introspection on which the idea of a distinctive 'teenager' identity depends. The nineteenth-century obsession with the superficial appearance of buildings was displaced by a revolutionary obsession on the part of 'experts' and states with what went on *inside* buildings—working, playing, having sex, sleeping, eating, marrying, growing, making, cooking, chatting, fighting: these all suddenly became objects of fascination for governments across the continent. And seizing control of the everyday environments of Europe's citizens gave these governments the technology and rationale they needed to intervene in the minutest details of people's everyday lives. Many states did this not in spite of their citizens, but at their behest. But this idea of planning, the notion that the world could be truly *known* and *understood*, and that based on that knowledge and understanding, a purer, righter, better world could be produced, had a downside too. The logic of the housing estate has lifted millions out of poverty and hunger and incest and disease and uncertainty; but it was also the totalizing, ultra-rational (but, this time, totally immoral) logic of the Holocaust, the Soviet Five Year Plans and the Great Ukrainian Famine, the Maoist Great Leap Forward and Cultural Revolution, Apartheid, and the Killing Fields of Cambodia. The mentality of the total plan, which started in cities in Europe around 1900, has been the triumph and the tragedy of the twentieth century, its guiding 'genius' and spirit, for better and for worse.

This book is not comprehensive—it is not meant to be. Much of Europe, like Scandinavia, Iberia, and the Balkans, is left out. And clearly, there were great cities in Europe before the 1890s—in Renaissance Italy, medieval Germany, Golden Age Netherlands, and Enlightenment Britain and France. But those cities were unique islands: they represented not what was typical of those societies, but what was exceptional. The history of Europe cannot be understood without, for example, the role of Paris in the revolutions of 1789, 1830, 1848, and 1870—but Paris was so radically different from France, and even from London, that it was always spectacular and unique, rather than ordinary and typical. Many important topics have been excluded too—most obviously economics, but many more beside. And the early 1970s marks the end of this book's story. But not because the transformation that cities bring has abated—it is a process which has not relented for over 150 years now, and continues with vigour from Rio de Janeiro and São Paulo, via Capetown and Mombasa to the megacities of India and China. But in the 1970s, important changes were afoot which lie beyond the scope of this book, and my expertise as a historian. Europe had, by then, largely completed its urbanization. Importantly, the demographic, technological, and economic changes which had driven urbanization, symbolized by the railway and the factory, slowed in the West. Europe's cities de-industrialized rapidly, and production shifted to the Far East: first to Japan, Taiwan, Singapore, Hong Kong, and South Korea; now to China, Vietnam, and India. In the West, many states began to doubt their ability to plan and to provide, and welfare and health systems stumbled, while worklessness, drug addiction, and crime soared as cities struggled to cope with the 'De-Industrial Revolution'. In Eastern Europe, and above all in Poland, communist governments could not assert effective control over their populations by the end of the 1970s. Meanwhile in China, the Communist Party left 'The Plan' to wilt on the vine from the early 1980s, and allowed the rapid free-market urbanization and industrialization that had begun to transform Britain 150 years earlier. Capitalism is no less rigid than socialist planning, no more inescapable for those caught up in it, no less rigorous in its pursuit of an inhuman logic. All of this lies beyond the scope of my expertise as a historian, and as a European historian at that. These histories must yet be written. And when they are written, I hope that 'where' is just as important as the 'what' and the 'why' of the story.

1

Revolution in the Streets

The 'man on the street' is so often taken as the barometer of the 'true' political sense of a situation that we sometimes forget that the street, for the people that are on it, is a very real thing. It is not a journalistic abstraction, nor an argumentative cliché. It is not a composite of all possible streets, all possible opinions and all possible experiences, but a unique time and place, lived and seen and smelled and touched and entered and left by specific, unique people. It is not the pure democracy of the Greek agora, nor the fervoured heat of an impetuous rush to the barricades, nor the pomp of a coronation procession, or the easily decoded ideology of a military parade, but the slow, wearing, cumulative force of a million and one lived experiences of a thousand and one very physical places and environments.

To speak of 'Everyman' is also to risk speaking of 'nobody'. To speak of 'everywhere' in this or that nation is to speak of nowhere. But transforming 'everyman' into 'someone', and 'everywhere' into 'somewhere', leads us to the coalface of power. And this is where most research into power in politics and sociology and history has pointed over the last twenty years: power is *local*. That certainly does not mean that it exists in, say, town councils instead of parliaments, or regions instead of nations (although it often does exist there). Instead, it means that power exists only in real exchanges in real places between real people. Power becomes real only when it is *applied* to something—it does not exist 'up there' in floating constitutions or states or institutions, but 'down there', in the encounter with the mother and the social worker, the trade unionist and the factory foreman, or the socialist and the secret policeman.[1] Until that moment of encounter between real people in a real place, all the power and might of both the state and the individual are bound up tightly and inaccessibly, as latent as the power at the heart of an atom.

Of course, the twentieth century was not the first time that cities and the spaces that made them have played a major role in shaping the political life of Europeans. In ancient Greece, the physical space of the agora was central to the political life of some of the communities there; if one could not get to it, or were not allowed into it, one could not participate. The politics of the Italian Renaissance, or the Dutch Golden Age, were focused on the mercantile cultures springing from the harbours, warehouses, and banking arcades of daily life. The French Revolution makes no sense without the destabilizing actions of groups of Parisian women searching for bread, the radical *journées* of protest, or gangs of toughs from the Faubourg St Denis or Faubourg St Antoine barracking 'provincials' on their way to the National Assembly; and the growth of the French state, and the emergence of a class system, makes little sense without an understanding of the rebuilding of Paris which started in the 1840s, reached its apogee in the 1850s and 60s, but continued apace until 1914. And any Marxist (and many who are not Marxist) will confirm the central position of the Paris Commune of 1870–1 in forming modern political identities. Equally, the industrial revolution makes little sense without a history of Manchester, Birmingham, or Glasgow. But the key personnel of European politics in the period right up to the transformative nineteenth century were aristocratic; they were landed; they were small-town. This was more and more true the further east from Britain one went, but even in Britain, the cabinet at the end of the nineteenth century consisted of nineteen members, and in this most urbanized of polities, eleven had hereditary titles of some sort.

But throughout the nineteenth century, this system was under massive strain. The French Revolution, the Chartist movement in Britain, the 'turning point at which Europe failed to turn' in the widespread revolutionary disturbances of 1848, and the Paris Commune of 1870–1, were all profoundly *urban* disturbances. There was no overnight revolution in 1900, like some magnificent shift change in which the aristocracy clocked off, traipsing sullen and exhausted back to their ancestral estates, past an eager, fresh-faced popular alternative, marching in from their factory shifts. But the early twentieth century does mark the decisive shift in European theories of sovereignty from the ancestral estate to the housing estate.

Of course, one could tell this story in the development of the ideologies of fascism, socialism, social democracy, liberalism, conservatism; one could tell it in the personalities of Lloyd George or Adenauer or Stalin; one could tell it in the institutions of the parliaments and the franchises and the parties. One could even tell it in the story of city politics itself—until the 1970s, town councils across Europe undertook many of the roles we associate today with the modern nation state, from housing to education, from health care to unemployment welfare. And many excellent histories have explored these frameworks. But all of these stories, important as they are, keep politics floating above and around the history of the people whose lives it determines. Politics, in these stories, becomes like the atmosphere: invisibly and unquestionably everywhere, a convenient, all-pervasive 'miasma' of power and belief and practice that is detached from its practitioners. It is a magical force which acts at a distance, without a clear mechanism for engagement, and without a direct explanation of why, say, specific instabilities might occur in a naval dockyard in Bremerhaven, but not in a similar dockyard in Portsmouth, or why a factory in one Moscow suburb might support liberal democracy, but another similar factory round the corner might fight for Bolshevism, or why one bar in Hamburg might vote communist, but suddenly change and support the NSDAP. This chapter starts with the everyday space, and works up to the politics, rather than starting with the politics and trying to work down into the everyday space. It is about mills and dockyards, streets and apartment blocks, workshops and community centres, and how the accidents of design and association and habit evolved in those places gave structure and substance to some of the most important political transformations wrought in the century, from the birth of democratic socialism to the struggle to promote fascism, from the Russian Revolution to the fall of the Soviet Union.

*   *   *

The end of the nineteenth century saw a revolution in formal politics, as across Europe, parties formed that were explicitly focused on representing a class: the working class. True enough, European conservative and liberal parties in the nineteenth century had tended to *serve* the interests of one class—the upper-middle class, or bourgeoisie—but they pretended to universality. But in February and March 1890, the German media and the Prussian landed elites that directed German national politics in Berlin had to contend with some unwelcome news. The idealist new German emperor, Wilhelm II, had decided to lift the ban on the organization of the Social Democratic Party, and allow it to fight in the 1890 election without impairment. City after city went 'red'. The 'Iron Chancellor', Bismarck, had imposed substantial restrictions on all ideologies and groups that challenged the 'national ideal' that he had struggled to invent. From the late 1870s, these restrictions focused on Catholics and socialists, both of which groups viewed themselves—or at least, their ideologies—as having internationalist, rather than national, underpinnings. This was a grave affront to Bismarck's unifying project in the 1870s and 1880s, and he declared a *Kulturkampf*—a cultural struggle against Catholics and socialists, outlawing many of the organizations of both in the years after German unification in 1870–1. In the 1880s, the new German state outlawed, for example, 155 socialist newspapers, and 1,200 other socialist publications.[2]

Big city, metropolitan living was relatively new to Germany, and by the first 'free' elections of 1890, cities had roughly doubled in size since the formation of the new nation in 1870. In the twenty years after German unification, Munich had grown from 169,000 inhabitants to 349,000; Leipzig from 107,000 to 295,000; Berlin from 826,000 to 1,579,000.[3] This transformation produced a totally new political landscape for the new kaiser. From the Maffei locomotive works in Munich North to the potteries of Leipzig; from the harbours of Hamburg Old Town to the chemical plants of Chemnitz (making their revolutionary artificial royal blues and cardinal's scarlets to be dyed into English cloth woven in the suburbs of Manchester and Leeds); through the mines and railways and smelting yards and slag heaps of the acrid Ruhr valley in the west of Germany, all the way to the AEG electronics works of Berlin Wedding in the east, civil servants and journalists and party officials were putting red pins in maps of the Reich, marking out nearly every large city in the country as a victory for the socialist SPD.[4]

While the Social Democratic Party was technically legal after 1890, the German state at every level (national, provincial, city, county, parish) hassled and frustrated the party's organization. One such case arose in Hamburg in 1892, after a long running battle between the party and the city state's prosecutor, Dr Romen. In the two years since the party's legalization, he had been trying to undermine the party's capacity to organize, regularly (and successfully) attempting to imprison party leaders and editors of the party's local organs. But in the summer of 1892, Romen extended his direct assault on the SPD to general criminal proceedings in the city's courts. He started asking defence witnesses in all sorts of non-political cases if they were social democrats, spreading the 'establishment' prejudice against the social-ists into the (theoretically) a-political arena of criminal justice—and with some effect. On one particular day, 17 July 1892, a witness was called—a working-class man. He attended court in his work clothes (called as he had been from his working day), not his Sunday best. Romen accused the witness of gross disrespect to the court arising from the spread of social democracy—and the witness was, indeed, given a formal 'severe reprimand' on his criminal record. On 28 July, Romen turned his attention to one of the leaders of the Dockworkers' Union, Johann Will, who was accused of malicious libel for a piece he had written for the union's paper, *Die Gerechtigkeit*—'*Justice*'. He asked every one of Will's character witnesses if they were social democrats, and declared their evidence to be invalid if they were, based on a 'pattern of gross disrespect' of social democrats for justice—which had already been demonstrated by so many poor people coming to courts to give evidence in their work-clothes rather than Sunday best. Will eventually received four months' imprisonment.

Thus far, this was a relatively run-of-the-mill situation, given the twenty preceding years of hostility on the part of the German state to the social democrats. But in cities across the country in the 1890s, the worm turned. The local SPD leadership declared a protracted conflict with the city state's authorities, which rapidly paralysed the city's administration and humiliated the police. It was clear to working-class Hamburgers that the courts and the legal system could not reliably be used to secure the freedoms of the party—their freedoms—and the national constitution offered little in the way of real power to do any-thing about it. The victories in the 1890 Reichstag elections had been little use to the party because the kaiser was under no obligation (as was the British monarch and the French president) to govern with the consent of the legislature; in the German constitution, the Reichstag's role was largely advisory, and the kaiser did not draw his ministers from it. In Germany, the empty 'formalities' of the trappings of power were, therefore, far clearer than in Britain or France. Thus, if the politics of the SPD was to be made 'real', it would have to come not from the organs of the state—the legislature, the judiciary—but from the actions of the party's members on the ground. This debate could not even be effectively conducted in the press, for Romen used the political police to raid the party's press organs repeatedly, and confiscated their print runs. Thus, the conventional 'middle-class' mechanisms of discussing and securing freedom and dignity were closed to the SPD in Hamburg.

All the SPD had left was the city itself: upon confiscation of their newspapers on 30 July 1892, the city organizers called for six simultaneous meetings at different locations in the city on 9 August, such that it would be impossible for the police to disrupt all of them. This was a deliberate strategy to crystallize and clarify the impotencies of the state that frustrated them. They used a spatial spread of meetings to make effective confrontation from the police impossible and ineffective. Chief of Police Rosalowsky proposed banning the meetings; City State Senator for Police Affairs (Hamburg was, and is, a federal state in the German constitution), Dr Hachmann, disagreed—his scribbles are all over the paperwork. He doubted it would be legal; he doubted it would be effective, given police numbers and the pledge of workers from all over the Hamburg conurbation to attend; and he felt that it would just increase the popularity of the SPD. Indeed, the bourgeois establishment was doing well to smother the conflict, starving it of the 'oxygen of publicity': while the socialist press could not publish freely, the city's dominant papers largely ignored the persecution of the socialist dockworkers, and the bans on the meetings. On 9 August, the day of the six planned meetings, the biggest papers, the *Hamburger Nachrichten* and the *Hamburger Correspondent*, led with a horse in Wansbeck that appeared to have influenza. But at street level, at all the meetings, resolutions were passed demanding Romen retract his views, validated by the judiciary, that SPD members could not give reliable evidence in court, and could therefore not appear as defence witnesses for each other.

The scandal went national, and papers in Berlin, Munich, and Cologne picked up the story in a way that Romen could not control. However, meetings in Hamburg quickly were banned on health grounds, as cholera broke out in the city in mid-August (see Chapter 5). Over the next year, the political police picked off and prosecuted the speakers at the meetings; but the meetings themselves passed into SPD mythology as a central moment of identity formation, and as the prosecutions rolled on, the SPD press across the whole of Germany pointed to the impotence of the state when the SPD took control of city spaces, and the corrupt double-dealing of the state when using the law. Hachmann, the local politician who argued that persecuting the SPD like this would make heroes of them, while revealing the impotence of the police to control urban environments and the moral corruption of the justice system, had all his fears realized.[5] Above all, it clarified that the politics of the new, urban age could not be confined to the council chamber, the court or the national parliament: the new politics had to be a politics of the street.

This close political networking in urban Germany was conspicuous in the period before the Great War, and central to the success of the Social Democratic Party. Party and urban fabric were utterly interwoven. One British visitor to Berlin formulated the organizational integration of ideology and place like this:

> the Social Democratic Party Executive could sit on the top floor of the *Vorwärts* building [the SPD's newspaper], pass a manifesto paragraph by paragraph, have it put into type and circulated to every tenement in the city of Berlin by the next morning. We cannot quite do this yet in London, but we ought to be able to do it. And some day we will do it.[6]

It is difficult for us to think of a place as an ideology. But the ability to turn a place—be it a factory, a marshalling yard, a dock, a street— into a coherent political ideology, *and then* gain control of the levers of the state was, across Europe at the turn of the last century, fraught with difficulties.

These were not necessarily abstract, 'global', or even national difficulties. One historian has shown how people in just one mill in the industrial city of Bradford—Manningham Mill, where S. C. Lister & Co. made velvet—could struggle to sort out amongst themselves who they were, and what they believed in.[7] In the autumn of 1890, male and female velvet weavers across Leeds and Bradford struck for a wage increase and won, and this led to a 'standing committee' of operatives, a proto-trade union. But in December 1890, after the USA introduced huge tariffs on British cloth, Samuel Lister, the owner of Manningham Mill, announced that all his workers would receive a pay cut of 35 per cent. The overwhelmingly female workers affected contacted local trade unions about organizing a strike, but local male union leaders counselled against it. There was no effective union structure in Manningham Mill, and organized trade unions, dominated by men, did not like the idea of militant women. A clear space— Manningham Mill—had isolated a social group, namely poor women. The paradox is that women were employed initially in mills like Manningham because women were *more* vulnerable to low wages and worse conditions than better-organized men. However, the very act of bringing these women together to 'exploit' them (or at least, pay them less than if the same number of unionized men had been brought together), backfired spectacularly. Brought together for the purposes of their cheapness and the absence of unionization, these women stood firm, and forged a new type of association.

Instead of accepting the pay cut, and the lack of support from male organized labour, the women promptly organized a trade union themselves, and went on strike. But rather than standing outside the factory on a picket line, the women were far more proactive. Hundreds of female weavers went door-to-door in the large industrial conurbations of Bradford and Leeds collecting funds for the strikers, and recruiting other weavers that they met at other mills to do the same. In total, they raised the exceptional sum of £11,000. Increasingly harassed by the police and prohibited from meeting houses and chapels, they met in parks and open-air ice rinks. It was this *spatial* issue which galvanized so many to support them, more than the 'simple' issue of wages and pay: the limitations on the women's right to free speech and free assembly, and their harassment by the police and municipal authorities, broadened the dispute and crystallized *other* union leaders' ideas of forming a coherent political interest to challenge this. A dispute in a nameable mill, followed by exclusions from chapels and public halls, led to meetings in the cities' new parks which produced the first coherent plans in Britain for a coordinated party of the working class: the Independent Labour Party was formed in Bradford in 1893, the forebear of today's Labour Party.

British parliamentary labour politics was born of the trade union— men (and it was almost always men) who knew each other from the factory, the mine, or the mill; or who were often so highly skilled that they could name all the other men of similar craft in a given city (like the master cutlers of Sheffield), and who organized themselves into political–economic–cultural units. But spaces are diverse, not homogenous, and class was not 'one' thing, but many. Within what might seem to be a coherent 'type' of person ('the' working class), conflicts between different workshops over status, pay, religion, politics, and ethnicity might proliferate. In the vast Belfast shipyards building the *Titanic* and the *Olympic*, and many more ships besides, 60 per cent of the workforce belonged to a union in the 1900s. But not just one union: there were seven unions of riggers and seventeen of sailmakers, and dozens more beyond that. After a period of 'vigorous consolidation', this had sunk to eighteen shipbuilding unions, and five societies of sailmakers and riggers.[8] In the course of the 1890s, inspired by the events in Bradford, disparate trade union groups organized themselves nationally, and under various auspices—Fabians, Co-Operators, craft unions, workers' unions, church and chapel groups—and founded the Independent Labour Party, which initially operated largely in local politics in the industrial cities of Yorkshire and Lancashire. In 1899, a railway worker, Thomas Steels, proposed amalgamating all the workers' groups into one national party, to stand for parliament. In 1900 the Labour Representation Committee was formed to link together all the local and regional parties of Labour, and contest national elections.[9]

Once workers organized with political intent, they had to find ways of spreading their message. To do that, one had to enter, and control, urban spaces beyond the workshop. This 1898 account by a weaving operative from Leicester explains how they would 'engage' with people from outside their own factories, and captures the bizarre drama and sound of this group of proselytizers. Primarily, they would take to the street:

> We paraded the ward with a home-made lantern three foot square, set upon two poles, with mottoes on each side and naphtha lamp inside, and accompanied by an ILP (Independent Labour Party) Brass Band. Others do canvassing…whilst we are canvassing, we are making Socialists, which is our principal object, and we insist on a good energetic canvass. Whilst one portion are doing this, and addressing circulars, the agitators are holding fifteen to twenty minute meetings and we

make a point of holding a meeting in each street in the ward, and often four or five on a good, central spot.... On the polling day, we insist that all poll and give them no peace until they do.[10]

Politics in this urban context becomes not just a battle for ideas, but fundamentally a battle about whose brass band played loudest, whose street discipline was clearest, whose 'canvassing' (it sounds more like mobbing) was most 'energetic'. The socialism which inspired the Independent Labour Party was marked out in a broad intellectual framework, and could be drawn from a variety of texts and arguments and discussions; but the capacity to lift it off the page and take it out of the chapel or the factory or the mill was measured in square miles of territories conquered, and numbers of streets occupied.

And where socialist politics failed—as it often did—to take root amongst the people whom it was supposed to liberate, socialists often explained this through the degradation of these very people by their environments. Thus, for turn-of-the-century socialists, the city explained both their successes and their failures. Edward Hartley was an Independent Labour Party activist in West Yorkshire's industrial cities, and when he came to explain the party's failure to do well in the 1890s in council elections in Bradford's desperately poor, industrial South Ward, he explained that its people were:

> ...bitter, intolerant, unsympathetic and insolent, prone to live on charity rather than on the rights of manhood and womanhood...not until the death rate, the insanitation and the horrible mode of life are changed, shall we ever see the South Ward of Bradford taking an intelligent interest in the things mostly concerning it.[11]

The living and working spaces of the modern city could create the physical and economic environment which would call socialism into being—but so could it produce an environment and a people so degraded that they were incapable of engaging with their own liberation.

The fertile grounds of the new urban environment did not produce only humane visions of social change, as with the British Labour Party and German SPD. In Vienna, St Petersburg, and Moscow, a different type of politics took root—one racist, and one revolutionary. To reduce the Viennese experiment in centre-right political innovation around 1900 to its extravagant anti-Semitic statements, though, would be to misunderstand it, for this was potentially the first conservative, democratic, urban 'mass' party outside Britain. The Christian Social Party founded in Austria in 1893 offered a political credo that was at once right-wing, religious, focused on the bourgeoisie and small traders, and yet was also populist, democratic, and urban. The distinctive feature of British politics in the eighteenth and nineteenth centuries had been a 'conservative' force that was psychologically and ideologically prepared to engage with cities and their inhabitants. But on the Continent, conservative politics at the turn of the century was dominated by parties obsessed by religion and agriculture. Whereas in Britain, the Conservative Party might break the interests of agricultural protectionism (in the reform of the Corn Laws in the 1840s) and choose a British Jew (albeit a baptized one) as their leader, Continental conservatives more frequently focused on anti-Semitism, extirpating socialism, promoting the Church's rights, and protecting agricultural interests against the free-trade campaigns of the new industries reliant on international trade in raw materials and finished products. As such, the whole of Continental Europe had few, if any, conservative organizations that could offer a plausible conservative programme to an urbanizing, industrializing continent. This disconnect between the right and the city meant that only two political alternatives presented themselves in the new cities: the first was socialism, of the type promoted by the SPD in Germany, the Section Française de l'Internationale Ouvrière (SFIO) in France, or the Labour Party in Britain; the other was an attempt at exclusion—typically, by grotesquely gerrymandering urban electoral districts to ensure the predominance of bourgeois parties, or by the vigorous actions of a secret police. One of the great tragedies of European history in the first half of the twentieth century is that it failed to produce a humane, suburban, conservative politics. The Conservative Party had not always been seen as a blessing for everyone in Britain, but viewed in the context of the last 150 years of European history, Britain and the world have a lot to be thankful for in its calm acceptance of both democracy and social policy. The Christian Social Party of Austria could have changed this catastrophic absence for Continental Europe, but it did not.

Karl Lueger's Christian Social Party was successful above all in Vienna, taking control of the town hall in 1897 on the back of a propaganda campaign focused on a bold social policy of improved schools, care for the elderly, and transport infrastructure, combined with rabid anti-Semitism. As such, they were perhaps the first popularly elected 'conservative' party to embrace the British Conservatives' understanding of the need for a coherent social policy and a bedrock of popular support. Their tragedy was that while the British Conservatives had been 'urbanized' by the traumas of Chartism, agricultural protection, and the Corn Law crisis of the 1840s, the Christian Socials had enough of the Viennese hinterland and Catholic anxiety at a secularizing world in them to have none of the British Conservatives' ability to advocate universal equality before the law. As such, the Christian Socials perfectly reflected the profound paradox of Catholic social thinking at the turn of the century, a paradox that it is important to understand because of its crippling effects on democratic conservatism. The depth of Catholic hostility to the modern world of the big city can be seen in the hugely influential Papal Encyclical of 1891, *Rerum Novarum*. This is a complex document. In it, Pope Leo XIII railed against the transformative forces of the modern city, condemning all forms of socialism, and all forms of social policy. By doing so, he paralysed attempts to forge an effective, popular, 'urban' conservatism on the Continent.[12]

Leo spoke for many conservatives when he summarized the revolution of the cities taking place in Europe at the end of the nineteenth century in a way many socialists would also have recognized:

> The elements of the conflict now raging are unmistakable, in the vast expansion of industrial pursuits and the marvellous discoveries of science; in the changed relations between masters and workmen; in the enormous fortunes of some few individuals, and the utter poverty of the masses; in the increased self-reliance and closer mutual combination of the working classes; as also, finally, in the prevailing moral degeneracy. The momentous gravity of the state of things now obtaining fills every mind with painful apprehension; wise men are discussing it; practical men are proposing schemes; popular meetings, legislatures, and rulers of nations are all busied with it—actually there is no question which has taken a deeper hold on the public mind.[13]

It is clear that Leo clearly 'got it' when it came to understanding the revolution that was underway across the Continent at the turn of the century. But while he was able to acknowledge poverty, he could only do so linked to the dangers of the 'closer mutual combination of the working classes' and 'the prevailing moral degeneracy'. He argued that:

> It is not easy to define the relative rights and the mutual duties of the wealthy and of the poor, of capital and of labour. And the danger lies in this, that crafty agitators constantly make use of these disputes to pervert men's judgments and to stir up the people to sedition.[14]

He went on to prohibit—in fact, to *damn*—the sorts of response proposed by the nascent SPD, SFIO, and Labour parties. While he, and so many others on the right in Continental Europe, could acknowledge 'that a small number of very rich men have been able to lay upon the teeming masses of the labouring poor a yoke little better than that of slavery itself', he would damn *with threat of excommunication* the socialists who sought to fix it. Their views were 'emphatically unjust, for they would rob the lawful possessor, distort the functions of the state, and create utter confusion in the community'. Socialists were 'a few dissentients'; he stated, 'we must not have recourse to the State' to put right the manifest wrongs. The family and the individual were the only mechanisms of change acceptable to God.[15] *Rerum Novarum*, then, eloquently focused Catholic minds on the horrors of the new urban world, and the particular classes of people that it called into existence; and it pointed out a 'duty of care' of the poor by the rich. But it ruled out specifically those new political mechanisms—parties of the poor, or social policies enacted by the state—that claimed to offer a solution to the problems he identified. Instead he insisted on more 'organic' models, based around family and a paternalistic small state. And few things seemed more organic to turn-of-the-century Continental conservatives than race.

In this context, and in the multi-ethnic Austro-Hungarian Empire, the Austrian Christian Social Party's emphasis on race took shape. Christian Social anti-Semitism seemed to offer an organic basis for social policy, rather than one which relied on the power of the state or the rise of a class. The tragedy of the Christian Socials' anti-Semitism was that, given their urban focus in Vienna, it was neither electorally necessary, nor was it a particularly strongly held belief of the party's leaders, like Karl Lueger (which, in German, means 'liar'—a problem he countered by insisting on pronouncing it 'lou-aiger').[16] When in power, the party actually focused on far more practical matters, like reforming provision for children in care and the elderly, hospital construction, building the city's underground railway, and a massive school-building programme.[17] The Christian Social Party were also expert campaigners, adept at using superficially democratic techniques to undermine the democratic process. When it came to the legal manipulation of the city's administrative spaces, the Christian Socials were highly effective. In bourgeois, rich districts of the old city like Mariahilf and Neubau, there were 66,838 and 76,760 inhabitants respectively, each with the same representation in the council as working-class Ottakring and Favoriten, where there were 173,761 and 145,530 inhabitants respectively. Not content with gerrymandering, they introduced compulsory voting—who could object to such a democratic measure? But voting was much easier for people not working a twelve- or fourteen-hour day, and many workers were fined for being unable to go and vote. Finally, they introduced a one-year residency requirement before one could vote. Working-class people were often highly mobile in *all* Continental European cities around 1900, and frequently moved before the one-year qualification period was fulfilled. But the party's mastery of the legal administration of urban space could not always hold up when it came to physical contest for urban space.[18]

The medieval core of Vienna is surrounded by a large belt of late-nineteenth-century development, built on the huge defensive zone of walls and ramparts which were demolished in the 1850s, in recognition of the long-vanished threat of Turkish invasion. Through the middle of this redevelopment runs the Ringstraße, a vast boulevard, fronting onto which are the grandiose buildings of the Austro-Hungarian monarchy in all its bourgeois pomp—opera houses, universities, palaces, parliaments, museums, stock exchanges. It also marked the closest to the city centre that the Social Democrats could get their supporters to demonstrate without arrest—and while letting them get back to their suburbs on foot in time to eat and sleep.[19] It thus represented a pragmatic and legalistic border for marking out political–spatial boundaries between law and disorder; rich and poor; old, established Vienna within, and migrant, new Vienna outside. It provided the perfect setting for large demonstrations and parades, whether by the Austrian military or workers at May Day.

The Christian Socials were a new party, keenly aware of the deeply socially embedded loyalties of the middle-class liberals and working-class socialists, and wanted to demonstrate their physical presence in the political city, moving out of the central districts, inside the Ring, and directly challenging the socialists on 'their' territory of the Ringstraße itself. They were keen to try to broaden their appeal to include more of the upper levels of the working-classes (which very frequently voted, and vote, Conservative in Britain), and realized some 'real and present' urban manoeuvring was necessary to achieve it. To this end, they organized a torch-lit parade along part of the Ring on the evening of 23 October 1904. Ostensibly to celebrate the birthday of their mayor, Karl Lueger, it was meant to bring the Christian Socials into the space of the city in the same way that the military, socialists, and trade unions used it. But in an act of foolish political miscalculation, Lueger claimed, half wryly, in the council chamber two weeks before that many poor parents had sold their children's clothes—bought with coupons issued by the City of Vienna. He managed to turn a piece of compassionate conservatism (the issuance of clothing coupons to poor children) into the focus of class conflict. The Social Democratic Workers' Party's formidable organizational machine in the suburbs swung into action, and squads of socialists beset the houses of notable Christian Socials on the day of the rally. Two hundred socialists from the outer suburbs crossed the Ring, and surrounded the house of the party's director in bourgeois Alsergrund. Another group draped a Christian Social's house with red flags, and banners bearing the slogan, 'Down with Lueger! Long live the working class!'[20] In the light of this, and the socialists' threats to cause substantial disorder disrupting the torch-lit procession, the police banned the conservative nationalists from marching. Their bourgeois underpinnings and inability to compete for the city on physical terms was laid bare, and their reliance on a gerrymandered electoral map was exposed. Faced with a physical contest over space, the Christian Socials could never compete with the Social Democrats, something which they would discover to their cost in 1918. Then, with a fair electoral system, Christian Social support almost disappeared from the city government.

The Russian city, and the Russian factory in particular, were different from those in Western Europe. There were fewer cities and

fewer factories but, rather than diminishing their importance by dilut-
ing their influence in a vast sea of agricultural peasant economy, in
some ways their concentrated form enhanced it. The Russian state
only 'freed' the peasantry from serfdom in the 1860s (in inverted com-
mas, because they had to buy their freedom with a loan, thus placing
most peasants in a lifetime of debt), and only when workers were not
tied, slave-like, to their lord and their land could cities really grow.
But Russian banks and stock exchanges were not well developed
enough to finance rapid industrial development, so it was only when
the finance minister, Witte, opened up the Russian economy to foreign investment in 1892 that overseas capital from Britain, Germany
and France could flood in, and cities could grow, providing both
workers and product markets for explosive factory growth, similar to
what we are currently seeing in south-east China.[21]

The twin-headed Hydra of Moscow and St Petersburg was thrown
into sharp relief by the peasant worlds that surrounded them, and
Russian factories tended to be much larger than those in the rest of
Europe.[22] Whereas in Britain and Germany, factories of 200 were
common, but most employed 50 or less, in Russia, the reverse was
true: over a half of factories employed more than 1,000 people.[23] In
St Petersburg, the number of factory workers in 1890 was 73,200; this
had tripled to 242,600 by 1914; and by 1917, it was 392,800.[24] The
78 largest metal works in St Petersburg averaged 2,923 workers each;
70 per cent of St Petersburg's workers worked in factories of over
1,000 employees, while in the USA—Russia's closest comparator in
terms of the development of large plants—70 per cent of industrial
workers worked in plants of less than 500 employees.[25] And in Berlin
and Paris in 1914, 94 per cent of industrial workshops employed fewer
than twenty people, while in London 66 per cent of industrial firms
employed less than twenty people.[26] So the 'space' of the factory in
St Petersburg (and to a slightly lesser extent, Moscow) was completely
unique in the world. And again paradoxically, St Petersburg's poor
lived evenly distributed throughout the city up to 1914, even in the
city centre, while in British, French, German, and Austro-Hungarian
cities they were segregated into suburbs where their own culture could
evolve. By contrast, St Petersburg's workers lived right in the midst of
breathtaking inequalities of wealth. This, then, was an explosive,
sudden transformation, intensively focused on the transformative

experience of the huge factory, with far fewer skilled 'craft' workers than in the evolving factory systems of Britain and Germany. These vast works were divided into 'shops'—the Putilov metal works, for example, had forty-one shops. Each shop would often have its own, unique character, employing workers who had migrated from one particular region, or who, as peasants, were regarded as particularly expendable. One worker recalled the life of an unskilled labourer, or *chernorabochii*, in one of the 'hot' shops of the Putilov works in the 1900s as being unbearably difficult:

> The chief characteristic of the work of a *chernorabochii* is that it is shockingly hard. It is one of the meanest, roughest, heaviest jobs which one finds in the factories. Apart from sheer muscle-power, nothing significant is required—neither literacy, skill, nor even simple quick-wittedness, since the gang leader, or senior *chernorabochii* will provide this. To carry iron, to load and unload wagons, to lift two hundred pounds of cast iron, to fetch and carry all kinds of heavy weights, to dig and prop up pits—these are some of the tasks of the *chernorabochii*. But his chief task is to be able to survive on seventy kopecks a day, to support a family, or from time to time to send ten or fifteen roubles to the countryside.[27]

They also faced a second task: try to stop their jobs being taken by the women and boys constantly arriving from the countryside, willing to work for far less than subsistence wages. Britain and Germany, where Marx and Engels had predicted revolutions, had cities full of craft-based workshops, contrary to the popular myths of industrial employment; but Russia had cities of plants on a vast scale. Because *any* form of union membership was forbidden in Russia, the politics which came from the work-spaces, shacks, and slums of the two great Russian cities was much more radical and desperate than that of Central and Western Europe. While in British and German cities, unions could organize semi-legally, Russian unions had to organize secretly and illegally—but they sometimes managed to do so with some success. The very act of making something secret can enhance its extremity, radicalizing ideologies and marginalizing individuals from socially 'normalizing' behaviour. But within the industrializing cities of Russia, conditions were exceptionally harsh, and the state's ability to deal with them exceptionally low. Almost as soon as 'accelerated' capitalist investment started to inflate Russian cities and industries, unions emerged, but what strikes the historian is the *timidity* of their demands, and the viciousness with which they were repressed by the state and its secret police.

For example, the Workers' Union had organized in about forty plants by the mid-1890s, and could manage to sustain a focused campaign, but 'only' to reduce the working day by half an hour (from 12 to 11.5 hours) for those working in unheated buildings—which, in St Petersburg and Moscow, could frequently be −20°C. Clearly, the physical location and conditions of work drove demands like this and supported the underlying alliances which allowed them to be pursued. And contemporary radicals were very clear about how this relationship between the process of industrialization, and the establishing of certain forms of urban environment, might work. Georgii Plekhanov, a close collaborator of Lenin's at the turn of the century, read two of the defining ideological texts of the modern world, Karl Marx's *Das Kapital* and Charles Darwin's *Origin of Species*, and merged them to try to understand the relationships between environment, economics, society, and culture. The new Russian city, driven by an explosive set of historical, environmental, and economic changes after the economic liberalization of 1892, seemed to be the perfect exemplar of this.

In subversive underground text after subversive underground text, Plekhanov furnished Russian radicals with a geography of revolution which did not pertain in Western European cities. It is hard for present-day readers to engage viscerally with the clichés and distinctive languages of revolutionary socialist political philosophy, but it is worth doing because when turn-of-the-century radicals talked about the 'relations of production' they were not reflecting just on some abstract economic theory: they were talking about real people in real factories in real cities, having very real relationships. So Plekhanov could argue in 1895 that:

> The character of the external…environment determines the character of man's productive activity, the character of his means of production. The means of production determine in turn the mutual relations of people in the process of production…And it is the interrelationship of people in the social process of production which determines the entire structure of society. For this reason the influence of the natural environment on this structure is undeniable. The character of the natural environment determines the character of the social environment.[28]

The shift between countryside and city, between wide open land farmed in established structures of politics, custom, and religion; and intense competition in the factories, with no accessible 'rule book' on how to proceed, represented the sort of radical environmental transformation which would destabilize any organism, human or otherwise. Thus the unique, sudden nature of Russian urbanization could give revolutionaries cause to translate Marx's theories, intended to describe the advanced, embedded capitalism of Britain, Belgium, and Germany, to the novel circumstances pertaining in Russia. The people who were in the factories of St Petersburg and Moscow were very often peasants in outlook, background, and life story; the only way that they could be converted into the proletarians necessary for revolution was if they were understood in terms of *where* they were, not *who* they were. Thus, people in the country were peasants, but people in a factory were proletarians, even if they had grown up as peasants, could not read, knew more about farming than metal work, and kissed icons every evening as they re-entered their homes (or rather, shared bedrooms, as most St Petersburg workers shared their dwellings, and even rooms, with other families). It was this vast leap—Lenin's (and his peers') application of Western European analyses to Eastern European contexts—which so profoundly destabilized Russian cities, and in turn, the world.

Above all, in Russian industrial politics at the turn of the century the central feature was *tsekhovshchina*, or loyalty to the shop. The place of work, and the encounters and loyalties found there, were at the heart of political organization—and it was an organization which made Russian workers and Russian cities the most disorderly and strike-prone in Europe in the years before the First World War.[29] Far from being a rigid authoritarian state, which is the picture painted by a political history of Russia, an urban history of Russia at the turn of the twentieth century shows a state in a violent, conflictual mess. Before the war had started, in just the month of July 1914, in St Petersburg alone a breathtaking 261,413 working days were lost through industrial action.[30]

A striking example of this pre-war militancy was the quasi-trade union, the Assembly of Russian Factory and Mill Workers in St Petersburg.[31] Paradoxically, the Assembly had been financed by the Okhrana, the tsarist secret police, as a way of creating loyal, monarchist, religious, anti-socialist organizations to campaign for reform, and offered a path to moderate change in the empire. But when leaders of the Assembly started to take their campaigning mandate seriously, the Okhrana began to harass and undermine them. When some workers were dismissed from the Putilov Metal Works in December 1904, *tsekhovshchina* discipline led to demonstrations and a large strike. Personal loyalty to workers in a specific workshop spread to the entire works, and then to other factories, and a demonstration was organized to start from six points around the city on the following Sunday. Carrying icons and pictures of the tsar, true to their moderate Orthodox monarchist roots, on 9 January 1905 the workers walked peacefully to the Winter Palace to request an eight-hour day and better pay, where they were fired upon. The setting provided a powerful urban theatre in which to 'present' such conflicts to newly literate urban publics across the continent—as in the Italian newspaper illustration in Figure 1.1. Over a hundred died; it became known as 'Bloody Sunday', and provided a revolutionary iconography and identity for twenty years, a codeword for governmental perfidy. We get some impression of the chaos of the scene, and the grandeur of the environment juxtaposed with the tightness of the crowd in Figure 1.1. It transformed the urban poor's view of the tsar and the foundations of his authority, and furnished a rhetoric of injustice focused on the whole the system, rather than with individual features of it, which would grow and grow until autumn 1917. By 12 January 1905, the strike had spread to Moscow.[32] The whole summer of 1905, the spaces and places of industrial Russia were characterized by strikes and intense labour revolt, usually focused on one, identifiable, specific workshop—and forming, ultimately, the event that historians have come to refer to as the '1905 Revolution'.[33] But this 'revolution' makes no sense without understanding the very specific concerns and dynamics of a very real place, like the Putilov Metal Works; and indeed, the Russian workforce was by far the most disorderly, rebellious, strike-prone and violent in Europe in the years between 1900 and 1920—a matter of no small importance for the country's (and Europe's) political development. Without understanding the unique organization of Russia's factories, and the micro-geographies within them, the Russian Revolutions make little sense.[34]

* * *

In the period between 1917 and 1924, almost all of Europe east of France descended into a period of intense political violence and

Figure 1.1 Massacre of protesters in St Petersburg, 9 January 1905. Interestingly, the victims here seem to be middle class, judging from some of the hats they are wearing—here depicted in an unknown newspaper, showing how urban unrest could be fixed to one place, *and* symbolize political chaos across the continent. The harsh repression of this peaceful demonstration crystallized both the secrecy and the fanaticism that characterized Russian urban political development.

disorder, focused on its cities. Revolutionaries from Adolf Hitler and the radical leftist Kurt Eisner in Munich, to Lenin in St Petersburg, to Mussolini in Rome, focused on the city, its secret spaces, its streets, its political and social aspirations, and its unpoliceability to destabilize established political structures. To explain the political life of interwar Europe without focusing on the personal, cultural, social, economic, and environmental devastation of war and its outcomes, the widespread disease which followed it, repeated economic collapse or sustained depression, or the catastrophic way that the multi-ethnic states of Russia, Germany, and Austria-Hungary were divided up, may seem bizarre—but excellent histories of these things are easily accessible. These were potent causes for disorder, chaos and human suffering in the 1920s and 1930s. But what these phenomena do not explain are the mechanisms by which political responses to these crises arose and gained their effect: losing a war might make someone angry, and place social organization under a lot of stress, but it does not of itself dissolve the state, and replace it with a new structure. Some other process has to be brought into play to do that.

The revolutions in Russia in 1917 and Germany in 1918 were sparked by the same particular forms of spatial relationship: warships moored near industrial cities and starving populations in urban centres. It was sailors in Petrograd (formerly St Petersburg) and Wilhelmshaven (just north of industrial Bremen) who initiated the first phases of violence which drove both revolutions. Semi-isolated on their ships with nothing to do, in close company with bands of other men of similar age and class, armed but not fighting, caught up in the day-to-day struggle of urbanites to locate food and coal, these men formed potent and volatile cadres of people with the capacity and know-how to enter nearby cities quickly and effect revolutionary change with violence. One historian has used space and place to characterize the different elements that made up long series of events throughout 1917, known collectively as the Russian Revolution. He distinguishes between 'streets, factories, workshops', 'fields, forests, villages', and 'barracks, battleships and the line'.[35] These were the central terrains of the convulsions of 1917–23 which defined much of the political century to follow.

Factories had largely made Russia ungovernable by early 1917.[36] It was a combination of commemorations of Bloody Sunday, women's campaigns for better food rations, and yet another strike at the Putilov metal plant in January and February 1917 that led to the abdication of Tsar Nicholas. But the failure of the replacement government to commit itself wholeheartedly to extricating Russia from the war under-mined the possibility of general urban consensus to support the liberal regime. However, the final form that the revolution would take was by no means certain: Social Revolutionaries (in fact, progressive, lib-eral socialists, despite their name), Mensheviks, Bolsheviks, and half a dozen more leftist subgroupings, could all call on specific workshops, garrisons, and warships to back them in their competing attempts to undermine the liberal government led by the Socialist Revolutionary, and deputy for the Petrograd soviet, Alexander Karenskii.

This confrontation reached a climax in August 1917 when Petrograd regional military commander, General Kornilov, drew up Cossack regiments and sent them into the working-class districts on 26 August to restore order and close down the Bolshevik printing presses and workers' organizations. Military interventions in urban environments are rarely effective, because cities are tough terrain for conventional armies to fight in. This one was such a failure that the next day, the government resigned. Those on the radical left, like the Bolsheviks, seized the opportunity to marginalize more moderate socialists, and their efforts were directed out of the Putilov Factory, Trubochnyi Factory, Metallikeschii Factory, and the Old Baranovskii Machine Construction Factory. The Putilov works had been engaging only in erratic production for months, but faced with the threat of Cossack intervention, the Cannon Shop there put out 300 heavy pieces in three days (three weeks' normal output) to arm their soviet. It sent out 8,000 of its workers too, tightly organized into eight Red Guard units alongside several fortification detachments and groups of agitators to go and foment disaffection in Kornilov's troops—which they did to great effect, as almost all of them melted away.[37] Thus at the begin-ning of September 1917 there was no meaningful central government because of the actions of the factory workers; and there were no effec-tive troops that any such government could call upon if it had existed. So to a degree the 'October Revolution' was not the vicious elimina-tion of one set of robust power structures by another, but the creation of the institutions of government ad hoc by factory workers, soldiers, and sailors in urban centres in a relatively anarchic situation.

The factories were not just important for the spontaneous organization of manpower and matériel for revolutionary violence—they had a central ideological role too. It was in the verbal discussions and meetings between workers in a quite limited number of factories that a specifically anti-bourgeois ideological strand of political thought was developed, and it was this anti-bourgeois stand that made the formation of an effective, humane, compromise government impossible, and which moved the Russian Revolution from its 'liberal' to its 'Bolshevik' phase. It sidelined the Mensheviks and Social Revolutionaries, who were more popular and preferred to avoid violence where possible. To attack the bourgeoisie (which was remarkably small, almost non-existent, in Russia) was in fact to invoke a codeword: it meant the rejection of democracy in the Western European sense, and a refusal to compromise with any of the centrist or leftist elements in the provisional government. In some instances, one can trace this back to specific *rooms* in specific factories. One of the first explicitly anti-bourgeois (that is to say, anti-democratic) statements emerged in July 1917—just before the Kornilov affair—and it was produced by No. 6 Shop of the Trubochnyi Factory. Following a protracted meeting and discussion in their shop, the workers there unanimously declared:

> On our part, we swear to die in the name of the liberation of the toiling class. And let the entire bourgeois clique not think that we have forgotten our tasks, that we are preoccupied by our party disputes. No. When self-sacrifice is needed, then let that vile clique [the bourgeoisie] know that we are ready to die or achieve victory.[38]

Yet while this sort of 'consensus' could be engineered in very specific workshops, where everyone knew each other and was in the same location, the wider Russian urban working class was very divided, and the majority of the country was neither urban nor working class—it was peasant and rural. Only this ideology's specific geographical compression in certain dockyards, workshops, and factories could give it the coherency to act as it did. Far from being a disadvantage, it was a key to success: for example, in Spain there had been a substantial radical, anarchist revolutionary political force in the country since the 1860s, but it was distributed throughout many agricultural regions, each with different languages, religious customs, landholding patterns, and climates, so never effectively brought about the type of crisis available to the more geographically circumscribed Bolsheviks.[39]

The real diversity of the urban working class in general (as opposed to its composition in individual factories or shops) is revealed in the elections of 1918. In one of the most industrial districts of Petrograd, Nevskii, elections in the summer of 1918 to the Petrograd soviet resulted in thirteen Social Revolutionary delegates (democratic social-ists, with a strong support in both cities and amongst peasants), one Menshevik, thirteen Social Revolutionary-Menshevik, and only seven Bolsheviks. The Nevskii Shipbuilding Factory votes broke down into 1,221 votes for the Social Revolutionaries, 200 for the Mensheviks, and 493 for the Bolsheviks. Yet this minority position was not neces-sarily such a disadvantage, in the light of the great concentration of Bolshevism in very specific workshops, like No. 6 Shop, Trubochnyi Factory. What made the Bolsheviks able to take power was their focus on very specific factories, and maintaining discipline there.[40] It was not the number of people in their army, but the tightness of their formations that was important, and it was the geography of the mod-ern city that underpinned these formations. This intimate physical proximity was crucial, and the value of establishing a well-disciplined, well-defined, highly active cadre of revolutionaries was central to the success of Lenin's party in the longer term. While the 'invention' of this idea of a 'vanguard party', so central to the Russian Revolution, is usually ascribed to Lenin and his 1902 essay 'What is to be Done?', many of the practical aspects of the idea were worked out without him when he was barely back in Petrograd, and had not yet established a convincing power base. It was in places like No. 6 Shop, Trubochnyi Factory where the ideas were first put into practice. Lenin returned and tried (and sometimes failed) to take control of these cadres; but he did not found them, and was not in a position to do so, because they were formed in worlds alien to him, in which he, as a bourgeois intel-lectual, could never have easily mixed prior to late summer of 1917.

Nor was the importance of place unique to either Russia, or the left. The mechanism of the fascist rise to power in Italy was equally a product of the conflicts of the city streets—in part because the author-ity and reach of the Italian state had always been so very circum-scribed, limited, and partial. Real power in Italy did not reside in office-holding in Rome. To capture the Italian state was not to capture a great deal; it was streets that mattered. And it was street fighting which formed the foundation stone of the Fascist Party. To read an account of the rise of the fascists is to read of squabbles over organized crime patches, fights on trams, contests over the rights to sell oranges in Milan's markets, and other apparent 'minutiae'.[41] Italian fascism sprang from a set of labour disputes in north Italian industrial cities, and represented a vaguely middle-class attempt to challenge workers' assertions of their collective identity. Mussolini had formed his first band of *Squadristi* to attack striking Alfa Romeo autoworkers at their factory in Milan in 1920. The party came to power after occupying major cities, then assembling all its forces outside Rome. Fearing imminent civil war, King Victor Emanuel made Mussolini prime minister. Thus, on the surface, it was the threat of a coup (the infamous 'March on Rome' that never happened) that put the fascists into power. But to make their power real, the fascists would have to take on the socialists directly, and more broadly: Mussolini knew that appointments in Rome were not at the heart of the movement, but confrontations at factory gates. Although the apparatus of liberal democracy was gradually removed up until 1925, when Italy became a one-party state, a precondition of that consolidation of power by the fascists was cowing the mighty industrial unions and cities of northern Italy which had rendered Italy ungovernable in 1919 and 1920, and neutralizing the threat that they posed to the political order that Mussolini hoped to establish.

This sort of assertion of power could not be done with anything as puny as laws. It meant entering the cities and engaging in physical conflict with industrial workers on their own turf. Furthermore, the fascists themselves were not a coherent group: they were only formed as a party in November 1921, although as a street-fighting outfit they had existed for longer than this. The fascists had no single constituency to which they could appeal for support, and no consistent ideology or political programme.[42] Something was needed to galvanize them into a solid identity, to give them a coherent *esprit de corps*, as well as dissolving the workers' organizations that continued to support communist and socialist groupings in northern cities like Turin. Donning the black shirt of a fascist follower was only the first step in producing a true fascist. True political commitment required the galvanizing force of direct action, and direct action requires a specific place; this is what shaped the party—especially the younger men on whom it relied—into a coherent political unit. The *Squadristi* themselves have left few memoires, but Italian historians have pieced together their ideology, for example from the popular stories that they bought and read. In them, this sort of view is typical:

> political struggle especially freed me from any negativity. Each night before going into action it totally took over my life. It made me unprejudiced and decisive in action, like the others, or even more so...I forgot everything else. I developed a will of iron which gave significance and purpose to my every move.[43]

Doing led to believing, in the slogan of the time (an emphasis on the 'deed' borrowed from communist revolutionaries, and which would be aped by the Nazis). Yet attempts to produce this 'real and present' power were hard to organize in the first place, and hard to bring to a successful conclusion. Nowhere was this more crucial than in the large industrial cities of northern Italy, where socialism was embedded into every aspect of everyday life, from the factories one worked in to the bars one drank in.

These industrial cities in northern Italy had been in turmoil since the war, with frequent worker occupations of factories, culminating in a series of occupations in 1920. It is not clear what the workers occupying the factories wanted—in Sesto, part of the industrial sprawl surrounding Milan, workers occupied the factory on the following grounds, described in a leaflet published by the strikers:

> the [occupation of the factories] does not represent a political or economic revolution by which one regime is replaced by another...It is in reality nothing but the affirmation by the proletariat of its right to existence which as of now is unrecognized by those who monopolize the means of production.[44]

So the workers wanted to assert their presence, but had not evolved a coherent programme. While workers in No. 6 Shop, Trubochnyi Factory were explicit in their rejection of democracy as a means of political organization, the workers in Sesto lacked this sort of precision or clarity. Fascism initially formed in the industrial centre of Milan and proliferated in similar industrial cities as a response to labour unrest like this, which seemed to be going nowhere yet doing a lot of harm. But such cities had a well-developed workers' culture of their own, and this was hard to penetrate or disrupt. Fascists' first instinct was to copy this culture, with its rallies and banners and songs and bars and brawls, but this ran up against a lack of 'space' for them to do it in. Workers did it in their factories and bars, but Fascists largely did not have access to these spaces. Once again, the 'grand narrative' is brought down to the level of the street.

At other times, early fascists (or proto-fascists—the movement coalesced over several years) could join in with socialists—as in the food riots that swept Italian cities in 1919 and 1920, or by backing the striking taxi drivers of Milan in 1922. But if fascism was going to become a political movement to challenge and destroy socialism, it would eventually have to do more than mimic it or collaborate with it. In fact, increasingly fights between fascists and socialists were breaking out on an ad hoc basis: in industrial cities and their suburbs, like Milan and Sesto—on the tram lines between Sesto and downtown Milan, Sesto, and Monza, and in a few town-centre cafés and bars. But in April of 1921, amid a huge wave of fascist violence, a fascist group from outside Sesto itself seems to have organized a set of violent attacks on the socialist social and cultural centre, the Casa del Popolo, in a more systematic way, indicating that violence was coming to be viewed by *Squadristi* as a specific 'means to an end'. At that stage, Sesto fascists were still keen to present themselves as being *with* the working class in its reasonable demands, and worried about the impact of the Milanese *Squadristi* coming onto their turf to initiate violent conflicts. However, with a wave of working-class strikes in August 1922, the local mood amongst Sesto fascists changed, and when, in September 1922, the Circolo Avvenire workers' club was raided, this time it was Sesto's own *Squadristi* which took the lead. But exerting pressure like this was not easy, and frequently unsuccessful: working-class knowledge of the industrial suburbs always put the fascists at a disadvantage. In Sesto, when the fascists organized their raid on Avvenire, they were not confident in doing so: they attacked the building suddenly and fled, anticipating that they could not hope to hold territory like that if workers' friends and families arrived, as they surely would.[45]

In industrial Turin, Blackshirts' initial attempts to attack individual socialists and union buildings were thwarted in the working-class quarters of Borgo Vittoria and Pozzo Strada, when communists organized roof-top surveillance to warn of approaches. Then the residents pelted the incoming Blackshirts with bottles, stones, boiling water, and excrement.[46] To celebrate the fifth anniversary of the Russian Revolution in the first week of November 1922—just after the fascists had taken power in Rome, and installed their man as chief of police in Turin—the communists organized meetings in the back rooms of bars in four of the main working-class districts. The fascist prefect of the city, Carlo Olivieri, reported to Rome that communists were still fully functioning in these districts, and that this presented a major failure of the Fascist Party. A fascist wearing his black shirt, Gustavo Doglia, was killed by communists in October; they shot and killed a *squadrista* in Burgo Vittorio, one of the working class suburbs of Turin, in November. In December, tram worker Francesco Prato attacked two fascists in the street and killed them— he was quickly hidden in the working-class Barriera di Nizza, and the wounded communist remained hidden for two months, before being smuggled first to Switzerland, then to the USSR. Government investigators concluded that the Fascist Party 'considered Turin to be a barrel at boiling point that must be surrounded by iron to prevent it exploding'.[47]

In order to attempt to reclaim the streets and re-galvanize their members, some form of concrete, coherent action was necessary to demonstrate the fascists' capacity to move about the city with impunity. On 29 November, two separate attacks by 300 fascists on the socialist leisure institution of the *Casa del Popolo* in Borgo Vittoria were planned, and executed with military precision; but the socialists and communists were waiting, and used guerrilla tactics to repel them. Weaker in numbers on this occasion, the communists used their better knowledge of the city's rat runs, and their command of the roof-tops and windows, to frustrate the fascist attacks. This was not some peripheral 'tidying' exercise, remote to the concerns of 'real' politics and the state; all this street violence was an integral part of the political process, not external to it. Mussolini was already prime minister, but had failed to make his power real. Power must exist in a specific place and a specific space. Power does not exist in offices or laws or systems, nor does it float like a menacing cloud above society, but lies in the moment of action in which that power is exercised.

Because of the command of windows, roofs—and loyalties—in the working-class areas, a defeat like this could not go unchallenged if Mussolini's power was to be made real. The fascists decided to escalate the confrontation, both in order to galvanize their own supporters, and destroy the communist opposition. From 17 December, the fascists started to pack the city with bands of *Squadristi* imported from outside. They plastered the city with posters urging fascists to avenge the murders at the hands of communists; they stole ten pistols and two rifles from a military warehouse. By the morning of 19 December, they had burnt down the House of Labour, and murdered eight communists, and the legend of the 'Massacre of Turin' was born. The communists were not entirely broken; but they could no longer organize freely on a large scale in the working-class districts of Turin. And the fascists had forced their own hands as a party of violence and dictatorship. There was no going back, and in 1925—while erecting the formal apparatus of the one-party state—Mussolini publicly 'accepted' responsibility for the urban violence through which he had consolidated his power. In reality, it was a boast, because it was in these 'excesses' that the fascist anti-liberal project was realized.

Ten years later, in the cities and bars and factories and alleys of Germany, similar battles were being fought for territory by another fascist party. The success of the National Socialists cannot be explained away just by people drinking in certain bars, however; to ignore the frustration Germans felt for the outcomes of their defeat in 1918, or to dismiss the distress of the profound poverty of the hyperinflation of 1923 or the Great Depression from 1928 onwards (it started early in Germany), would be to do an injustice to the anxieties that preoccupied Germans in the Weimar Republic. But the *mechanisms* by which the Nazis could take these anxieties and preoccupations and convert them into the power it took to destroy the KPD (German Communist Party) and SPD (German Social Democratic Party) were real and physical; it will not do to rely on the phenomenon of one man, however fascinatingly nightmarish his vision may be, and however important his role certainly was. Anxieties and resentments and hatreds and aspirations, whether of one man or of many, do not turn themselves into political parties and governmental power by some mystical process of political sublimation. The connections must be made real. For anything to be made real, it must occupy a very specific place.[48]

NSDAP leaders were anxious about their inability to penetrate the big cities, and their reliance on rural and small-town support. They knew that if they wished to control an urban, industrial society like Germany, they had to penetrate the cities.

The slum areas of Hamburg's docks and poorer quarters around the Reeperbahn had long since been impenetrable to the Weimar Republic's police, and these areas consistently voted for the KPD and the SPD—the two parties polled between 60 and 80 per cent of the vote there up until 1930.[49] The Nazis felt that they had to organize a presence in places like this—especially the significant part of the Nazi Party that took the 'Socialist' and 'Workers' part of the party's full name seriously: National Socialist German Workers' Party. It was the goal of Hamburg Nazis to break into this area and organize there; it was the goal of the KPD and SPD to stop them. As one of the leading historians of interwar Germany has noted, 'the electoral success of both Nazis and communists directly related to their effectiveness in conducting the political struggle in the neighbourhoods'.[50]

The communists usually did well in acquiring and defending terri-tory—but not always. When in 1932, Rosa Erdmann's husband took over the bar at 155 Breitstraße, he told his communist customers that they were no longer welcome there—they were barred from their local *Stube*, where they had been accustomed to meet. A campaign of harassment was begun. As the local police chief noted:

> From the moment when the National Socialists turned up in Erdmann's tavern, the attacks against it by political opponents increased...The unconcealed efforts of the Communists were obviously aimed at wear-ing down Erdmann...or at driving the SS from the tavern. The leader-ship of the KPD felt it unbearable and dangerous for their survival in the area concerned if it came to the National Socialists remaining per-manently in the tavern.[51]

It was a wise analysis—one which would have been familiar to many urban policemen across the continent. When a local KPD man, Witt, was found shot dead, and SA men from Erdmann's were suspected, communists decided to act. Drawing up support from other suburbs, the Red Front Fighters' League and the Red Youth Troop, placed squads in houses around Erdmann's tavern during the afternoon so that their build-up would go unnoticed, and agreed to meet at 10 p.m.

They attacked—over sixty shots were fired; no one was killed. The attack failed, and the Nazis remained at Erdmann's.

Socialists were far less ready and willing to use street violence than either communists or Nazis, preferring to organize in factories, docks, warehouses, and works, based on their well-established presence there developed over fifty years. Far more interested in 'respectability' than either of the newer communist or Nazi parties, they failed to defend their territory in areas of traditional strength in Hamburg, like Carl-Theodorstraße and Große Brunnenstraße. On 12 July 1932, about twenty or so SA men hid behind trees and in side streets on their way back from a drinking session and attacked a group of men on the way back from a Reichsbanner meeting—the socialist 'fighting' organization to defend democracy. Outnumbered, the socialists were quickly overcome; but another group of socialists on their way from a different paramilitary group meeting, the Iron Front, also passed by, evening out the numbers. But instead of joining in the fight, they stood back and merely shouted insults at the SA men. This was profoundly indicative of what happens when one cedes control of the streets—although, paradoxically, the problem may have been caused not on the streets, but in the docks and factories.[52] Widespread unemployment caused by the Great Depression meant that the usual, day-to-day association of socialist men suddenly became voluntary—now that their workplaces were shut, they had to *choose* to go to a socialist bar. While NSDAP places of association were voluntary too, it had always been so, and had grown out of bars and beer halls, because the SA had targeted the unemployed from its inception. The SA stormtrooper movement grew out of bar space; the SPD retreated into it. The NSDAP never penetrated docks and factories effectively, but once deprived of this territory by the Great Depression, the SPD could not function. One by one, SPD bars in Sankt Pauli and Altona (both effectively docks districts of Hamburg) shut down, and with them, the capacity to meet, to organize, to socialize, evaporated. The identity and *esprit de corps* on which collective action depended no longer had places in which to coalesce. In short, the SPD's presence in public life was eliminated along with the spaces they occupied, and once-solid socialist wards went over to the KPD or the Nazis, both of whom were resolved on the destruction of the Weimar Republic.

But the city was not only an instrument through which power could be seized; if a grip on this power was to be held, it had to embed itself into the urban cultures—or rural cultures—which it hoped to govern. All the totalitarian regimes of the 1920s and 1930s had good reason to fear the cities. Mussolini, Hitler, and Stalin were all aware of the role of cities in producing the specific forms of political instability that had enabled their acquisition of power. They knew too that it was in the cities that the well-organized roots of socialism still remained buried, always a potential threat to their authority. But Stalin was faced with a somewhat unique problem: Marx's theories proposed that socialism would occur in a capitalist, urbanized economy—he started by thinking Germany, Belgium, or Britain, but ended his life unsure where this prospect was realistic. Russia, however, certainly was not a candidate. It was far too agricultural; its population was far too dispersed, religious, illiterate, superstitious, and conservative. Paradoxically, it was many of those features which made effective revolution in Russia possible, and effective resistance to it impossible. But this still left an anomaly: socialism was supposed to be modern. It was meant to be productive, distributive, industrial, technological, and Russia—especially its countryside—was none of these. If Stalin and the other leading communists around him wanted to make Russia conform to their ideal of a modern society, and also ensure that their ideological programme was not vulnerable to the same sorts of instability that brought them to power, then they had two main options: either they could move the rural population to the cities; or they could move urban life into the countryside. They did both, rapidly growing the urban population of the USSR and catastrophically forcing urban, industrialized models of production onto the countryside. Between *c.*1926 and 1939, about 26 million peasants moved (or were forcibly moved) to Soviet cities.[53] There, they did not abstractly 'observe' socialism; they physically built it, and by doing so, became the proletariat that the theory required.

A concrete example of this would be the construction of the metro in Moscow. It was in the underground, deep under Moscow, that rural peasants became urban technicians, engineers, and proletarians. It was the metro (and the thousands of urbanizing projects like it) that taught many peasants to read, to join the Comsomol, to find proletarian partners, and have truly urban children. It was something as real as the metro which showed them the capacity of the state to act coherently and to produce something on a vast scale. While highly geographically specific, the metro also was experienced as a 'national' project: suitably ideologically enthusiastic employees and their families were drafted from the countryside by the 100,000—a strategy which called the physical city into being, *and* produced a proletariat to populate it. Physical and social processes were profoundly, and self-consciously, combined. City, class, and nation were being melded into one experience, at once site-specific and universal. One English visitor to the USSR in 1937 noted:

> I was told by an English-woman that a peasant in Tiflis [Tblisi] had asked her whether she had seen 'our' metro? She said that she thought the only metro was in Moscow. 'Yes' said the peasant, 'our Moscow metro.'[54]

The population of Moscow in the first *three* years of the first Five-Year Plan—so between 1929 and 1932—leapt from 2.2 million to 3.7 million, more than 50 per cent.[55] The process of building Moscow was intended to produce the 'new citizen', to transform the crude peasant into the precise, committed, dynamic instrument of labour.

A story—likely apocryphal, but who knows?—in the *Moscow Daily News* told of a young worker who had been drafted in from the countryside to work on the project. At night, when he returned to his collective barracks, he was so crass, so vulgar, so unaware of the ideological commitment to progress that he was supposed to display, that he slept with his boots on, muddying and dirtying his bed. Gradually, he started to recognize the efforts and tolerance of his barrack-mates and workmates, and took the boots off. Eventually, he began to use the bathhouse. He married, then brought his parents to live in Moscow. He had been transformed, the story claimed, into 'a Muscovite, a Metrostroi shock worker, an enthusiast in his difficult and noble work'. But this transformation worked beyond Moscow alone, bringing in the rest of his peasant family. As one historian has observed, 'the physical transformation of the city was also to serve as both the means and the metaphor for the transformation of the new Soviet citizen'.[56] As the *Pravda* headline once exclaimed, 'How many people recreated themselves making the Metro?'[57] Projects like this forged the 'community of labour' on which the entire Soviet vision of a new society was predicated, and so were central mechanisms in converting ideology into power. Cities, their sociability, their construction, their very fabric—above and below ground—were not accidental by-products of an abstract communist philosophy; they *were* that philosophy made real. Even once the process of completing the metro was complete, once the vast, transformative social upheaval of migration, literacy, engineering, and labour had been effected, the everyday *use* of the metro was carefully choreographed so that to move through it was to relive aesthetically the experience of the production of the socialist citizen.[58]

In Nazi Germany, the task was not so much to construct city streets—although plenty of such construction did go on. Rather, the task was initially to supervise, surveil and regulate them. National Socialism was a new movement; Nazis' hold on the cities was tenuous and erratic. Far from being all-pervasive masters of every level of society, for most Germans it would have been difficult to detect the presence of the NSDAP in their everyday lives in the 1930s, and this 'failure' of penetration was something which bothered the party hierarchy profoundly. In the spring of 1933, with the failed boycott of Jewish businesses, and in November of 1938, with the staged riots around *Kristallnacht*, the Nazi leadership was confronted by conspicuous public rejection of a core plank of the ideology of the party faithful. Both were specifically *urban* attempts to organize the German population (or that part of it which the Nazis thought mattered, there being hardly any Jewish businesses and synagogues outside the cities), and every housewife who continued to shop at Jewish grocers in 1933, and every middle-class lawyer or doctor or engineer who complained about the riots surrounding Synagogues in 1938, spelt out the failure of the party to promote one of its core ideologies effectively amongst the wider public. When the NSDAP came to organize the formal extermination of the Jewish people from January 1942 onwards, they made sure that they did not do it in Germany, but in Eastern Europe.

Instead of showing a regulatory confidence in Germany's cities, the NSDAP was so anxious about urban opposition that it developed a sophisticated system of urban supervision—at least initially, for it largely disintegrated in the face of the Allied aerial bombardment. If city blocks were daily incinerated, 'block supervision' would become a meaningless concept. A district like Altona, an industrial part of Hamburg, was typical. There was a strict regime of party surveillance, to ensure that the communists would not be able to re-establish themselves there. At the top of the urban surveillance and party organization in big cities was the *Kreisleiter*—'district leader'. In Hamburg-Altona, he supervised 32 'district groups', who managed roughly 250 'cells'. A cell was a population unit of about 1,000, and these were further subdivided into a 'block', each with its own leader, supervising about 50 households. On the fifth of the month, each *Blockwart* (block supervisor) would present a report to the cell; the cells would report to the district leader; the district leader would submit it to the *Kreisleiter*, who would in turn report to the *Gau*, or regional administration.

This system was effective in a *negative* sense: it was good at providing information to disrupt formal political opposition, like the Communist Party. But it was weak at securing the proactive support of the urban working classes that the Nazis desperately craved. Communists were so impressed by its disruptive effects that it was broadly copied in East Germany after the war, as it provided a remarkable capacity for micro-supervision of even the most mundane aspects of day-to-day life: which girls were going out with which boys, which women were keeping slovenly homes, which men swore at Nazi Party functionaries. It mixed the structure of the party into the structure of the city, creating an overlap between the spaces of everyday life and the spaces of political power. Whereas previously, going into a communist or socialist or Catholic bar or skittles club (Germans were—and still are—obsessed with skittles) was an act of choice, requiring the citizen to engage and disengage with alternative identities while moving through the city, this system of systematic penetration of the spaces of everyday life meant just the reverse. No amount of 'retreat' from a specific public space on the part of the citizen could allow them to escape this gaze. Often, a 'gaze' was all it was; lives were lived relatively unmolested by the authorities (terrifying knocks on the door in the dead of night were extremely rare in National Socialist Germany, but common in the USSR), but always with the vague and unspoken threat that 'something' might happen. Thus in August 1935, the area group leader in the Hamburg-Altstadt, Piwitt, instructed his block supervisors to start compiling names of Jews; he did the same again in 1937.

These lists were distributed to other block supervisors, and they tried to persuade others to boycott Jewish businesses based on these lists, by hassling housewives not to go to them. This was not as part of a major national campaign, but as part of the steady process of penetrating the everyday lives of the working-class communities there.[59] A simple and 'innocuous' question from a *Blockwart* to a housewife going into a Jewish shop might encourage her to walk elsewhere. No threat was made, no shouting, no reporting, no secret police—just a remarkably soft yet penetrative strike to the heart of the mundane habits of every-day existence, by accompanying them with a courteous, but meaning-ful, glance, question, or suggestion. Urban structures were not just for producing disorder; if used imaginatively, they could be powerful mechanisms to establish control and conformity too. But equally, stripped of the might of the state, the SS, the Gestapo, the Abwehr, and all the other instruments of terror, many housewives treated these 'little Hitlers' with contempt, humiliating them, and shopping in the Jewish shops anyway. The SPD, now banned by the Nazis, kept an underground organization going in Germany until about 1936–7, and their members sent reports on the situation on the ground to the SPD in exile, reports which are remarkable for their overlap from the Nazis' own secret observation organizations. One member from Munich reported in May 1935 on an attempt by some local Nazis to stop people shopping in a Jewish shop:

> On the night of 1 May 1935 large stones were thrown from a car at the windrows of the shop belonging to the Jew Pappenheim in Weisenburgplatz and smashed the panes. The following day a large crowd gathered outside the store and openly opposed these excesses. One heard comments such as, 'Incredible goings-on', 'cheek', 'vandal-ism' etc. Thus it was clear that the population had no sympathy with the tricks of the Nazis...It was clear to the observer that this incident was not the resolve of mass discontent, but an act planned by a few criminals....National socialists also appeared in front of the Jew Schwarz's shop, and warned customers not to enter the shop. But it was noticeable that no-one let themselves be put off; in fact, one could see that some customers demonstratively carried the goods they had bought with hardly any wrappings.[60]

It seems that the while the NSDAP was effective at destabilizing cities in order to seize the instruments of the state, they did not succeed, in the ways that the Bolsheviks or the Italian fascists did, at politicizing the street thereafter as a way of producing a political power base: too many shoppers behaved confrontationally to arrest them all. Once in power, the Nazi regime was always remarkably select in the enemies it made amongst German 'Aryan' citizens.

If the NSDAP apparatus, however, found leaders of the SPD, the communists, or trade unions, they were harsh because such people, well-embedded in the fabric of urban life, could often evade the supervision of the *Blockwart*, and their opposition was so much more dramatic than that of the housewives in Weisenburgplatz (and countless other *plätze*). Recent research by one German historian on Berlin during the Nazi period shows not a totalitarian megalith, but the traces of literally thousands of resisters working to undermine the Nazi state—the files of successful and unsuccessful Gestapo (Secret State Police) and Sicherheitsdienst (Security Service) operations reveal that leaflets, protests, small moments of sabotage, and disruption proliferated, especially after the beginning of the war. And this first piece of comprehensive research on Berlin's everyday resistors—spreading to nearly 700 pages—covers just socialists and communists: such research for Berlin on the ways professional men, ordinary women, gay people, Jews, and young people resisted is largely waiting to be done to the same level of detail. As one Gestapo report from Berlin complained in 1937:

> They ['Marxists' and 'enemies of the state'] sit around in the evening and drink beer. They meet with people who used to share their perspective in the residential districts, they dress up meetings as 'family visits'. They avoid all formal organisations, and try in the methods mentioned above to keep 'friends' in agreement with them. At these get-togethers people naturally discuss the political situation, swap stories, and spread what one might call 'fluster'-propaganda, which currently represents the most effective illegal operations against the state.[61]

The Gestapo report from 9 January 1938 about the 'Berliner Liederfreunde'—the Berlin Friends of Song, a choral society—in the working-class district of Neukölln, states bitterly that, 'The members and guests are recruited almost exclusively from known office-holders and members of the SPD and the trade unions. They were all friends with each other, or knew each other, so the impression was of a large family.'[62] SPD member Hildegard Schönrock, who died in 1998, confirms that this was exactly the case. At a choir meeting of the local youth choir, she recalled regularly seeing the local SPD leaders there, as well as well-known NSDAP spies. They would sing songs about 'solidarity' to keep their spirits up, and when the singing was over, melt away into the city, having established contacts with others of a like mind—not always for subversion: perhaps more often to make friends, meet a girlfriend or boyfriend, find a job. But while the choir meetings were easy to observe, they formed a public network which the richly diverse environment of the city could immediately cover up in bars, stairwells, clubs, and workplaces. Towards the end of the war, the US government was especially concerned about the deep reach of Nazi ideology into German society, and thought that there would be an extensive resistance after the war: but it was not to be. National Socialism's grasp of the cities was superficial, and democratic politics quickly re-established itself in Germany in 1945.

Nor was it the case that it was only the 'losers' of the Great War, the disordered and broken states of post-war Central, Eastern, and Southern Europe whose political stability could rest on their ability to understand or manage what happened on city streets. After the French parliamentary elections of May 1932, there was a period of weak and varied political leadership. As was common in the Third Republic, ministries came and went—though five ministries in eighteen months was 'good going'. The fundamental tensions which democracy can produce were writ large in the National Assembly. Struggling to cope with an economy in profound difficulties, the leftist parties refused to countenance circumscribing the pay of the vast army of people in the employ of the French state, while the centre and right parties refused to countenance raising taxes. Democracy looked to be paralysing the French state, just as Hitler was taking power in Berlin that January. As the democratic process revealed itself unable to resolve the crisis in a stable, resolute, and permanent way, the very concept of parliamentary government came under extensive attack.

The moderate right called for a sort of 'authoritarian' president—elected, but unaccountable to any but the electorate and his vision of the destiny of *la France*; the moderate left called for socialization and nationalization. The extremes of right and left called for revolution in some form or another, and these extremes were extensive. There was a long tradition in France of explaining complex political situations as the result of a conspiracy—typically, of Jews, secret societies, and Freemasons. Often, all three were assumed to overlap. After the publication of Edouard Drumont's *La France juive* in 1886, the nationalist idea of 'France' and 'Frenchness' increasingly focused on the idea of a secret Jewish plot to destroy the nation; the harder the plot was to find, the greater the evidence of its cunning secretiveness. If a grotesque, malign spirit such as Drumont's can be said to have created anything perfect, then his Jewish conspiracy theory was it. The most famous outcome of this theory was the framing of the personally unappealing Jewish army officer, Alfred Dreyfus. But this plot—so devastating to the political life of France, the reputation of French values, and the reputation of France itself from 1894 until well into the twentieth century—was not, in essence, urban. It was conducted at the highest levels of the French state, in elite circles. A populist urban press was certainly important in prosecuting both sides of the argument, but the real business of the affair went on in secret trials and amongst the highest ranks of the army. It was a *salon* affair. But such was the nature of the transformation of politics in the early twentieth century that the next great anti-Semitic scandal to shake France was no longer an affair of the elites; it was a contest for the streets of Paris, and reflected a fundamental shift in the mechanisms of authority in the French state.[63]

As the Third Republic struggled incompetently to find a coherent solution to the economic collapse blighting Europe since the end of the war in general, and the Wall Street Crash in particular, the French right explained the 'problem' in France in terms of a Jewish conspiracy combined with the corrupt nature of parliamentary government. In particular, they focused on the case of Alexandre Stavisky as exemplifying all that was wrong with France. Stavisky was Jewish-Ukrainian in origin, and a swindler of the first order. He, along with some idiotic and/or duplicitous Radical Party politicians had become embroiled in a swindle in provincial Bayonne, first coming to light in 1927. The Paris prosecutor charged with bringing the case had delayed Stavisky's trial nineteen times—it still had not been resolved in December 1933—and the right-wing press screamed conspiracy, oscillating between suspecting Freemasons and Jews, sometimes both. But at the end of 1933, it was clear to Stavisky that he could not escape trial forever. He fled Paris, and was found in a mountain chalet by the police, squirming in agony. He either committed suicide (the official verdict), or was shot by the police either because they were casual racists who had no respect for human life; or on the orders of Camille Chautemps, the Radical Party prime minister, to silence Stavisky's revelations—depending on one's political preferences. Both the suicide and murder explanations remain plausible. The Paris prosecutor's office which delayed the prosecution for so long was headed by Pressard, who was a Freemason, and also the brother-in-law of Chautemps. Such was the scandal that Chautemps was forced to resign, and Edouard Daladier became premier in January 1934. So far, so 'un-urban', so 'high political'.[64]

The hysteria about a Jewish–Masonic–Radical–Secret Service plot grew amongst the far right, while on the far left, the plot was explained as bourgeois–Jewish–Masonic–Radical.[65] Over the next two weeks, there were a series of demonstrations which often erupted into violence. The demonstrations oscillated between left and right, each side trying to demonstrate a greater capacity to mobilize on the streets. On 3 February, Jean Chiappe, the populist but right-wing Paris chief of police was sacked by Daladier for his indulgences to the right on these demonstrations. On 6 February, Daladier presented his cabinet to the Chamber of Deputies to be sworn in—but outside, there was a vast, well-organized, coordinated attempt to invade the Chamber by 50,000 extreme-right 'leaguers', which caused the collapse of the government and the widespread belief that France, like Italy, Germany, and in fact almost every other Continental European state, would become a dictatorship.[66]

Explaining the riot of 6 February 1934 is a complex business, because it is hard to perceive 'sides' in it. Superficially, it looks highly coordinated because apparently incompatible political groupings organized themselves to march to the centre of Paris from different directions, as can be seen in Figure 1.2; however, their mutual antagonism provides the key, because this confrontation was supposed to 'resolve' the conflicts between these groups—and it did. The main groups that organized the first marches on 6 February were the 'leagues' of the far right. The Croix de Feu ('cross of fire') and the Action Française were quasi-fascist nationalist organizations drawing support from veterans, small tradespeople and big business. The goals of their leaders are unclear: they certainly wanted to destroy Daladier's government; they certainly wanted the reinstatement of Chiappe; they certainly wanted to destroy the parliamentary system of government as a whole. They succeeded in their first goal; they failed in their second and third. But whether they wanted to destroy *all* of France's republican values (rather than just the clumsy parliamentary method of administering them) in the way that Mussolini and Hitler exemplified, and whether they could have done so even if they *had* wanted to, is a matter of some debate.[67] Contemporaries, though, were convinced they wanted to, and could.

There were a plethora of rioters offering a variety of views, so demons were easy to identify in the February Riots. The Jeunesses Patriotes were more directly inspired by Mussolini's Blackshirts, and wanted to protect France from 'the left'. Solidarité Française was funded by the cosmetics millionaire Coty and more directly imitated the Nazi party in its anti-Semitic goals, but had no coherent ideology.[68] The hugely popular veterans' associations, like the Union Nationale de Combattants (on the right), or the much larger Association Républicaine des Anciens Combattants (ARAC, essentially a branch of the Parti Communiste Français) also took part. Rag-tag units of communists and socialists also went along, aiming to disrupt the rightist 'leagues'. But above all, the well-disciplined ranks of the ARAC were deployed in a deliberate attempt to make the rightists' goals impossible.

To understand the leagues' goals, it is not much use looking at their ideological documents—partly because several of them, like so many fascist groupings, did not have any; and partly because when they did, they contradicted each other so much. The Croix de Feu probably aimed at a very authoritarian version of French republican democracy; the Solidarité Française had no specific goals, but probably wanted to destroy democracy altogether; the Jeunesses Patriotes wanted an Italian-style dictatorship with strong social policies. If one wants to establish what their objectives were on 6 February, it is more informative to look at their disposition on a map of Paris. What this shows is that their clear objective was to converge on the Place de la Concorde, opposite the National Assembly, in such a way as to render the normal parliamentary administration of government impossible, the police impotent, and the communists irrelevant. Most of the leagues stressed

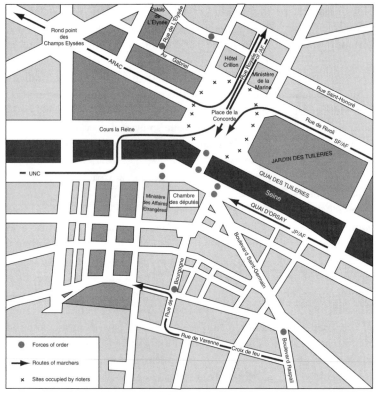

Figure 1.2 This diagram shows how the French '*forces de l'ordre*' tackled the 'Stavisky' Riots in Paris, February 1934, and emphasizes the protracted, mobile nature of the conflict moving through the most famous spaces in Paris. It is tempting to view cities always as sites of *dis*order, and indeed, the French government fell as a consequence of this well-managed attack on the Assemblée Nationale. But a new one was promptly and effectively formed. A well-organized state, combined with many citizens genuinely committed to the French Republican ideal, could, as here, defeat urban instability. Russian, Italian, and German cities lacked all three: effective state organization, a unifying idea which people believed in, and a citizenry willing to defend it with equal violence.

their view that the entire democratic process of any parliament was anathema to them, based as it is on compromise; therefore, the rightist groups focused on the physical destruction of the Assemblée Nationale, and called for an '*homme grand*' to lead France to efficient glory. Thus, the Croix de Feu gathered on the boulevard de Raspail to the south-east of the Assembly, and routed itself round the back of the building, then along its western flank. The Jeunesses Patriotes and the Action Française assembled in three blocks: to the east, on the Quai d'Orsay; to the north-east, in the rue de Rivoli (behind the Louvre); and to the north, behind the Place de la Concorde, on the other side of the Ministry of the Navy. The conservative Union Nationale des Combattants approached from the military establishments at Invalides, just to the west. Their goal was to converge on the National Assembly, making Daladier's swearing-in impossible, and possibly destroying France's parliamentary system.

As the crowds approached the Place de la Concorde in the late afternoon, as shown in Figure 1.2, it became clear that the various police units were surrounded—and also dissipated in a disadvantageous set of hard-to-defend locations in a very 'open' part of Paris. When the communist Association Républicaine des Anciens Combattants approached from the north, a vast riot broke out in which, at heavy loss, the communists and the police effectively prevented the leagues from achieving their objectives of invading the National Assembly, occupying government buildings, and massacring the communists. However, this was at substantial cost. By 5 a.m. on the morning of the seventh, Daladier's government had resigned, and most of the top layers of the French state were convinced that the republic might disintegrate. There was a vast amount of bloodshed that night, too. There were about 6,500 members of the 'forces of order' there, as they are always called in French histories. However, many of these were beat bobbies and firemen; a good third of them were from outside Paris and had little experience of the city; very few were the elite riot squads of the Garde Républicaine, and Paris's police chief had just been sacked, leaving them leaderless. The fighting all night was exceptionally hard, as surrounded police units sought to disperse the crowd and defend the National Assembly, while communists and 'rightists' sought to kill each other, and often the police. A favourite tactic was to slash the tendons of the police horses with blades, immobilizing parts of the Garde Républicaine and forcing the more experienced forces of order to dismount and tend to their beloved animals. Then, the men were attacked, and had to shoot their horses, which brought an enhanced sense of butchery and carnage to the streets. Eventually, lethal force was used, and the police opened fire—but in a chaotic and haphazard way. Nine hundred and sixty-nine injuries were experienced by the 'forces of order', and one death. Such was the chaos on the Place de la Concorde that the Garde Républicaine's commander there, Col. Nicolet, had to send his officers back out to fight with concussion. A total of 1,421 civilians were injured—14 mortally.[69]

While governments falling and nearly 2,500 injuries and so many dead would indicate a grave crisis—and indeed it *was* a grave crisis, far more violent than the threatened 'March on Rome' Mussolini had organized—this incident demonstrates something else of profound importance to understanding the dynamics of state power in the twentieth century: states which can, even at high cost, defend and control urban space, can preserve their political systems intact. While in Berlin, St Petersburg, and Rome the state had been *un*able to control the urban terrain, in this particular instance it was so able. Between 7 and 9 February, the Garde Républicaine quickly regrouped, called up reserves, used their cavalry capabilities and successfully contained the follow-on protests, arresting wholesale such league members as ventured out on the streets. The French state proved to be efficient and decisive in its response to urban political disorder in a way it had frequently not previously managed to be, and thus preserved itself. Furthermore, the rioters on the political left in February 1934 were fixed on preserving the French Republic and its values, and they too were adept at mobilizing to control city space. Communists were not afraid of a street fight: it was frequently their *modus operandi* of choice. Even leaderless, confused, and surrounded, such was the ideological commitment of the police officers, republican guards, and firemen—not to mention the communist veterans—to the fundamental institutions and values of the Third Republic that it could control the city and survive, even when a specific administration might fall.[70]

Sociologists and historians argue that, far from producing the collapse of the Republic and its democratic values, it was the events in the streets around the Place de la Concorde of February 1934, and subsequent urban conflicts throughout that spring and summer, that allowed an anti-fascist, democratic, republican ideology to coalesce in France around a common set of values, and a shared set of fears.[71] It is a cliché that the 'politics of the street' are inherently unstable, but the events of February 1934 in France help us understand the street and participatory action not solely as a site of *opposition* and *in*stability, challenging any contemporary tendency to view democracy as a 'passive', 'discreet', or inherently orderly process. One of the most potent outcomes was a series of violent actions in all large French cities— Lyon, Lille, Marseilles, Bordeaux, and above all Paris—by leftist groups intent on defining and defending French Republican values, and excluding the right from a 'field of debate' in the run-up to May Day 1934, and then reaching forward to the formation of the Popular Front government in France in response to the Spanish Civil War. One historian has shown how the number of deaths in political violence in France in 1934 was on a similar scale to the deaths in street violence in Germany in the run-up to Hitler's seizure of power in Germany in 1933.[72] The major difference was that in Germany, both communists and fascists sought to use the city to effect the destruction of the state, while democratic socialists struggled weakly to defend a space for their politics, and the police and the army oscillated and were ambivalent; while in France, effective communist and socialist street violence and coherent control of urban space by a Garde Républicaine also committed to the Republic supported the democratic status quo. Above all, these planned acts of violence, of political identity formation and exclusion, were not confined to, or even associated with, large 'set piece' confrontations like that around the Place de la Concorde, but were dispersed between specific locales in working-class neighbourhoods in urban France.[73]

* * *

While it is very much *not* the case that the war provided an apolitical *entre-acte* to the twentieth century, the politics of societies in a uniquely total and global war took on a dynamic in which 'normal rules' were suspended. However, in the period after the war, new political structures rapidly re-established themselves, but took on a global significance as two competing political visions organized on either side of the Iron Curtain. While the 'big players', like Truman and Stalin, remained

important, and while no historian could doubt the psychological, economic, and political impact of the war itself, historians of international
relations and global conflict have also started to realize the importance
of the day-to-day, for it is in the day-to-day that decisions take effect,
and it is from the day-to-day that much 'grand principle' also derives.[74]
For example, the fear of nuclear destruction in the USA was fostered
most not by the news or politicians, but by the drills and routines in
shops and schools that highlighted the imminence of Armageddon. But
for a global political conflict to become real, it needs a place in which
to do so, and few places are more central to the international politics
of the second half of the twentieth century than Berlin. It is tempting
to narrate the story of *all* the politics of the post-war world just by taking a walk through the streets of that city. It would trivialize the convictions of either the democracies in the West or the socialist bloc in the
East to say that there was *nothing* to their forty-year confrontation but
a street encounter in Berlin; but without Berlin, it is hard to see the
defining global political polarization of the twentieth century taking the
shape that it did.

Berlin started to figure large in the post-war political settlement
largely by its absence, when Eisenhower made the calculation, in the
closing months of the war, that the city was not an important military
target—and indeed, it was not. It did not fulfil the administrative function for Germany that London or Paris fulfilled for Britain or France.
It was not the main industrial city, or an important infrastructural
centre—few important train lines or rivers or canals ran through it or
to it. It has no natural resources, and is not near any other cities that
were militarily important. Above all, most American planning overestimated the level of commitment to National Socialism in the German
population, and anticipated that substantial groups of fighting forces
would retreat into Germany's and Austria's substantial impenetrable
mountainous terrain and conduct a sustained military insurgency from
there. So rather than focusing on cities, Allied—and especially US—military
planning focused on areas remote from them, and fantasies of a mountain resistance. In fact, US military planning right through the war
imagined a 'ruralized' Germany after it, recognizing that contemporaries understood well the link between cities, and an effective military—
industrial complex. The American 'Morgenthau Plan' for Germany
proposed an entirely pastoral, de-urbanized, rural Germany of small

towns and pre-modern agriculture. It was briefly US official policy, until the panicked British government calculated what a post-war European economy without an industrial, urban Germany would look like.[75] So American peace planning did have cities at its heart—but focused on their abolition. British peace planning also had cities at its heart—but focused on their reconstruction.

As the wartime alliance fell apart, it became clear that Roosevelt's hopes for an accommodation with the USSR were only to be as long lived as Roosevelt himself; they shared the journey to the grave. Recent historical work does not show the USSR to be entirely cynical after the war however, and it seems that the Soviet Union was ready to countenance some sort of de-militarized, depoliticized democratic Germany, as they did with Austria.[76] The 'island' of French, British, and American Berlin, deep inside the Soviet-dominated Eastern Zone of Germany, always posed a paradox, and it was the attempts to resolve this paradox that gave form to the great political conflict of the cold war. It is important to understand that many of the disagreements about Korea or Cuba or Vietnam or Angola first found their expression in the spaces and places of Berlin. As one cold-war historian has concluded, 'Berlin functioned as the point at which two competing trajectories of power, each to end in a new German state, most directly confronted each other and produced their most explosive conflicts.'[77]

Initially, it was the Soviets that dominated the city, as it was deep in their zone. American planning for the post-war order was disastrous in 1945, and the Americans disestablished almost all their entire overseas intelligence networks at the war's end. The abrupt disbandment of the Office of Strategic Services in October 1945 meant a sudden collapse of the American intelligence presence in Berlin as personnel were rapidly withdrawn—a deficit that would not be remedied until the establishment of the CIA in 1947. But while it might seem that espionage, infiltration, exfiltration, and subversion happen in a sort of 'no-space', running like invisible threads through a hidden and ethereal world, this was not the case. Such activities happen in a very real space—and the US essentially vacated it for two years, with catastrophic geopolitical consequences. Thus the Soviet Union and the nascent security services of what would become East Germany (or 'democratic' or 'free' Germany, as the Soviets insisted on calling it) had free rein, both inside and out-side East Germany. The personnel of X-2—the counter-intelligence division of the Americans' wartime intelligence network—was reduced, in October 1945, to a staff of five individuals in Berlin; five individuals in a city of four million people of central strategic and political importance to global geopolitics, to deal with the entire Soviet military-intelligence complex.[78]

The first US military commanders in Berlin, Dwight Eisenhower and Lucius Clay, had little time for the types of espionage activity managed by the Office for Strategic Services, and actively promoted its disbandment. They assumed that manly dialogue with fellow soldiers in the Red Army would resolve most issues, most effectively. Thus the remnants of the OSS that were handed over to the military command as the US's intelligence organizations were wound up at the end of the war were given minuscule resources, and their activities were largely confined to filling out dossiers on German conservatives and trade unionists that the Allies thought potential candidates to construct the post-Nazi German polity. But as the situation in Berlin soon made clear, a neat path to demilitarized collaboration in the administration of Germany was not possible; Soviet plans to develop a nuclear bomb to match American capabilities were heavily dependent on German scientists and scientific installations. By January of 1946, the Berlin Operations Base of the slimmed-down, rag-tag remnants of the OSS was the only coherent operational unit of overseas intelligence gathering that the USA possessed. Faced with vast tank and anti-aircraft formations along the zonal demarcation lines, the Allied command in Germany quickly realized that it had no idea how big these formations were, what armaments they possessed, what their battlefield disposition was, or what the Soviet order of battle might be, should it come to that. Churchill's 'Iron Curtain' had fallen, and the US Military administration had neglected to ensure that it had any intelligence-gathering capabilities behind it. The city of Berlin took on, in this context, an outstanding importance. While the Americans failed to understand this (the British seem to have understood it better, but had less capacity to do anything about it), the Soviet intelligence networks focused ruthlessly on Berlin in this period, operating out of their base at Karlshorst in the south-eastern suburbs.

This tension between the superpowers experienced its first real test not so much in Berlin, as around or over it. The issue which triggered the crisis surrounding Berlin, though, was one of currency. The British and Americans concluded in 1947 that economic reconstruction in Germany was not possible without a currency in which investors could have long-term faith, and the USSR was unwilling to countenance a new currency separate from an all-encompassing deal for the whole of Germany, a deal which the archives show they were remarkably ready to make. In a hurry, and with little warning to either the French or Soviet occupation zones, Britain and America formed 'Bizonia', and introduced a new currency—the Westmark. They knew they would have to introduce this currency in the *whole* of the Allied part of Germany, for if they did not, the people of West Berlin would not be able to buy anything, rendering them effectively de facto citizens of a unified Eastern Zone with no distinctive Berliner economy. The Moscow government knew this too. One report from the Berlin residency of the Soviet security apparatus from 31 December 1947 advised that information derived from 'well-informed Americans' indicated that:

> the Berlin question causes the Americans much concern. They recognise that the realisation of a currency reform limited to the western zones will deprive them of the possibility of holding on to Berlin, even within the framework of the present four-power administration. At the same time, all of the anti-Communist propaganda carried on by them illegally in the Soviet zone originates in Berlin…They want to hold on to Berlin at all costs, even to the point of making concessions to the Russians.[79]

Stalin was, it seems now, ready to countenance a de-militarized, neutral, democratic Germany. But in 1948, Stalin became increasingly frustrated with his inability to shape the outcome of negotiations over the final destiny of Germany, and cut the Allied zones of the city off from the west. In itself, this was a vulgar test of strength—a deliberate strategy to attempt to humiliate the Americans (and their junior partners, the British), but not provoke such a crisis that the USA would exploit their nuclear monopoly to mask their massive deficits in conventional forces (and their complete intelligence vacuum). Berlin became the site of this test—and in being used that way, fixed itself as the index and measure of two globally competing political ideologies for forty years.

But it was not an abstract index, or an arbitrary measure: the contest was real, and happened in real places and real time. First, units of the Red Army began to block, occupy, and disrupt road and rail routes to the West in March, 1948. Trucks would 'break down' in strategic places; roads would be 'repaired', making them impassable. On 20 March, the Soviet delegation walked out of the Allied Control Council. By 31 March, the Soviets were demanding the right to search all trains going into West Berlin. On 6 April, a Soviet fighter collided with a British passenger plane flying to Berlin in what seems to have been a genuine accident—although confrontations about why a fighter jet was so close to a civilian plane were vigorous. On 20 June, the Allies introduced the Westmark just in their own zones. The Soviets cut off electricity supply to West Berlin, and closed road and rail links. Thus the city of Berlin turned a currency crisis and a foreign policy crisis and an ideological conflict into a real interaction at a real place at a real time. A city made the defining geopolitical conflict of the second half of the twentieth century very, very real.

The blockade was a disaster for the Soviet Union. It highlighted the oppressive nature of their approach to their zone of Germany, while heroizing the British and Americans—who had recently been bombing German cities in carpet raids, killing many thousands. It emphasized American air superiority by providing a constant parade of it in the form of the Berlin Air Lift (often called the Air Bridge at the time) over a major European capital. It underlined Soviet military impotence, for to have escalated this into a real conflict, as US commander Clay anticipated, would have left the USSR exposed to unanswerable nuclear attack. A secret assessment produced by French intelligence summed the problem up clearly:

> They [the Soviets] cannot tolerate an administration in the centre of their one that is hostile to them, which, with its freedom of the press and speech, is an unfortunate example for the entire Soviet zone population that cannot be prevented from having contact with Berlin.[80]

This intolerance shows the USSR's leadership acting far more from a position of weakness than of strength. In the Berlin city council elections in October 1947, the SED (the 'Socialist Unity Party', created by the USSR as a puppet in the East) came third, a grave humiliation. But they maintained important posts in many trades unions, and this meant that they had access to substantial forms of patronage both at work and also in the form of distribution rights to additional food and clothing coupons. So important was this that the elections to both city council and the executives of the city's trade unions became an intense focus of activity for all four powers in the city.

But cities in general—and Berlin in particular—were not just important in giving shape to the global political conflicts that determined the last century. It might be tempting to see the Soviet Bloc as a monolithic structure, but it had a complex internal dynamic, and one which often hinged on street politics. The binary nature of the confrontation between two superpower blocs has obscured the complex urban politics of the East, and what it can tell us about the fragile nature of Soviet power. The political elites of states in the Soviet orbit had mobile and transformative relations with their supposed political masters, and the capacity of cities to transform and define these should not be underestimated. One of the central projects of the East German State was the physical reconstruction of East Berlin—and in particular, the vast, lifeless ensemble that is the Stalin Allee in Friedrichshain. It was a continuation of Unter den Linden, the main ceremonial thoroughfare of Imperial and Third Reich Berlin; a substantial prestige project for a young nation with something to prove. But throughout the city, in both East and West, physical reconstruction of dwellings, sewers, hospitals, schools, and infrastructure was a central feature of urban life, and a major source of employment and economic activity, and Friedrichshain was at the heart of a heavily bombed, working-class area.

The German Democratic Republic, the final recognition of the division of Germany, was only established in 1949, and it took a few years for the SED, the USSR's puppet party, to develop a coherent programme and impose itself on the country. By the summer of 1952, the party had committed the country to radical Stalinization and set out a long-term policy framework: farms were to be collectivized, and industrial output was to be increased as 'a basic precondition for social development'. But in spring 1953, Stalin died—the great tyrant disappeared, just as the SED had announced a programme of tyrannical Stalinization. The government vacillated: it announced that a

'New Course' would be followed, with more emphasis on consumer goods. But it undermined that by insisting on increasing output in line with the Stalinist plans. At the heart of these outputs was urban reconstruction—the GDR's cities, just like the Federal Republic's, were desolate and devastated. In June 1953, it was announced that Berlin's builders had to increase their output by 10 per cent; Otto Lehman, the union leader, backed the government up. On 16 June, as workers arrived on sites along the Stalin Allee, it was announced that the 10 per cent target—or 'norm'—had to be met by the end of June, in just two weeks, with no pay rise, and no food ration rise. This set off a process that, within twenty-four hours, led to riots, lynchings of security officers, widespread disorder, and regime change in Moscow. It was the first test, of many, of the USSR's empire-building strategy from within the empire itself.

It is worth engaging with some of the minutiae of what actually happened on the morning of 16 June, because in the mundane details of the interpersonal dynamics of a building site, we can see carefully dismantled many of the clichés of a 'Western' understanding of the quest for 'freedom' in the Soviet zone—and also the idea that the USSR offered an effective, monolithic power. This, in turn, will demystify a little the collapse of 1989. When describing the events of June 1953, the Western press led with extravagant, romantic claims about freedom. *The Times* in London led with, 'East German Workers Shout for Freedom'; the *New York Times* headlined with ' "Spirit of Freedom" is Seen'.[81] A visit to the building site where it all started reveals that there was no such preoccupation with abstract political theory. A quick assessment of the details of the situation on the Stalin Allee building site on the 16–17 June 1953 by someone with a knowledge of DIY or building would reveal a very different set of concerns and processes in play, to those highlighted by someone with a training in political science.

On the day of 16 June, when the finalized norms became known, the first disturbances took place on the building sites. That afternoon, local union leaders (who were, it should be remembered, responsible for securing order in industrial settings, not pursuing their members' interests) were required to submit a report on what had happened to the local party leadership. Artur Liebenau, one of the shop stewards, wrote it, as he experienced the day unfold. This report is fascinating because it was written on the afternoon of 16 June, before widespread violence erupted, and therefore views events on the building site as an 'interesting local difficulty', rather than 'the cause of the biggest rebellion in the Eastern Bloc since the war'. The local leadership asked the Construction Industry Union 'Stalin-Allee Division' to report on difficulties with the Carpenters' Brigade in their area, and voiced their concerns about whether the Brigade might cause 'complications' on the site.

At 9 a.m., during morning break, the Carpenters' Brigade of the Stalin Allee Division of the Construction Industry Union held a meeting, and the union officers (including Liebermann) attended. The meeting was heated, and focused entirely on the issue of production norms—but not from a philosophical or political perspective. In particular, there was a lot of anxiety from workers with man-made boards—chipboards, plywoods, hardboards etc. All of these workers got the same hourly rate, based on the same hourly output—a bureaucrat somewhere with very little building experience had decided that 'a board is a board is a board'. The workers with plasterboard, however, complained that their material was more breakable than fibreboard or chipboard—something which any DIY enthusiast will confirm—and thus there was no way that they could work to the same speed as someone working with laminated chipboard or plywood. For some time they had been agitating for a correction to this from experts, union leaders, and the city council. The publication of new norms that week underlined the extent to which the concerns of the plasterboard workers over several months had been ignored. The union leaders, themselves all experienced builders, concluded directly in their report on the 16th that this was, indeed, a reasonable cause for anxiety within this brigade, because currently workers with plasterboard could not achieve the norms, and as such their wages were sufficient only to pay for food, but not rent, heating, and clothing. So at this stage, before a general rebellion has taken place, union leaders seemed clear that the workers' demands were very fair.

As the meeting on the site continued, some people blamed the government, saying that they acknowledged the problem but were unwilling to undertake the fundamental revisions to address it—a contempt for workers revealed by the publication of new norms. Casual comparisons between past and present should be avoided, but it should be noted that when civil society organizations—charities, unions, pressure groups, lobbying organizations, churches, employers' associations, civil rights associations—get into socio-economic conflicts, frequently governments are blamed for them whether it is their responsibility or not. This happens in 'free' and 'unfree' societies. It is a standard position in all sorts of social, cultural, and economic conflicts for participants to say something along the lines of, 'Those in power well understand the fundamental causes of this conflict/problem, and, if they chose to, they could resolve it with the reforms we suggest. They choose not to take this "common sense" approach. We therefore have no faith in them.'

In democratic systems, states are very able to ignore this sort of thing by corralling such concerns into four-yearly discussions, or 'elections'. Elections provide a safe zone for everybody to get things off their chest, and for conflicts of interest to be resolved (or dismissed) in a way which people find acceptable. This means that a 'lack of faith' in the state in democratic societies is relatively easy to manage through the jamborees of democracy. But in one-party or totalitarian systems, no mechanism exists for managing confrontations like this. Thus, in totalitarian systems, even *small* concerns about the state cannot effectively be managed or corralled, because there is nowhere for them to go, and so they take on far greater concerns for the government than in democratic societies. It is important to understand how small the discontent with the state was at these early meetings. A sense of the limited radicalism of this break-time meeting comes in the union leaders' concluding sentence on it in their report:

> As the meeting by this time had long over-run the breakfast break, the employees concluded that they would work the missing time as overtime, but demanded some answers to the questions they raised in the meeting.[82]

The fact that the workers volunteered to make up the time spent in this meeting shows how orderly and limited this process was. Up to this point, the shop stewards felt that the workers' demands were fair and that they were in reasonable control of the 'situation', such as it was. Workers were rebellious, but not so rebellious that they did not work a full day.

But then, at 10.40 a.m., the shop stewards (who were working in the interior of the building), spied through a window a passing cluster of men heading down from Wasmannstraße. They were carrying a banner declaring, 'Building Workers Demand a Reduction in Targets'.[83] The builders working around the shop stewards jumped up, shouting, 'Come on, let's go and demonstrate—show solidarity!' Given that worker solidarity was a prime rhetorical device of the GDR state apparatus, the builders would have been thoroughly primed by the state itself to use arguments like this. The shop stewards followed the demonstrators as they collected workers from each site, and headed into the city centre, estimating their numbers at about 1,200. They were shouting things like, 'We demand lower targets, we demand lower prices', 'We are workers, not slaves', and 'Construction workers, join us! Solidarity is strength!' On one occasion, the shop stewards heard someone shout 'Down with the Unions!' and 'We demand a free Berlin', but they were lone voices—the demonstration was disciplined, and seemed planned, but the union leaders could not work out from where. Interestingly, the slogans the workers used were slogans redolent of 'socialist unity' rhetoric, not 'Western' liberal rhetoric. Around lunchtime, the shop stewards thought they had better report, and walked back up to the building sites, meeting lots of building workers who had not demonstrated at the canteen vans. At the Strausberger Platz, they chatted to some of them—the overwhelming majority of building workers—who agreed that the protesters were right, but that they 'couldn't be bothered with that rubbish'.

The middle phase of the day seems unclear—it is hard to ascertain who went back to the sites, and who was new in the demonstration. Observers reported that the afternoon demonstrators were 'youths', and not building workers. But later in the afternoon, groups re-coalesced as the working day came to an end. As the workers moved through the city, their numbers grew in a sort of snowball effect—but culminating only in about 2,000. They went down through Stalin Allee to the Alexanderplatz, along to Marx-Engels Platz, and then up Unter den Linden.[84] By this stage, the working day was drawing to a close on building sites—around 4 p.m.—and lots of people were milling around in the city centre. Apparently initially intending to present their views to the trade union leader, Lehman, they were substantially angered to find that no one in the trade union association directorate was actually at work at all—so they resolved to move on to the House of Ministries, and present their case directly to Fritz Selbmann, the minister for heavy industries. By this stage, there were a few thousand building workers. Selbmann came to a balcony at the ministry, and workers shouted for him to come down—which, with some courage, he did—whereupon he was mobbed. A couple of arrests were made, but the demonstrators were promptly released when the police could not control the crowds—one of many demonstrations of the limits of power of the authoritarian state in an urban melee. A small group of the workers used the chaos in the city to break away from the main crowd, cross over into West Berlin and go to the American broadcaster, RIAS, to present a list of four demands: an end to the productivity rises; reduction of food prices in state-owned shops; free and secret elections; and no recrimination for the demonstrators. These demands were broadcast, leading many to assume that the rioters had American backing and that the Americans may intervene. Note that only one of these demands focused on abstract political principles.

Riots developed sporadically in many central districts in the night of the 16–17 June—excited by the fact that some demonstrators had captured a van from the HQ of the SED which had loudspeakers on it; they patrolled the streets and announced a general strike for the next day. Observers reporting back to the political centre found that those people who were most interested in 'abstract' political demands were very young workers. On the morning of 17 June, at 7 a.m. (shift start on building sites in summer), more workers joined, and youths chanted slogans (which rhyme in German) like, 'We're at the end of our ordeal, we want to vote free and for real', 'This is all pointless, Down with Beardy' (Walter Ulbricht, leader of the Party in East Germany, had a goatee beard), and 'Butter not Guns' which had been a socialist chant in the late 1930s in German cities, as the NSDAP pushed industrial rearmament programmes over consumer goods.[85] Minute-by-minute reports from the police from 6 a.m. on 17 June show that in factories across East Berlin, workers were refusing to work, and meeting together in a chaotic and unmanageable way. They also confirm the proactivity of young people in organizing this, and that outside the city-centre setting of the Alexanderplatz, the focus of comments and placards remained production targets and pay. In the KWK Metal Works, one worker, K, ran through the cable machine hall at 7.45 a.m. and pulled out the electricity supply of workers who continued to work; but in the central abattoir, workers continued to work, except in the refrigeration room.[86] As news leaked out, it looked like these street demonstrations—coming at a moment when the Soviet Union looked leaderless after Stalin's death, and springing from the unique and unpoliceable cultures and spaces of the building sites that were distributed throughout the city in both East and West—might cause the East German government to topple.

The CIA has recently released the reports that it hastily tried to gather from its young intelligence network that night, and they make grim reading. At 4.30 a.m. on the morning of the 17th, a West Berlin police unit observed twelve Russian tanks pulling up to the western border of West Berlin. It was an ominous prelude to the sealing of the city in 1961. Half an hour later, another unit of twenty Russian tanks was seen approaching from the east, through the suburb of Adlersdorf. By about 11 a.m., a full scale riot emerged in the Alexanderplatz, with kiosks being overturned and set on fire, while West Berlin telephone and transport workers noted that both networks had been closed down in the East; the call for a general strike seemed to be being observed. As the rioters turned towards the House of Ministries, fifteen Soviet medium tanks, twenty armoured cars and thirty machine-gun trucks appeared, and began to fire. At 2.20 p.m., East Berlin radio announced that a state of emergency had been declared; all people in groups of more than three would be liable to be shot; as would those venturing outside at night, and those trying to enter the Western zones.[87] What is clear is that this was not 'an' uprising. This was a *composite* of dispersed uprisings, and while the *effects* of it can be summarized as one rebellion, the causes of it only make sense in the plural mess of, say, an abattoir, where most parts could function, yet, for reasons we will never know, the workers in the refrigeration unit chose to down tools and join a demonstration, or a metal factory where the cable workshop continued to work, until other workshops disconnected their power. Why one part of a factory should strike, and another should not, is hard to know in this instance. But cities allow us to see the mess of history, rather than its neatness.

These events transformed the nature of Soviet rule throughout the entire Eastern Bloc. First, the repressive aftermath showed demonstrably and measurably and in full view of the Western media, that any idea that the SED government in East Germany—only four years old at this time, and operating in profound policy confusion—was anything other than an imposition through force was wrong. This was more of a shock than one might think; Soviet and SED leaders genuinely thought that what they were doing was the wisest, most rational way of understanding the world, and organizing it politically. File after file released from the archives after 1989 shows that they really believed that what they were doing was right and humane. For them, free-market capitalism had led to National Socialism and the Second World War; its claim to rule was non-existent, given where it had led. Secondly, it made the tentative steps towards liberalization in the 'New Course' promised by the East German government on 9 June irrelevant, because now policy would be developed in order to maximize security, not consent.

Perhaps most interestingly, in the faraway Kremlin, the disorder about production norms and the difference between plasterboard and plywood made the position of Stalin's most likely successor and temporary Soviet leader, Lavrentii Beria, untenable. Strangely, this grotesque murderer and co-conspirator with Stalin as head of the Soviet secret services since 1938, turned out to be a compassionate, humane reformer when he got close to power in 1953.[88] But these twenty-four hours of madness on building sites and public squares clearly spelt out the chances for regime survival if one genuinely engaged with the concerns of ordinary people in Soviet satellite states. Beria was a paradoxical figure. He had organized the deaths and deportations of millions in the late 1930s, while consistently opposing anti-Semitism. On becoming deputy prime minister on Stalin's death, he exposed the fraud of many show trials (which he had helped organize), started the process of releasing millions from gulags, and quickly banned torture in the Soviet penal system. As a resolution to the 'German problem' (i.e. the division of the country into two), so clearly drawn into focus by the riots in Berlin, he proposed unifying Germany as a neutral power, with full, free elections—just as they were doing in Austria.[89] He was promptly arrested and shot in a coup led by Nikita Khrushchev. With a bit more of his previous murderous brutality in pursuing his reformist agenda in Moscow in 1953, the riots in East Berlin could indeed have had a very different outcome for the political history of the twentieth century.[90]

No one would experience the crackdown in Eastern Europe more than the people of Budapest, just three years later. While in 1953 it was the city street that fed into Moscow politics, in 1956 it was Moscow politics which helped radically destabilize the city street. By 1956, Khrushchev—deposer and probably murderer of Beria—had himself reached the conclusion that Stalin had been a disaster. On 24 February 1956, he gave a 'secret speech' to the 20th Congress of the Communist Party of the Soviet Union and, crucially, leaders of the Communist Parties of the USSR's satellite states. In it, he spelt out the dangers of a 'cult of personality'; of 'violations of socialist legality'. He spoke of wartime blunders, the cruelty of deportations, of purges, and of deaths and disaster. He used words like 'murder' and 'excess'. And he blamed Beria for being a primary agent in this— sometimes fairly, sometimes not. The effect was profound, not least because the CIA soon obtained a copy of the speech, and published it. But for the effects of something like this to become truly real, they need a place in which to become so—and the first place was in the Stalin Locomotive Works in Poznan, Poland's fourth-largest city.

At the end of the Saturday morning shift on 23 June, some workers met together in the factory, and formulated a set of demands that they would physically take to the capital, Warsaw. First amongst them was not 'freedom', or anything so nebulous, but a 20 per cent wage increase. The delegation left for Warsaw, but no meetings were held. Fearing that the delegation had been arrested in Warsaw, the 12,000 employees of the locomotive plant in Poznan voted, at the end of both the night and the day shifts, to have a demonstration on 28 June. They raided the city's prison, freed the prisoners, and 'armed them- selves with monkey wrenches, sticks, crowbars and sometimes even with pistols'. They moved on to the military radio station engaged in trying to block Western broadcasts, before moving on to destroy the local secret service offices. The riots spread to other Polish cities, but at heart the problem was economic: when the Polish regime responded by sending a high-level ministerial delegation to Poznan and, essen- tially, meeting the workers' demands, the crisis was resolved—though not without 53 deaths (including 9 soldiers and employees of the State Security Ministry), and 300 injuries. The responses of the army, mili- tia, and police were chaotic and ineffective. Senior Stalinist officials were dismissed, and economic 'errors' were admitted in public.[91] The lesson was clear: action in a locomotive works in one city could change policy directions in another.

But another lesson was also clear: the communist leader that the protesters wanted was Władysław Gomułka, who had fought the war in Poland as a communist resister, and thus was viewed as a national hero. He had also won popular votes for the communists after the war, before being caught up in the paranoid machinations of Stalin's brand of East European communism and imprisoned for being a 'deviationist'. Thus he had nationalist, military, democratic, *and* anti-Moscow credentials, while still being a staunch communist. With the Polish government paralysed by the conflict around the Poznan works, Gomułka was due to re-assume control of the party at the Eighth Plenum of the Central Committee on 19 October in order to restore popular credibility. But that morning, the leadership of the USSR suddenly arrived in Warsaw on a plane, and organized Soviet troops to move 'on exercise' towards the city. The implications were very clear—and Polish streets and workplaces were plunged again into disorder, this time anxiously focused on Soviet occupation. Catholic songs were sung (Russians were Orthodox), nationalist claims were made to territory (the USSR had annexed several provinces in 1939), and claims were made for military autonomy (Russian officers were placed at high ranks of the 'sister people's' army).[92] Gomułka's popularity grew—and Gomułka was a party apparatchik: the issue was visible Russian control and presence, not the one-party state in general, or communism in particular. Thus, at the heart of the second wave of riots in Polish cities was a profound geopolitical problem: Soviet power in Polish territory. Gomułka openly resisted the Soviet military threat, while promising, from conviction, to stick hard to the Communist Party line and remain in the Soviet Bloc. He kept his job.[93] This showed people across the Eastern Bloc that street politics worked. So by 1956, there was clear evidence that street politics could change governments in Moscow, and policy in satellite states.

In Hungary too, there was a profound power struggle in 1956 between the men who owed the Stalinist system everything, men like Mátyás Rákosi, who spent the war in Moscow as leader of the Commintern; and men like Imry Nagy, who had a more volatile relationship with the Soviet Union, and who were keen to follow a more 'humane' set of policies.[94] Nagy had spent the war as a scientist in a Moscow agricultural institute; he was not a hero, like Gomułka, but a quiet man of learning. Prime minister between 1955–6, Nagy was sacked for deviating too much from Moscow's wishes. On 23 October 1956—crucially, just after the start of the academic year, when students are congregated in their lecture halls, and just as it had become clear that the Polish had secured so much by resisting Soviet military force and focusing on a popular communist leader—a group of students at Budapest's university organized a march to the statue of General József Bem, a Polish hero of the revolutions of 1848 and symbol of the locomotive workers of Poznan. The initial demands were formulated between 14 and 19 October—so, *before* the outcome of the government crisis in Poland, but *after* the effective riots in Poznan—and focused on the Education Ministry's decision to enforce compulsory study of Russian. It is important to note that students did not want 'freedom'. They wanted to abolish compulsory Russian. This demand was accepted by the ministry, and, emboldened, on the morning of Monday 22 October, several independent student groups established themselves outside party control.

In response to this, in the main hall of the Building Industry Technological University in Budapest, the local communist youth organization held a meeting, ostensibly to discuss reduced public transport fares, improved food at student halls, and subsidies for text books. However, 5,000 people turned up, and the meeting lasted for eleven hours, and over the course of the evening, workers from the building trade—with which the university was allied—began arriving as their shift ended. In that hall the demands evolved, arriving in the early hours of Tuesday 23 October at a demand for the removal of Soviet troops from Hungary. We do not know exactly what was said in that hall, or by whom. The students formulating this demand were primarily members of the communist youth organization; they published their demands on the university's duplicating machines, and distributed them throughout Budapest on the morning of 23 October. If they had not been in the university buildings, they would not have had access to duplicating machines, and could not have published their demands. They organized an enlarged march to Bem's statue—a march which the government banned, then allowed, then banned again. The simple act of organizing a march through a city showed, not the *strength* of communist dictatorship, but its vacillating weakness.

The march itself was a relatively cerebral affair: the students arrived in Bem Square at about 4 p.m., and hung flowers and Polish flags on the statue; poetry was read; demands were articulated. But unlike in Poznan, the students' demands were more overtly political, which meant that they were less easily diffused. While in Poland the demands were from workers about wages (which could be met or not met in any political system) and the preservation in power of a popular communist, the students' demands in Bem Square were the dismissal of the hardliner Ernő Gerő from the government, and the return to power of Imre Nagy. Localized demands (local in this sense being a statue, a lecture hall, a shift change, unique access to duplicating machines which a university afforded) for changes in the head of government cannot generally be met in *any* political system that wishes to preserve stability, whether democratic or authoritarian. But the students in Bem Square went further: they wanted the USSR to withdraw its troops from Hungary, and for the country to become neutral, as Austria had just become. Thus, students were generalizing from their local demands about Russian language classes and bus fares, to make important claims about global geopolitics—again, remarkably difficult for any system to accommodate, democratic or authoritarian. Whereas there is a clear mechanism for people on a building site or a lecture theatre to derive, formulate, and present claims about pay, production norms, rent, and working materials, there is a fundamental mechanical disconnect between building sites, locomotive factories, and lecture halls on the one hand, and the global disposition of armed forces in superpower conflicts on the other.

The students on Bem Square were trying to use streets, squares, and lecture halls to make just such a mechanism for connecting the two systems. As such, their demands were not so bizarre, but they failed to understand the changing dynamic in Moscow where Khrushchev was engaged in a struggle for his own supremacy. Prime Minister Gerő was away in Yugoslavia until the morning of the 23rd, when the demonstration was taking place, and failed to get the advice of military commanders on the ground. Crucially, at the march— which took place in silence—there were about 800 uniformed cadets from the military academy. This led military leaders to doubt the loyalty of the armed forces to the state. Then, instead of returning to the universities, some of the students walked over the Danube to the parliament building. From 6 p.m., crowds grew—up to about 250,000. Gerő arrived back that day, but his 8 p.m. broadcast was a disaster:

his truculent, imperious tone stimulated thousands more out onto the streets, and around 9.30 p.m. the crowds started to attack Stalin's statue, which they rapidly destroyed. Commemorative statues provide powerful settings for political street theatre. They moved on to the Radio Building, where the secret police opened fire. When ambulances attended the scene to tend the wounded, the crowds parted—until the ambulances themselves opened fire, with secret police in doctors' and nurses' uniforms. At about 10 p.m., one van of Red Army soldiers was sent to help protect the Radio Building, and promptly deserted.[95] The street scene then embodied a profound international geopolitical crisis: the local military seemed unreliable, and could be *seen* to be unreliable, as evidenced by the cadets marching in uniform; conspicuous urban symbols of the occupying power (Stalin's statue) had been attacked, highlighting a fundamental problem with the occupying power's *own* view of Stalin; streets were filling up *because* of the approach taken by local leaders; and the occupying army—the Red Army—was apparently deserting. All of these features link in, of course, to other systems—of ideology, political ritual, power politics—but these things become real and material only when they are fixed and enacted in a specific place by specific people.

Meanwhile, news of the riot was spreading to the bars and homes of the working-class industrial districts of Czepel and Újpest. A group of workers at the benignly named United Lamp Factory stole some trucks, and broke open the factory, knowing its secret: it actually manufactured rifles, of which they captured more than 1,000, and drove to the city centre. Secret police and regular army offices were turned over, liberating more light weaponry into the hands of the urban rebels. At 2 a.m. the first Soviet tank was seen, and the Red Army, alongside the Hungarian army, attempted to break out of the Kilián barracks, and were prevented from doing so by a group of workers and students who had fortified the Corvin Cinema opposite the barracks. Workers' Councils rapidly took over most of the factories and collective farms across the country, rendering the existing party infrastructures irrelevant and redundant. Even the parade in strength of entire Red Army tank battalions through the streets on 24 October did not end the evaporation of political power—largely because of vacillation in Moscow, but partly too because it seemed that Nagy himself may have invited the Soviet tanks to defend the parliament building, where they had opened fire on protestors. On 27 October, Revolutionary Councils organized themselves in most government departments too, meeting in ministries in Budapest. On 28 October, Soviet troops agreed to withdraw from Budapest. Nagy, now installed in office as prime minister by a panicked Soviet government recoiling from humiliation in Poland, recognized these councils on 30 October; on 31 October, the military reorganized itself into Revolutionary Councils, and pledged themselves to Nagy's new government. Having no effective military chain of command, on 1 November, Hungary withdrew from the Warsaw Pact, and it seemed that the entire Soviet foreign-policy settlement was being unwound by a set of students and workers—a cinema was penning in a barracks. So, very rapidly, a set of concerns about Russian language instruction at one university had, in less than seventy-two hours, transformed a whole capital city into a sort of revolutionary melee, and a Stalinist authoritarian system and foreign policy network had evaporated. Encouraged by broadcasts from Radio Free Europe, many in Hungary assumed that military support would be forthcoming from the West.

Soviet troops' initial engagement was rolled back as the Kremlin expressed its faith in Nagy, a committed communist of huge popularity in the factories and barracks. This disintegration in power across the country—a largely agricultural country—happened because of a collapse in a city; and so it was in a city that power would have to be restored. Soviet troops built up both in Hungary, and surrounding Eastern Bloc states in readiness. On 4 November, the order was given to take Budapest back, and fighting was fierce—initially in the city centre, which was quelled in about three days, then moving on to the working-class industrial districts, where fighting continued until 11 November. In particular, Soviet vehicles found it difficult to operate in urban combat, because they were particularly susceptible to Molotov cocktails being dropped on them, and could not manoeuvre their guns to point far enough upwards to fire at the sources of the assaults. To look up, the tanks had to open their hatches, and when they did so, they were fire-bombed. In Czepel in particular, fighting in the factories and the warehouses continued, resisting sustained Soviet heavy artillery fire from Gellért Hill; on 9 November, an emissary to Czepel laid down an ultimatum that unless they surrendered no one would be spared, and they fought on until 6 p.m. when, with no ammunition left, they surrendered. The 'revolution' was over; the clumsy assertion of military control of the city meant that the Soviet Union and its agents could re-establish political authority in the whole country. The two-way links between 'high politics' and 'street politics' could not be drawn out more clearly.

The geography of a city was not just about defining 'them and us'—them being the evil Soviets, and 'us' being the vulnerable Eastern Bloc states. A large part of the escalation which grew between 1958 and 1961 that culminated in the erection of the Berlin Wall was a result of the East German political leadership's attempts to 'bounce' Nikita Khrushchev into fulfilling their own policy objectives. Berlin could determine the relationship *between* socialist dictators, and it is important to understand the huge significance of the Berlin Wall. The build-up to the construction of the wall was longer than is usually assumed; while there was some surprise on the morning of 13 August 1961 when the wall actually went up, there had been plenty of warnings and expectations in the run-up. First of all, all the major players knew that Ulbricht, leader of the East German government, was trying to enhance his position vis-à-vis Moscow, and so any crises he could engineer around Berlin would increase his leverage over Khrushchev. It was actually the East German state which was responsible for carrying out the mundane activities of servicing the autonomous region of Berlin, for all the legal niceties of 'Four Power Occupation'. It was the GDR that supplied the city with electricity, and which took away its rubbish, not the USSR, and thus the GDR had more influence over it.

The problems with Berlin were myriad, but central among them was the spatial fluidity it provided, which undermined an ideological rigidity that others—on both sides of the Iron Curtain—were trying to develop. These problems were drawn into sharp focus when during summer of 1953, and again in November of 1958, the border between East and West Berlin was sealed due to disturbances in East Berlin.[96] In particular, in the aftermath of the riots of 1953, the US government set up food distribution centres in West Berlin that proved hugely popular with East Berliners, reinforcing in a very concrete way the key American ideology of 'material plenty'. When attempts were made to seal off the west of the city, they had to be rapidly revoked after 150 women hijacked a train in the Berlin suburb of Groß-Schönebeck to take them to get their *Amipaket*—'American Packet', a parcel of US aid. People from all over the country were flooding through the 'portal' of Berlin to experience 'American plenty', then returning to their factories and farms to spread word of what they saw.[97] The flow of people out of East Germany in the late 1950s was increasing; typically, 4–5,000 people a week after the closure of the border with West Germany in 1952, spiking around 25,000 a week at moments of intense crisis. And the primary route for that flow was into West Berlin. This route out was experienced by the East German and Soviet leaderships as a sort of ideological 'black hole', sucking out credibility, legitimacy, security, and economic prosperity. And with good reason; the thousands who left each week were those with mobile marketable skills—engineers, machinists, intellectuals, craftsmen. Those with immobile assets—farmers—or unmarketable skills (or no skills at all) were often the ones left behind.

The reasons people left were complex, and a look at the Berlin 'traffic' yet again undermines a dominant Western narrative of a 'quest for freedom'. Many people wanted more money (which is often the true referent served by the rhetorical substitute 'freedom'). But when one historian of modern Germany tried to get behind the rhetoric of both sides of the cold war and understand why 'real' people left, the answers were more prosaic. The VEB Electrical Works in Köppenick in East Berlin kept extensive personnel files which, because they were internal, were largely free from political jargon, and they noted the comings and goings of their employees. The files say things like: 'Trip to West Germany rejected, fiancée left Republic shortly beforehand'; 'Had pro-West attitude, which meant he could not be delegated to study. All relatives in West Berlin and West Germany'; 'She was in factory only six months, was work-shy and led very immoral life. She had many debts and wanted to escape them by fleeing the Republic'; 'Returned from West Germany in January 1959...Fled Republic again probably for family reasons, because he did not get along with his mother.' In fact, only 20 per cent of the refugees from the eastern part of Germany were given the category 'C' in West Germany, which signified political reasons for flight. Most wanted to leave to be with families, and earn more money.[98]

The openness of the border was something that sophisticated East Germans used to their advantage, as the secret files show. For example, one man, a Wilhelm W., wrote to the East German president,

Wilhelm Pieck, to complain about not receiving a housing allocation. He ended his letter with the following comment:

> If the allocation should prove impossible, I would like to request your assistance in the acquisition of an exit permit to West Germany, since my relatives there can offer us suitable accommodation at any time.[99]

Pieck would have known that all the man had to do was find a way into East Berlin, and his 'exit permit' was assured. Indeed, paradoxically the mass exodus towards wealth (or a fiancée, or away from an irritating mother) may well have stabilized the East German regime, because it took potential opponents out of the country in a market-driven way far more effectively than the mass murder and deportations which had, for example, characterized the Soviet Union's attempts to deal with potential internal opposition in the 1930s. Meanwhile, it left behind a 'rump' of citizens who, by the nature of their choice to remain, acquiesced in some way to the GDR's project. While the 'black hole' of the permeable city of Berlin might have threatened East Germany, both as a source of political rebellion as in 1953, or as a method for skilled, mobile young people to leave, it may too have been essential to the successful functioning of the repressive security apparatus.[100]

But one area where it most definitely undermined the successful functioning of the security apparatus was in the field of espionage.[101] While Soviet and other Eastern Bloc agents could move freely in the West, the reverse was not true, and infiltration of agents into the Eastern Bloc was exceptionally difficult. The importance, therefore, of Berlin and Berliners to American global strategic thinking and capacities cannot be overestimated. While Western intelligence agencies were thoroughly penetrated by the USSR, the secret services of Britain, France, West Germany, and the USA had great difficulty in establishing even basic data about Warsaw Pact capabilities: the design of tanks, the layout of airfields, orders of battle, and so on. Almost the only manageable interface that could take place between Western agents and inhabitants of the East (the only plausible surveillance and communications agents imaginable) came in the traffic of ordinary citizens between East and West Berlin. Since the end of the cold war, former senior CIA and KGB agents in Berlin have used declassified archives to document the contest that was played out there, between the late 1950s and the 1970s.

In March of 1960, the CIA's Berlin Operations Base received a letter from a man who codenamed himself Sniper. Subsequent communications from Sniper contained references which, although obscure, confirmed that whoever they were from was fairly well-informed about espionage measures in the West. In particular, Sniper identified senior KGB penetration into MI6, the British security service, and the West German Federal Intelligence Service—tips which, once decoded and checked out, led to arrests. It was clear that Sniper was a high-quality asset. Sniper's identity was, however, still unknown. Using dead-letter drops in Warsaw, Sniper established a go-between who, at 5.30 p.m. on 4 January 1961, phoned the special number established for him at the Berlin Operations Base switchboard; a safe house was warned that a Mr Kowalski (the activation code that Sniper had established) was coming to visit— and would be bringing Mrs Kowalski. No one knew who either person was, but the CIA was anxious about the sudden addition of an untested person. Sniper, Kowalski *and* intermediary turned out to be Lt. Col. Michal Goleniewski, previously deputy director of Polish military counterintelligence and currently director of the technical branch of the Polish foreign intelligence service. He and his mistress sought refuge in the West. In some ways, this fascinating personal story of subterfuge and daring is of minor importance to the argument being made here—even despite the subsequent unfolding drama of being able to roll up major Soviet penetration into all the Western security services. What is perhaps of most importance is how Goleniewski managed the mechanics of his defection: he called a taxi, and directed it to West Berlin.[102]

When the wall went up on 13 August—actually a barbed wire fence, initially—the Berlin Operations Base of the CIA effectively had to be wound up. The wall was rapidly constructed—and it was not a political abstraction for Berliners, but almost an intimate process, tangible and real—as can be seen in Figure 1.3. The wall had a paradoxical effect on the security of the Eastern Bloc. The closure of the border limited the capacity of 'normal' espionage activities in the East, and meant that agents could no longer be cultivated there. This heightened the necessity of collaboration with a foreign intelligence service for a meaningful chance of escape; building the wall heightened Eastern dissidents' dependence on overseas intelligence services for escape. Thus, the higher up within communist establishments one was, the more valuable one knew oneself to be to the West. The wall made conventional espionage all but impossible—defection was the only route. Thus the wall may well have prompted more defections of high-value assets than it prevented.

East German nuclear physicist Heinz Barwich operated at the highest levels of the Eastern Bloc's civilian nuclear programme, directing the major research initiatives in the late 1950s in the USSR. Barwich was frequently allowed to travel to the West, and as such belonged to a privileged class of person in the Eastern Bloc which had relatively unfettered lives. He, like everyone else, supposed that something would eventually be done about defections, but assumed that that would be stricter travel controls—which he, from his privileged position, would

Figure 1.3 The construction of the Berlin Wall in 1961 shocked many in East Germany. It highlighted the importance of Berlin in global geopolitics, underlined the threat which urban environments posed to totalitarian regimes, and transformed the relationship of East German citizens to the state in which they found themselves. We are used to 'open vistas' of the wall, with a well-established no-man's-land, but here we see the intimate humanity of the hasty construction.

be able to circumvent. But when the Wall was built, Barwich realized that he would *not* be able to travel in the way that he had; he lost his scientific contacts in the West. The Wall transformed the view of the 'privileged' in the East about the regimes in which they lived, both damaging their status as scientists, athletes, or performers, and simultaneously making them more dependent on overseas intelligence agencies to re-establish that status.

Barwich had been a relatively willing, even enthusiastic, collaborator with the communist regime of East Germany, but by about 1960 he had concluded that while capitalism rested on man's exploitation by man, 'real, existing socialism' rested on man's exploitation by the state—or so he claimed afterwards. But one intelligence historian has pieced together an alternative story, using evidence not just from Barwich's claims, but also from his interrogations in the USA, and the newly opened Stasi and KGB files that reveal how British and German intelligence focused in on 'high fliers' losing their privileges after 1961. Barwich was profoundly angry that the Wall destroyed his privileged, mobile position in society, as well as that of his young, new wife, whom he had married in 1960. However, in 1961, he was given such a prestigious job that his concerns were allayed somewhat, becoming deputy director of the Soviet Bloc's Joint Research Institute for Nuclear Research, near Moscow. But while in Moscow, his home institution lost its Faculty of Nuclear Research, and with it he lost his comfy job to return to when his Moscow placement ended. So he found himself isolated in Russia; he and his wife could no longer come and go as they wished; and the 'insurance policy' against ill treatment (the permeable Berlin border) that all privileged apparatchiks in the Eastern Bloc possessed was withdrawn from him. The glamour of travel disappeared, along with his job security and social status—and with the construction of the Wall, the Stasi was given free hand to surveil his every move. He was painfully aware of this sudden intrusion into his life associated with the wall. At this point, the KGB and Stasi files show that he started to receive their attention as a potential security risk: informers around him reported he had made comments critical of the Socialist Unity Party, the GDR's monopoly party; Soviet agents in MI6 and the West German Intelligence Service had reported that they were interested in him in early 1962. In fact, the Wall emboldened Western agents, as they knew that 'insiders' would now have to rely on overseas agents to preserve any hope of escape.

In the summer of 1962, at an International Atomic Energy Authority conference in Vienna, he established relations with the CIA—just after the KGB and Stasi thought he might, but which they could not confirm. Barwich second-guessed how the KGB and Stasi would behave and, in 1964, defected while visiting a conference in Switzerland. Once out, the CIA broadcast a pre-arranged piece of music, followed by a numerical code which contained instructions for his wife. This directed her to a 'dead letter box' in Berlin containing money, identity documents and instructions for her exfiltration. She escaped to the West too.[103] What is important about this story is that changing the layout of Berlin changed the way even privileged people and communist apparatchiks thought about socialism and the system in the East. The Wall was a profound admission of defeat that undermined the resolve—by undermining the privileges—of the Eastern Bloc's elites. Psychologically, the Wall transformed the athletes, scientists, musicians, and dancers of the Eastern Bloc from privileged citizens on a global stage into constantly surveilled citizens of an ideological prison. Thus, this wall through the middle of the city produced a profound intellectual crisis throughout half of Europe.

But it was not simply in supposed 'repressive' regimes in the East that the politics of cities and city streets shaped the ways that societies organized and conducted themselves. The explosion in suburban building across Western Europe between 1950 and 1980 gave to millions of Europeans a patch of city to call their own and to turn into a repository of material acquisition and accumulation: cars and garages and drives; gardens with exotic plants from new garden centres; fridges, freezers, dishwashers, cookers, and microwaves in newly fitted kitchens; televisions first in living rooms then in bedrooms. Millions of post-war homes constituted sites of accumulation that tied citizens into the well-planned prosperity of 'capitalism with a human face'. Across Continental Europe, a political phenomenon emerged to represent this new urban geography: Christian Democracy. Christian Democrats (and perhaps the MRP in France), tied the fortunes of conservative parties to the prosperous, well-to-do areas of the post-agricultural Continent. These were conservative parties which eschewed violence, embraced civil liberties and the rule of law, supported market economics *and* strong welfare policies. And instead of relying on the support of an established Church and an agricultural interest, the pre-war bastions of Continental conservative politics, these new parties emphasized the social and familial side of 'Christian' values while refusing to speak for a specific Church, and represented urban districts as well as rural ones. This potent combination was new outside Britain and the USA—a novelty that contemporary Anglophone analysts were quick to comment on. One American scholar struggled to characterize this force in 1949, commenting that 'CHRISTIAN Democracy is a comparatively new political force that has emerged from the chaos of World War II to challenge the old Liberal, Socialist, and Communist forces.' But he struggled to define exactly what the phenomenon stood for, stating that the Christian Democrat believes:

> that democracy, to avoid becoming associated with either capitalism or socialism, which tend to deny or ignore man's moral nature, must be Christian, with the idea that man is created by God and that society is determined by the natural law. The Christian Democrat therefore rejects Hegelian idealism and Comteian positivism, Marxist historical materialism, agnostic pragmatism, and historical relativism, all of which have sought to replace the moral code with a political absolute.[104]

The 'absolute' had done such harm in Continental Europe that it is a wonder that anyone would *not* reject it. Frustratingly, though, I have been able to find breathtakingly little historical research on the mechanics of how this new political force, which has dominated European politics in the second half of the twentieth century, became 'real' in people's everyday lives in the 1940s, 1950s, and 1960s. We know 'where' the left happened; we know 'where' the radical right happened. We have little idea 'where' or 'how' the democratic right took on physical form.[105]

The most extreme expression of this transformation was in Italy and Germany. Italy, in particular, shifted from being a largely rural, agricultural economy (with substantial cities in the north) in 1945, to being a largely urban, industrialized economy by 1963. In 1951, 42 per cent of the population was engaged in agriculture; in 1961, 30 per cent. The fall was even greater in the north: migration to cities was so intense that rural employment fell from 48 to 26 per cent of the total in ten years.[106] Huge state enterprises and a relationship (frequently

corrupt) with the Christian Democrats were central in this process—
but when it comes to how it actually worked itself out in everyday life,
or what the role of everyday life was in this breathtaking revolution,
historians have been strangely silent.[107]

In the late 1960s, it seemed that urban disorder was as much a
feature of supposedly stable, democratic societies in the West, as
oppressive fragile ones in the East. In the USA, vast conflicts around
the issues of race and social inequalities in large cities dominated the
headlines in the late 1960s, most conspicuously in the extreme and
widespread urban violence in Los Angeles in 1965 and Detroit in the
summer of 1967, which caused profound anxiety in the USA. They
involved curfews over huge areas and millions of people, violent resistance to racially motivated 'law' enforcement, hundreds of millions of
dollars of property damage, the use of paramilitaries and live ammunition, the residential evacuation of American cities by whites in the
long term, and the transformation of American politics in a profound
way. But few examples of street politics have become more iconic for
Europeans than the *événements* of May 1968, above all in Paris.

As the generation which took part in those events has risen to the
top levels of European society, a mythology of a great 'revolutionary
moment' has been emphasized. But far from being a radical act, there
was little that was genuinely revolutionary about the events of May
1968—at least in Europe. Instead of establishing a clear voice for a
counter-culture, or taking on the vested interests of 200 years of racial
discrimination as in America, the *événements* should perhaps best be
considered as a triumphal parade of bourgeois self-indulgence, in
which the fundamental values of Western bourgeois democracy
acquired a consensual finality. Having no meaningful goals other than
their own self-expression, they were relatively swiftly achieved. Contrast
the riots in Detroit of 1967, focused on police brutality, racial humiliation, poor-quality housing, and poverty, with the riots which emerged
in France and other many other European countries a year later. Far
from advocating change, the riots in the universities of Germany,
France, and Britain of 1968 promoted a strange sort of status quo,
branded as a radical assertion.

In the case of Paris, the myriad of groups, grouplets and '*groupuscules*' which emerged into the public arena in 1968 made grand claims
indeed. They claimed, in short, to reject *everything*. It is worth surveying

the gamut of groups—just of students (for there were workers' groups too)—which took to the streets in May 1968, and nearly seemed to bring down the French government. There was UNEF, the National Union of Students of France, which was divided into two: the 'minos' (who were in the majority), who were on the extreme left, and the 'majos' (who were in the minority), who were more politically neutral or conservative. There was the FNEF (National Federation of Students of France), who were conservative. The other large student groups taking to the streets were the PCF (French Communist Party), the PSU (Unified Socialist Party, extreme left), and the FGDS (Federation of the Socialist and Democratic Left, mainstream left). Then, most radical of all, there were the *groupuscules*, an army of transitory battalions, coming into existence for sometimes a few days at a specific street corner, café, or riot, but sometimes forming a sustained bloc capable of taking control of a situation and dynamizing it. There was the UEC (Union of Communist Students), the ESU (Unified Socialist Students), and the PC(ML)F (Communist Party [Marxist Leninist] of France) who were pro-Chinese—as were their competitors, the equally pro-Chinese UJC(ML) (Union of Young Communists [Marxist Leninist]). Then there were the two strands of Trotskyite groups, each divided into mutually antagonistic *groupuscules*: on the 'Lambert tendency', there were the OCI, the FER, the CLER, and the ORJ. The equally hostile 'Franck tendency' also was divided: there was the PCI, the JCR, and the UC (also sometimes called the Voix Ouvrière—Worker's Voice). Then finally there were the anarchists and the situationists.

How to make sense of this apparent chaos? The most obvious way to do so would be to link them (or contrast them) not through the arcane distinctions of whether one was a 'Guevariste', a 'Maoiste', or a 'Leniniste', but the far more pragmatic category of where one was on a map of Paris. For it was the geography of Paris, and the use of space in and around universities that caused the escalation and particular features of much of the violence, which tended to revolve far more around the opening and closing of university campuses, and the arresting and freeing of individuals, than any significant political convictions. Where people were is more important to understanding what they were doing than what they thought. While the symbolism of the barricades in the Quartier Latin is etched on the minds of many, the problem actually brewed in the western suburbs of Paris at a new university, Nanterre—a privileged bastion of middle-class students, who mostly hailed from the richest *quartiers* of Paris.

But the beginning of the story of the violence lies not on a university campus, but in some of the most prestigious business streets of Paris. At 3.00 a.m. precisely on the morning of 18 March 1968 outside the Chase Manhattan Bank at 39, rue Cabon, there was an explosion. When the first police van pulled up, a second bomb went off—at 3.10 a.m.—at the Bank of America on the Place Vendôme, destroying primarily the shop window of Henri Maupiou's cloth and fabric shop opposite. A third bomb went off at 4.40 at the offices of TWA. The police identified a group of suspects—a communist cell which supported the Viet Cong's campaigns against the USA in Vietnam, the Comités Viêt-nam, and the Jeunesse Communiste Revolutionnaire. Over the next few days, the police arrested various members of these groups, and their *groupuscules*—so far, so ordinary. But the ways they executed the arrests were particularly spectacular: rather than quietly raiding a flat at night, they opted for hugely conspicuous arrests in public. One suspect, 22-year-old Xavier Langlade, was snatched as he descended the stairs at Opéra metro station, in the morning rush hour of Thursday 22 March. That afternoon, one of the students at Nanterre, Daniel Cohn-Bendit, ran round the campus, announcing that there was to be an occupation of lecture theatre B2 at 5 p.m. that day in protest at the manner of the arrests. This occupation, one way or another, led to the eruptions of May 1968—though, of course, with a break for the Easter vacation. Revolutionaries need to see their parents too.

To understand why such an apparently unprepossessing set of circumstances—a group of students at a new university occupying a lecture theatre in support of some arrested terrorism suspects—could lead to such a potent eruption of street violence, it is important to explore the geography of Nanterre's campus. Nanterre's campus was located in an industrial wasteland in western Paris and was, in 1968, completely isolated. There was an old railway station relatively nearby, called 'La Folie'—or, 'Madness'. It was a dilapidated, wooden station, with infrequent services. The last train left at 10 p.m. The campus was surrounded by mud and railway lines on one side—mud which one had to cross to get to the station. On the opposite side, the thousands of students living in the concrete blocks placed there looked over a *bidonville* of 10,000 North African immigrants—a shanty town of self-made shacks with little or no sanitation, one of many such which ringed Paris (and which can be seen in Figure 5.8). On the third side, there were derelict warehouses and fully functioning factories—in particular, the Peugeot car factory. In the first year of operation, 1964, there were 2,000 students. In 1968, there were 22,000 milling around, and Thursday was the day when most sociology lectures took place.

There was one café on the campus; there were no bars. There were cafeterias with automated vending machines, but they opened at bizarre hours—often people on campus were hungry. There had been sustained agitation on campus already over petty rules: political and religious posters were banned from the notice boards; males and females were not allowed into each others' dormitories; no one was allowed to have guests of any sort in the bedrooms; re-arranging the furniture in the rooms was forbidden, as was the hanging of things on the walls. As one female student, Wanda S., said when interviewed in 1968:

> Many times I've opened my window and leant right out of it, asking myself it I was going to decide to jump or not. I didn't do it. I don't know why.[108]

The students were not acquiescent in this situation—a women's dorm was 'invaded' by the male students in 1967; the opening of the university swimming pool was disrupted by protesters in 1968. Both were led by Daniel Cohn-Bendit, a sociology student from a wealthy Franco-German family. So the place was characterized by relatively extreme environmental hardship by middle-class standards (hunger, mud, filth), spatial isolation, boredom, poverty (surrounding it), extreme wealth (inside it), and a vast panoply of rigorously enforced, petty, anachronistic rules. The students who attended it were amongst the richest in Paris, and they focused on relatively 'new' subjects, like sociology, with little in the way of tradition to bind them to an established intellectual core. Thus at 5 p.m. there was nowhere for people to go—physically, it was hard to get away from the muddy building-site campus. They might as well go to a meeting.

Lecture theatre B2 was in the sociology department, and so when students met there, one proposed that, in order to give the meeting less of an air of a sociologists' clique, they should instead occupy the administration building. After all, the administrators would have gone home. They agreed they would move, but a discussion broke out about whether theirs was a political agenda, related to the arrests of young people in public for the bombing. One person said:

> If it's militants of the Comité Viêt-nam National that have been arrested, then it's because they're the ones that are most dangerous for the bourgeoisie...[109]

Daniel Cohn-Bendit interrupted, and spoke:

> Everyone is agreed with the struggle against imperialism, along the political lines of the Comité Viêt-nam National, and everyone here is for the victory of the Vietnamese people, in fact, that's the basic reason we're all here.[110]

This relatively simple exchange dynamized a situation, for it turned boredom, frustration, and isolation into grandiose politics. Lousy cafeterias (easy to resolve) became the global struggle against imperialism (hard to resolve). On 29 March, there was a day of discussions on 'the anti-imperialist struggle'—but in fact, the day of 'debate' was dominated by a contest over territory. The administration of the university energetically tried to prevent the students from continuing the occupation of their building, and called in the police to help when the students refused to leave. After the Easter vacation, the students returned to campus and formulated their demands and, besides the occasional references to the anti-imperialist struggle, most were focused far more closely on territory close to home. They wanted the right to be able to use the university to hold political meetings; they wanted the police off the campus; they wanted such students as had been arrested to be freed; they wanted normal classes to resume: 'For us, the most important thing is to be able to discuss these things at university', they declared.

Onto this, they tacked some other complaints: they felt 'trapped' by capitalism; they disliked the mechanization and 'cybernetization' of society. They objected to the use of psychology and time-and-motion studies in factories—'for which many of us are training'. They announced that on the 29 April, their day of discussion, if they were disrupted they would 'respond in a more and more radical way', and to that end they were preparing a demonstration in front of the prefecture of Hauts-de-Seine—i.e. they would take their protest *off* the campus, and into the industrial suburbs of western Paris in which the university was located. In this context, the counter-leaflet by the Union of Young Communists (Marxist Leninist) (UJC (ML)) seems to make some sense:

> This movement [the student movement] is reactionary because they criticize in words the bourgeois university but try to ignore the fact that the university exists to serve the bourgeoisie, because universities assist in its exploitation of the working class masses. What you learn at university is to scorn workers.[111]

Given that few of the students at Nanterre were seriously destined for work in factories, the UJC(ML) seem to have made a valid point. On the 29 April, at the Sorbonne in the central Latin Quarter, they too held a day of debates, and occupied the university to do so. Cohn-Bendit attended; the university tried to close the buildings. The pattern of spatial conflict around universities was established; the importance of *university* spaces is demonstrated because, for ten days either side of 14 April the demonstrations abated. Why? Because for most of that time, the universities were closed, not by order of pseudo-revolutionaries, nor by frightened university rectors, nor by the police—but by the long advertised Easter vacation. Take the students out of the space, and the students seem to have become neutral.

A set of leaflets announcing yet another occupation of Nanterre appeared on 26 April—but more problematically, it also contained instructions on how to make Molotov cocktails. Clearly, this is illegal, and could be viewed as an incitement to commit very extreme violence. On the day after, on a Saturday morning, Cohn-Bendit was arrested at his chic house in the wealthy 15th arrondissement. He was on his way to a radio interview, but as he left, at 8.10 a.m., the police moved in and arrested him as he came out of his front door for incitement to violence. By 2 May, both the Sorbonne and Nanterre were closed to preclude rioting; students tried to reopen them. The police cleared the students with increasing violence, and by 3 May, the CRS, the French riot police, had effectively sealed the campus at Nanterre. Nanterre now being essentially 'out of bounds', the confrontation moved to the Sorbonne in the Quartier Latin in central Paris, and escalated. It focused on the space of the university, specifically the central courtyard:

university authorities banned students from the campuses; the students forced their way in. The police cleared them out, and arrested students that resisted, which turned the police stations themselves into sites of violent campaigning by students besieging them to free their friends.

The experienced riot police, the CRS, were not employed to disperse students in central Paris—it was felt that their presence there would be inflammatory, and they were engaged at Nanterre. Instead, minibus R831 of the standard police got stuck in a crowd outside the Lycée Saint Louis—one of the most prestigious preparatory schools for the elite French universities. The policemen inside did not have their helmets on when two cobblestones crashed through the windows. A full scale riot ensued, and barricades were erected, as can be seen in Figure 1.4. A myth was born. On the night of the 10–11 May, the police stormed the barricades at substantial cost: 274 police and 116 demonstrators were injured, and 60 vehicles set on fire.[112] Yes, students wanted to free Vietnam; but primarily, they wanted to establish their parity with rectors in running and organizing universities, and often at a very micro level. They wanted to be able to visit their girlfriends, use the notice boards in the corridors, arrange the furniture in their rooms as they wished. When they were given these things, they went back to class. Much is made of the alliance with workers in this escapade—and it is certainly true that many workers in France used the urban disruption to their own ends.

But the workers at the metal plants and car factories which are dotted along the northern edges of Paris began their street campaigns *after* the government had 'given in' to the students—if opening universities so students can sit their finals is 'giving in', in the context of some students' declared goals of eliminating 'bourgeois' examinations from the university curriculum. In this context metal workers announced a so-called general strike—'so-called', because only 19 per cent of metal workers took part. There was, however, widespread disruption—although with no particular objective—and these strikes grew on subsequent Mondays (when absenteeism was high anyway), on 20 and 27 May. Increasingly, local shop stewards amongst the *métallos* used these strikes as bargaining positions: early posturing on the part of union leaders about destroying the system by installing *autogestion* (workers' management) in the factories rapidly unravelled in

Figure 1.4 The *Événements* of Paris, May 1968—here in the rue Gay Lussac in the Latin Quarter. The rioters here were remarkably geographically contained in the old university district, and had few concrete objectives—yet de Gaulle struggled to manage the phenomenon. Visually, such scenes evoked revolutionary potential; yet the student demonstrations oscillated with the rhythms of university life, and the geographies of university locations across Paris. The most extreme protests were remarkably restricted—both in their location and ambitions.

the Renault factories of Boulogne-Billancourt and the Avions Marcel Dassault plant, where workers quickly shifted their rage from 'the system', and began to focus on their wage packets, length of working week, and job security. Car workers at Citroën demanded low-cost car rentals during their vacations. In other factories, equal pay for women and non-French workers was the objective—and, indeed, the

French employers' association, the Conseil national du patronat français, did agree to a 10 per cent pay rise for metal workers, and a 35 per cent increase in the minimum wage across the board—good and noble outcomes, but not ones won by the students.

At precisely this point, for reasons that have always remained unclear, President de Gaulle left Paris in a sort of 'flight to Varennes' moment, reminiscent of the panicked flight of Louis XVI from Paris in 1792 during the radicalization of the French Revolution, and the transformation of Parisians from loving subjects into a hopeless lost cause. The scale of the disorders in the student quarters was relatively contained yet, in an age of television news, had a remarkably 'spectacular' impact—a flavour of which can be seen in Figure 1.4. This gave what was admittedly France's most sustained period of labour unrest a far more political colour, and introduced, on the one hand, an air of panic but, on the other, a general realization that given the material progress that had been made in workers' lives since the war, this really was not worth the collapse of the Republic. When de Gaulle, on 30 May, made clear that the instruments of the French state would not acquiesce to the workers' demands—indeed, there was no coherent set of demands for the government to acquiesce to—gradually, a return to work began. In particular, the occupations of factories in Paris's industrial suburbs slowly began to dissipate: although it should be noted, that at the huge Renault factories in Billancourt, employing 30,000, only 300 workers occupied them; and amongst the 15,000 Citroën workers in the 15th arrondissement, only 100 regularly turned up for union meetings in this period.

What stands out from these demonstrations and factory occupations is not a fundamental *dis*satisfaction with the liberal democracy and social market pursued by the French state for a hundred years, but just the reverse. The workers of Paris, and the other large industrial cities of the north and east, did not want to destroy the French state; rather, they wanted more of what the French state had already secured for them, and, rather more nobly, they wanted more people—immigrants, women, young workers—to have it too. While only 40 per cent of French skilled workers—which the *métallos* were—had cars in 1963, ten years later, 75 per cent had them. And young workers wanted to borrow them during paid holidays. Thus, in their demands for higher pay for the poorest, and equal pay for the non-male and the non-white, the marchers and occupiers actually advocated the best values of French republicanism, not the abolition of it. And in their interest in material benefit, far from wanting to destroy capitalism, they wanted to enjoy it more. One leading French news review at the time pointed out how targeting the consumerist dream actually undermined the strikers' objectives:

> Five weeks on strike has created an emotional strain between the married couple, Pierre and Nicole. They lived in two different worlds. He is a union representative, a devoted militant who is always active at the workplace. She is stuck in the housing estate, dealing with personal problems, with unpaid rent, and with kids to feed. She feels abandoned. Suddenly their relationship turned sour.[113]

For every man engaged in a riot, leading a demonstration, or occupying a factory there were thousands of both men and women resenting the disturbance of their lives and hoping to acquire fridges, washing machines, and cars. The police gained in confidence in clearing factories, and when the main union organization, the CGT, called people out on the streets for one hour on 12 June to protest at 'military dictatorship', almost none turned up. An empty street, unused for political protest, can be a potent space for confirming the legitimacy of the status quo.[114]

When French workers emptied the streets to support social market capitalism, those on the other side of the Iron Curtain occupied their factories to try to attain it. Disorder is increasingly regarded by historians as a feature of the Soviet Bloc in Eastern Europe after the war.[115] Far from being a successful monolithic oppressor in Eastern Europe, the USSR emerges, in an urban history of that half of the continent, as a paper tiger facing constant humiliation at the hands of bricklayers in Berlin in 1953, locomotive engineers in Poznan and students in Budapest in 1956, men who had rowed with their mothers in Berlin in 1961, the crowds that pelted Soviet tanks in Prague in 1968, and shipbuilders in Gdansk in 1970 and 1980.

Poland was, throughout the 1970s, the most ungovernable of the Soviet satellite states. On 14 August 1980, a strike broke out in the shipyards of the adjoining industrial cities of Gdansk and Gdynia on the Baltic coast of Poland. The workers wanted an independent union to negotiate for them, outside of the party structure. While in 1970, workers in Gdansk and Gdynia had rioted and burned down the party headquarters, and seventeen of them were killed when panicking troops opened fire on them as they alighted from a train, this set of actions was altogether different in 1980. The strikes spread quickly to other cities—to steel mills in Warsaw in particular. And within two weeks, the government had agreed to recognize an independent trade union; in fact, a multiplicity of trade unions were established, under the collective name of Solidarity. But it is important to understand the very circumscribed *locality* of the origins of this movement—a movement which ultimately, although indirectly, led to the collapse of the Soviet regime.

When Alojzy Szablewski, a foreman in the Gdansk shipyard (and participant in the 1970 riots), started the process in 1980, he was not concerned with anything as abstract as 'freedom', or even the more concrete 'Soviet Bloc'. The movement was concerned with working conditions in a fabrication chamber on his shipyard. As he explained:

> I went to a room where there was no ventilation and the workers were breathing smoke. I told the director that if the situation didn't change by the next day, I would stop work on that ship. The next day the ship had many plastic sleeves, and great ventilators were taking the smoke out. In one of the huge work rooms, the heating was out of order and the temperature was very low. We went to the director and told him it had to be repaired, and it was.[116]

From this sort of very local, place-specific protest, other similar ones emerged. Students at Łodz University demanded the right to form their own organizations without interference. In another port city, Stettin, a tiny incident is illustrative of the massive transformations in power dynamics that can happen just by changing the ways a room or a place is laid out. A union leader in Stettin during the strikes, Aleksander Krystosiak, was in his office when the district attorney came in to speak to him:

> There I am sitting on the side of the desk that normally was his; he is sitting in a pleading position on the side of the desk where I would normally sit. He is telling me that they caught a worker who stole something. He is asking me if I'd object to this worker being arrested. For some reason, I stand up. He immediately jumps to his feet and stands at attention. This is a psychological study of an official! A few

days earlier, I wouldn't have been able to look at him, he was so self-important, and so puffed up. And there he was standing in front of me, just a worker—and he looked like a sick rat—one of those you could step on and crush its spine...[117]

For all that people spoke of 'global' superpowers, for power to work, to reach into people's everyday lives, the geography of a desk, and who sits at which side, can be pretty potent. The disorder this created in Poland—the collapse in confidence and conviction amongst the ruling elite—was profound. And once the regime had conceded the right to form independent trade unions, and shifted power from the party to the military, they had signalled their inability to sustain their vision of the world. The collapse was not sudden. The collapse in the 'total' claims of Eastern Europe's Communist Parties came, not in a grand tumult in 1989, but in the fabrication rooms and offices of the Gdansk and Stettin shipyards in the 1970s and 1980s. From 1980, the unions built up funds; and with the funds, they built houses and reading rooms; and with these, they created pluralism and legitimacy. And the grip of the Communist Parties of Eastern Europe did not have to wait until 1989: between 1981 and 1983, there was martial law in Poland. This may seem like a constitutional nicety, but it was important: first of all, it stopped an invasion of Poland by the USSR, and secondly, it showed that government by an organism other than a Communist Party was perfectly possible.

But we should not be smug here: the rights of minorities—black people, gay people, migrants—were not 'granted' out of the goodness of elite hearts in Western Europe either. In Britain, poor people, many of whom were black, in the late 1950s in London's Notting Hill; poor Catholics in the 1960s and 1970s in Belfast; poor people again, again many of whom were black, in London, Birmingham, Liverpool, Bristol, and Manchester in the 1980s seriously shook the political establishment. In some accounts, the riots of the 1950s and 1980s are dismissed as 'race' riots; as if the problem was somehow the rioters' 'race'. This is not what they were. In every instance of disorder, there were white people there, and the source of anger was not race, but poverty, hopelessness, environmental degradation, and rac*ism*. A rac*ism* riot is different from a race riot. Equally, in France the *banlieus* have regularly resorted to violence and disorder in order to construct a political voice—most recently, and in some ways most seriously, in October and November of 2005.[118] In this set of violent disturbances across French cities, social housing projects—themselves often unpoliceable due to the designs of the alleys and bridges and tunnels and towers that make them up—around every single sizeable French city erupted into violence. Its universality was remarkable. One part of the reaction in both Britain and France to urban disorder was to call for a more perfect expression of 'order' and force; but a liberal regime will know that it cannot govern a city through force, and that freedom, as a technique of government, is more effective than control. Britain's and France's systems of government will not collapse in the ways that others have, because freedom as a *technique of rule* is so very effective.[119]

Following these disturbances, there were not threats of violence or summary executions in Britain and France. Instead, the concerned governments of France and Britain wanted to *help* the rioters; they wanted to *study* and *understand* them. So they invited them to hearings and inquiries and, when they had found out what bothered them—economic hopelessness, racism, overbearing police strategies, bad public transport trapping them on their decrepit housing estates—the liberal states set about putting these things right. And in doing so, they became more liberal, more free, more tolerant. Thus, the processes of street politics and urban politics when driven by the marginalized and the impoverished can actually drive and reinforce the central political projects of 'freedom' which the French and British states profess to pursue. Viewed like that, the rioters of Broadwater Farm and Clichy-sous-Bois can be seen as deeply conservative in their politics. Their goals were not to overthrow the state, but to make it live up to its best ideals.

Perhaps the story presented like this is triumphalist—the first half of the century saw cities collapse into the horrors of National Socialism, fascism, and communism, while the true spirit of freedom burned quietly in British and French cities; the second half of the century saw cities confirm the victory of liberal democracy, and undermine the pernicious empire of the USSR. In some ways, this is true: not many people remain fans of Soviet communism, or National Socialism, or the Roman Catholic encyclicals of the 1890s, no matter how appalling their experience of war or the fall of the Iron Curtain. But the picture is more complex than that, and the 'happy ending' is the fortuitous outcome of chronology—drawing the finishing post in 1989 rather than 1939. In all the messiness of urban life and urban politics, we can see that the distinctive features of urban social life have negotiated the particular features of the urban landscape to drive politics forward. European politics, and occasionally global polities, have been shaped by cities in a profound way, and in surprising constellations and with many paradoxes; for while cities can serve to affirm the values of liberal democracy, they are just as capable of making a liberal democratic outcome impossible. And whatever we define our problems to be, any policy to solve them which does not focus on our urban lives is destined to frustration and irrelevance. This urban focus goes above all for our history: we need to be more attentive to the messy, untidy mechanisms of real politics if we want to understand how it works in people's lives, rather than the grand abstractions of the state or geopolitics.

2

No Place for a Lady?

All the world's a stage,
And all the men and women merely players;
They have their exits and their entrances,
And one man in his time plays many parts.[1]

In 1898, the *Daily Chronicle* sent an undercover reporter to Stoke-on-Trent, the sprawling industrial conurbation known as the 'five towns' at the heart of Britain's pottery industry in the north Midlands. What the paper found there caused a national scandal, and challenged any assumptions about the delicacy of women's lives, minds, and bodies that contemporaries might have been tempted to make. In the factories making the most prestigious luxury porcelain and pottery goods in the British Empire, most of the employees in glazing and enamelling were women. And amongst those women, 80 per cent of their babies were born dead. The journalist went to meet a group of women workers being secretly treated for lead poisoning by the company they worked for, and noted that resultant from just *one company's* enamel shop there were:

> 9 totally blind, 2 of which are insane and helpless; 6 dead some little time; 3 dead since reported; 2 are insane and helpless; 2 in bed paralysed and totally helpless; 5 are, according to medical authority, 'liable to go blind' and six have paralysis of arms and wrists called 'wrist drop.'[2]

And this was not an anomaly. This level of vulnerability to a poisonous world was typical in new, urban worlds coming to characterize Europe in the first half of the twentieth century. If 'a woman's place is at work', many women and men around 1900 worried that work meant harm, vulnerability, exposure, and neglected children.

One thousand three hundred miles to the east, Aleksandra Kondrat'eva was a peasant from Novgorod who fled to St Petersburg when her father died and she was orphaned. She stood for literally millions of women migrating to Europe's suddenly expanding cities at the same time. Faced with disaster like the death of her father, she attempted to find work in a factory, but quickly became pregnant three times. The rapid sequence of pregnancies led to sickness in 1901, whereupon the Schtiglitz factory sacked her. Up until then, she had lived with two other families in the corner of a room, a room from which she was evicted.[3] So, if a woman's place in the new urban Europe was not at work, the home hardly provided an unproblematic place for her to be: for so many women, 'home' as we would recognize it barely existed. Most women could claim something that we would view as 'shelter', but for millions of women in the rapidly growing cities, these were not places of safety, health, comfort, or rich family life. And this situation—caught between the 'rock' of work and life outside the home, and the 'hard place' of house and home—has been one of the defining frameworks of the twentieth century for millions and millions of European women. But this idea of a separate 'home' and 'work' is relatively new, and it is a product of urbanization. The process began in Britain in the early nineteenth century as factories separated home and work, for both men and women. The growth of transport infrastructures, like railways, buses, trams, and undergrounds, led to this spatial segregation—especially for men. In the sudden explosion in urban living which occurred in Europe between 1870 and 1900, millions more women had to adapt to this new spatial 'architecture', and ask questions like 'what is a woman's place?' and 'what should a woman's place be like?'

While feminism in the last forty years has stressed the importance of getting out of the home, feminism in the preceding hundred years focused far more on the quest to get into one. Yet each of these views on 'a woman's place' remains highly politically charged; in this chapter, I want to move away from a view of where women 'should' be to emphasize the dynamics of where they actually were, what they did when they were there, where they wanted to be, and what they wanted their environments to be like. A huge literature on this topic exists on the late nineteenth century, and it is time to turn focus on the twentieth.[4] As we see women taking decisions about where in the city they want to be, we can grasp better the changes they have effected in their lives, the *mechanisms* and *locations* of that struggle, as well as the powerful restrictions on their abilities to meet their own objectives.

Stories like those from Stoke or St Petersburg were powerful indictments of the effects of urbanization on women, as they were uprooted from conventional rural property structures, social organizations, and cultural expectations. The move to a city 'liberated' many European women into poverty and desperation, and left them outside the traditional systems of honour, duty, and obligation which, although oppressive in themselves, had also given women a framework in which to make claims on the world, and resist some of the claims the world made on them. There was, at least, a system of rights and responsibilities in rural, village, and small town life which were well established, even if highly discriminatory and poorly enforced. Cities stripped women of both this oppression and the niches of self-preservation that it offered. For some women, urbanization was profoundly liberating in a positive sense, freeing them *to* earn their own money, *to* go where they pleased, and *to* live how they liked. For other women, the move to a city was liberating in a negative sense, freeing them *from* constant observation, *from* oppression, *from* starvation, and *from* generations of grinding poverty. For yet more women, like Anna and the enamellers of Stoke, the move to the city was the start of a string of catastrophes and impoverishments. For most women, the truth was probably a combination of all three. And for all women, where they were, and what they did in the spaces and places that characterized their lives, determined so much. 'A woman's place' is perhaps one of the most fraught issues of the twentieth century, and it is an issue raised primarily by urbanization.

Higher education illustrates well this paradox between our assumptions of a woman's 'place' and those of our grandmothers and great-grandmothers. While today, it is a commonplace to assert that women's progression depends on their participation in education in every field of academic endeavour, and at the highest levels, this was not the case a hundred years ago. Few women in Europe in 1900 would have put access to universities at the top of their list of priorities (and for many poorer women today, such talk may still seem irrelevant to their lives and worlds). There were only 48,000 university students in the whole of Germany in 1900, out of a population of 27,737,000 males; France sent 29,000 young men to university in 1900, out of 18,917,000 males; in Britain, no one even bothered to count properly, but it was fewer than in either France or Germany.[5] University attendance was such a remote objective for *men*, that 'normalizing' it as an aspiration for women would have seemed bizarre, wilful, and perverse. Neither men *nor* women could, for the most part, envisage careers in 'the professions', a career of rewarding, independent, intellectually challenging, flexible work; and women in particular did not necessarily expect to find fulfilment outside the home, as well as less work in it. Rather, paid work for most women around 1900 (and for many today) represented an unfulfilling career in menial work, often in a dangerous environment, usually for a low wage, *and then their huge burden of unpaid domestic labour for their family on top of that.* This is what feminists rightly call the 'double burden' of modern womanhood: women are expected to leave the home and get jobs, but do not enjoy a corresponding alleviation of their household chores.

Another clear example of the paradox of recent views of women's 'place' focuses on the idea of civil rights. It seems to us instinctive to focus on rights derived in legislatures—but these very often turn out to be rights primarily for the middle classes, who both view the world in terms of rights *and* who are adept at enforcing them in courtrooms and bureaucracies. Very often in current popular debate, people fix on the acquisition of the right to vote as being of prime importance to women a hundred years ago. But that was not always the case. Not all men could vote in Britain in 1900, and no men could vote in Russia in 1900, so those 'rights' too might have been seen—in fact, *were* often seen by many women—as the self-absorbed obsession of a few middle-class cranks.[6] For most women in 1900, and for many working-class women today, their goal was a safe, comfortable, happy home in which they could raise their families free from material privation. For these women, the home was and is a key index of their 'citizenship', not the exercise of political rights, or the acquisition of knowledge, or the performance of a professional job. And the home is a place—a real experience located in a real world. We need to turn to more realities like these if we are to understand the fraught nature of feminism, and the class dynamics which can sometimes dominate it. Ultimately, the history of women is highly place-specific.

* * *

Looking at working-class women in Europe at the turn of the twentieth century illustrates just how important the home was to women, and how infrequently older adult women were involved in paid labour outside their own or someone else's home. In Britain, only one-third of women worked outside the home in 1900, and even then, usually only until they got married in their mid-twenties. In 1911, 69 per cent of all *single* women in Britain worked outside the home, falling to 9.6 per cent after marriage—though the idea that they usually stopped doing paid work in their own homes should be discounted: cleaning, cooking, taking in children, laundering, match-box manufacture, lace-making, sewing, and many light-industrial tasks were often done in the home across Europe.[7] And in Britain, half of the women that did work outside the home before the First World War, worked in *somebody else's* home as servants and maids.[8] One way or another, a woman's 'place' was in the home. Apparently, inescapably so—and yet, over the course of this chapter, we will see that many ordinary women struggled hard to change their 'place'.

Perhaps surprisingly to us, many women in European cities in the late nineteenth and early twentieth centuries explicitly opposed the idea of women's 'rights' at work. Instead, they agitated for what was called a 'family wage': a wage for men sufficiently high that women would not *have* to work because of family poverty. Many women argued that if women worked, they would drive men's wages down (a process economists call 'dilution') and, furthermore, cause male unemployment. But if women were excluded from the labour market in cities, men's wages would rise to allow a 'family wage' to be paid, and male unemployment (a constant blight on the lives of millions of Europeans from around 1890 to the 1950s) would disappear. One prominent (male) progressive in Britain in the 1900s, spoke for millions of men and women when he wrote:

> The nation must set its face against the employment of married women in factories and workshops, and gradually extend the period of legal prohibition. There is only one proper sphere of work for the married woman and that is her own home. In the case of factory workers the employer must be made to furnish a maternity fund if he wishes to employ married women. Thus penalized he will probably prefer not to employ them—to the very great advantage to the labour market and the nation.[9]

Some disagreed with him, viewing home as a sort of prison, and the 'family wage' as a licence for men to behave tyrannically. The scale of debate on this issue in the 1900s was vast, and not organized solely around gender lines.[10] One woman wrote in a lively newspaper debate on the topic in 1909:

> Man has never objected to women working. She has borne her share of the world's burden since history began. It is her wage-earning which distresses the masculine mind. Let a woman slave, in some apology for a home, at any sweated, unorganized trade and no man is troubled. But once let her come into the open market, trained and capable, asking that her services be given the usual recognition—Scandalous! Down with her! Make room for the man![11]

But plenty of women, especially in areas of heavy industry and away from areas of textile production, would contradict her. In Germany, in the metal and porcelain industries that were heavily unionized, there was substantial progress towards a 'family wage' in the 1900s— even though young single men complained hard and bitterly. Workers for the vast metal concern IG-Metall in Berlin were paid a basic rate, and then a supplement for the size of their families; bachelors just passing their apprenticeships shouted 'equal pay for equal work', but wives and mothers of older men supported the family-wage principle.[12] And many French trades union meetings throughout the 1890s and 1900s concurred: the family wage was essential, if the home, as a special place, was to be created and sustained—although French cities were somewhat exceptional, as in the 1900s 40–50 per cent of married women worked outside the home. But this symbolized not the achievement of equality, but the poverty of all wages, and the prevalence of short-term employment patterns for men in urban France.[13]

While wages in Britain at the turn of the century were the highest in Europe by a long margin, even in low-wage urban economies like Stoke-on-Trent, far from seeking employment and employment rights, women across the Continent struggled hard in order not to have to work outside the home. They would risk substantial poverty to avoid it because of the problems that such work might pose—in particular, the long hours and the damage it did to their health and their relationships with their family. At the opposite end of the economic scale to Britain, proper statistics for Russian cities are not widely available for the first thirty years of the twentieth century; governments there were either too uninterested in the poor or too chaotic to collect them reliably. But individual philanthropists and doctors did investigate specific streets or buildings, as and when they were able, and some kept assiduous notes. For example, at 18 Zabalskanskii Prospekt in Moscow, there resided twenty-six working-class couples. One-third of the men were unskilled labourers—the poorest-paid category of workers, existing around or below the subsistence level, and constantly hungry; just the sort of people one might expect to depend on dual-income households. Yet twenty-two out of the twenty-six wives were recorded as 'dependents', and only seven of them had children, meaning that fifteen of the wives stayed at home even though there were no children to care for. A couple of doors along and across the road, at number 21 Zabalskanskii Prospekt, there were forty working-class couples. Twenty-one of the men were in the poorest category of unskilled labourers, yet only one of the women worked outside the building of the entire forty, and only nine women had children. So while skilled male British urban workers were the highest paid in Europe and thus their partners might afford more readily to reject paid work outside the home, even the *lowest* paid workers in Europe either forced their wives not to work outside the home, or accepted their desire not to do so—or, most likely of all, a combination of the two: a deeply-held belief on the part of most women that 'home' (however squalid) was where they should be, especially if they planned to have children, backed up by a readiness to enforce that belief by men (and other women) should it be challenged.[14]

So how were women to respond to this poverty, to the dangers posed by the workplace, the dangers of the home, to the chaos that urbanization wrought on their lives? The new factories that came with urbanization meant that by the 1890s poorer women were increasingly grouped together in new ways, as women of the same class in factories keen to employ them as cheaper replacements for men, as was seen in the velvet mills of Leeds and Bradford, and the early stages of organizing the Labour Party (see pp. 20–3). Many of the industries that emerged around 1900 and which shaped the twentieth century in profound ways, like automobile manufacture, telephony, photography, and electrical goods, also began employing women as new firms like Siemens, Kodak, and Hoover sought new labour supplies at low wages. And around this time, shops too began to change radically, with a long decline in owner–proprietor shops, where the family lived on site and worked in the shop, to chain and department stores employing large numbers of staff on low wages, like W. H. Smith, Boots the Chemist, Prix Uniques, Woolworth's, Schocken, and Bon Marché. These environments also brought women together in new ways. Finally, in the last twenty years of the nineteenth century, there was an explosion in office work, to manage the new chain stores and industrial concerns that emerged into the multinationals that we know today, like AEG, BASF, Lever Bros., and Bayer.

But above all, employment grew in administration in the rapidly expanding state, most conspicuous at city level, as it grew into areas of welfare, transport, health, education, taxation, and policing that it had never before occupied. All of these activities required typing pools, and these too brought women together as a 'class' on a scale and in organizations that were entirely new outside the textile industry. This grouping together meant that women's mobilization and collective action became possible, as for the first time large numbers of women were brought together in unique circumstances. Often, this meant that the first confrontation was not with their employers, or the state, but with labouring men. In many cases across European cities, women were deliberately excluded from trade unions, so they had to negotiate new factory, shop, and office experiences outside the formal, legalistic frameworks in which historians have traditionally tried to understand the 'rise' of the working class. If women were to 'rise', they had to find other techniques to do it than classic trade unionism, because often the working class, in its political, organized form, was highly committed to ensuring that women, if they worked at all, remained low-paid and low-skilled.

Along with the cotton and woollen mills in northern England, the match factories of the East End of London became, in the 1890s, amongst the first places to produce coherent, directed, sustained action amongst women—especially in the Bryant & May and Bell's factories in Bow in London's East End, some of the strikers of which can be seen in Figure 2.1. They employed 3–4,000 people, three-quarters of them women, all on shocking wages. One social investigator, Clara Collett, found out that girls started at the age of thirteen, and earned 4 shillings a week—roughly £16.10 in today's money, or about three hours' work on the current minimum wage.[15] This was for working eleven hours a day, five and a half days a week, using highly poisonous sulphur and white phosphorous. Nor was this level of pay essential to turning a profit. The Salvation Army's Safety Match Factory worked nine hours a day, used the less harmful red phosphorous, paid 10 shillings a week minimum, and still turned a profit. The women and girls at Bryant & May often suffered from a terrible disease, 'phossy jaw', due to the presence of sulphur and white or yellow phosphorous. Their gums rotted away, their teeth fell out, as did their hair. Their jaws swelled up, twisted and eventually crumbled inside their skin, which was itself yellowed and flaked. They were docked half a day's wages for being late, and were not allowed to go to the toilet. In 1888, some women complained about this—and they were sacked. Unusually, the rest of the employees—staggeringly poor as they were—went on strike, demanding an end to dangerous forms of phosphorous and sulphur, and the docking of wages. They did *not* demand the vote—their concerns were more immediate, more environmental—although they did march from the East End to the Houses of Parliament, staking a claim to be heard in the legislature by staking a claim to be present in the 'wrong' part of the city.

The *sine qua non* for this sort of collective action was the way factories brought these women together, which is highlighted in an image like Figure 2.1. This process of segregation into class and gender in Britain was far from new, as the large cotton- and woollen-mill towns of the north were also seeing nascent female political militancy (see Chapter 1). But so many thousands of women segregated by sex and class was a new phenomenon, and factories of unskilled labour on such a scale in London were new (northern textile workers were more skilled). The girls and women at Bryant & May (they always called themselves 'girls', and their union was called the Match Girls' Union) seem to have had a profound sense of their solidarity—but also, initially, their inferiority. Charles Booth, one of the East End's foremost social investigators, noted the match girls' anxiety about their social status, observing that 'they would withdraw themselves from the company of others whom they consider too aristocratic to associate with on equal terms'.[16] Gilbert Bartholomew, the managing director of Bryant & May, observed that 'they [the girls] would not associate with others employed in the jam, pill or other branches'. Their solid sense of sorority was deeper even than this. Describing lunchtimes at the

Figure 2.1 The 'Match Girls' of Bryant May, going on strike to stop the erosion of their working conditions. Industrial employment grouped women together in unique ways, which enabled them by the 1890s to organize to resist working practices which harmed them physically, mentally, and financially. Such experiences transformed the ways women staked a claim to citizenship by bringing them into situations where they were all together, and crystallizing their 'inferiority' in repeated attempts to worsen their working conditions. Factories which brought them together also enabled them to take new forms of collective action, far more immediately effective than, say, acquiring the vote.

Fairfield works, Bartholomew observed that: 'Each body of workers have their own table, nor will they allow any others there. Each know and maintain their place against all comers.' At the Victoria works, by contrast, he claimed that *all* the workers were Irish, either by birth or lineage.[17] These were tight communities indeed. So when one part of this community was victimized, the mechanisms and frameworks to deal with that victimization were in place; created, as Karl Marx and Friedrich Engels observed during the first phase of urban industrialization, by the very people who exploited them.

In 1848 Marx and Engels pointed out how cities and factories and commerce dragged millions from the countryside, compressing them into new social and spatial formations which would eventually become radically unstable because of their own inherent contradictions, and because the exploited would, eventually, realize their common situation if they were aggregated together. The product was modern bourgeois society, which 'with its relations of production, of exchange and of property, a society that has conjured up such gigantic means of production and of exchange, is like the sorcerer who is no longer able to control the powers of the nether world which he has called up by his spells'.[18]

This type of spontaneous organization brought about by urbanization and industrialization did not go unnoticed. Anxiety about the ways that cities were bringing women together to organize outside the control of men in trade unions or families was intense at the turn of the last century, and the twenty years before the First World War were characterized by extensive discussion of the 'woman question'. There was a widespread sense of panic, amongst both men and women, that women were taking over, promising to destroy all sense of the 'natural' order of things. This was a sense which roused both men and women into action. In Britain, female anti-suffrage campaigners, like the prominent Liberal, Violet Markham, launched vigorous, well-planned, rational campaigns against women's votes, arguing that women could much better enhance their positions in the world in all sorts of ways that addressed a whole range of different concerns: by focusing their efforts on ensuring that they were more fully in command of the home; by focusing on their roles as imperialists; and above all, by intervening more decisively in the many 'feminized' roles that the state was developing in education, health care, welfare administration, and social work.[19] Similar concerns were expressed by many women in Germany, many of whom were amongst the NSDAP's earliest supporters.[20] Many early feminist campaigns repeatedly emphasized that the vote was a sideshow; eliminating domestic violence, stabilizing domestic budgets, obtaining maternity leave, eliminating noxious working conditions, and developing women's roles in 'feminine' careers like nursing, teaching, and social work should be prioritized. But above all, the main goal was to obtain and then keep a home.[21]

In the new industrial cities of northern Italy like Milan and Turin, more sinister attempts to celebrate the modern city did so by vigorously declaring it a 'male' space, characterizing cities and the industries that drove them in terms of masculine muscularity. An extreme form of a relatively typical set of European anxieties, the Italian Futurists founded an enormously influential artistic, literary, and political movement focused on violence, anti-feminism, and anti-liberalism, exalting in the technological paraphernalia of the modern world—street lamps, steam trains, skyscrapers, aeroplanes, and power stations—and eagerly sought a purifying war which would expose women for the 'appendages' they were, and expose liberal men as no better than women. In this hyper-masculine, anti-feminist world, machines took on a sexual attraction—Tomaso Marinetti, principle ideologue of the Futurists, described how he approached steam trains in a shunting yard to 'caress their breasts', and describes factory discharge as 'maternal'.[22] Urban space took on a female quality, not to be 'venerated' or 'protected', but only in order to be mastered and conquered by a man; cities could be feminine only if they were vulnerable to masculine control and penetration. The Futurists had a profound impact on the artistic avant garde in Europe's great cities, but reached further. *Futurismo* was no la-di-da artistic trifle—their founding manifesto was published on the front page of the major French daily, *Le Figaro*, on 20 February 1909, such was its resonance with contemporary concerns. Futurists spoke for millions of anxious men (and a fair few conservative women) when they feted an aggressive masculinity, muscularity, movement, and warfare. Their manifesto declared:

1. We will glorify war—the world's only hygiene—militarism, patriotism, the destructive gesture of freedom-bringers, beautiful ideas worth dying for, and scorn for woman.

2. We will destroy the museums, libraries, academies of every kind, will fight moralism, feminism, every opportunistic or utilitarian cowardice.

3. We will sing of great crowds excited by work, by pleasure, and by riot; we will sing of the multicoloured, polyphonic tides of revolution in the modern capitals; we will sing of the vibrant nightly fervour of arsenals and shipyards blazing with violent electric moons; greedy railway stations that devour smoke-plumed serpents; factories hung on clouds by the crooked lines of their smoke...[23]

They spoke for a widespread strand of European intellectual thinking at the time, anxious at the 'feminization' of the world, which stood also for the effeminization of men increasingly concerned with 'soft' liberal values, anxiety, and neurosis. This anxiety at a 'feminine' or 'feminized' world cropped up in almost every sort of document or debate, ranging from the Scout movement in Britain, to the promotion of rugby football in France, to the building of hospitals in Germany. It pervaded discussion of almost every other issue in the 1900s. The *Futuristi* saw feminism, and the idea of women taking an active role in the world, as sitting right at the heart of the problems of the modern world—its pacifism, liberalism, book learning, and crass, directionless, lazy reverence for the past. 'Scorn for woman' was a widespread political position amongst working-class political organizers, as well as the avant garde intelligentsia.[24]

But at the heart of this widespread view of the world stood a distorted vision of women, inspired by the increasing demands of women of all classes to be treated in a different way (although the *Futuristi* also loathed socialist men, and called for a war that would purge the working classes; in short, they loathed anyone trying to assert themselves against what they perceived to be the 'natural order of things', with their own masculinist sexual fantasies of modernity at its peak). The small claims some women were staking to a life with stable incomes, or to fulfil their intellectual curiosity and move freely outside the confines of the home so radically threatened conventional middle-class and working-class models of masculinity that such claims often engendered a deep and aggressive suspicion of anything which smacked of feminism. Across Europe around 1900, an imperialist culture mocked

effeminate urban men and their book learning, feting a militarist, racist, sexist masculinity which focused explicitly on 'the blessings of war',
and eliminating womanly influence. For many men, there was a 'flight
from domesticity', and a concomitant understanding that women
should show greater commitment to it. And it should not be thought
that Britain was any different: the number of articles in mass-market
British newspapers in the 1900s affirming things like, 'That England
is at war shows an amount of energy and superabundant spirits that
go a long way to demonstrate that we are not a decaying race', is
breathtaking. Edwardian newspapers were positively obsessed with
masculine violence and muscular force.[25]

Yet it was in France, perhaps, that anxiety about women's role in
society was most keenly felt, most tightly linked to urbanization, and
most vigorously acted on. Titles at the turn of the century, like Jacques
Bertillon's *La dépopulation de la France* in 1909, had a profound impact,
because mainstream politicians, commentators and voters drew a
direct line between the changing habits of women in France's rapidly
growing cities and the capacity of the French state to survive at all.[26]
The French social and political elite noted a strong decline in birth
rates in the new cities growing fast in the last quarter of the nineteenth
century, and feared that this would leave France in a situation doubly
perilous: urbanization meant that there would be lots of women *not* at
home because they were out doing paid work (dangerous enough!),
and also that there would be insufficient sons to fight the next war
with Germany and preserve the 'race' (a catastrophe). The solution:
explain to women with ever greater force that they should remain in
the home and breed more. The vitriol poured out against French
women was remarkable, and their perceived 'failure' to serve the state
and the nation in childbirth was a potent argument used to exclude
them from the public spaces of the city, where they might assert their
rights and manage their destinies.[27]

Ultimately, though, it was an effort that failed, and French women
managed their fertility with increasing success. In fact, in the first
twenty years of the twentieth century, Europe's women in general,
and Europe's urban women in particular, managed a spectacular revolution in the ways that they controlled their own bodies; it was a
revolution effected in direct correlation to the level of urbanization.
Demographers refer to it as 'the great demographic transition' in

Europe, which started in the late nineteenth century, suddenly picked up pace in the 1890s–1900s, and culminated around 1910–20.[28] Birth rates per thousand adults each year in 1900 were thirty-seven in Austria, thirty-six in Germany, twenty-two in France, and twenty-nine in Britain. But in 1922 (just after the post-war baby boom had ended) they settled down to about twenty-three in Austria, twenty-three in Germany, nineteen in France, and twenty-one in Britain. Then the process continued more gradually: by 1960, still well before the pill, they were eighteen in Austria, seventeen in Germany, fifteen in France, and seventeen in Britain.[29] There, give or take a few births, they have remained ever since. The statistics show very clearly that in the first twenty years of the twentieth century, women were transforming their understandings of, and attitudes to, their own bodies, with little birth control available except abortion and withdrawal. Historians still struggle to explain this clearly, but they have come to some tentative conclusions, all of which upset popular views of 'restrictive' sexual knowledge and 'Victorian values' in the past. First of all, the 'great demographic transition' undermines our image of the 'ignorant bride' of the past. It indicates an increased rejection of the late-nineteenth-century taboo about oral sex: 'Victorian values' generally praised penetrative sex, and abhorred oral, and that switched around in the 1900s and 1910s, it seems. Secondly, abortion, until the introduction of the latex condom in the 1930s, was the only reliable form of dealing with unwanted pregnancy, and historians have concluded that it must have played a major part in effecting such a massive change so quickly. It disrupts our ideas of the past, perhaps, but research has shown that potions for the inducing of miscarriage were advertised widely at this time in newspapers and magazines, even on their front covers, and abortifacients were available on full view in chemists', pharmacists', and apothecaries' shops across the continent's cities—much less so in rural areas.[30]

The more that women lived in cities the earlier the decline in birth rates, and the greater the scale of the change, but the role of urbanization was significant in changing birth rates in a further regard, because urban children had to go to school. The introduction and extension of universal schooling in Western Europe between the 1870s and 1890s had several consequences. It meant that urban women by 1910 were much better educated than their mothers and their country cousins, and we know from more recent studies in the developing world that as girls' education improves, birth rates drop. But the increase in schooling also meant that children represented *not* more hands on the plough or at the loom, but simply more unproductive mouths to feed for longer. Historians have struggled to understand precisely how women achieved this change in their own fertility across Europe at this time because people did not leave records behind about it. But it seems from the evidence that two techniques were central: first, there was a transformation in sexual practice involving both coitus interruptus, which also implies a change in the ways that women were relating to men during sexual intimacy, and a shift to oral sex; and secondly, abortion on a vast scale.[31] Neither fit the popular image of Victorian values, naivety, and prudery that is often used to frame debates about modern sexuality, but the statistics are clear: the pill had little or no meaningful effect on fecundity, and women (especially urban women) in the 1900s and 1910s were making decisions about their bodies in ways their mothers and grandmothers had not.

But even this anxiety over women's increasing control over their bodies overlooked the urban reality for most women, which was focused on a very difficult home and work life. For many urban women, home and work were one and the same place. When the Office du Travail tentatively began to investigate the conditions of life for Paris's thousands of home-working seamstresses in the 1900s, they gave us a picture of what 'home' was like for millions of urban women across Europe. While women may have been taking more control of their bodies, their worlds of work and home were more difficult for them to manage. Unlike the women in the match factory in London, Parisian seamstresses were dispersed throughout the city, not brought together by capitalism. The majority of the women the Office du Travail surveyed earned less than 600 francs a year, while their rent averaged 150–300 francs a year. One of the investigators the French government sent to interview one of these women concluded matter-of-factly:

> This worker, who is forty-seven, looks as if she is sixty. Her food is made up of little more than little balls of minced pork, salted herrings and the cheapest of vegetables. She says that she gets no help from anyone and that life for her is an unalleviated burden.[32]

Work for these women—and there were millions of home workers in turn-of-the-century Europe—was fixed to the home, and did not mean a 'career' in the sense we mean it today. It did not even mean leaving the confines of the dwelling, necessarily. Barely able to feed themselves or their families, what liberties these women could secure for themselves had to be secured in the context of their courtyards, blocks, families, bars, and streets, not national legislatures. Nor was this pervasive anxiety about women in the cities confined to Paris. It was a structuring drive behind much of the politics of the period, in Weimar and Nazi Germany, Third Republic and Vichy France, Soviet Russia, and Fascist Italy.

*　*　*

The First World War temporarily transformed the position of women in European cities, but not for the reasons often assumed. The war, in its own catastrophic way, also transformed the lives of many men— something that women then were keen to recognize. In some of the stories we tell ourselves about the war, there is sometimes a sense that women's position was reinvented through heavy labour and skilled factory work, and that thereafter they refused to accept a life of unpaid domestic labour typical of the many wives of, for example, Zabalskanskii Prospekt, discussed on p. 107. It is tempting to think that 'a woman's place' moved from the home to the factory, from maternal background to militarized foreground. This is not the case. One of the main reasons that the war shifted people's thinking on women was because it transformed so radically the situation of men: the masculinist bravura prosecuted by the British imperialist, Rudyard Kipling, or the Italian Futurist, Tomaso Marinetti, made little sense when thousands of men were daily losing their minds to the extent that they were wetting themselves where they sat. The war should stand as an immovable challenge to anyone who seeks to formulate a past—or a present—in which women are fundamentally oppressed, and men are fundamentally the oppressors. While the balance of power has always tipped in men's favour, the simple fact of being a man signifies nothing on its own with regard to the oppression of women; men could liberate, and women could frequently argue against their sisters' ambitions. The early twentieth century was a singularly bad time to be a man.

It is important to pause a moment and focus on the war, because it undermines an easy narrative of 'progress', for either men or women. In particular, the war was an especial disaster for men, and it did serious harm to the idea that men were emotional rocks, women emotional weaklings. In just the final offensive against the Germans, between late August 1918 and 11 November, the British lost 69,000 men dead, 23,000 missing in action, 287,000 wounded in action; while the Germans at the same offensive lost 78,000 men dead, 348,000 missing in action, and 360,000 wounded in action.[33] Virile fighting may be, but it does not give the individual the power to shape their destiny, the true measure of freedom. Men's continued physical vulnerability through their work (in mines, metallurgy, shipbuilding, and other highly dangerous industries), or through warfare, highlights just how little control *any* poor European citizen could exercise over their destiny. A man who made it to fifteen in a shipbuilding city like Bremen or Glasgow might expect to live another forty-six years in 1905; his wife would expect to live five years longer than that, despite the risks of childbirth. A man born in a small city like Bristol in 1900 could expect to live to see forty-seven—a year more than the English average; a man born in Manchester, a large industrial city, could only expect thirty-six years, his wife five or six more.[34] Being a man at a time of war, and being a man in a big city at all, could be a deadly business.

While many women did take up work outside the home during the war, they did so with the express knowledge—indeed, often the *aspiration*—that they would leave this labour at the end of it. Research on women workers in France and Britain during the war shows that many were keen to return to the work of motherhood and domestic management, and that there was no expectation that the situation would last beyond the end of the crisis.[35] It is clear, of course, that many women did not wish to do so too. One historian has investigated women's lives in factories before, during, and after the war, and concluded that in this area of women's lives, very little changed, and women's labour during the war was generally understood as being mainly about caring, in the form of nursing, just as it was before and after the conflict. Employers, governments, conscripts, and women themselves often explicitly understood the process as temporary and reversible.

And when women did finally make it into (relatively few) factories, they were not always welcomed. For example, in one engineering plant in Glasgow, the self-styled 'second city of the British Empire', in 1915, the workers had stuck up posters saying 'When the boys come, we are not going to keep you any longer girls.'[36] Far from being welcomed as noble contributors to a national effort by the men who remained behind in reserved occupations, women employees were resented as threats to their pay, because they were un-unionized. In the language of economists, men feared 'dilution'—the suppression of their wages, their status as bread winners, and their masculinity as muscular labourers through the introduction of a cheap female labour force. Yet only about 1,500 women were working in engineering positions in Glasgow by the middle of 1916 (in a city of about 400,000 adult women), and they were not employed in either heavy or skilled workshops. The situation in John Lang & Sons, a Glasgow metalworking firm, was typical of many workplaces in wartime cities. One of the managers at Lang's issued instructions 'to start women on the small machines which are at present worked by lads, to transfer the lads to heavier and more intricate machines, and then to shift the men on these machines onto the nightshift'. Women were being treated as cheap, weak, and stupid, but not through some abstract gender politics: 'a woman's place' was central again. It was the specific machines they stood at, and the specific times they stood at them that made clear to them that they were doing children's work. And this was always done at lower wages: the records of Wm. Beardmore & Co engineering works in Glasgow stated tersely: 'Semi-skilled and unskilled men to be paid not less than 28/- [shillings]; All female workers, 20/-.'[37] Women workers, no matter how good they were at their jobs, were never any better than cheap replacements for the 'real thing'.

Yet women were not powerless in this situation. The mechanics of their resistance in the particular example of the factories in Glasgow are uncertain, but once brought together in specific factories, they sometimes managed to persuade their fellow male workers that paying all women a uniform inferior rate would devalue *all* skilled work. After all, once employers had successfully abolished skills distinctions for women, as at Wm. Beardmore's works, men were likely to be next, and so in February and March of 1916, male engineers began to agitate for equal pay for equal work in several factories in Glasgow. This protest was not seen as trivial: it resulted in the arrest of male shop stewards at Albion Motors and Barr & Stroud engineering works, on charges of sedition. Eventually, employers yielded in Glasgow, as subsequently they were often forced to do across Europe—at the Renault plant in north Paris, for example, a similar conflict erupted in the war, with a similar outcome. In many plants in Europe, equal pay for equal work was a principle on which women felt confident during the war. It was not a permanent victory as the situation was promptly reversed after the conflict, but it was a victory nonetheless, and it was won in the workplace.

And finally, while some women did take up heavy industrial labour, and many more became nurses, this was far from the most shocking transformation in women's working lives in the war for contemporaries. The most challenging forms of labour that women undertook in the war was not when they went into the factories, but was when they donned 'masculine' clothes, and went into that most 'masculine' of spaces: the street. They put on the uniforms of traffic officers, ticket collectors, tram drivers, police officers, postal workers, and they went out into the city streets to organize the everyday aspects of urban life left, literally, 'unmanned' by conscription—a striking image of which can be seen in Figure 2.2.[38] The women working here for the Berlin-Charlottenburg Tram Company were part of a huge army of postal workers, ticket collectors, railway officials, tram drivers, messengers, and traffic officers that not only left the home and 'walked the streets', but bossed men around while doing so. In terms of its radical effects, the First World War marked, not the assertion by women of their right to do men's work, but the assertion by women of their right to men's space.

This shift of women from the interior worlds of both home and work, to the exterior realms of the street, shocked contemporaries for two main reasons: first of all, women in uniforms—even if only postal or tram uniforms—made them look automatically more masculine; it somehow militarized their bodies, as can be seen with the Berlin-Charlottenburg tram workers in Figure 2.2; secondly, these women were out in the city, organizing streets and streetlife, managing the public, dynamic aspects of urban existence. A woman's place was thereby transformed in profoundly radical ways. First, streets were so singularly associated with men in European culture at the time, and it

Figure 2.2 In the Great War, relatively few women undertook industrial work—contrary to the myth of wartime transformation—but many, as here with these tram drivers, inspectors, and conductors in Berlin-Charlottenburg in 1917, donned uniforms and took control of urban spaces in ways which men and women alike found striking and shocking. Seeing women 'in control' and giving orders in city streets, fully mobile, and wearing masculine clothing in the form of uniforms, was made all the more spectacular by their devastating role in revolutionary change at the war's end.

was so normal to classify women's capacity to occupy street space merely in terms of a shady lack of respectability at best, and sex for money (the 'streetwalker'—there is no equivalent pejorative for men) at worst, that the symbolism of women actually *managing* streets by driving trams and directing traffic was fundamentally shocking. It was this presence in city streets (not out of sight in factories) that highlighted women's capacity to move about in societies and spaces that were suddenly emptied of men; it showed that women in no way *needed* to be protected; and that the city was women's for the taking. Secondly, women vigorously engaged with their new urban roles, and pursued their right to the city—right up to the point when, at the end of the war, they drove revolutions through every major city east of France, destroying royal houses that had ruled for centuries.

And in this delicate matter of revolution, rioting, political violence, and disorder, it was not women's new employment status or
the pursuit of rights to vote or go to university that drove them on,
but their 'conventional' roles as household managers, responsible
for securing food and coal to bring up children, that underpinned
their revolutionary decisions to take to the streets in Munich,
Vienna, Berlin, St Petersburg, and Moscow in 1917 and 1918.
Food rationing, extra policing, supervision, and harassment 'on
behalf' of their absent brothers, husbands, and fathers, and increased
susceptibility to disease (the death rate for Viennese women increased
by 64 per cent between 1914 and 1919) hindered them;[39] but their
penetration into the bars, trams, streets, cinemas, and dance halls
alone and unchaperoned, yet still respectable, allowed them to stake out
a space in modern life undreamed of by many middle-class suffrage
campaigners.

The experience of transforming 'a woman's place' was not uni-
formly positive, however; women tram workers were regularly attacked
in Vienna as they took up their war work in the streets of the city.
One woman justified her assault on a female tram-worker like the
ones in Figure 2.2 to a policeman, saying, 'If they had stayed at home
and got their stockings in order, the war would have been won a long
time ago.'[40] Sadly, the policeman did not enquire further as to the
underlying 'logic' of her position—or if he did, did not note it in his
pocket book. We have to conclude that opposition to a transformation
of women's roles in the early-twentieth-century city was as likely to
come from other women as it was from men.

The war left millions of women unchaperoned in the cities of
Europe, and contemporaries (many women as well as men) viewed
'roaming' women as a potent threat to the entire social order in all
its forms—economic, political, familial, social, and sexual. To go out
'unchaperoned' at night had been the height of unrespectability for
many women, both middle-class and working-class, since cities had
started to separate the worlds of work and living.[41] Thus strict controls on leisure pursuits were introduced—famously settling on 11
p.m. closing time in Britain. In Prague, Vienna and Budapest, there
was a 2 a.m. closing time, although women's groups in all three cities campaigned for a more restrictive 11 p.m. closing time, as in
Britain.[42] Part of this debate about closing pubs and bars focused on

productivity—men needing to get up early to work. But another part of it focused on women 'cavorting' without their husbands, and in spite of the sacrifice men were making; women 'out of control' in the playground of the city, with no man to ensure their honour. One historian has combed the archives of the Viennese police force, and found that they read as a story of a growing conflict between women and men—and women and women—about how they should behave when out alone in the city at night.

Individual women could be as conservative as many men, like a certain Fanny Freund-Markus, who complained to the police that the sustained efforts of the Viennese to preserve a vibrant night life was an assault on the truly patriotic population. Thus she aligned herself fully with the military commander for Vienna, who complained:

> Often even officers cannot resist the temptations of the many nightspots. These officers, who have come here from the theatre of operations, whose wounds have not healed and who have not yet been restored to health, would do better to save their strength and get a good night's rest in order to return quickly to fitness. A radical remedy of this unfortunate situation, the redress of which is of great military importance, could be achieved by closing such locales at an earlier hour...Surely such places of amusement provide profit for their owners and tenants; for the general public they spell only harm.[43]

The suggestions of women like Fanny and the military commander were acted on, and most leisure establishments imposed voluntary restrictions on women coming into them unchaperoned. This was reinforced by a decree of 1 December 1914 banning all 'prostitutes' from going to cafés, restaurants, or anywhere where there was singing or dancing. A prostitute could be defined as more or less any woman on her own—a strategy for shaming middle-class women into staying at home that had been widespread in Europe since the mid-nineteenth century.

But women did not, of course, accept this bar to the city and its nightlife. They vigorously resisted attempts to confine them to their homes through an overt moral discourse, in which they had to sacrifice leisure, to compensate for the ways their male relatives were sacrificing their lives, limbs, and sanity. A Frau Zschörner went out for a drink on her own one night in Vienna in 1916, and was refused service in the Café Carlton on the grounds that she was on her own and therefore not 'respectable'. So rather than slope off home, she went and gathered some of her friends, and returned to the bar, and again demanded service. She was so angry about her treatment and what she felt to be the impudence of the waiters, that she made a formal complaint to the police, arguing:

> There must be the same rights for all. Either no lady without accompaniment can be served, or all ladies of all rank!... It can't be demanded of a young, vivacious woman that she'll stay cooped up at home for two years, since the beginning of the war—she'll just become melancholic.[44]

In another example, a certain Anna S. brought a lawsuit against a coffee house for refusing to serve her. Karl Attila, the waiter who had asked her to leave, explained to the court the coffee house's policy on how to deal with 'certain ladies'. It was to make single women wait a long time to be served, serve her abruptly, then present the bill with the coffee—very inappropriate behaviour. As the judge concluded, 'Even for a waiter, it is terribly difficult to decide on first glance if a lady belongs to the so-called "easy world".'[45]

These women claimed a bold sort of equality, based on doing and going and drinking and enjoying, and they became visible to the historian because they used the formal legal process to back them up in it. Frau Zschörner demanded equal rights for women, and equal rights between classes (although she did, in the same letter, say that some of the women in the bar were behaving coquettishly, so she was not above reproving her peers for their sexuality). Anna S. resorted to the courts to resolve her conflict with Attila, and his casual disregard for her rights to go where she pleased, and be treated with dignity when she got there. But far from expressing their freedoms primarily in terms of rights about, say, voting, they expressed them in terms of their right to go to a bar, the right to be vivacious, the right to have a drink, and the right to have a waiter speak to them courteously. For each case like this that makes its way into the archive, many millions more must not have done so. But the first cause of their resort to law was about the city and its spaces; they demanded access to them. These women were winning their rights in very specific places—ones which are conventionally left out of history.

Similar attempts to 'control' women in cities were seen across urban Europe—and in British cities, particular anxiety emerged over the cinema. There, in the dark, and exposed to fantasy worlds (discussed more fully in Chapter 3), women could be, do, and fantasize about anything they chose. The overwhelming favourites at British cinemas were melodramatic exploits, frequently featuring young women—serials like *Hazards of Helen*, *A Munitions Girl's Romance*, *The Shop-Soiled Girl*, *The Girl Who Took the Wrong Turning*, and *Exploits of Elaine*, which often showed women as competent, socially mobile, and physically vigorous. *A Munitions Girl's Romance* shows a woman dealing with a spy in her factory—the kind of proactive, female heroism which was typical of wartime films, though often this 'heroic' wartime woman in a factory evaporated in 1920s British cinema, to be replaced with demure, vulnerable 'heroines' at home. This association of femininity with the cinema led directly to claims that the darkness fostered immorality. This legitimized placing thousands of urban locales across Britain under suspicion, supervision, and surveillance because of the worry that 'people of a low standard of morality' were likely to congregate there. Leading suffragettes agreed that places where women congregated needed especial surveillance, Mary Allen claiming that cinemas aroused women to 'breathless excitement'. Allen misrepresented women's cheers, gasps, and boos—which were the norm for audience participation in the era of the silent film—as a dangerous 'loss of control'.[46]

For the 'feminist' Mary Allen, such engaging behaviour in public by women was seen as such a worrying social disorder that it led her and many other 'feminists' to demand greater police surveillance of these spaces across British cities, and government censorship of the films' content—drawing out neatly for the historian just how divergent the interests of working-class and middle-class women could be. Charlie Chaplin came in for especial criticism in Allen's circle: his films were 'vulgar and suggestive of evil'. Women's Police Service officers across Britain drew up lists of women whom they considered to be behaving frivolously, frequently barring them from entrance to cinemas in many cities. In the case of the temporary armaments cities of north-west England, the factories of Gretna and Carlisle stopped running trains and buses in the evenings to cinemas, isolating their inhabitants in their quasi-urban industrial sprawl and attempting to confine them to their barracks. While agreeing to show their female employees films, they noted that 'having regard to the *exceptional nature of the audience*, [we] stipulate that every precaution should be taken to avoid pictures in which the sex problem might be unduly involved'. Immobile in their camps, young women workers could do little but watch what was given to them, their physical isolation rendering them vulnerable to greater scrutiny and management.[47]

Some feminist critics of urban planning and development have suggested that the post-war suburbs that emerged in the 1920s–1930s and again in the 1950s–1970s across European cities were based on this sort of 'isolation' strategy, as a way of keeping women 'in their place'—at home.[48] And from the left at the time, the cinema could be seen as inculcating a sort of passive, capitalist vacuity that penetrated the home. One revolutionary Berlin poet, Bruno Schönlank, wrote dismissively of the city's factory-girls around 1920:

> ...Factory workers, tired
> from the drudgery of the day.
> Salesgirls, seamstresses, spinning
> golden fairy tales of luck and the wages of true love....
> Beautiful girls ceaselessly follow the pictures
> and swallow in the lies.
> They gladly let themselves be led astray
> by that which enchants their souls.
> Drunk with the glitter they reluctantly return home
> and in the dark room see yet a light,
> which breaks through their dreams as bright as the sun...
> till grey everyday life puts it out again.[49]

Some historians have agreed with this sort of comment, concluding, 'unquestionably the chief interests in the lives of young women workers in the Weimar period were romance, sex, and those aspects of mass culture relating to personal emotions'.[50] This trivialization of women's concerns about their own lives has been a consistent feature of the ways that women's views are marginalized throughout history: while men have 'serious' concerns about national policy frameworks and class conflicts, women have supposedly focused on ephemera, like dress codes and childcare. History and politics are often dominated by 'serious' and 'masculine' verbs, like 'fight', 'eradicate', 'build', and 'defend'; it has been harder to formulate many women's concerns about 'putting together a home', or 'going out and about unmolested' in the same clear-cut way. But cinemas in wartime offered women a space to explore their own emotional priorities—and women's use of urban spaces like this could prove profoundly revolutionary.

Yet it was actually in their 'homely' roles as mothers, carers, cooks, and cleaners that the wartime city brought women into greatest conflict with authority. The ways that women behaved in cities during the war often transformed how they were perceived by the state. For example, in Berlin at the beginning of the war, women who caused public-order problems were dismissed in police reports as just 'women'—which, in the shorthand of the typical European state at the time, was to say that they did not count. But two years later, with widespread food riots a regular occurrence in Berlin by the middle of the war, the Berlin police changed the ways that women were referred to: instead of being dismissed because of their sex, crowds of women were now referred to as 'persons' and 'the public' in police reports. These words had previously been reserved for the male 'citizen classes', implying that women, through their frequent rioting and rampaging through the city's streets, had altered their position in the eyes of a masculine state.[51]

Women most frequently came into conflict with the organs of the state in the war when they attempted to obtain food, reaching an extreme in Russian cities in 1916–17, and German and Austrian cities in 1917–18. Particularly for the powers with no direct access to the Atlantic—Germany, Austria-Hungary, Russia—food was a central issue, the one which led perhaps most directly to their inability to sustain warfare. Early disputes in the war arose around the curtailment in supply to the cities of 'luxury' goods, like butter and pork; at the end of the war, the struggle was over potatoes and flour. Between 14 and 19 October 1915, the Berlin police noted more than fifty riots over food, primarily focused on butter due to a price rise in the previous month from 20–60 pfennig/kg to over 3.40 marks. In riot after riot—often involving 5–6,000 people—women were at the centre of the action. They were not always the ones throwing the stones, but they organized the protests and encouraged or directed their adolescent sons. By the end of the war, the consequences of these actions were serious and striking, as can be seen in Figure 2.3, which shows a woman, some adolescent males, and some older men butchering a horse in the streets of Berlin in 1918. These riots were reported daily in the national newspapers, giving them, in the words of one leading historian of Berlin, 'the power to create a picture or theatre of the street for millions of Berliners as well as for the millions of readers outside the city'.[52] Centre-stage in this theatre of the street were women, adopting the main roles in the unfolding political dramas of modern Europe.

Figure 2.3 Starving Berliners butcher a horse in the street in autumn 1918—led by a woman, and some adolescent males. For all that the trenches evoke the Great War most clearly, it was lost due to political collapse in nearly all major European cities east of France. Starvation in Berlin, Munich, Vienna, Budapest, St Petersburg, and Moscow led to the discrediting of the *anciens régimes* in the eyes of many civilians—especially those who had often previously been excluded from political life: women, children and young people, conscripts. It was from urban experiences such as these, as much as (and often more than) the traumas of the trenches, that the revolutions of 1917 and 1918 emerged.

The concluding act to this drama was the role these urban women played in central and eastern European cities in destroying the empires in which they lived. It was not just in the specific revolutions of February and October 1917 in the case of Russia, or November 1918 in the case of Germany and Austria-Hungary, that women's role was so central, but also in the political work they did leading up to them. It was in women's permanent presence on the city streets that those states' utter illegitimacy became a public reality, because they could not tend to the basic needs of their citizens: food and warmth. By the end of the war, the authority of the state in these cities was dead, not because of some abstract political principle developed by great men and acted upon by revolutionary heroes, but because women had declared it dead; indeed, they had killed it by a thousand cuts. In St Petersburg, now called a less Germanic and more Russian Petrograd, it was women who secured the abdication of the tsar in February, 1917. While trade union leaders asked women to remain calm, women from across the city used the occasion of the International Women's Day to march to the city centre. There, they chanted, 'We want bread', 'No more war', 'Down with the tsar' and other such slogans. When the Cossacks were ordered to disband the women, the women used their status as 'vulnerable' to humiliate the Cossacks into mutiny, rather than fire on their 'mothers and sisters'. The Cossacks did mutiny, and the next day the tsar abdicated. At every stage, the women spoke from their position as women: it was from the authority of the homemaker that these women elaborated a theory of citizenship, and dissatisfaction with the state.[53] In fact, women had been rioting in Moscow and Petrograd with terrifying frequency, from the spring of 1915.

When one woman tore up her as-good-as-useless food coupons in front of the Viennese mayor, Richard Weiskirchner, and said to him, 'Why don't you burn these coupons and shove them up your arse?', she did not need the vote to do this. And when women organized their adolescent sons to go and 'hunt' horses in the street, as in Berlin in Figure 2.3, they did not need the vote to do that either. And the fact that some men had the vote in German and Austrian cities did not make them any less hungry. The woman telling Weiskirchner to shove his coupons up his arse spoke with the peculiar authority that derived from her *domestic* role as the manager of her family's diet.

Another woman wrote to Weiskirchner anonymously from a working-class district:

> Dear Mr Mayor! Meat is very expensive and in very <u>short supply</u>. <u>No</u> vegetables. Potatoes one per day per person. Instead of ½ kilo of flour per week we get more potato flour—to do what? From day to day <u>hundreds of thousands</u> are waiting for sauerkraut and one sees a tub only once every fourteen days…Why so seldom? We can't hold out any longer. We have already shown enough patience and sacrifice, it can't go on. <u>In the whole world, Vienna is the saddest off</u>. Peace at <u>any</u> price.[54]

She signed her note, 'A Mother starving with her children.' From early in the war, the Viennese police counted queues outside grocers' shops every day, calculating the probability of a women's riot at each individual spot, so that they could plan for it later in the day when the shop sold out. These regular shows of force by women, in which the forces and authority of the state was demonstrated to be dead on street corners throughout cities, killed off the chances of these political systems surviving the war. No elections were necessary. The houses of Habsburg, Hohenzollern, and Romanov fell not just because of revolutionary ideologies, but also because of some remarkably conservative ones: urban women unable to manage their home lives as they saw fit, women in queues, and women in riots were central to the process.

These advantages gained in the war were biggest where women were boldest, and their attacks on the state strongest; yet they were, like those of their British cousins working in Glasgow engineering works, transient gains. Hypothetical political rights—like the right to vote, attend university, practise a profession, apply for social housing alone—were granted in Russia, Germany, and Austria in 1919 but persistent poverty and political chaos meant the exercise of them was often fairly meaningless. Even in Western Europe, the formal process of rights acquisition was remote from most women's lives. In Britain, women obtained the vote soon after the war; in France, they had to wait until 1945. Yet as the rest of this chapter will show, 'possessing' abstract rights (like voting) was not the deciding factor in deciding whether this woman or that woman could shape her own destiny. Frequently, this revolved again around the issue of space: where women could go, under what conditions, and wearing what sort of clothes. The years between the wars represent the period when women secured the biggest changes in their capacity to 'own' the city, by maintaining the rights won in wartime to move about alone.

*   *   *

The most impressive feature of the transformation of women's lives between the wars was marked by the fuller engagement of women in paid work outside their own and other people's homes, and cities were at the heart of that change. In Britain, Germany, and Russia, the twenty years between the wars mark the movement of women into paid employment on a massive scale. Economic data from Britain and Germany shows roughly the same number of women in employment after the war in 1921 as before it in 1911, showing that the war had little lasting effect on women's employment. But the following fifteen years transformed many women's worlds. In Germany, the number of women in paid employment outside the home rose by 64 per cent;[55] in Britain, it rose by 68 per cent;[56] in Russia, the absence of meaningful statistics for the pre- and post-war periods makes direct comparison hard, but the second Five-Year Plan viewed them for the first time as workers. Only in France was there a decline in the number of women working, especially in industry. Fifteen per cent fewer women worked outside the home in 1939 than in 1921.[57]

Increased presence in the workforce and the collapse in domestic service as a source of employment across the continent meant increased opportunities for women to network, to ally, to discuss, to earn cash, and to work a shorter day. Factories, shops and offices were rarely unionized environments for women, but the people that worked in them were not passive. Historians have generally concluded that there is a fundamental difference in male and female industrial organization: once men are brought together in single-class industrial work places, they have tended to organize in order to pursue a specific set of 'improving' objectives which they define for themselves: better pay, shorter hours, more benefits, safer conditions. Women were often excluded from this agenda, and so when women have undertaken industrial militancy, it has often been focused more defensively, on resisting the *removal* of rights or the *degradation* of their status or salaries. Put crassly, men strike for better pay; women strike to stop pay cuts. Efforts by women to deal with this formally, through trade unions, met with resistance from women workers. As one Manchester cotton operative commented when asked about how women responded to worsening conditions between the wars, 'you muttered and mumbled amongst yourselves but—you hadn't got the confidence. You weren't brought up at school to be confident, not at home…seen and not heard.'[58] But informal networks were important to factory women, and they could learn a lot through them, especially about sex, avoiding pregnancy, and handling men at home. Equally, women on piecework in weaving or automotive industries were quite capable of negotiating with foremen for pay rises if they felt that machinery failure or poor quality raw materials had slowed their work down.

Women were most successful at achieving positive change in the workplace in the new, technological industries of the interwar cities. At Lucas Automotive in Birmingham, one of the largest manufacturers of car parts in the world, men were represented by the Amalgamated Society of Engineers, a union which explicitly prohibited women's membership. So when the company introduced a new set of working regulations designed to improve efficiency (a universal shorthand for reducing labour costs) in 1932, its more than 5,000 women workers had no formal avenue to resist them. When the wage-cutting reforms were introduced the women seemed to be shocked, yet they struck quickly, almost instantly. As one woman recalled, 'the rumour started to fly round. The [new] system is coming to Birmingham. Coming to Lucas's.' The rumours ended when 'all of a sudden the door opened and a girl run in, she says "come on, we're all out!"' They quickly adapted popular songs to their cause, picketed in an ad hoc way, and organized sit-ins, claiming that they would not be 'slaves', and nor would they yield to their husbands', brothers', and fathers' desire that they return to work. The company was quite taken aback by the women's action, as it had prided itself on its paternalistic relationship with its workers, and in fact, quickly yielded. The women organized a victory parade through Birmingham city centre, again reinforcing the perception that public space and public participation outside the home were central features of the transformation of women's lives underway.[59]

When the workers in the trim shop at Rover Automobiles, one of Coventry's largest automobile manufacturers, went on strike in September 1930, the union—in this case, the Transport and General

Workers' Union (TGWU)—supported them from the outset, and insisted on equal pay for equal work across the gender divide as a *quid pro quo* for accepting 'modern', non-craft-based, production-line working practices. At the Rover works, the shop stewards of the TGWU, Britain's largest union, decided to include women in their negotiations. Male union members in the trimming shop realized that if men's output was to be transformed from 'the skilled product of a gifted craftsman' into a 'unit', then their interests were best served by getting all 'unit generators' paid a high wage; once one accepted that a 'unit generator' might be paid differential wages, all male wages would be phased down to the lowest female wages.[60] Thus it was imperative to ensure that women's wages were high, because in the de-skilled, production-line systems being introduced from Ford in the USA, men could no longer charge a high premium for routine, but highly skilled, tasks. The union was successful in its 'equal pay for equal work' dispute—but such practices persisted in the wider motor industry until well into the 1970s, and strikes by female workers at Ford's Dagenham plant. One of the reasons why the dispute proved difficult to resolve in 1930, and caused so much rancour in Coventry, was that other industrial manufacturers in the city were outraged that one company might formulate a set of agreements that would potentially deprive *all* companies of cheap, non-unionized female labour. In the technologically advanced sectors of British industry, women were relatively successful in 'humanizing' the new scientific management, stimulating greater consultation and provision of minimum income guarantees, as was the case with the 'Bedaux Time and Motion' system in the trimming shop at the Rover works.[61] Women's ad hoc experiences of the 'rationalization' of labour in the 1930s, based in trimming shops or assembly lines, had a huge impact on the 'formalization and extension of semi-skilled workers' rights and privileges', yet was very site-specific: distinctive workshops, like the trimming room, in particular car plants, were where such action took place.[62]

However, women could often experience the industrialization of the 1930s as a disaster, a massive 'race to the bottom', as migration from the countryside picked up pace—and in French cities, mass migration from abroad was also a distinctive feature of the interwar years. Many thousands of women homeworkers in Paris found the move to ready-to-wear clothing, produced in factories on production

lines, catastrophic. First, their autonomy was removed, and their place
of work too. Then, with massive immigration into Paris from North
Africa, the Middle East, and the Far East between the wars, these
women could not even secure employment in the new 'sweatshops'.
One Turkish entrepreneur in Paris marvelled at the ways Chinese
migrant labour undermined even Serb migrant labour, which had led
to widespread unemployment amongst Parisian women, wondering
out loud:

> How do they do it?! Us, we kill ourselves working. But them, they must
> kill themselves even more than we do, because they manage to accept
> work at prices 20 to 30 percent lower than us. We really can't under-
> stand anything any longer...[63]

So for many women, the new worlds of work experienced by people
in new, technological industries might be liberating; but for those
women still working in conventional female roles in the garment
industry, the world outside the home could be very impoverished.

Even in situations where the whole concept of 'rights' was, in
effect, non-existent, women could use the opportunities afforded by
work outside the home to make powerful statements about themselves as humans, though. One of the distinctive features of Russian
life in the period between the wars was the elimination of the spaces
and places of peasant life, and their replacement—even in the
countryside—with industrialized, urban or semi-urban environments. Peasants there still were aplenty in 1939; but they no longer
lived isolated on self-sufficient plots. Urbanization and collectivization transformed the patterns of everyday life. The population of
Moscow in 1920 was about 1 million souls; by 1928, it had doubled
to 2 million, and by 1940 it had doubled again to 4 million. The
population of St Petersburg was artificially low in 1920 at 720,000
as citizens fled back to ancestral homes in the chaos that followed
the revolution, in order to forage and stave off starvation, but by
1930 it was 1.7 million, and by 1940 it had also nearly doubled to
3.2 million. Donetsk in the Ukraine registered as a small town of
32,000 between 1900 and 1920, but by 1930 it stood at 174,000,
and by 1940 nearly half a million. Similar progress was made by
Stalingrad.[64] Women were disproportionately highly represented
amongst the millions drawn into this process (largely because women

were disproportionately highly represented in urban Europe, even before the carnage of the war), and in a 'system' where all human life was counted cheaply, it was especially hard for them to assert themselves. If a man's life is worth nothing, what claim to dignity might a woman make? And yet women tried to use where they were to make spaces of autonomy and control within the city, even amongst the chaos of the revolution, New Economic Policy, and Five-Year Plans.

In the squalid conditions of Soviet cities, 'home' was rarely a place that was physically fixed—a feature of everyday life that particularly affected women, who endeavoured to remain at home even in the poorest families. People could move in and out of 'home' unpredictably, and resources were so scarce that women who could achieve 'one family, one room' were regarded as skilful social and economic operators. Much policy in the USSR in the 1920s was oriented towards excluding women from the workforce—indeed, excluding them from all public life. There was a deliberate ideological focus on the 'worker', and gender was thought by most Communist Party officials to be a tedious, self-absorbed, self-centred, divisive diversion from the real business of the revolution: class warfare and the veneration of the worker-producer. The early representation that women's interests secured in the Communist Party structure in the form of the 'women's section', the Zhenotdel, was systematically eliminated over the 1920s.[65]

The Five-Year Plans were central to changes in women's lives, however, and at their heart was a rapid urbanization and industrialization of Soviet society. And while each of the first three plans impacted in different ways, the transformation of women's physical place in society was crucial. The first plan, from 1928 to 1932, committed the USSR to a vast programme of urbanization and industrialization. Women were understood as 'appendages' to this plan; essentially, they existed outside it. A careful piecing together of the records by one Russian historian has shown that at the end of the 1930s, the USSR had a female urban population of about 30 million (versus 26 million men in the cities—an indication of just how catastrophic the First World War, civil war, and the first two Five-Year Plans had been for men in particular); of these 30 million urban women, about 17.5 million were of working age. Of these 17.5 million, about 53 per cent worked by 1939—and about 85 per cent would be gainfully employed outside the home by 1959.[66] Unplanned for, women in Soviet cities in the 1930s moved into the factories and entered into direct contests with men for labour and status. Stripped of their gender, but ascribed a class in the productive system of Soviet planning, they staked a claim to proletarian citizenship by entering factories and collectives.

The Five-Year Plans impacted on women in several ways. First, the plans created massive inflation, requiring dual incomes in households to survive, such that by the end of the first plan, in 1932, one-third of workers in heavy industry were women—a proportion that has never been equalled. Secondly, by halfway through the second plan (1933–7), so much urbanization had already taken place, and so many peasants had been starved to death, that the countryside ceased to be an effective source of labour from which to attract migrant workers, so shop-floor managers had to cast around for additional labour supplies within the cities themselves—and they found them in women. But this presence of women at the heart of the industrial, urbanizing, modernizing project was treated with some concern, by both women and men. The state was worried that women were entering into the public life, spaces, classes, and occupations of urbanizing Russia in an unplanned (and therefore destabilizing, dangerous, volatile) way; their word for it was '*samotek*'—unplanned, accidental. This apparently haphazard status carried with it profound danger. In Stalin's Russia, to exist 'outside the plan' was a precarious place to be—almost amounting to being against it.

Some women recalled being very pleased to obtain work like this. Mariia Aleksandrovna Igleiko was a lathe operator in the rapidly growing city of Minsk. She recalled that in 1930:

> We mastered this profession—completely new to us—with great pleasure...The factory seemed big to us, although then about four hundred people worked in it. With our participation new shops were created at the factory—a foundry, mechanical assembly, and pattern shops. We began to produce drilling machines, lathes, and different equipment for the new construction. I loved my profession very much. I took great joy in the fact that I was producing a product the country needed, in turning the different details of difficult shape [on the lathe]. I looked over the results of my friends' work with pride. We always went to work very early, got our tools, arranged them comfortably around us so as

to economize on our work time. We stayed at work after our shift, helping one another when someone was late.[67]

For many women, like Mariia Aleksandrovna, this labour could be a pathway from meagre agricultural existence to genuine prestige and a technical education. In the second plan, women were slightly more integrated into governmental policymaking, and women were explicitly conceived of as being located in the public realms of men—factories, tram depots, gas works. Yet by the mid–late 1930s, the underlying structures of Russian urbanization and industrialization had been laid down, and the process began of moving women out of factories and shifting their 'place' back into the domestic sphere. The turning point was the 'Decree for the Defence of Mother and Child' in 1936, which widely circumscribed access to birth control, and emphasized the idea of the mother 'at home'. This also meant re-imagining the home as essentially the Western, bourgeois, 'one family, one home' model (or at least, 'one family, one room'), and rejecting the widespread experiments in dormitory collective living that had characterized the first fifteen years of Soviet urban construction. Because of this focus on acquiring a defined home, many women found the 'new conservatism' in Russian policy a positive step, helping them realize their goals more easily—although urban women resented the disappearance of reliable birth control (in the form of medical abortion) to which they had become accustomed in the 1920s.[68]

Others, on similar career trajectories to Mariia Aleksandrovna's, found that their new status as skilled labourers and technicians drew them to the attention of the deadly NKVD, Stalin's secret police. And all women found that the task of running a household in chaos, when all resources were being directed towards the construction of heavy industry, was extremely difficult. It was easier, though, in urban areas than rural—in Soviet cities, basic food rationing ceased in 1935. Anna Dubova was the daughter of a '*kulak*', the notional rural Ukrainian class enemies supposedly destroying the revolution. During the Great Ukrainian Famine (organized as a deliberate genocidal extermination policy by the Soviet government in the early 1930s), somewhere around 2.6 million peasants were starved to death, and a further 1 million forced from their land and deported.[69] Anna, like millions of others, fled to the cities—in some ways, this was a deliberate goal of the famine: to force peasants to become proletarians. Anna found nowhere to live in Moscow in the winter of 1932–3, and slept on floors wherever she could—as did so many others. Determined to resolve this massive instability brought into her life by her forced transition from the country to the city, she took matters into her own hands. Campaigning for 'rights' was not an option open to her, so she married a young Komsomol member, and eventually they got a tiny room of their own. 'When I went to bed, I would think to myself, Dear Lord, I'm in my very own bed. I experienced such happiness; it was like being in seventh heaven, I was that happy.' Getting space, and keeping others out of it, produced and defined her happiness in a state in constant geographical turmoil.[70] The quest to acquire 'a room of one's own' has defined the struggle of many working-class women in European cities in the last hundred years. This is perhaps a troubling conclusion in much current popular debate about women's lives which characterizes home, and staying there, as somehow problematically conservative. For many women across the last century, home has been a radical assertion of who they are and what they want, not a negation of it.

Yet the experience of the Soviet Union was perhaps not typical; few societies have urbanized that fast, or that chaotically. For women in many Central and Western European cities, the twenty years between the wars was a time for the radical assertion of their 'right to roam' in the city, a freedom which was symbolized in the ways women dressed too. As can be seen in Figure 2.4, in clothing, they exposed their shoulders and wore loose-fitting sack dresses, rejecting the body-shaping principles of the corset (a predominantly middle-class garb; the types of physical labour working-class women did was not possible in one). Hemlines rose, and perhaps most spectacularly for contemporaries—male and female alike—hair was cut short. In Germany, the talk was of the 'new woman'; in France, the dominant image was of the *garçonne*, a feminized boy or masculinized girl. Historians have struggled to interpret this phenomenon. Some have classified it as the 'visual' liberation of women, a direct statement based on individual behaviours and commitments, and springing from new-found wealth and leisure time. Others have concluded that short haircuts do nothing to resolve low pay or sexual violence, and that fashion is a form of oppression, compelling women to adorn themselves in order to be acceptable, and requiring that they constantly invest and reinvest in ever-changing clothes, hair products, and make-up.[71]

Figure 2.4 Café 'la Coupole', Paris, 1920s. This shows how women transformed their attitudes to their bodies between the wars—contrast the ways these women present themselves, to the tram workers in Berlin, or the 'Match Girls' in London. The hair is short and 'boyish', the shoulders are bare, and the dresses are baggy, not tight. Stylish urban locales like this provided fora in which women could take more control of their self-image, and demonstrate a revolutionary attitude to their bodies. Images of well-known haunts like this fed into countless less-famous urban locations, as an inspiration and source of legitimacy—assisted by new technologies in picture printing and the rapid growth of women's magazines between the wars.

Women committing themselves to the new leisure spaces of the interwar world in short dresses, bare shoulders, and bobbed hair; and appearing in the cinemas, dance halls, cafés, streets, and bars—as can be seen in Figure 2.4, at the fashionable Parisian nightspot 'La Coupole'—provoked profound shock amongst contemporaries. The bobbed hair and the short dresses prompted some in the 1920s to reclassify the city as a whole into a feminine artefact: one American guide for rich tourists to Paris could conclude, 'It is, one must grant, primarily a women's city we are observing. Paris's chief and most characteristic concern is with the outer adornment of women.'[72] A British visitor in 1927 echoed:

> Paris is above all, a woman's town...Paris much more than (say) London ministers to the amusement of shopping—a specifically feminine employment....Back in Paris, after a sojourn in London, I realise that France is always politely murmuring, 'Place aux dames!'[73]

This last phrase is telling: 'make space for the ladies'. It reveals that although the true flappers and *garçonnes* were relatively few in number, cities and femininity could work together to effect powerful symbolic transformations of the understanding of womanhood. And images of nightspots like La Coupole in Figure 2.4 were transmitted in women's magazines and 'women's sections' of newspapers like the *Daily Mail* and the *Daily Express*, which modelled a use of urban space, and use of the body in that space, to audiences far and wide. 'Superficial' as fashion may be, the surfaces it represents can symbolize profound transformations for the people that wear it—and the people that opposed it being worn. As one woman, Elsie, recalled of London in the 1930s:

> I'd rather have had a pen in my hand than a bloody machine on my knee. And this 'walking tall'...I thought, 'I'm going to hold my head up like anyone else, and nobody's better than me'...If I'm dressed and I feel good, that's what I feel and I can hold my head up...I did feel I wanted to be better.[74]

For Elsie, a rejection of factory work in favour of the new opportunities opening up for women in clerical work, combined with the feeling that she was well turned out, provided a real sense of increased dignity and self-worth. New ready-to-wear fashions that became widespread between the wars were part of a 'democratization of taste' which allowed women to make powerful statements about themselves through their clothes; and urban spaces, ranging from offices to cafés, to cinemas, and the streets themselves, furnished a setting for some women to show off this new confidence in a public way. These transformations in self-presentation were transmitted through the new post-war explosion of women's magazines, and newspapers like the *Daily Mail* which set out to speak directly to a female audience. When dynamized by the post-war explosion in 'women's media' this symbolism could take on a powerful ideological charge even if relatively few women adopted *all* of its features, from bobbed hair to bare shoulders. But these realignments were not uncontested: they might be easy to secure in trendy nightspots like La Coupole, but the Maison Poiret was the fashion house and shop in Paris most closely associated with the rising hemline, and it was regularly stoned and had its windows smashed by people (we do not know their gender and class) who belonged to that substantial portion of the public who saw this trend as *deeply* destabilizing.[75]

But perhaps one of the best ways to understand the specific nature of women's aspirations is to situate them in women's own realities, and the dreams they had for their future. There, the iconographic 'new woman' barely touched most European women's lives, despite Elsie's experience. The explosion in employment in the rapidly growing cities of Britain, Germany, and the USSR often cemented, rather than challenged, women's subordinate status. As one young woman in Berlin explained about her life in 1932:

> At 4 o'clock I get off work. When I get home, I start cleaning the flat with my mother, as my mother also works. My mother cooks dinner while I clean and tidy up a bit. In the meantime my father comes home from work. When dinner is ready, we eat. My big brother gets home at 7. When he has eaten, Mother and I do the dishes. Then I read the paper a bit. At 9.30 or 10 I go to bed. At 6 I get up again and go to work. That's how it goes the whole week long.[76]

The grind never ended, and many women had to shape out fantasy futures within very narrow parameters. One working-class girl in her teens in Berlin expressed her dream world like this in 1926:

> When I come home for lunch, I'd like something good to eat, like beefmarrow soup with dumplings, then ox meat with some side dishes, then wide-band noodles with braised beef, and for dessert ice cream with sweetmeats. In the shop I'd like white rolls with ham, and in the evening to go to the gymnastics club, Wednesdays as well as Mondays. Thursdays back to the shop. In the evening I'd like to take a stroll with my family. I'd like nice clothes and shoes. (Fridays) Back to the shop. In the evening I'd like to go to the theatre with my friends. (Saturdays) I'd like to work in the shop until 1 p.m. and then help Mother, so we

can go out at 5. Every third Sunday I'd like to go to the woods, every
second Sunday to the theatre, and on the last to stay at home.[77]

It is striking how closely related the dream was to everyday reality.
The young woman in Berlin proposes no formal political revolution—
she still aspires to work in her shop. But she does want free time in
the evening and at the weekend; she yearns for white bread and to be
able to afford meat and sweets. She would like to move from a six-day
to a five-and-a-half-day week. But there is a revolution that she is
implicitly proposing if one contrasts the 'reality' with the 'dream' for
these female Berliners: in the home, they must be relieved of their
second job. Contemporary surveys across Europe in the 1920s and
1930s told the same story: leisure was a reward for *paid* work, and so
men had more right to it than women. So in Liverpool between the
wars, 46 per cent of working class men under twenty-four went to the
cinema once a week or more, while only 37 per cent of young women
did. This meant that if women were to profit from paid employment,
the most fundamental change had to take place not 'out there' in the
big wide world, but back at home. Otherwise, women would simply
be cursed with the 'double burden': two jobs, only one of them paid.

*   *   *

Statistics for women's labour during the Second World War tell similar stories to those of the First World War: there was a substantial rise
in the number of women working outside the home during the war
itself, but when the war ended, employment outside the home fell
back to similar levels, before beginning to rise again more perma-
nently from around 1950. It has been peacetime work, not wartime
work, that has transformed (or enlarged) the working environment of
women.[78] Despite the potential resource for defence that women might
offer in the war, their inclusion in home guards was vigorously resisted
in European cities during air raids.[79] Only in the Soviet Union were
women fully integrated into urban defence functions.[80]

Furthermore, despite the opportunities offered by the war for work
and a life outside the home, there was sometimes no general desire
amongst many women to sustain this when the war finished.[81] And
viewed in the longer term, across the whole first half of the twentieth
century, the underlying structures of women's working lives were

largely untouched by *either* war. For example, in Britain in 1901, 86 per cent of the women that worked outside the home did so in jobs characterized by 'femininity' and where women were in subordinate positions—nurses (not doctors); primary school teachers (not second-ary); social workers; shop assistants; domestic servants. In 1951, this figure had 'fallen' to 84 per cent—hardly any change over fifty years, despite two wars. While the number of women working had risen substantially, the *status* of women in work in Britain had changed little, or not at all.[82]

The war was not neutral in its consequences for women in general, and urban women in particular. Cities became targets of geopolitical conflict in the Second World War in ways never equalled before or since and, while many children were evacuated and many men con-scripted, women had to stay precisely where they were: in cities, and in harm's way. While in Britain there is a sort of 'folk memory' (albeit often false) of the war positively transforming women's working hori-zons, the same could not be said for Continental Europe, where the 'folk memory' of the war is always mingled with a more conspicuous pain, and often with shame. The experience of warfare for the women of major cities from Marseilles to Moscow could shift between early unawareness that there was a war going on at all, to incineration, rape, humiliation, aerial bombardment, siege, and starvation. Britain was much less affected by any of these features, despite the potent 'myth' of the blitz in the British national psyche, and concomitantly, the populations that 'stayed behind' in Continental cities were far more exposed to these threats.[83]

The suffering of women on the home front in Britain was certainly great, and any attempt to relativize it is fraught with dangers—but it is essential to understand the European urban context for women in the 1940s, and using Britain as a yardstick for this may help under-stand the difficulties that the predominantly female and infant popula-tions of Europe's cities endured. Being bombed is always hateful, but many German, Polish, and Russian cities were bombed to a far greater extent than British. Gender-specific figures are hard to come by, but in aerial bombardment women figured disproportionately amongst the victims because many men were away fighting and many children had been evacuated. Relativization is always morally problematic, not least because Holocaust deniers use the gap between British and

German deaths from bombing to suggest a moral equivalence between British and German war crimes when the two are not morally equivalent at all. But some statistics may help understand the magnitude of women's suffering in Continental cities, especially if we bear in mind that women were disproportionately affected by it. Contrasting British suffering with German is not intended to minimize the suffering of the British, or heroize the Germans—it is intended to allow a conception of suffering about Britain in the war to be appropriately multiplied to suit Continental circumstances.

The Germans destroyed about 600 acres in London, and London was the most heavily bombed city in Britain; the allies destroyed *at least* 600 acres in *at least* 27 German cities.[84] For the 66,000 Britons killed by aerial bombardment, the same number were killed by Allied bombs in French coastal cities in the attempt to end submarine warfare and prepare for D-Day, while roughly 500,000–600,000 Germans died from aerial bombardment.[85] In the raid which obliterated Coventry, 568 people died;[86] in the raid which caused the firestorm in Hamburg (Operation Gomorrah—the name says so much), 31,647 corpses were *recovered* (many were left in the rubble), and 125,000 were wounded.[87] The raid on Dresden in February 1945 killed about 25,000 on a conservative estimate.[88] If 600 acres were flattened in London, then 6,000 were destroyed in Hamburg and Berlin, and 2,000 in Cologne and Düsseldorf. When people are reduced to writing 'Wir leben—Hilde, wo bist Du?' ('We are alive—Hilde, where are you?') in chalk on mounds of rubble to find their loved ones, association of war work or the war experience with words like 'liberation', 'dignity', or 'progress' in terms of women's capacity to decide their own destinies just makes no sense on the Continent.[89] Given that these cities were people's homes, and that substantially more than half the people in them were women, we are talking about a major, devastating disruption to the capacity of women to organize the world around them in a way which satisfied their needs and wishes. We need to integrate this destruction of homes and lives into the history of women, and overturn once and for all the idea that the war represented an opportunity for them.

Against these figures, Soviet civilian deaths are of a magnitude almost impossible to comprehend: the Siege of Leningrad (formerly St Petersburg) cost an estimated 1 million civilian lives, mostly women, in one city alone, and total Soviet civilian losses were around 26 million, at a conservative estimate.[90] And in many respects, it was women that provided such resilience as there was in a city like Leningrad. One woman, Anfisa Kharitonova, was sixty when, having knitted a scarf, she was taken to the front on the outskirts of the city in the midst of the siege. There, she asked which man had shot down most German planes. When he was indicated to her, the sixty-year-old woman put the scarf round his neck, saying, 'My dear son, this is for you, for your bravery, for your love for the motherland and for Leningrad.' She then spoke to a larger group, saying:

> No words can express all the boiling hatred for the damned fascist curs. When I hear of all the evil deeds, which they have committed against our brothers and sisters and against our little children, my heart bleeds...I cry with hatred for the enemy of my Motherland. We know that the wilderness has lions, tigers, and jackals. These innocent creatures, transformed by the swastika, have ransacked the wilderness and seized our flourishing land. If I were younger, I would grab a gun and mercilessly kill those beasts.[91]

It looks like crass propaganda now, but women in the city were often recorded rousing soldiers to ever greater efforts like this, and the organization of survival often came down to women's skills in making 300 grams of bread a day stretch into a life-saving meal.

One popular German song from just after the war summed up the situation for the people left in the country's bombed-out cities:

> A wind blows from the north.
> It blows us back and forth.
> What has become of us?
> A small pile of sand on the beach.
> The storm throws the grain farther, just like our lives.
> It sweeps us from the ladder.
> We are like dust, so light.
> What shall be?
> Life must go on.
> There is still enough hope for us.
> We shall all start from the beginning,
> because this existence can also be beautiful.
> The wind blows from all directions.
> So let the wind blow!
> For above us the heavens won't let us down.[92]

In this context, a central aspiration of most 'ordinary' women after the Second World War was to acquire a stable, warm place which would resemble the idea of 'home' for them. The idea that 'a woman's place was in the home' was, in this context, *massively* liberating—because it assumed that she would have a home (the problem of overcrowding and homelessness is discussed in Chapter 5). What is striking about the thirty years after the war is that, when it came to acquiring and keeping a home, women in Europe's cities were remarkably more successful than they had ever had been before. The level of destruction of homes in Central and Eastern Europe was profound, and women were left primarily to deal with this situation in the short term, prolonging the impact of aerial bombardment on women in particular. Before the war, the population of Cologne was 775,000; at the end of the war, that had fallen to 40,000 as remaining women, older people, and children fled to the surrounding countryside to seek food and shelter from sustained bombardment. But by the end of 1945, the population was 400,000—overwhelmingly women and children—as those who had fled to the countryside returned rapidly. And these women set about forming, in every city in Central and Eastern Europe, the brigades known to Germans as *Trümmerfrauen*—'rubble women'. It was these women which set to the task of clearing sites like that in Figure 5.7 on p. 368.

They began, often on their own initiative, to clear the rubble from streets, to strip and prepare and dress the bricks so that they could be reused. Germany is famous for the quality of its technical education, but the *Trümmerfrauen* were explicitly prohibited on building sites from acquiring skills or trades that would allow them to work in the future. They were there for donkey work, like shifting rubble, and repetitive tasks, like dressing bricks. In the first weeks of the peace, the wives of known Nazis were compelled to do this work, but this was a small supply of labour for a huge task, and soon a universal female conscription was introduced in Germany's big cities, which largely governed themselves in this period. Many women volunteered, for heavy labour meant extra rations.[93] Women in Frankfurt, for example, were living in 1945–6 on 1,533 calories a day while doing heavy labour, compared to 3,241 calories a day in 1935. In Hamburg, they were working on 1,180 calories a day in spring 1946; the requirement for a sedentary woman is 2,000 a day.[94]

But while they were compelled to labour on the cities in the 'crisis years', the popular press was drenched with anguish about what damage this might do to the 'German family', catching these women in the 'Eve/Virgin Mary' dichotomy in which women are so often represented in popular and high culture. It was made clear to women again and again that in their roles in urban reconstruction, they were just ersatz men; but many women longed not to have to work like that, and to return to family life, and family space. As the *Süddeutsche Zeitung*, one of Germany's leading liberal quality dailies, opined in January 1948:

> Strikingly many *women*, whose husbands are still in prisoner-of-war camps, developed a tremendous élan in reconstruction. They want to create a home before the husband returns.[95]

When the men came back, the women would return to motherhood. Many must have wanted to do so, given the nature of rubble work and the chaos which characterized family life in the protracted process of establishing widows' pensions and awaiting the return of millions of POWs. The same paper in April 1946 had already celebrated the exclusion of many women from the world of work under the headline, 'No Girls in Uniform—Men's Jobs for Men Again'. Celebrating the decision by the City of Munich to start sacking female tram workers, the paper observed that the women were being sacked, 'to make room for returning men...since it has been established that the constant vibrations [of the trams] are dangerous to women's organisms in the long run...men will in the very near future again dominate the transit system'.[96] Was this a set-back for women? The issue is fraught: the big goal that most women had was getting somewhere to live; undertaking jobs like tram driving would have been for many a secondary concern. We do not know how many, though, would have liked a home *and* to continue working on the trams in Munich—an option that was never presented to them.

Knowing that they would soon step back from the actual rebuilding of Germany's devastated cities, these women patiently began shifting vast tonnages of debris, salvaging every brick, beam and girder that could be reused to build the homes they hoped to inhabit, and the public buildings they hoped to use. To understand the quantities of rubble dealt with by these women, it may help to visualize it in the way that Germans visualized it themselves. If the amount of rubble collected in Cologne were piled on a field a hundred yards long by forty yards wide, roughly the size of a football pitch, it would have formed a tower four and a half miles high.[97] One of Germany's most famous poets, Günter Grass, watched them work and immortalized them thus:

> Rubble woman, rubble woman
> Sing the children—
> Make a bet, make a bet,
> With the brick kiln, with the brick kiln,
> It's a matter of rubble,
> Amen, amen.
> Berlin lies strewn about,
> Dust flies up,
> Then a lull.
> The great rubble woman will be made a saint.[98]

The vast level of self-sacrifice of these civilian populations in Central and Eastern European cities is hard to underestimate. Urban construction and reconstruction has so long been an icon of masculine heroism—but in the post-war years in German, Polish, and Russian cities, it is a fraudulent iconography, and these women have only recently been made saints, despite Grass's prediction.

On top of the vast work of urban repair in Eastern Europe, there were enormous population movements as people sought to adjust to redefined borders—and sought to escape the Red Army. In strange ways, although on different scales, victory or defeat could bring about humiliation and degradation for women, as men sought to explain both their victories and their defeats in terms of their capacity to abuse women's bodies. The widespread shaving of women's heads in the public squares of French cities, and the systematic rape on a terrifying scale in Berlin, Leipzig, Dresden, Warsaw, and Budapest are not equivalent: rape is worse than humiliation; millions of rapes are worse than 40,000 humiliations, sickening though it is to try to quantify either. And yet they are related, because they belong to the same family of misogynist instincts: they are powerful assertions of how men can treat a woman's body as a lump of flesh rather than the vessel of a real person; they are both intended viciously to subordinate women in a hierarchy; both have the effect of scaring women indoors, denying them their 'place' in public space; and both of them used urban space to produce a powerful theatre in which to enact their hateful purpose. And in the case of the shaving of women's heads in France, women were often at the forefront of the mobs.

Towards the end of the war, de Gaulle's first priority was to secure the city of Paris: this was central to all his political ambitions for himself, and for France. But de Gaulle was far from the only person in France seeking to reconquer the city in order to reassert a 'rightful' order. The issue of the *Tondues*—'the shaved women'—is one that has only recently been fully addressed by French historians. Indeed, it is only since the 1980s that the French have fully started to examine their role in the Nazi horror, and the shameful self-forgiveness of so many French in the immediate aftermath of the war. The paradox here, which again challenges the relevance of the acquisition of formal rights, is that just as French women were being given legal equality, they were also made to bear the shame of French defeat on their bodies, a shame so torturous and evident in Figure 2.5.

The *mise en scène* for this calamity was typically the small square that is so prevalent in French urban design. In a British cityscape, such theatrical rituals would be much harder to enact, but the network of *places* in any French city makes perfect theatres for this sort of spectacle. The square is a city space which structures and contains the 'set-piece' performance in a way the haphazard layout of British cities cannot do. Squares shifted from being the site and symbol of occupation, with Germans sitting with impunity drinking in them, to sites of celebration at the liberation, to the theatres of a macabre and vengeful misogynist performance. Many women had, of course, compromised with German occupiers or the hated Milice police of the Vichy regime. Many French men were forcibly removed to Germany as labourers and hostages; many were overseas in Britain or the French colonies; and many French men used the chaos of the war to abscond and reinvent themselves elsewhere. In this context, urban women were particularly vulnerable in occupied France: they had far less access to food than the substantial French peasant, rural population, and far more access to Germans. If a French woman accepted a drink from a lonely German soldier to brighten a drab existence in a miserable situation, she could easily be branded a collaborator. If she slept with a

Figure 2.5 Urban space is not just about freedom: if is often used to humiliate and intimidate women—as here, with this '*femme tondue*'. Many thousands
of women were humiliated in France in 1944–5 as part of a bizarre urban
theatre, whereby the bodies of women and the settings of cities were made
to carry the 'shame' of France's capitulation and collaboration. Such images
suggest that any simple opposition between 'oppressive' men, and 'oppressed'
women is difficult to sustain: many of this woman's persecutors are smiling
women. The layout of French cities, with long boulevards focused on small
squares, provided the ideal theatre for this macabre drama.

German in order to earn money or food stamps ('*collaboration horizon-
tale*'), few French troubled themselves to enquire deeply as to whether
the money was spent on food for a fatherless family. A woman might
turn a trick for a *milicien* (a Vichy policeman) to get a visit for her child
to the Milice doctor. But to understand this would mean viewing
women as determined agents driving the success of their families in
hard situations; viewing them as shameless harlots, embodying everything that was wrong with a cowardly, unmasculine, collaborationist
France was much easier.

The disturbing thing revealed by many of the photographs taken of this mass-humiliation is the very visual, performative nature of this brutality, and the shrill 'silence' of the suffering that these women endured, as can be seen in Figure 2.5. This visual composition of silent suffering produced publicly in city squares served for a generation to underline the paradox of women's renewed rights in France, and their frequent inability to escape humiliation and violence in both the private sphere of the home, and the public one of the modern, urban, industrial, technological France. The humiliation of women and the *site* of that humiliation formed an indelible structure in the memory of liberation for millions.[99] In photo after photo of this process, women are fully represented in the angry mob, and recently (only in 2002), one French historian has gathered together the vast amount of evidence on this topic: sickening films, disturbing photos, sanctimonious police files, mean-spirited placards draped round the women's necks. One witness, Mélinée Manouchian, described an incident in Paris:

> Near to the métro stop Danube [in the working-class 19th arrondissement of Paris], a crowd was following a woman who was entirely naked. Her head had been completely shaved, and on her breasts two swastikas tattooed in Indian ink. I trembled at the idea that this woman would no longer be able to undress herself in front of a man without showing the shame that was on her body. On her back she also had tattooed a portrait of Hitler. The crowd which was out of control were throwing stones at her, pushing her and insulting her.[100]

In case after case, women were as likely to instigate and perpetrate these acts as men—which can be seen clearly in Figure 2.5. There were three spates of 'purification' (as the French euphemistically called it) between 1944 and the end of 1945, and in each one streets and squares formed a structuring agent in this vigorous attack on women's dignities and their right to shape their own destinies.

In the cities of Central and Eastern Europe—Budapest, Berlin, Dresden, Leipzig, Warsaw, Vienna—the threat to women (beyond starvation, disease, aerial warfare, cold) did not come from the men from within their own cities, but from the invading Red Army. It is only in the last few years that historians have begun to understand or investigate this vast tragedy, and they have been stimulated by two major factors. First, these women are now at the end of their lives; the burning shame, anger, humiliation, and internal rage has somewhat abated, and they have begun to talk of what they lived through so that its memory does not die with them. Fifty years of painful silence can only be seen as a double burden on them, for Germans in East Germany were not allowed to describe themselves as 'victims' in the war; specifically, they could not be 'victims' of their 'liberators', the Russians. But a yet more tragic reason, if that is possible, has driven this issue to the fore. In the Rwandan genocide in 1994, rape against both men and women was widespread in the aftermath. In the 1990s, as Yugoslavia collapsed into hateful anarchy, one of the most regular features of Serb and Bosnian military tactics was the systematic rape of women in the towns and cities they occupied. Men raping in large numbers to subdue civilian populations has recently come to be understood, not as a recidivist embarrassment confined to a comfortingly distant past, but as a persistent feature of male violence—and, therefore, the human condition.

Women in the countryside were raped too, but armies rape most where they stay longest, and where there are most people, and that means cities. Armies pass through the countryside. They stay in cities. It is hard to put a number on the scale of the crime, and attempts to do so have broken down due to the secrecy and shame of the crime, and difficulties that historians have had counting rapes by whole regiments, or repeated rapes over days and weeks. Should a rape by a dozen men register as one? Or twelve multiplied by the number of times the woman was raped? If a woman is raped eight times by three men, how many crimes have been committed? One vast crime? Or eight smaller ones? Or three medium-sized ones? And what if, as often happened, the woman lost consciousness while being raped? How should one count them then, when the woman had at, say, twelve rapes, or twenty-four rapes, 'ceased to be a reliable witness'? Or if the woman was not a woman at all, but a nine-year-old girl? What sense do her numbers make in the harsh light of her pain? Historians have had to step back, and observe merely that there were millions of rapes, and they were all, in their own way, uniquely terrible. In Budapest, mothers tried to disguise their children, as 'Márta' recalls:

> There were three of us who were fourteen and fifteen years old. We were dug into the coal in the cellar, so that only our noses stuck out.

Moreover, we were doing this for a week, when the procession of Russians came in every night. My mother and the mother of the other girls smeared our faces with coal...[101]

Failure to disguise children could have terrible consequences, as 'Erszébet' noted calmly:

I well remember mother dressing me as an old lady, just to make sure that no one would attempt...to take advantage of me, although I was only nine years old. But with good reason, because my best friend, her mother didn't do it, and the child was grabbed and when she didn't let go, they shot her in her mother's arms, because the Soviet army officer took a fancy to her...[102]

In stories after the war, these women's male compatriots often explained that they (the women) *enjoyed* this process; that it was not rape at all; that, in fact, these women had voluntarily gone with these soldiers: they were harlots, tramps and slatterns, just like the *Tondues* in France.

Indeed, for ambitious young communists who knew which way the wind was blowing, the 'Nazi' and 'Western' and 'bourgeois' lies of rape could be a useful tool to climb the slippery pole in the new state. One man, 'Sándor', recalled (or rather, conveniently forgot) after the fall of communism in the 1990s:

Well, I mean, I don't know whether I did hear about them raping people and so on. We *now* know they did. But this wouldn't have necessarily reached a young man...wearing a red armband. And by March or April [1945] when school started we already had guns so nobody would have told me what they thought about it. And for us I think they remained the 'liberators' certainly for some time.[103]

He cannot quite bring himself to claim he did not know: 'I don't know' whether I heard about hundreds of thousands of rapes; 'this wouldn't *necessarily* have reached a young man'; it *may* have reached young men that their girlfriends and sisters were being raped, but he cannot be sure, is what he wants to say. Surely, rape on this scale must have been obvious to everyone with female friends or relatives. Or anyone that had eyes or ears.

One German woman, who wished to remain anonymous and whose identity was recently cruelly revealed by a self-righteous German tabloid press, wrote her experiences in a diary, which has been recently translated. She will remain anonymous here, and her English-language publishers have rightly left her as Anonymous, as she wished. For Friday 27 April 1945, Anonymous headed her diary entry, 'Day of Catastrophe, wild turmoil.' It was the day the Russians arrived in her apartment block in Berlin, where everyone was hiding in the basement, and it details the attempts—some successful, some not—of the women to avoid the soldiers. Twelve women were raped in that block that day, including the author. It makes painful reading:

> I scream and scream…I hear the basement door shutting with a dull thud behind me. One of them grabs my wrists and jerks me along the corridor. Then the other is pulling as well, his hand on my throat, so I can no longer scream. I no longer want to scream, for fear of being strangled. They're both tearing away at me; instantly I'm on the floor.…I can feel the damp coolness of the floor tiles. The door above is ajar and lets in a little light. One man stands there keeping watch while the other tears my underclothes forcing his way——[104]

And so it goes on. 'Day of Catastrophe' indeed. One Berlin hospital estimated that 130,000 women were raped that spring in Berlin alone. If one is working on a ratio of twelve women raped in each apartment block (which was Anonymous's experience), the idea that a young man would not 'necessarily' know seems even more ludicrous than at first glance. Many—we do not know how many—became pregnant. Only erratically granted medical abortions by local medical boards, they either had to mutilate themselves to force a miscarriage, or have the baby and live with the stigma for the rest of their lives. It was hard to be a 'saintly woman' in the cities of the mid-twentieth century, whatever legal rights one had.

* * *

Given the grave dangers which the urban environment had posed to so many women during the war in one form or another, it is little wonder that a long-standing interest in focusing on unpaid domestic labour and domestic space came once again to the fore in the postwar decades. The proudest achievement of the 1950s and 1960s for most women in European cities was the securing of a suitable home; their second major goal was to secure fair pay for a day's work. One of the central challenges which women had faced in industrializing

Europe since the beginning of the process of urbanization was to establish a home that would secure them social prestige and power, a space in which they could more effectively assert their own authority, preserve their health and that of their families, and manage and protect the family's assets in the form of furniture, coal, books, and the other paraphernalia of everyday life which is of such central importance to the individual. For some individuals, this could be a particularly painful, yet particularly important, experience.

Surviving Jews returning to France found that their apartments had been requisitioned and their furniture confiscated. Thus, to acquire their previous dwellings, they had to evict other French families; to acquire their possessions, they had to find out who had looted them. The autumn and winter of 1944–5 saw dozens of organizations formed in French cities to 'protect' wartime acquisitions at the expense of deportees. As French Jews returned to Paris, a series of anti-Semitic riots in traditionally Jewish areas ensued—the 3rd, 4th, 11th and 20th arrondissements in particular. It was the lost personal effects which most preoccupied returnees, however, and the French government did establish an infrastructure to try to sort out the depots of confiscated furniture and personal effects.

Returnees had to submit precise lists of every item in their homes at the point of their expropriation—and, of course, they could do so with remarkable detail, for it was often dreaming of these things which had sustained them through years of misery. One is tempted to conclude that the mental space of the pre-war home of the memory helped many deported Parisian and Lyonnais Jews create an internal, mental refuge of calm from which to escape the disaster all around them. It was a long, painstaking, and emotionally difficult process making such lists—but the evidence in the archives shows that surviving Jews clearly kept a detailed mental map of every knick-knack, every wardrobe, every chair that made up home. Many petitioners provided detailed drawings of inexpensive furniture, scrawled on the back of paper bags or whatever materials they could get. These articles, though, meant something *more* than 'just' things: the petitions were often accompanied by preambles in which survivors used the lists to establish their Frenchness, their dignity, and their sense of themselves. Petitioners linked their identity with their things with their homes. One historian has concluded that:

petitioners used the letters accompanying their inventories to articulate to both themselves and to the state their place in France, their at-homeness in Paris. Petitioners used the inventories as memory-maps, as props to reconnect with a lost past; and the letters to make claims on the French state.[105]

Securing a wardrobe could be a potent symbol of love and marriage—and a murdered partner. It was common in France to put off marriage until a wardrobe could be afforded, so a petition for a wardrobe could be a petition of grief and loss, or an assertion of love and fidelity. Often met with hostility or laziness on the part of the authorities long after the war, many were left to rant, with Félix J., 'I want to know why someone stole our apartment. I want to know why French institutions allowed it to happen. Who can answer? Who wants to answer?'[106]

In every city in Europe, between 1950 and 1970 there was an expansion and improvement of the housing stock on a huge scale, and while women were not unambiguous beneficiaries of this process, benefit they did. Indeed, inside the domestic sphere women could actually be integrated into the consensus of nation-building, whereby the post-war virtues of privacy, the nuclear family, and the acquisition of durable consumer goods and appropriately tasteful furnishings could allow women to stake a claim to a new form of 'respectable' citizenship, without necessarily challenging conventional gender hierarchies head on. Alternatively, one could see it as a successful marginalization of women, fobbing them off with fridges instead of degrees, Formica worktops instead of careers.

When women did achieve the goals of bourgeois feminists, and establish for themselves careers based around fulfilling work outside the home, it could still be experienced as a new form of constraint, because of what feminist scholars have highlighted as the 'double burden' of paid labour outside the home, without alleviating unpaid labour inside it. The USSR is an extreme example of a relatively typical process, but after the Second World War, there was a ratio of women to men in that society of roughly 60:40; and of the men, many were injured and unhealthy. Women therefore represented a potent labour force—they were the healthiest, strongest, and most plentiful supply of workers. And yet their duty to reproduce was not diminished with the increase in their duty to produce; production and reproduction were not alternatives, but dual obligations. The factory, the hospital, and the classroom did not *replace* the home as a site of women's labour, but merely doubled the number of places in which women were supposed to work. The Moscow Komsomol constantly pressured women to achieve yet greater targets in industry, while also stressing again and again that their duties in the home had also increased if the Soviet Union was to replace the men it had lost in the war.

When one historian of the USSR interviewed fifteen predominantly middle-class women about their youths in post-war Moscow, they stressed the centrality of work outside the home to their identities. They were proud to have achieved what they did—senior positions on factory technical committees; teachers of literature at secondary schools; successful chemical engineers. And yet the success of women like these can obscure both the underlying situation for women, as well as the difficult situations success outside the home put these Moscow women in. So during the war, while 75 per cent of the workers in textiles in Moscow were women, within two years of the war's end all but one of the female technical directors, floor managers, and plant directors had resigned, and left the spinning mills.[107] However, there was also scope for personal agency in the urban parts of the USSR. The Soviet Family Law of 1944 was supposed to impose once and for all the model of the family as a man, a woman, and children, attempting to erase forever all the memories of the chaotic experiments to reinvent the family in the late 1920s, which tried to reduce women's domestic labour by focusing food preparation on canteens and childcare in crèches—and in some urban experiments, even the concept of 'home' altogether, in the form of barrack housing.

But while women did work, and while women did accept (if not embrace) their role as 're'-producers as well as producers, Moscow's divorce statistics show a steep rise in the few years after the war, despite rigid legal constraints on family structure. From 680 divorces in Moscow in 1945, the number rose to 4,395 in 1947, jumping again to 8,889 at the time of Stalin's death in 1953—showing a remarkable level of freedom for Soviet urban women in their organization of their family life (divorce rates were only a fraction of this in the countryside). The home, though, remained central in cities across

the continent. Overcrowding was a massive cause of divorce and family stress across the whole period. One Moscow woman, Katia, whose
husband had been murdered in the frenzies of the 1930s, complained
that the other people in the apartment (her apartment—not her
apartment block) treated her and her family very badly, locking her
out of the kitchen and shouting insults. Another woman, Alla, reported
that before the war, four people lived in her apartment, but by the
1950s it was twelve. Another, Elena, lived with her husband, mother,
and uncle in one room—it was the lack of privacy that led her to seek
a divorce.[108]

The social stigma of single motherhood (through choice, rather
than death of a partner) was much less for women in Russian cities
than in western Europe; most of the Muscovite women interviewed
after the opening up of Russian society, remembered knowing several
deliberate single mothers, and they were not regarded as exceptional
or problematic people. Most were not divorcées, but women who had
deliberately had children outside marriage in a more flexible form of
relationship. Only one of the women interviewed thought this was
shameful or problematic, and she was a peasant from a collective farm
who had moved to Moscow after the war, a powerful indicator of the
ways that rural and urban living could shape attitudinal horizons.
One teacher recalled having a row with a colleague, in which her colleague said, 'Don't you dare gossip about me! Yes, it's a difficult situation. Men are scarce, but I have a child, and I'm raising him no
worse than a family would.' The ambivalent teacher admitted that she
and others were slightly scandalized, but not condemning, concluding,
'It was a wonderful thing to see such daring.'[109] However, these wom-
en's access to resources was, of course, severely restricted, although it
seems to have been a restriction they accepted. Nor was this struggle
for resources and home restricted to the USSR—my grandmother
had similar restrictions, being billeted in a shared dormitory on a
disused airfield when she married after the war. Plenty of Britons, the
most prosperous Europeans until well into the 1960s, will have similar
family stories.

While single mothers were generally accepted as normal in Soviet
cities, even amongst these largely well-educated women in this historical survey, women who did not have children were regarded as unfor-
tunate and to be pitied—though all the married working women

experienced work inside the home as a doubling of their labour—they called it the 'double shift'. Amongst one group of women interviewed, only one man helped his wife with household chores, and was substantially mocked for it by his workmates and other women in his block. Equally, all the women interviewed lived initially in dormitories or ill-defined living spaces in which conflicts and compromises with other families were part of the daily routine. The aspiration for a private home was a central one for them in their quest to manage their own destinies.

This quest for domestic bliss—or just a dry, warm space that women could assert some control over—often met with substantial scorn from male intellectuals. Orwell characterized the suburban home—the dream of many women—thus:

> You know how these streets fester all over the inner-outer suburbs. Always the same. Long, long rows of little semi-detached houses...What *is* a road like Ellesmere Road? Just a prison with the cells all in a row.[110]

Yet when a new generation of sociologists set out to understand these places, that is not at all how the women that lived there conceived of them. Two young sociologists, Peter Willmott and Michael Young, went to a new suburb of social housing in the 1950s, designed to resettle the people from the cleared slums of London's East End. They observed there a more affluent working class, in which women were asserting new forms of control over the domestic sphere—often positively insisting that they would not leave it. These women often pursued types of identity not through their job, or their religion, or their kinship networks, but through their consumption: how they organized their home, and what they bought to put into it.

First, they interviewed women in the 'traditional' East End area of Bethnal Green. It was a world of hard labour and often forced, unwelcome sociability for many women. A Mrs Flood described her living situation, with husband, unspecified number of children, and mother-in-law matter-of-factly:

> I've got two rooms with my mother-in-law. I have to go down three flights for every drop of water, and as soon as I come into her kitchen,

she turns her back. We never speak to each other even if we meet in the street.[111]

The situation in German cities was similar. The West German Federal Office of Statistics confirmed that in German cities, similar living conditions prevailed, noting that there were 1.6 families per apartment in German cities in the early 1950s; and 'family' did not mean mother–father–two children. Family typically meant three generations, as it did for Mrs Flood.[112] It also meant children out of wedlock. In Frankfurt, 9.1 per cent of children were born 'out of wedlock' in the years 1935–9, and after the war this figure soared to 16.8 per cent in the years 1945–9, with a celebratory peak of 21 per cent in 1946—nine months after the end of the war.[113]

Clearly, women were sleeping with men in all sorts of situations and with all sorts of outcomes—and not by mistake, either. The public was largely supportive of single mothers in Germany in 1949, again confounding our views of a prudish past. When asked, 'Do you approve of single motherhood?', 32 per cent of women and 33 per cent of men approved of unintentional single motherhood, while 52 per cent of women and 54 per cent of men approved of intentional single motherhood. Most men and women in Germany seemed to agree: children should be planned, and not accidental, but it does not really matter if the parents are married. Most people also thought that abortion laws should be either abolished (14 per cent of women, 19 per cent of men), or at least 'lightened' (43 per cent of women, 33 per cent of men). One nameless secretary in Frankfurt was interviewed in the late 1940s. She went to evening classes and met a man (there was a 2,400,000 'surplus' of women to adult men in post-war Germany), whom she fell in love with. It turned out that he had a family—they were refugees from the East. Things were awkward at first, but 'then we struck a "gentleman's agreement": no divorce took place, he stayed with his family, and we continued our relationship'.[114] Indeed, whenever historians have gone looking for rigid morality in the first half of the twentieth century, they have seldom found it in any pure form. The world in general, and housing in particular, was too chaotic for the kind of inflexible, universal morality that some social commentators seek to impose on 'the old days'.

While present-day news reports and pub conversations about the 'breakdown of community' 'these days' evoke a past of solidarity, friendship and community, and rigid moral codes, the reality for our mothers and grandmothers was often very different. A tight-knit 'community' could easily be experienced as a sort of punitive prison—as well as a relatively 'light-touch' environment, when it came to personal morality, as in London, Frankfurt, or Moscow. When sociologists Willmott and Young went to 'Greenleigh' (Dagenham) in east London, a new estate built for the residents of Bethnal Green, they expected to find a dissolved, atomized, alienated community of women displaced from their traditional East End networks, but in fact they found that many of the women there were luxuriating in the activity of 'keeping themselves to themselves'. When similar research was done on new estates in Liverpool, the conclusions were similar:

> The main issue for most people was, however, the importance of maintaining a distinction between a friend and an acquaintance, and of keeping neighbourly relationship within the bounds of acquaintanceship... 'It's bad policy to make friends on the estate, because sooner or later you fall out with them and that creates unpleasantness.'[115]

As another British sociologist concluded in 1959:

> For the first time in modern British history the working-class home, as well as the middle-class home, has become a place that is warm, comfortable, and able to provide its own fireside entertainment—in fact, pleasant to live in. The outcome is a working-class way of life which is decreasingly concerned with activities outside the home or with values wider than those of the family.[116]

Middle-class intellectuals and historians have often decried this as a 'retreat' into the private world, and condemned it as antisocial and anti-civic. One of the most famous, Richard Sennett, entitled his book, *The Fall of Public Man: The forces eroding public life and burdening the psyche with roles it cannot perform*. In it he has argued that this shift into suburban houses (houses that were warm, self-sustaining, entertaining and quiet) is part of a grand historical tragedy, at the heart of many of contemporary society's woes. But the consensus is beginning to change.[117] For the women who sought to occupy these new suburbs across Europe, new dwellings represented for them very real gains in status, health, and material well-being.

Many people were keen to move from places like Bethnal Green, in the heart of the East End, tightly packed together, and tied to 'dying' industries like dock work. And they longed to move to places like 'Greenleigh' (Dagenham), with its gardens, space, and 'futuristic' industries, like the vast Ford car plant. In particular, women loved not living in flats—'flats are all right if you believe in communism'—and they were particularly pleased with the effect that moving seemed to have on their children.[118] Joyce Storey, a working-class woman from Bristol, marvelled at her new world when she moved to a new estate after the war, and felt it to be distinctively *hers* when she took the keys to her council house after the war:

> I wandered upstairs to view the bedrooms and to stand at the door to look around and imagine all of them carpeted and furnished in differ-ent colour schemes. When I came to the bathroom, this home was the ultimate in luxury. Never in my whole life had I lived in a house with a bathroom. At South Road and at Repton Road, the tin bath was housed on the wall in the back yard and hung on a six inch nail, usu-ally opposite the privy door, which was also outside. No more having to drag it down every week and boil up saucepans of hot water to have a bath. I closed my eyes in sheer ecstasy.[119]

The choices that people make about what they want in life have been too often dismissed as merely possessing a sort of peripheral status, and women have sometimes been characterized as victimized shop-pers, dupes of the capitalist system intent on selling them a suburban fantasy. But some scholars increasingly view the choices that people make about consumption (however limited) as embodying a deep sense of identity, and so the ways people furnish and manage their homes can no longer be dismissed as 'womanly ephemera'.

Historians have observed a parallel process in Germany after the Second World War, in which the ways in which women asserted con-trol over the hundreds of thousands of new homes in the many rows of flats built in belts round bombed-out city centres, the ways they furnished and managed them, were a measure of their contribution to the new German nation—a democratic, stable, inclusive, urban nation.[120] The difficulty here is that writing about the home as a space of liberation, as a space for the assertion of identities, challenges a powerful—and rational and plausible—strand of feminism since the 1960s which has focused on the desire of many women (especially middle-class women) to leave the home and understand their destiny in terms of education and fulfilling paid work. It sounds conservative or reactionary to state that many women's goals have been focused not on getting out of the home, but getting into one, alongside securing the resources to enable them to get by without paid work outside the home, and acquiring the things that indicate prestige in the shaping of the home. This focus on domesticity, reproduction, and material acquisition, however, reflects the aspirations of many women as they were, rather than as they 'should' be, and highlights that even within feminism, different spaces reflect different priorities and ambitions. Even in the Soviet Union, the idea of a consumerist woman building a new society by governing her own space in the city—a private, domestic, homely space—could have a powerful impact. Single-family occupancy apartments could transform women's capacity to organize both their own lives, and those of the people around them as much in Leningrad and Moscow as in Liverpool or London. What many women really wanted was a kitchen, and separate bedrooms for themselves and their children.[121] In the words of that great feminist, Virginia Woolf, they wanted 'a room of one's own'. In these rooms, they might find at least as much freedom as in legislatures, academies, and boardrooms.

In a recent polemic, one cultural-studies specialist has attacked the scorn poured on much women's fashion by feminists, and has called for us to reappraise the ways women of different classes and ethnicities have used fashion to display and identify themselves when they have engaged with the masculinized world of the city street.[122] There has been research done on miniskirts, for example, as a design phenomenon, but little is known (beyond questions posed to bemused parents) about what they really meant to the people wearing them. Apparently, though, dress could mean a great deal in the post-war city, just as it had in the 1930s. One woman, Hilary Fawcett, described her childhood in the 1950s and 1960s in the industrial city of Newcastle-upon-Tyne. Fashion, far from being either peripheral or superficial, provided her with a potent way to re-present herself to the city in which she lived, allowing her to transgress boundaries of class and status:

My lower-middle-class background provided me with few social advantages, but my ability to read fashion and place myself 'ahead of the game' gave me an edge that felt powerful in a world in which as a young woman I still felt essentially powerless. The changing fashion system allowed young people like myself to reinvent ourselves in terms of social status through the ever-changing subtleties of fashion, and for a moment enjoy the possibility of uniqueness and difference that the dynamic popular market allowed the newly enfranchised consumer.[123]

This uniqueness and difference only becomes real when it is presented to the world, when it becomes public, and goes 'out on the town'.

The craze for Elvis in Germany after 1956 led many women to change how they dressed and how they moved, becoming more expressive with their bodies. Women styled themselves to look American and did 'American' things like dance in public moving their arms, which emphasized their breasts and waists, and drank Coke. Conservatives were appalled, regarding Presley as a source of delinquency and Marilyn Monroe as a 'stripper'. There was a widespread belief in Germany that performers like Presley were turning women into unrestrained sexual predators, roaming unchaperoned through city centres and suburbs hunting emasculated men to do their bidding, and that this was a specifically *urban* phenomenon, with frequent youth riots in German industrial cities between 1956 and 1958, often involving up to 4,000 *Halbstarken*—'half-strengths', or 'idiots', who modelled themselves on Bill Haley, James Dean, and Elvis Presley.[124] This, of course, was an exaggerated scare, exaggerated deliberately to legitimize the restriction of women and girls to the domestic interior (which paradoxically their mothers were so keen to define), and their exclusion from dance halls, parks, pleasure gardens, and city centres, that conservatives sought to impose. Women caught boogie-ing, jiving, samba-ing and rock'n'roll-ing were often considered racial traitors for dancing to 'nigger music', and often faced substantial hostility to their actions. In East *and* West Germany, officials tried to restrict women publicly dancing in the new style, for they thought it released uncontrolled sexual drives, debased the racial purity of Germany, and undermined attempts to produce rational, striving, upwardly mobile women. One local newspaper in West Berlin complained about a radical disturbance to the natural order of things. In October 1956, they carried a report into what was happening in the Hot-House, a trendy club in the city, and which the newspapers took to symbolize all the spaces of the modern city where young women were 'out of control'. It could stand for any one of a thousand examples of similar anxiety about Germany's urban women.

The Hot-House in Berlin was a world in which women were becoming accomplished rock'n'roll dancers, much better than the men; they insulted the men as clumsy, and berated them for treading on their shoes; they danced with other girls, one taking the man's role, and throwing and pitching her partner. They even bought their own Cokes. Judged superficially, this just looks like pompous outrage, but if we 'unpack' the various assumptions in this situation, we get a different impression. By becoming accomplished rock'n'roll dancers, they were exhibiting a physicality generally associated with men, especially in football. In using their arms outstretched to dance, they stated a claim to physical freedom. By insulting men as clumsy, they humiliated them in public, and refused to be demure and deferential. By dancing with the other girls, and taking the 'male' role in the dance, they were indicating that men were superfluous and women sufficient. By buying their own Cokes, they were rejecting the small rituals of financial dependence that defined (and in many cases, still define) much heterosexual courtship.

The Berlin newspapers were appalled: they were 'wild barbarians in ecstasy', 'degenerate', and 'vulgar and erotically expressive'. It may be hard for us now to understand how much the 'deportment' of a woman's body mattered in the public performance of a gender order. This new form of behaviour, however, when performed so publicly in the politically charged environment of the city, actually threatened to undermine an entire gender order: women were asserting their independence and rejecting the male supervisory role that conventional dancing (with the male lead) had imposed for generations. Buying one's own drinks—and offering to buy men their drinks—challenged an entire process of deference that had underpinned courtship rituals for as long as anybody could remember (or invent, if they could not actually remember).[125] And this challenge took place *in public*. Rock'n'roll dancing was unstructured, autonomous, expressive; everything that women's role in society was not 'supposed' to be.

While one area of 'women's work'—service in other people's homes—almost completely disappeared during the Second World War, never to return, most women since the war have gone on to work in 'conventionally' gendered jobs: hairdressing, childcare, shop work, secretarial work, teaching, and nursing. Is that because that is where they want to work? Or is that because all other avenues have either been culturally drilled out of them in their early years, or more formally closed to them in young adulthood? There are few definitive answers—but many avenues of social mobility did open up to women in the 1960s and 1970s, especially at the new university campuses built across Europe from the mid-1960s. But even there, women mostly did (and still do) 'womanly' subjects, like art history and anthropology, while men did medicine, law, and engineering. But the doors to universities were newly open to men too, and even when women graduated in the same subjects as men, their pay in the 1980s, 1990s, and 2000s was still, on average, lower than identically qualified men.

While the revolution of unstructured dancing in public places, or the widespread popular acceptance of single motherhood in European cities, is rarely part of the 'folk memory' of women's post-war liberation, a different aspect of their 'corporeal' freedom is. The pill looms large in 'folk' memories of the liberation of women's bodies—certainly larger than rock'n'roll dancing—and if the pill has a 'place' or space associated with it, then it is in the laboratory, one of the places from which women are most likely to be absent. And yet the academic history of women's attempts to control their fertility focuses not on the 1960s, but the turn of the twentieth century—as discussed on p. 115.[126] And often, women's corporeal freedom, say, to wear what they want or nothing at all, is often suspiciously close in outcome to other trends which have sought to highlight women as objects for the gratification of men, as in Figure 2.6 in which 'freedom' for women can still sometimes be the same as revealing some of the more sexually charged parts of their bodies in public (although the fans at this pop festival in Rotterdam seem to be studiously avoiding staring—something the photographer did not do). The consequences for the topless men around her are not the same: the 'politics' of looking, and the ways that men and male agendas can control 'the gaze' in a way that women just cannot, is fundamental.

Figure 2.6 Women are perhaps 'freer' than ever before, as here at this pop festival in Rotterdam in 1970. But as many feminists have pointed out, this freedom is often little more than a freedom to be sexualized in different ways; the freedom not to be sexualized at all has not yet been won. Nudity may seem like a freedom—but it is also, just coincidentally, profoundly gratifying to many men.

Some investigators of the impact of the pill on women's capacities to control their own destinies have emphasized that it could be something of a double-edged sword. The capacity to render themselves infertile reduced women's capacity to 'rationally' object to having sex with a man, and enhanced men's views of women as solely sex objects. Mary Quant, inventor of the miniskirt, might declare that the pill was liberating, putting women 'in charge...She's standing there defiantly with her legs apart, saying, "I'm very sexy...but you're going to have a job to get me. You've got to excite me"'; but another fashion designer, Karen Moller, concluded at the end of the decade that in 'swinging London', 'The alternative society pretended to be more equal, but...women were still doing the back-up jobs, the menial jobs and not getting any credit for it.' And more radical feminists questioned the impact of the pill, for making sex an activity with no consequence—emotional or biological—and thereby making women's objections to having it also of no consequence. Sheila Rowbotham, one of Britain's leading contemporary sociologists, wrote in 1969 questioning women's attempts to 'prove that we have control, that we are liberated simply by fucking', adding that she and other women 'could be expressing in our sex life the very essence of our secondariness'. American feminist Dana Desmore complained that in the post-pill world women were defined merely by their sexuality, and mocked a freedom 'that includes no freedom to decline sex, to decline to be defined at every turn by sex'.[127]

Problematically, though, this strand of feminism has also felt awkward with the types of 'working-class' feminism that has emphasized the acquisition of a home to remain in, a male wage sufficient to raise a family on, and a rejection of the significance of degree-level education and success in masculine 'professions'. This more 'immediate' feminism, focused on the demands of everyday *family* life, has struggled to find a voice more recently and this has had a problematic impact on women, especially in Britain, since the late 1980s. In the mid-late 1980s, the Conservative government de-regulated the banking and finance sector. Decisions taken by banks and building societies after this deregulation to lend on multiples of *joint* incomes, rather than the highest *single* income, fuelled rapid house price inflation, first around London, and then across the whole of Britain. This impacted on middle-class women (with high professional incomes to multiply the ratios) very positively, and on working-class women very negatively. The ratio of house prices to incomes has soared spectacularly in Britain. From 1974 to 1985, the average house price was roughly twice the average income; but from the mid-1980s this began to rise sharply in a world of liberalized credit.[128]

On the one hand, this liberalized credit extended home ownership to millions of people who would not have been able to achieve it before—there were roughly 320,000 mortgages given a year in the late 1970s, but 600,000 a year in the late 1980s. But on the other hand, increasing the amount that could be borrowed increased the amount that could be spent; and it is basic economics that prices will rise to fill spending capacity. House prices have inexorably risen, such that in 2007 the average house cost 3.39 times the average income, up from two times the national income in the 1970s.[129] This has made it more and more necessary for women with children to find paid work outside the home, in a society in which skilled and unskilled working-class jobs have become more and more scarce, which has been less and less willing to pay for early-years childcare, which has been more and more hostile to trade union membership (to push up salaries, and campaign for childcare), and without offering a solution to the 'double burden' for women of paid work and unpaid domestic labour.

The pill also means that often a woman must express a rejection of a man in terms of a rejection of him 'as himself', rather than a rejection of the potential 'consequences of him'. This, allied to a growth in hard- and soft-core pornography in the 1960s and 1970s, has (it is often argued by liberal feminists) meant that women are now expected to have sex at any time, or all the time, or anywhere. 'Liberation' still seems to be curiously organized around the gratification of men, at least as much as women—something implied in Figure 2.6, which shows some of the ways that 'freedom' from the constraints of, say, corsets and other such constraining clothing, might 'coincidentally' also provide more visual gratification for men. According to this argument, this 'commodification' of women has not enhanced women's status or their freedom. Instead, it has transformed a capacity to manage their own fertility, achieved in fact around 1900–1920 and not in the 1960s, into the *loss* of arguments they once had at their disposal to control their bodies, without replacing it with anything better.

Conservative feminists have pointed out that the soaring rates of abortion since the introduction of the pill show that it is not properly achieving what it set out to do, and that the widespread use of abortion as a form of birth control is a risk to the physical and mental health of women.

The debate about abortion is morally and politically fraught, too often conducted on the extremes of the argument, whereby it is viewed either as an unspeakable evil, or a 'neutral' right, as if the right to vote and the right to abortion carried the same emotional consequences for the people exercising either. It can seem from the statistics on abortion and childhood pregnancy that clearly many women are very much not intellectually or emotionally in charge of their own bodies in the post-pill world, and are trapped between men who want to have sex without consequences and a masculine medical profession which regularly operates on women who are not actually sick. In the final analysis, though, where a woman (or a man, for that matter) is born, and the social, material, and cultural environment she is born into, are still the best predictors of where she will end up. And the struggle to afford accommodation, especially in British, Spanish, Russian, and Italian cities—but also now in French, German, Dutch, and Belgian cities—compels women still to accept the 'double burden' of work both inside and outside the home, and frequently to live with their partners and their extended families.

Women clearly still have a long way to go before they can claim truly to be the arbiters of their own destiny—as do men. We might usefully ask whether men enjoy seeing so little of their children, just as we ask that of women. Barriers of class, race, ethnicity, culture, and custom all make it just as hard to analyse what 'the' problem is facing 'the' woman in Europe at the beginning of the twenty-first century. It is clear that women have more capacity to manage their own destinies now than they did at the beginning of the twentieth.

But it is clear too that this 'progress' is problematic in three important ways. First of all, *relative* progress has been limited. Women's position has improved—but so has men's. European men today are much less likely to face death in armed conflict; they are unlikely to be dragged into doing jobs like coal mining or shipbuilding, which were so violent to their bodies that they could expect to die in terrible pain before they were fifty. The fact is, women's lives need to improve *more quickly* than men if the progress is to be real. Secondly, most of the advantages that have accrued to women have accrued disproportionately to middle-class women—especially those that have had access to a university education. Even they face discrimination, but less so than working-class women who have seen many skilled and unskilled jobs disappear. Finally, there are still major limitations on women's capacities to map their own destinies, both 'real' and cultural.

The fact that 7 per cent of all pregnancies in Manchester in the period 2001–7 were of 'women' who were still in fact children, seventeen years old or younger, does not speak of girls having a sure sense now of their destiny in life, or a sure sense of the purpose of delaying sex, or the consequences of sex, or a sufficient understanding of their bodies—and those of their partners—to use contraception effectively.[130] Recent research in Britain showed that only 4 per cent of the population could suggest anything like a realistic figure for the prevalence of rape in this country. Shockingly, 5 per cent of respondents thought a woman was totally responsible for being raped if she was alone in a deserted area at night, and 20 per cent thought she would be partially responsible.[131] If we pause to rephrase this data, it takes on a terrifying import: a quarter of people in Britain today think that women should *not* have complete freedom of movement, a fundamental civil right, the type of freedom that Viennese women, for example, struggled so hard to obtain in the 1910s. The greatest tragedy of all, perhaps, is that the poorer the person, the more faith they have in the criminal justice system's effectiveness to punish the men who do this, the more they underestimate the level of rape (which is conservatively estimated to be one in every 200 adult women *every year*), the more likely they are to blame women partially or totally for being raped—and the more likely they are to be raped themselves.[132]

It is perhaps wisest to give the final word to one of the most respected sociologists and feminists writing today, Ruth Schwartz Cowan. She has made a bold argument about the twentieth century and women's experiences of it. At every turn, she claims, liberation and oppression went hand in hand. Work outside the home did not free women from vast amounts of labour inside it; labour-saving devices in the kitchen cost a lot of money, which meant women had to work outside the home to obtain it, and households bought TVs and video recorders before they bought fridges and freezers; women overwhelmingly still work in 'feminized' jobs on 'feminized' wages; such publicly funded childcare as there may be is timed *both* to justify the demand that women work, *and* is too short to allow them to work full hours and therefore develop a full career; careers have been demanded *in addition to*, rather than *instead of*, unpaid domestic work in a way that is not true for men. There is, she concluded in the title of her most famous book, always 'more work for mother'. Women's lives have improved over the twentieth century—mass rape, humiliation and aerial bombardment notwithstanding—but sadly it is hard to argue that they have improved disproportionately more than men's. The fact is that there were many ways in which women might use the spaces and places of the city to free themselves a hundred years ago, and there are many ways in which the spaces and places of the city constrain them now.

3

The Cultured Metropolis

In 1927, a woman wrote to a record company in Wardour Street, London's 'Tin Pan Alley'. We know nothing about her, other than what she included in her letter. She was a new consumer of a new technology, which had enjoyed its first (relatively brief) boom: the gramophone record. She was a 'fan' (a novel concept in itself) of 'Whispering' Jack Smith, one of the most popular performers of the time. She opened her heart to him:

> When I'm feeling blue and all alone I get one of your records out and play it softly until it seems that you are sitting here with me understanding all the rotten things that make up my life. I don't know what you are like to look at; I don't very much care. I lost both my sons in the War, and there's a big ache left where there used to be a feeling of gladness. I'm writing to tell you...that you have done more toward soothing that ache than anyone else in the world.[1]

She describes here an inner world of profound significance to her: an emotional interior life, desolated at the death of her two sons in a war which lost much, and won little.

At the end of the twentieth century, the capacity of popular music to reach into the most secret, terrifying realms of the human heart and mind was just as strong. The British pop star Robbie Williams had a hit with the song *Angels* in 1997. It ran:

> And through it all,
> She offers me protection,
> A lot of love and affection,
> Whether I'm right or wrong.
> And down the waterfall,
> Wherever it may take me,
> I know that life won't break me,

When I come to call,
She won't forsake me,
I'm loving angels instead.[2]

The song, it seems, makes little 'sense' and has little 'meaning' in the way that Purcell or Bach or Wagner or Stravinsky have 'meaning'. Through all of what? What waterfall? Loving angels instead of what? Instead of the person he has already told us that he loves? It seems to be a fairly clichéd song about unconditional love; the lyrics seem to have been selected for their scan and rhyme, rather than their meaning and coherence. It is a song like thousands of others, and one which does not make clear semantic sense. On one level, it is as superficial and disposable as all the other ragtime, cakewalk, boogaloo, rock'n'roll, hi-energy, rap, *chanson*, *Schlager*, and power ballad hits of the twentieth century—as likely to be unremembered as the words of 'Whispering' Jack Smith are to us now, despite their capacity to soothe the anguish of violent death. Even Robbie Williams's most devoted fans have little sure idea what the song is 'about', because it makes little grammatical or syntactical sense.

So are these songs, these paradigms of twentieth-century culture, then meaning*less*? Are they disposable, commercial ephemera? This question has dogged the interpretation of urban culture. Yet a survey in 2005 by a TV music channel of 45,000 Europeans showed that many people in Britain want *Angels* played at their funerals, and there is anecdotal evidence that it has gained some prominence as music at the funerals of children in particular.[3] The video to the song can be seen at the YouTube website. After the song, there is a message board where people can leave their thoughts on it. One woman wrote: 'this was played at my mums funeral. she was 61 at time and she loved him. wat a man he is beautiful. xxx'. Another noted, 'i really like this song…helps me'. One more said, 'Dedicated to my baby girl who cannot be with us as she was stillborn 30th Jan 2007. Named Angel, she was my whole world and I will always love her forever! Sweet dreams sweetheart xxx.'[4]

But if songs like this are capable of moving people through grief and love and death and loss; if they can explore or express the loss of a child a woman has carried for months only to die in her womb, or two children shot to pieces on the Western Front, one thing must remain absolutely certain in any reasonable analysis of the songs: they are only as meaningless as grief and love and death and loss and consolation and war are. If those things are meaningful, then these songs must be meaningful too. But the significance lies not in the words of the songs, nor their artistic 'merit', but the *use* of the songs by their 'consumers'. Just as a car's tyres do not interest us because of their chemical composition, but because of the ways they do something for us (like steer or stop), so the culture of the last century needs to be understood in terms of the ways it was used by its participants. From the beginnings of recorded music to the end of the twentieth century, cultural artefacts like these take us into the crematorium, the delivery room in a maternity ward, the trench, and the private grief of the living room. Such a passport cannot be ignored.

However, few things united left and right in the twentieth century like their contempt for modern culture. 'Modern life', declared 1990s British pop band Blur in the title of their 1993 album, 'is rubbish.' The words appeared on the album cover over an image of a streamlined 1930s steam train travelling at speed—an archetypal symbol of man's conquest of space, time, technology, raw materials, and nature in the modern world. At the end of the century on which this book focuses, Blur were making a knowing comment on the widespread condemnation of that century's culture as junk. They were middle-class men with art school educations sneering at the sneerers: those 'wise' minds of the commentariat that have found little to love in the worlds of the night club, cinema, football stadium, or suburban living room.

Far more common has been the sort of opinion offered here by a British Conservative MP in the 1960s, when characterizing the cultural life of the twentieth-century citizen:

> It is a life without point or quality, a vulgar world whose inhabitants have more money than is good for them. [It is] barbarism with electric light, a cockney tellytopia, a low-grade nirvana of subsidised houses, hire-purchase extravagance, undisciplined children, gaudy domestic squalor, and chips with everything.[5]

Nor can this MP's words be dismissed as reactionary right-wing rage. The liberal left could be far more condemnatory. As the editor of the left-wing *New Statesman* magazine wrote in 1964, when he watched a televised pop concert:

While the music is performed, the cameras linger savagely over the faces of the audience. What a bottomless chasm of vacuity they reveal! The huge faces, bloated with cheap confectionery and smeared with the chainstore makeup, the open sagging mouths and glazed eyes, the hands mindlessly drumming in time to the music, the broken stiletto heels, the shoddy, stereotyped, 'with-it' clothes: here, apparently, is a collective portrait of a generation enslaved by a commercial machine...Those who flock around the Beatles, who scream themselves into hysteria, whose vacant faces flicker over the TV screen, are the least fortunate of their generation, the dull, the idle, the failures: their existence...is a fearful indictment of our education system.[6]

Cameras were 'savage'. Faces of pop fans indicated a 'bottomless chasm of vacuity' and 'vacancy'. Drumming one's hands in time with the music is viewed as some sort of offence. These people were not looking at 'culture'; they were cogs in a capitalist machine which 'enslaved' them. Stilettos and the Beatles equalled slavery, and this slavery had been enabled—or even caused—by the total failure of the principal project of the Western state for the previous one hundred years: education.

One view from 'on high' of culture in the twentieth century has been that it has been a worthless, debased currency; a decline into 'meaninglessness' and trite commercial drivel. It has imprisoned its consumers in a capitalist framework; it has sated humanity's yearning for truth and meaning in an ersatz patchwork of faux signs, symbols, and signifiers. It has replaced depth with shallowness, truth with sparkle, and beauty with sentimentality, which James Joyce reportedly defined as 'unearned emotion'. Whether expressed with the verve and humour of an angry Tory in full flow, or the pious, pitying contempt of the progressive for those whom he claims to champion, the conclusion has been the same. This has been a century without culture.

However, in the last twenty or thirty years, some historians, sociologists, and anthropologists have transformed their definition of culture. In this new framework, culture is not what one finds in museums, opera houses, and art galleries (although many of these have always attracted 'ordinary' citizens by the hundreds of thousands). Culture is not what one visits once a month. Culture is not the best or the most typical or the most authentic expression of a national genius. Culture does not require a degree to understand it, or a government subsidy to produce it. Above all, culture is not a sort of 'medicine' which is good for you. Instead, many scholars have insisted that culture is not what one *learns to master* or *suffers for* at all; it is what one *does*. It is the way one represents and explains the world, and one's own place in it, to oneself and to others. It is time that this definition of culture was extended beyond academia, so that we can understand who we are and how we got here without the moral baggage of fears about 'dumbing down' or Americanization.

Setting to one side the question of what is 'good', and focusing on the question of what 'is', has freed up debate about what culture might be—and crucially, *where* culture might be, moving beyond salons, galleries, museums, and opera houses to a variety of transformative spaces produced for the first time in the twentieth century. While some historians, sociologists, and media scholars have long recognized the importance of the lived culture of the last century, some have dismissed it as 'leisure'. Instead of seeing football, dancing, television, and jazz as ways to represent the world to yourself and yourself to the world, they are sometimes seen as methods to dissipate time, akin to 'hanging about' or 'going to the pub'. Important as hanging about and going to the pub might be, they do not contain within them the types of mysteries that the listeners to 'Whispering' Jack Smith and Robbie Williams found in the music and song, and so they are not part of this chapter.

And in the twentieth century, this culture was the culture of cities, and its agents and facilitators were a range of totally new spaces and places which shaped what was seen, heard, used, and experienced. The culture of the twentieth century can seem at first bewildering, but it came into being in a very circumscribed set of less than ten specific places, spaces, and locations: music halls; cafés, bars, and pubs; football stadia; cinemas; dance halls; living rooms; and discos and night clubs. These spaces, each produced at a specific historical time in a specific geographical place, have marked out the parameters not just of *what* we consume as our culture, but *how* we consume it, and the impact it has on us and our relationships with each other. This chapter will look at these sites of culture and explore how they transformed our window on the world.

* * *

If one form of culture from the start of the last century is 'remembered' in the collective consciousness, it is the music hall. Yet the music hall of 1910 was largely unrecognizable from that of 1880. The revolution in music hall was profound in the 1890s: a revolution in capitalism, space, and bodily behaviour dramatically recast the audience's relationship to the show being produced, their relationship to each other, and their relationships to themselves. This revolution set a cultural, social, and economic course which would define the twentieth century. It defined culture in terms of 'separation' rather than wholeness, and capitalism in new and challenging ways—terms which I will come back to again and again.

Highly commercialized music hall was, until the 1900s, primarily a phenomenon of British and American cities. The layout of British cities—with gardens, back alleys, lax (or often, entirely absent) building controls, low-rise construction, and above all lots of space at the edges with no green-belt restrictions meant that it was far easier for an enterprising publican to build a large box in Manchester or London than it was in Paris, Vienna, or St Petersburg. These Continental cities were organized more vertically into apartment blocks, which pushed up land values and made halls uneconomic. The earliest music halls in the 1830s and 1840s were just rooms in larger pubs or cafés. By the mid-century, larger rooms—'halls'—were built in back courtyards in British cities. They had large areas of tables and benched seating. 'Punters' faced each other, not the acts, and the landlord made his or her (for many publicans were women) money, not on charging an entrance fee to see the show, but on food and drink sales. Many halls had no furniture whatsoever, making 'audience management' close to impossible. Artistes would go from pub to pub, table to table, doing their acts of magic, singing, dancing, or comedy. People drinking in the pub would tip the people they admired, and this was the usual way performers would 'earn'. Without either lighting or amplification, nocturnal entertainment was difficult to do in any other way than 'up close and personal', and the role of the landlord or landlady in choosing and paying the performer was present, but not all-determining. Crucially, performers, owners, serving staff, and customers were all spatially jumbled up.

The mid–late-nineteenth-century music hall would sometimes have a stage or a raised platform (sometimes more than one in the same hall) for the artistes who might occasionally be booked by the landlord and advertised by name—some indications of what was to come, both in terms of impresarios and 'big name' artistes. But people would still be ambling about, fetching their own food and drinks, or being served by an army of waiters, wandering in and out of the adjoining pub, and moving around the hall socializing. The hall would be filled with smoke, heated by fire and bodies, and illuminated with either gas, paraffin, or candles: it would be dim. A stage, had it been present, would have been an obscure, distant thing, and to ensure that everyone could see the performers, there might be more than one stage, or the performer might be down among the customers—especially if doing magic tricks or playing pranks on audience members. There would be talking and singing constantly—sometimes amongst the customers, and sometimes between customers and performers, sometimes between customers and owners, and between owners and performers. Words like 'melee' and 'hubbub' characterize what was going on in them.

Some enterprising landlords would make more of a coherent effort to 'manage' the entertainment. Shows at many halls regularly dramatized the court-room trials of major sex crimes and scandals, with all the parts played by men. So salacious stories of sexual deviance and private vice would be dramatized by men, often in extravagant drag, performing the roles of very knowing women, with the audience joining in as jurors or throwing in put-downs, heckles, and details for the entertainers to ad lib with. Witnesses' testimony and credibility were joked, played, and jested with. Performances were fairly riotous by all accounts—and of course very, very funny. Customers would still be wandering in and out, and round and about, chatting, flirting, eating, drinking, urinating, fighting, and singing their own songs as and when the mood took them—which the performers might integrate into their act, or might not.

The idea that audiences should be either silent or stationary in these halls would have been thought of as bizarre; in fact, it would simply not have been thought of at all. The nature of the space made that impossible. A fundamental cleft between artist and audience was almost unimaginable. Even at the classical music concerts growing in popularity amongst the bourgeoisie in the mid-nineteenth century, promenading around the room while they were going on was still relatively common—a feature still preserved at Europe's largest classical music festival, the Proms in London, where a mobile audience in the huge pit joins in with patriotic songs or imaginary cannon blasts. And at the opera, the other bourgeois obsession of the mid-nineteenth-century city, while the audience was still, they were arranged to look at each other as much as the stage. They sat in boxes furnished like small parlours, where they could lounge, talk, visit friends they could see in other boxes. At the new opera house in Paris, built by Charles Garnier as part of Napoléon III's and Haussmann's reconfiguration of Paris in the 1860s and 1870s, one cannot fail to be impressed by the small impression created by the performance room in comparison to the vast scale of the areas outside it for socializing and wandering about. Huge, palatial promenades, halls, staircases, and assembly rooms surround a theatre room which, although it seats 2,000, looks like an overstuffed settee. The Grand Foyer of the Opéra Garnier would put the Hall of Mirrors at Versailles to shame (which perhaps is what it was intended to do).

Within the new music halls, the promenading structure meant that they were used as much for flirting, getting together with friends, meeting prospective partners, or prostitution, as for seeking out entertainment. The Empire in Leicester Square in London's West End was perhaps the archetypal big music hall at the end of the nineteenth century. It offers a picture of a mobile place, full of hubbub. One visitor (a moralist keen to stamp out prostitution) gives an indication of what the Empire music hall was like to be in:

> There were very few persons in the promenade but by-and-by, after nine o'clock, I noticed to my astonishment, numbers of young women coming alone, most of them very much painted and all of them more or less gaudily dressed, numbers of young attractive women...They did not come into the stalls, but either sat on the lounge sofas, or walked up and down the promenade, or took up a position at the top of the stairs and watched particularly and eagerly who came out of the stalls...I noticed that in no case were any of these young women accompanied by gentlemen or accompanied by others, except of their own type.[7]

This particular observer, Laura Ormiston Chant, had dressed up like one of these women in order to pass amongst them—contemporary cartoonists exploited the possibilities of a middle-aged, upper-middle-class woman dressed up in what she thought to be a trollopy outfit, when she started her morality campaign. She clearly assumed they were prostitutes—and well they might have been. Prostitution was so common in European cities before the Great War that it is hard to comprehend the numbers involved, or even estimate them. Historians usually measure the number of women involved in prostitution in large cities (and increasingly, they are discussing the number of male prostitutes too) by the tens of thousands. But this genuine 'abundance' of prostitutes meant that middle-class contemporaries frequently assumed that *any* women that were out and about were whores, and so it is hard to tell from accounts whether one is dealing with a street full of hookers, or a street full of women out for a good time that an outraged bourgeois moralist is labelling as hookers. However, milling around in this promenade was also a middle-aged woman, who came up and tapped a man on the shoulder:

> I noticed she came up and tapped him on the shoulder and I followed them. She introduced him to two very pretty girls who were seated on a lounge...one of them very much painted and beautifully dressed... I saw this man and this girl go off together...an attendant called a handsome cab.[8]

What is overwhelmingly clear from this account—and many others from the time—is that the actual show or routine or artistic presentation was only one part of the general milling about, cruising, laughing, and socializing that went on in a music hall. The 'culture' of the music hall was a 'culture' of integrated sociability and sexuality, not one of passive spectatorship and separation.

But in 1885, however, a quiet revolution took place which would profoundly transform twentieth-century culture. The London Pavilion closed for refurbishment, and with revolutionary consequences. The Pavilion's owners were not seeking a cultural transformation: they were seeking to increase the number of people they could get inside the hall, while still complying with new, tighter fire regulations, designed to prevent the major blazes that could (and did) kill hundreds at a time in music halls in the late nineteenth century. The risk was the use of limelight, which came to be used widely in theatres in the 1860s and 1870s. Limelight revolutionized entertainment because it meant that suddenly many more people could see an individual performer, and that the light could follow them if they moved around. It is produced by blasting a flame of highly flammable oxygen-hydrogen gas onto a block of calcium oxide to produce intense heat and light of very clear whiteness. The risk of fire with the new technology was obvious—but so too was the new capacity the technology offered to put on larger shows more distant from the audience, which would take place in a glaring white light, rather than a dull candle or flickering gas light. If more people can physically see a performance, then more people can be charged for it. And if you can get rid of tables and chairs, and space for 'wandering', *yet more* people can be charged for it. Thus the technology of limelighting meant that for the first time more money could be made from the performance itself, than from the food and drink served at it.

The owners also wanted to attract more middle-class customers, to throw off the accusation that they were boozy, smutty, or politically subversive, and thereby avoid the attentions of censors and reach a more lucrative market with deeper pockets and more 'respectable' tastes. The cruisy, sociable music hall was not a place for 'respectable' folk; or rather, it was—they were hugely popular with the middle and upper classes—but they could not be marketed as 'family' entertainment, and so a premium could not be charged for them. To use a contemporary phrase, hall managers wanted to 'add value by developing a premium product'. The owners of the Pavilion resolved this collection of issues with a music-hall revolution, which through one adjustment of the interior space of the hall, repositioned the bodies—and the attitudes—of the audience: they introduced fixed, rowed seating and stopped serving food and drink around tables.[9] For the first time, the 'normal' 'man in the street'—and his wife or girlfriend—turned away from each other. They sat in still silence, and did not commune directly with either the artistes, or each other. Sociability and mobility were taken out of culture. Food and drink was taken out of culture. This was a transformation that would rapidly work its way across Europe: fixed-row seating produced a new bodily stillness that would be developed by the cinema, and which would ultimately underpin television. Culture was separated from its consumers; its consumers were separated from each other.

The first of the large capitalist companies to seize on this idea was Stoll-Moss Theatres. As the new format for the halls spread rapidly across Britain between 1890 and 1905 (and then France, from about 1905 to 1930), only such large conglomerates could afford to build them and fit out their opulent, fire-proofed, government-inspected designs, and in the 1890s big chains moved out across the cities of Britain. This process placed yet another wedge between consumers and producers of culture, as the role of the personal relationship between publican/hall-owner and artiste dissolved, to be replaced by a corporate set of impersonal negotiations, based on profit optimization and national marketing campaigns. Thus, the 'star', represented by an agent and marketed as a brand to a centralized management team (rather than a local music hall proprietor), was born and 'culture' became a 'product' to be 'consumed' rather than the lubrication of social interaction. Changing the space and the layout changed the economics *and* the culture of the music hall, and laid the foundations for the form of twentieth-century culture in general. Twentieth-century culture was not a culture produced by people for people: it was a culture produced by companies for markets, although consumers often 'twisted' commercial products to meet their own ends—the goal of Williams' song, *Angels*, was not to express grief at the loss of a baby. That is something the consumer put into it.

Music halls proper in Paris were more expensive than in Britain until the First World War, and so attracted a more up-market, less diverse clientele—something which was to transform itself completely in big French cities between 1910 and 1930, when French music hall rapidly anglicized.[10] Instead, French urban culture at the turn of the century was dominated by the *caf'conc* (pronounced 'cafconse', short for *café concert*), which were similar to smaller, earlier British music halls—freer in shape and layout, and more like a café with an area for singing or telling jokes. In Paris around 1900, a conservative estimate suggests there were at least 260 *caf'concs*. Their audience suggests a similar profile to the earlier halls in Britain: the Gaité in Montparnasse catered for shopkeepers and workers in blue blouses—often from the railway station nearby. The Folies-Rambuteau attracted workers from the large market complex at Les Halles, as well as a Jewish clientele from the Marais. The Cirque d'Hiver charged only 50 centimes for entrance; the Cabaret Alcazar d'Eté was free, and beer was only 50 centimes—similar to the price of a beer in a normal workers' café. The cafés could be minuscule: the Père Lunette was two tiny rooms, with a raucous singer in each.

This smallness was central to popular entertainment before the music hall revolution: it took little or no money to set up, and an entertainment 'industry' as such was therefore unnecessary. Sure, culture was still about making money, but all the people taking money, and paying it, could talk to each other, touch each other, drink with each other. If the workers in such a café did not like what they heard, they could explain that clearly and directly to the artiste or patron, or wander into the other room. And such entertainment was aimed squarely at the worker. An unskilled labourer earned about 4 francs a day; a skilled mason about 7 francs a day, so 50 centimes for entrance or a beer might be affordable once a week. Only the few large halls—like the Olympia and the Eldorado—attracted a predominantly well-to-do audience, charging around 5 francs for men and 2 francs for a woman.[11] Most *caf'concs* were never even formally registered as such: they were simply bars where people did turns, called *beuglants* ('bellowing places') or *bouis-bouis* ('dives').[12]

By the turn of the century, Germany was heavily urbanized, but the music hall and *caf'conc*, important as they were, did not rule the roost in the same way as they did in large French or British cities. While the layout of cities in Germany was remarkably similar in many ways to the layout of those in France (that is to say, dense blocks of flats on wide, straight streets) Germany's industrial and urban explosion after 1870 meant that the population of the new conurbations was, in 1900, often a population of peasant migrants. This was true in France as well, but the modern French Republican project since the defeat of 1870 had focused on homogeneity and uniformity throughout France, the opposite of the obsession with local particularism which underpinned the German national project. Thus German peasants brought with them from the countryside a vibrant culture of carnivals and religious festivals which competed with the emerging beer halls, cafés, bars, and drinking venues—a diversity of folk culture for which the country can still impress today, although it is more carefully managed by tourist boards.

But music hall, or *Tingel-Tangel* (named onomatopoeically after the ways acts were applauded, by clattering spoons in tin beer pots), followed the same pattern in the 1880s and 1890s as the itinerant performers in Britain and France had done, crystallizing in the 1900s into what Germans called 'Vaudeville' or 'Varieté'.[13] The new spaces of music halls, with rowed seating, spread across Europe. Gradually, from 1900, more and more culture—music, drama, comedy, dance—was consumed in a physical environment which silently and surreptitiously disciplined the body of the consumer, displaced social interaction between consumers, and separated out consumer and producer of culture. Across Europe, more and more people were turning away from their friends, and facing towards the stage. They were disciplining their wandering bodies, cutting out their shouting and singing, and learning 'to behave'. But no law or custom was demanding this: no religious or morality campaigner ever achieved as much in this regard as the revolution driven by capitalism and fire safety, which led to fixed-row seating.

What people actually saw from this fixed seating was pretty varied. Some of it was good—some of it was just fun. Much of it was just plain average—as most of everything is average. That is the nature of average, and the nature of things. Some of the big stars in Paris in the 1900s illustrate the type of acts that do not occur in the 'those-were-the-days' narratives which sometimes crop up in popular nostalgia for the music hall. Amongst the biggest draws in 1900 were female wrestlers (in which their breasts sometimes 'accidentally' popped out of their leotards); Pétomane ('Fartmaniac'), who played popular tunes on a whistle with a tube stuck up his anus, and who claimed to 'fart like a bride on her wedding night'; Dufay, who was a popular singer who could crack nuts using her breasts—one of her competitors went on to do the same with her buttocks; or dancers like Violette, who responded well to (and even orchestrated) chants of 'Higher! Higher', 'Show it! Show it!' and 'Get yer knickers off!'[14] In Britain and America, male bodybuilders were a big hit with women, as were *tableaux vivants* across ages and sexes—they were, in effect, an excuse to show semi-nudity by 'tastefully' staging great works of art in which people did not wear much. The Palace Theatre in London in 1893 reproduced a series of paintings by Jean-Léon Gérome, like 'The Moorish Bath', in which a naked black woman attends to washing a naked white one. In the words of one tongue-in-cheek reviewer:

The 'Moorish Bath' tableau is a perfect dream. In fact, I dreamt about it for several nights. The lady stands there clothed in flesh-coloured tights and her native modesty, and a very charming vision she is too.

During the 'Moorish Bath', the auditorium is also bathed—in darkness, so that your girlfriends cannot see your blushes or your eagerness in using the opera glasses. This is a distinct advantage.[15]

What did this 'mean', in the sense of a cultural analysis? From the historian's perspective, when the music hall repertoire is viewed as a whole, it means that any claim that either there was a particularly erudite, conoisseurial approach to culture in the past which we have 'oh-so-tragically' lost is plain nonsense. It also rather bursts the bubble of a sort of robust, chirpy, authentic, earthy, uncorrupted working-class folk culture that was subsequently lost to commercialism. From a more cultural perspective, it is hard to tell what this culture 'means', but clearly the body and its exploration and celebration were far more central to people in 1900 than clichés of Victorian prudery might lead one to believe. Farting, nudity, bodybuilding, acrobatics—they were all central features of the entertainment offered to the newly still spectators.

Yet the apparently trivial reform to the design of this urban space through the introduction of rowed seating, and the types of bodily stillness and reduced sociability that this enforced, had profound effects on the nature of the culture of the twentieth century, sparking off three revolutions by about 1910. First, the move to fixed seating spatially separated off producers and consumers of culture. They were no longer mixed; they could no longer touch each other, talk to each other, look each other in the eye. Secondly, it made the audience sit still. They were turned away from each other—from the capacity to walk up to a beautiful woman and tap her on the shoulder, or give an old friend a cheer and talk to him—and they faced the same way. Indeed, the seating being fixed to the floor as in a classic theatre *forced* people to sit in only one configuration, and the narrowness of the rows compelled an audience to remain still. This arrangement of space restrained both bodily freedom and conventional sociability, but without anyone ever rewriting a law, or starting a campaign for it. And finally, such theatres were no longer cheap sheds thrown up in back courtyards. They were hugely expensive, requiring a new, fireproof architecture, new seating contracts (with new ironmongery and upholstery firms capable of fulfilling them), new lighting technologies, new management structures, and new catering arrangements. This meant that their construction was out of the reach of the well-to-do publican, and could only be accomplished by large companies who could raise capital with banks and stock markets. Culture had become impersonally capitalist, but the agent was not so much capitalism itself, but the way that space was laid out.

The other great cultural revolution in Europe around 1900 was in the field of sport, and in particular, football. It is necessary to dispel a few myths about football. First and foremost, it was not a residual survival of an ancient game. Sport was not widely or regularly played in European cities at all up until the late 1880s, for a variety of reasons—and it was not watched either. Most sport, if it was played, was the preserve of the rich. Cricket, for example, required whole days to be set aside to play it; while in the slow months of an arable farmer's summer in southern England, it makes sense, in the year-round grind of the smelting shop or the spinning mill, it does not. Hunting (if that can be called a sport) required horses; fencing, a popular support amongst the young and rich in Germany, required expensive blades and access to doctors.

For the majority of Europeans, especially those who lived in cities, there were several reasons why sport as a way of understanding the world and one's body was simply an impossibility until the very end of the nineteenth century. First, people were just too tired. The working day for men in industry and offices varied between ten and twelve hours (often longer in Russian cities); the day in domestic service could be substantially longer, and work was physically demanding, so the idea of running around at the end of it would have seemed bizarre. Frequently, the middle classes across Europe desired that workers would play sport: they felt that it would 'improve' them physically in a 'Darwinian' sense, and make them fitter and stronger. It would also commit them to following a set of rules and an honour code that could not be casually ascribed to Church or State, so would seem classless and separate from the economic system, while at the same time underpinning it. But in most cities, workers could not be induced to play sport. One middle-class investigator of workers' lives in German industrial cities in 1898 aimed at a sort of physically and mentally stimulating workers' culture, including sport, but found:

> A person who has to be at work from early morning until late in the evening, mostly badly or insufficiently nourished, is exhausted by the

evening and stops in the next pub before going home for a beer, a glass
of wine or schnapps to give him strength. As he sets down his limbs, he
feels even more tired, and stays there.[16]

As for the formation of manly bonds and friendship, and the patient
process of learning 'to be a man' which consumes so many men's time
and energy between the ages of about ten and thirty, sport played little role in the nineteenth century. Masculine identities in particular
were formed largely by and through work and/or military service, in
a hierarchical, trans-generational way. If a young man wanted to
acquire prestige amongst his peers, fighting while drunk always
remained an option from the shipyards of Glasgow to the steel mills
of St Petersburg, but more durable would be acquiring status in the
workplace through skills or moving up a factory hierarchy.

Secondly, until the very end of the nineteenth century, cities were
laid out in a way which made spatially demanding sports hard to
play: alleyways, courtyards, narrow streets (with a lot of traffic, covered in horse excrement and the effluent of local industries), and an
absence of parks meant that any running or team game would be
spatially impossible, even if one existed and one were inclined to play
it. But by the late 1880s, working hours were being restricted, and
the '*semaine anglaise*', with its Saturday afternoon off, was becoming
common across Europe's cities, especially in industries with effective
union organization, such as metal work and railways. Parks were
being built. Waste from butchers, horses, and the like was being better managed. The spatial and temporal requirements for football
were suddenly put in place.

Finally, the social structures and formations that dictated the way
teams had previously constituted themselves for sport were dissolved
by the industrial revolution and the process of urbanization. In a factory city like Manchester or Birmingham in the 1840s there were no
guilds in the traditional sense; there were no villages, each observing
similar saints' days or holy-days on which they conventionally competed; there were no long winters when arable farm workers had little
or nothing to do during the day, and had to find a way of keeping
themselves alert, entertained, and fit for spring. There were no fallow
fields on which to play. And then, quite suddenly, a set of unrelated
factors came together in the thirty years after 1865, such that the
game in its modern professional form was conclusively shaped when

Newton Heath Lancashire and Yorkshire Railway Football Club—now Manchester United Football Club—went professional, and started paying its players in 1892.

Far from being passed down since ancient times, the rules of association football were formulated quite suddenly in the 1860s. In the 1840s and 1850s, elite private schools in Britain, like Rugby, Winchester, Harrow, Eton, and Shrewsbury, placed a new emphasis on 'games' as a method of 'forming character' at least as important as what happened in the classroom. Britain's growing empire, industrial revolution, commercial growth, and new professional civil service transformed the role of schooling: education, not just birth, was more important than ever in getting on, and these 'public' (that is to say, in Britain, private) schools boomed. As Headmaster Haslam of Ripon School said to his boys on speech day in 1884:

> Wellington said that the playfields of Eton won the battle of Waterloo, and there was no doubt that the training of the English boys in the cricket and football field enabled them to go to India, and find their way from island to island in the Pacific, or to undergo fatiguing marches in Egypt. Their football and cricket experiences taught them how to stand up and work, and how to take and give a blow.[17]

Violence was at the heart of these games—but that made them games for the wealthy. For the poor, though, breaking an arm or a leg in a football match might mean their children would starve.

In the 1840s and 1850s, these 'character-forming' games were most akin to the modern game of rugby in the ways they were played. This meant that they were essentially fighting games, in which a ball, which was often carried, was battled forward. They were similar to cricket in that, at any one time, most people in the game were not actively involved in moving the ball around—passing was rare: a cowardly act, effeminate and 'French' (although ultimately, it was in Glasgow that the passing game of football evolved in the 1880s and 1890s). When working-class men did master the game, especially from the mid-1880s, they were promptly accused of being cheats and ungentlemanly. The number of comments in the press about the awfulness of working-class football, and its corruption of the values of public school football, are so numerous as to be impossible for the historian to count. Comments like this in 1898 were typical:

the artisan differs from the public-school man in two important points:
he plays to win at all costs and, from the nature of his associations, he
steps onto the football field in better training…his strong desire to win
leads him to play up to the rules [and] to indulge in dodges and tricks,
which the public school man is apt to consider dishonourable, while it
is difficult for him to realise that you can be defeated with honour.[18]

The trouble with working-class men, it seemed, is that they were
unreasonably strong, obeyed the rules and tried hard. Factor in the
observations from many contemporaries that most men were so physically exhausted after a day delivering coal or smelting steel, that many
could barely move, and the achievement of the devious working-class
footballers becomes even more impressive. The 11,000 men from the
Great Eastern Railway Repair Yards and the 3,200 men of the
Thames Iron Works who founded and supported West Ham Football
Club in industrial east London in 1895 finished each day of metal
bashing and coal hauling, and *then* played football.[19]

In public school games, once a boy had the ball, he had to fight it
to the other end of the 'pitch' against a very limited group of people
from the other team trying to stop him. The emphasis was on one-on-
one conflict, as befitting gentlemen, and in the same spirit as cricket
or baseball. There was no passing; should he be about to lose the ball
in a conflict or through 'hacking', as it was called (which was a combination of tripping, kicking, and tackling), he offered it to the oppo-
nent, or held it out to a team mate, who began his run forward—this
is still the rule in rugby football. This lack of passing meant that while
'teams' existed, everyone's role in them was very similar: 'positions' on
the field did not exist in firm ways. The rules of these games were
particular to each school, and varied in team size, and how much
violence and ball-handling they allowed. Some focused on throwing,
some kicking, and some carrying. When these young men arrived at
the rapidly growing universities of the 1850s and 60s, they could not
play sport with each other, because they all carried radically different
rules in their heads. At that stage in England, there were effectively
only two universities, so all such young men would be in roughly the
same two places: the conditions were ideal to spread a custom or
habit. So, at Cambridge University, a draft set of rules was formulated
to enable the various public school boys there to play one coherent
game, and by 1871 the sports of association football and rugby football

had been clearly defined as two separate games, depending on whether one carried the ball or not. It was association football that abandoned carrying and fighting, not rugby football which invented it. The myth that Webb Ellis picked the ball up at Rugby School and carried it, 'inventing' the game of rugby is just that: a myth.[20]

As these men left university, and went to work across Britain, they encouraged the playing of football at the Sunday schools they patronized and, as these Sunday school boys matured in the late 1870s and early 1880s, they made the sport popular amongst working-class men. As rich young British gentlemen went to port cities, like Hamburg, Lisbon, Bilbao, Amsterdam, and Buenos Aires; or industrial centres like Hamburg, Milan, Barcelona, or the Ruhr; or joined the diplomatic corps and were sent to Vienna, Rio de Janeiro or St Petersburg, they took the game with them, and instructed their employees how to play it.

In the 1890s, the virtuoso one-on-one, dribbling English game merged with the Scottish passing game, to produce something like the modern form of football by about 1895, seven years after the first League was formed in Birmingham, by teams from the industrial cities of Northern and Central England. In the 1890s, goalkeepers and defences were formalized as norms (and not 'ungentlemanly', devious, and cowardly attempts to thwart a noble individualism), 'hacking' and other forms of violent high tackling were increasingly outlawed, and by 1905–10, a game of football would have looked roughly like it looks today, and would have been played in every major city in Europe and Latin America. Almost overnight (in historical terms) a central form of working-class cultural expression was born for a post-religious world, and it was, in this pre-media age, site-specific. It was fixed in three particular environments: the street, the park, and the stadium. Not until the 1980s would the widespread 'consumption' of football culture outside these three sites be in any way normal—though perhaps one should add the pub, *zinc*, or *Kneipe*, for while football was not played there, it was certainly discussed, re-lived, and refined there, especially after the introduction of mass-market newspapers in the 1900s.

Crucially, by 1900, stadia were being constructed in Britain—at Crystal Palace, in London, and throughout the industrial cities of the north. By the 1920s, stadia were being constructed in other European cities specifically for the playing of football. Just how quickly this happened can be seen in the history of perhaps the most famous football club in the world. In 1878, the workers at Newton Heath Depot, Lancashire and Yorkshire Railway formed Newton Heath L&YR FC, and for fifteen years thereafter, they played on a piece of scrubland off North Road. In 1892, the club went professional, and ceased to be attached to the railway yard, paying its players directly (rather than letting them rely on the Lancashire and Yorkshire Railway's salaries)— the club moved to a special pitch laid out adjacent to Bank Street in the industrial suburb of Clayton, and became a limited company. In 1902, the club was nearly bankrupt, but the managing director of Manchester Breweries invested in it, changed its name to the Manchester United Football Club, and remained its chairman until 1927. Driven by business money, they achieved promotion to the first division in 1905, and won their first league in 1908. The rest, as they say, is history.

This spatial dimension of building a stadium had a radical effect, because it transformed football from a participatory sport into an entertainment business. From its inception in 1895, West Ham United Football Club played on a piece of scrub land that was a long way from the railway and iron works which provided players and supporters, wedged in-between the docks and slum dwellings of the area, in the industrial east of London. But in 1904, the club bought the Boleyn Ground off Green Street in West Ham itself, and this was within walking distance of the iron and railway works. There, raked stands were constructed, allowing more men to see the matches, which transformed the game for spectators and made it profitable for owners. Furthermore, it was on the tram lines from Canning Town, and the semi-shanty settlements which housed London's dockers in Millwall and the Isle of Dogs. The West Ham Tram Company sponsored the new programme booklet covers, selling tickets for Saturday matches. Local hotels and snooker halls sponsored billboards advertising their services, as did a bicycle shop. This shift from improvised space to specific stadium was revolutionary. An £800 loss in 1904 was transformed in one year into a £400 profit in 1905.[21] One gets some sense of the ways that stadia could crystallize both the player as star and the spectator as part of a 'mass' in Figure 3.1 from the 1930s: the goalkeeper's agility is framed as much by the stadium as the photographer. In this, the physical space of the stadium in cities was profoundly

Figure 3.1 Manchester City's keeper attempts a save against Leeds United at Maine Road football ground, Moss Side, Manchester, 1938. Football transformed masculine leisure cultures in cities across Europe between the wars, placing male physical agility and skill at the heart of many men's identities, and stimulating the production of new urban spaces—stadia—to enable, celebrate and marketize this form of identity. The stadium draws out more than almost any other space the emerging 'gap' between the small number of producers of modern culture, and the vast number of consumers.

instrumental—but stadia had to be the products of big money, and so in producing football they had to split participants and observers in an economic sense as well as physical.

Nor was it solely in capitalist Britain that football and big business were close—it has been a feature of the game since its inception. Football in Moscow was played on fenced-off fields at the edge of the city from about 1910. The fences were designed to keep spectators away, the secret police fearing subversion from large crowds. Krasnaia Presnia ('Red' Presnia, given the epithet because of the residents' revolutionary and criminal vigour in the revolutions of 1905 and 1917), the forerunner of Spartak Moscow, was formed in 1921 in a working-class district of Moscow famed for its crime syndicates and huge steel mills and foundries. Krasnaia Presnia spent its early years playing on semi-arable fields on the urban periphery to small audiences largely consisting of extended families and gang members. But in the period after the civil war, the Soviet state experimented with a 'New Economic Policy' (NEP), allowing limited capitalism. Ivan Artemev and Nikolai Starostin, two wheeler-dealers who typify the 'NEP-men', used the new opportunities afforded by the NEP to charge people entry to see the game, now played on a disused potato field. With the money they made, they applied to build a stadium, and by the mid-1920s, crowds of 10,000 were common.

The stadium, though, remained unbuilt, until in 1926 the government allowed unions to 'sponsor' football teams; Starostin secured the Food Workers' Union—Pishchevik. The team became Pishchevik Krasnaia Presnia, and built the 13,000 seat Tomskii stadium in Petrovskii Park. Starostin wheeled and dealed sponsors until 1934, when Krasnaia Presnia sought a more powerful patron and a new stadium to rival Dinamo's 35,000-seater built just opposite the Tomskii. He brokered a deal with the wealthy Promkooperatsiia, the organization of independent tradespeople (like tailors, barbers and shopkeepers), and the powerful Alexander Kosarev, head of the Komsomol, who was desperately seeking a way to appeal to young men. The product was Spartak Moscow—but also the Spartak Society, a sort of sports 'franchise' that undertook team development in many Soviet cities. A year later, Starostin persuaded the Soviet government to accept a fully professionalized league. Starostin became enormously rich, and began renting Dinamo's stadium for Spartak matches. Millions watched football in the newly urbanized USSR weekly, especially the various forms of the Spartak franchise, and especially in new stadia, but the archives are completely silent as to why. Places like football stadia clearly must 'mean' something, but what, exactly, it is hard to say. Scholars have complained of 'social sites of hidden transcripts', where clearly some sort of significance is at play—but where the particular space hides, rather than reveals, the underlying importance or meaning.[22] The stadium, then, could transform a peripheral activity into a central one; a participatory activity into a passive one;

an amateur activity into a commercial one. They might not look radical, but the spatial transformation of football effected by stadia makes the stadium a revolutionary site indeed.

In the spaces of the field, the stadium and the pub, men became men. But still, the 'meaning' of football remains somewhat obscure. Something which takes up so much time and effort, which is so important to *billions* of men and boys around the world, cannot really be utterly meaning*less*, but its real importance has been difficult to specify. The relationship of the vast crowd watching the graceful, athletic footballer, as in Figure 3.1, was transformative of culture, but in ways it is difficult to specify. That many thousands of men should focus and identify with the athletic endeavours of a few is not easy to explain. Perhaps this is because most academics were the last to be picked for football teams at school, and so football has little 'meaning' to them. Often, football has been used as an index of some other, separate problem in men's lives—conflict between Catholics and Protestants, or the state and the individual. In particular, football in societies with dictatorial regimes (like the USSR, Nazi Germany, and Austria and Fascist Italy) or religiously divided cities (like Liverpool or Glasgow), has been studied to try to discover if this arena of working-class, masculine self-expression provided a way of resisting the totalizing ambitions of these regimes or religious identity. The results have rarely confirmed that it was.

Conclusions have been mixed: football has, despite the attempts of many inside and outside the game, rarely been successfully politicized, in the sense of being linked to the specific policies or objectives of a regime, ideology, or pressure group. There is some evidence that, say, Catholics might cluster at one club, and Protestants at another, but the identity was rarely as well developed as some of the clichés might suggest.[23] Football has been just as poor at representing even class-based political ambitions. When one historian investigated the German club which dominated the interwar years, Schalke 04 (pronounced 'shalker null-fear') from the industrial Ruhr valley, he found that while there was a strong sense of masculine identity amongst fans, or of the identity of being mine, metal, and chemical workers, or of the identity of being working class, nevertheless the Social Democratic Party and the Communist Party did not find a way of attaching itself to Schalke, or Schalke to it. The team's ground, Auf Schalke, remained a politics-free zone, in the formal sense of politics, despite the apparent common interest of the working-class men who went there.[24]

But what football has done across the last century is provide a sort of 'bubble' in which a set of other concerns about masculinity and pride and respect can be played out, without regard to the prevailing political winds. The Nazis were not keen on football initially; they felt it was too sectional, too divisive, and too masculine to serve the interests of universal racial unity. For the NSDAP leadership, there were no Sankt Pauli fans (in the docks of Hamburg) and Eintracht Frankfurt fans and Herta Berlin fans, all male. There were just 'Germans': one sort of person under one sort of leader. Above all, football was too individualistic for the National Socialist ideologues: the star footballer was a difficult figure to integrate into an ideology focused on collective submission to one man's great vision. Club sport was often suppressed by the Nazis, who wanted *everyone* to participate in 'race-improving' physical activities, not twenty-two men to do it and 50,000 others to shout about it.

When Austria joined Germany in *Anschluss*, contemporaries in Vienna mourned the loss of street football, as youths were forced into the Hitler Youth, and professional football was rapidly prohibited—but the situation did not last.[25] Soon, playing football during Hitler Youth meetings became a standard way of underlining the irrelevance of National Socialism to people's world views, whatever they might have been. And it became clear at the meetings of the smaller amateur clubs that survived that anti-Prussian sentiment flourished on the terraces and in the dressing rooms, indirectly challenging the idea of 'Ein Reich, Ein Volk, Ein Führer'. When professional football re-emerged as the war started, there were huge fights and disruptions on the terraces at Rapid Vienna when they welcomed the champions from the 'old' Reich, Schalke 04.

The next month, Rapid were playing another team from the *Altreich*, Fürth, and the SS security report noted:

> No sports event involving teams from the Ostmark [the name the Nazis gave Austria upon incorporation] and the 'Altreich' [Germany 'proper'] or even a referee from the 'Altreich' goes by without confrontation or unwanted scenes.[26]

And when Schalke 04 came to play at Admira Vienna a couple of months after that, the 'Prussian' referee disallowed two goals that

Admira fans were convinced were fair, and a substantial riot ensued, in which seating was ripped up and thrown, glass windows were smashed and the Gauleiter (Nazi Governor) of the region, Baldur von Schirach (former director of the Hitler Youth), was mobbed and had his car tyres slashed.

It seems the violence was entirely premeditated: it stemmed not so much from anger at annexation, but from an anger that the perceived Viennese style of football—daring, virtuoso, stylish, individualistic— was seen to be punished by a machine-like, thuggish, mechanical 'German' style. Viennese men felt emasculated and humiliated, and responded with violence. As one fan, Karl Stuiber, told a historian, his gang had decided the following before the match:

> If we did not win the return match, we would destroy everything and beat up the Piefkes [derogatory Austrian slang for Germans from Germany]…And then the game was over—it was a tie—and we ran onto the field and hit all those from Schalke, and before they left, we threw things at their buses, and then we ran into the Prater and hid from them.[27]

Often, formal politics and formal protest is seen by working-class people as a type of bourgeois obsession, using bourgeois means. This can sometimes be taken as demonstrating that the 'proletariat' do not care or do not understand what is happening. But viewed in the terms of their own cultural horizons, and the priorities of their everyday lives, what was happening in Vienna was not a *political* problem in the formal sense, but one of a collective urban identity and an injured masculine pride, and one which found vigorous expression. It is not very susceptible to 'meaningful' interpretations in the ways we are taught to interpret in university degrees and subsidized art galleries, but clearly it meant something.

In the last third of the twentieth century, football has come to be associated with violence and hooliganism. Yet historians have shown in city after city, that violence and hooliganism were a normal part of football right from the start. What changed over the century was not violence, but attitudes to violence. In particular, rising incomes made travel to away matches much easier, and when the ensuing confrontations were refracted through the new mass media, they suddenly acquired the flavour of inexplicable, vast, inter-communal violence, whereas before such behaviour had seemed merely a part of life's everyday drunken rowdiness. It is a commonplace of serious criminology, and has been since its invention as a discipline at the same time as football, that very often sudden 'increases' in problem crimes can often best be explained as a sudden 'decrease' in tolerance for hitherto normal behaviour. The idea that in the past, football crowds were calm, and composed of a sort of 'chirpy' salt-of-the-earth types is, according to one leading sociologist of sport, 'an entirely speculative view of the past' which disintegrates with historical enquiry.[28]

In Moscow in the 1920s, violence was so widespread at matches that the Soviet authorities considered banning football altogether—riots at matches in the 1930s were extreme, and the forces of order were regularly overwhelmed by surging crowds of gatecrashers without tickets.[29] In Glasgow, bottles and rivets (from the vast ship-building industry along the Clyde) were thrown regularly at players and officials in the 1890s, a type of behaviour that would not be tolerated at all today, but which was normal then. At the Scottish Cup Final at Parkhead in Glasgow's East End in 1898, a crowd of 50,000 persistently invaded the pitch, and could not be controlled by the police—eventually, the game was abandoned. Throughout the 1890s and 1900s, and again in the 1920s and 1930s, there was persistent violence and disorder at matches of both of the big Glasgow teams, attracting national headlines because it seemed so vicious, based on a knife culture and hatred between Rangers and Celtic, but also between other clubs. In 1920, Celtic fans invaded the pitch and attacked Dundee United players and the match officials. The violence was not necessarily *between* the two clubs' fans, but amongst them. Major violence and public disorder was an absolutely standard feature of football right through this period. While some press reports emphasized the knife culture and riotous behaviour characteristic of the violence in Glasgow between the wars, others emphasized not the violence, but a sense of surprise that tens of thousands of fit, strong, young lads, many scarred by conflict during the First World War, could be so orderly, given the horrific conditions that typified life in 'the second city of the Empire'.[30]

In the last third of the twentieth century, what changed was not the nature of the violence, nor the prevalence of it, but the perception and organization of football violence. A willingness to tolerate physical violence in general declined in the 1960s—and not just in the field of football. War was increasingly condemned per se, and violence towards women and children by men in the home came to be seen as more and more problematic. Violence in public—a feature of urban life previously so common that it was infrequently recorded—had been tolerated widely in the one hundred years before the 1960s. Up until the 1960s, should the police encounter violence, rather than prosecute it, they used violence to resolve the situation—yet another day-to-day use of violence which, by the 1960s, was viewed as unacceptable and so escaped the statistics. We romanticize the violence of Admira Vienna fans, because we can place it in a story of the 'good' working classes fighting the 'bad' German Nazis; but they were not. They were rioting because they hated Schalke 04, they were men, and they wanted a fight. The working classes of Vienna had found plenty of other people to hate before they could fix it on Germans, and have not done a bad job of finding people to hate since the Germans left in 1945.

But the recent story of football obscures the fact that between 1900 and 1925, football suddenly came to dominate the ways that working-class men described the world beyond work, experienced it, and demonstrated membership of it to such a degree that only the experience of work and the affinities that it created could compete with it. But by the end of the twentieth century as a source of masculine identity, work would largely fall by the wayside, and only football would remain. Football is today, as it was a hundred years ago, urban, masculine, and central to becoming a man in Europe (and beyond) for millions and millions of men. As such, it is one of the defining cornerstones of culture, and the ways people place themselves in the world, however obscure its meaning. The spaces of music hall orchestrated a revolution in the ways that people used their bodies, in that they forced stillness upon it. The space of the football stadium transformed the ways men saw their bodies, deriving status not solely through work or violence, but through physical grace, agility, and skill—or encyclopaedic knowledge and fanatical following of their team.

Perhaps the most conspicuous example of this was in Red Square, in Moscow. From July 1936 there was a yearly Physical Culture Day, when the players in various football teams—but always including the tanned, athletic Dinamo Moscow team naked to the waist, and the more 'entertaining' Spartak team doing trick shots and set pieces—

would parade in formations, do gymnastics, and play exhibition games. This was filmed, and the showings in newsreels across the USSR were spectacularly popular—the stills of the oiled, tanned Dinamo Moscow men's bodies in particular were avidly collected by young men and women, and pasted onto their dormitory walls.[31]

* * *

A final pair of revolutions emerged around 1900, though they would not reach full fruition until the 1960s. 'Black' music and 'black' dancing were to transform the European culturescape, and cinemas were to define many people's window on the world. The breakthrough for black music occurred in the mid-1890s in New York, when two hit songs and three hit musicals suddenly transformed white people's attitudes to black people's music, allowing black artists access to the infrastructure of music printing (and eventually recording, when it was commercialized), and performance. Racism is almost always a 'spatial' project: denigrating or destroying a race almost always involves separating 'them' from 'us', and putting 'them' 'in their place'—the compound, the ghetto, the reservation, the estate, the camp, the project, the colony, the plantation. But these songs and musicals put 'them'— black people from the rural South of the United States—in the middle of 'us'—a city in the North. Most important were the musicals opening in New York which showed black people, not as one-dimensional comedy backdrops to the lives of white folk, defined by their servile position as cotton pickers or servants, but as having richly coloured, deeply emotional lives of their own, in which black people interacted as emotional and social equals with other black people. And this American influence was one which would inflect almost all other cultural developments in Europe from the 1920s onward.

In 1896, *Oriental America* was a Broadway hit, typical of its time; it showcased black music, but with some 'blackfacing' in the cast. It was produced and directed by white people. It typified the way black cultures were packaged in a white world: it showed an exotic other, which often could not even appear as itself even in a subordinate role. White people had to play black people, because black people were not even competent enough to represent themselves in servility and exoticism. But in 1898, a revolution began: *Clorindy: The Origins of the Cakewalk* was the first all-black show to feature in a major New York venue, but lasted only an hour. It featured black performers performing a show written by black people, and it gained access to one of the most prestigious venues in New York, the Casino Theatre. It presented a white audience not only with black music, but black dancing. This was dancing which emphasized, not turning in pairs or moving in pre-organized patterns across the floor, but a freer, more bodily and unstructured response to a musical stimulus, in which each performer expressed the emotions inspired by the music freely in the movements of their body.[32] Soon after it, *A Trip to Coontown* was a massive Broadway hit: a full-length musical written by black artists, and performed by them. There were no blacked-up faces, no comedy idiot black people, but fully developed characters having fully formed relationships with each other.[33] This was the real breakthrough: despite the unappealing name, it showed that black people could create culture, perform culture, be themselves in culture *and* sell it to a white audience.[34]

A similar story can contemporaneously be observed in popular music. In 1895, Ernest Hogan, a black entertainer, managed to break into the sheet-music market with his ragtime, *All Coons Look Alike to Me*. The sheet-music market in the 1890s and 1900s was vast, and the money to be made there equivalent to the sort of sums made by singles artists in the 1980s and 1990s. *All Coons Look Alike to Me* represented a huge achievement for a black artist; it was a huge seller—but it was clearly based on playing to racial stereotypes. But in 1899, this too was to change: Scott Joplin's *Maple Leaf Rag* was the first piece of sheet music to sell a million copies, but succeeded not because of its willingness to play to white stereotypes, but because of its exhilarating syncopated swing. This challenged the beat and rhythm of conventional 'white' music by emphasizing the 'off' beats (in recent music, most conspicuous perhaps in reggae), while retaining the same overall structure of three or four time as conventional popular music. The ragtime, or just 'rag', was the foundational musical form of the twentieth century, and it was black.

Europeans rarely heard this 'authentic' sound before the Great War. They were aware of it, and snippets cropped up in some musicals and music hall acts. But recording technology was such that it was difficult for musicians in European cities to grasp the true sound of what ragtime was, although they attempted to play the sheet music relatively frequently. But without the syncopation, it lost its magic. The sounds of ragtime were initially transmitted through printed music and seem to have produced some odd results, which people realized after gramophones became widespread after 1923.[35] German ragtime records had begun to appear around 1906, but were expensive and difficult to get hold of. They were also short, and pressed on only one side, and there was no electrical amplification. What sound there was came out of the horn of a gramophone, so they could not be widely heard. In particular, it would be hard to dance to them, as the noise of several people's spirited dancing in shoes, which were typically hard-soled, on a wooden floor would easily overwhelm such a device. But the music itself spread widely, albeit in a corrupted form. The major orchestras which laid down ragtime-inspired tracks in pre-war Germany were all named after dance halls in Berlin: the Odeon-Tanzorchester, Kapelle vom Palais de Danse, Tanzpalast-Orchester, Ballhaus-Orchester. So it seems that the Berlin dance hall was a place and a space of influence well beyond the perimeters of its own walls or cloakroom, for it was a space which lived in the imagination of the people—mostly middle-class, at this stage—who heard the very expensive *records*. Opening the door to a dance hall and entering it was like entering a worm-hole linking the life of Berliner or Hamburger bourgeois respectability with the carnivalesque exoticism of New York, Chicago, and New Orleans.[36] These 'worm holes' made the idea of a global culture possible: for the first time, *every*where could become *some*where, and that *some*where was the *same*where for everyone inside the dance hall. After the war, as dance halls spread, at eleven on a Saturday night, thousands of drunken revellers from St Petersburg to Paris could imagine themselves in New York or New Orleans.

In London, the first 'authentic' ragtime was heard from about 1912 onwards—and the authenticity is important, because European musicians rarely understood the syncopation when reading sheet music, so their early attempts were fairly dull. The 1912 tour of the US vaudeville act, The Original American Ragtime Octet, of large British cities was a defining moment. Just one year later, there were seventy-five ragtime revues touring in Britain, the first of which alone, *Hullo Ragtime*, was seen by 400,000 people. In 1911, the *Dancing Times* printed instructions to the Boston, the most popular of the ragtime dances, but, stemming from written instructions, it was not widely emulated. Instead, such 'free' dancing as there was tended to be tango, and done by the rich.[37] J. B. Priestley, writing some time later, recalled the impact of seeing a rag in Leeds in 1913:

> hot and astonished in the Empire [a music hall], we discovered ragtime…It was as if we had been still living in the nineteenth century and then suddenly found the twentieth glaring and screaming at us. We were yanked into our own age, fascinating, jungle-haunted, monstrous…Out of these twenty noisy minutes in a music hall, so long ago, came fragmentary but prophetic outlines of the situation in which we find ourselves now, the menace to old Europe, the domination of America, the emergence of Africa, the end of confidence and any feeling of security, the nervous excitement, the frenzy, the underlying despair of our century…here was something new, strange, curiously disturbing…[38]

While Priestley may well have been over-emphasizing his foresight retrospectively to enhance his status as 'sage', it is clear that these fragments of transformation were profoundly unsettling in a continent of empires.

It was the American soldiers that took their rest leave in Paris during the First World War that left behind the most important heritage in terms of transmitting black American music to Europeans. The black soldiers in particular—segregated rigidly in the US army—often found more acceptance and tolerance amongst white Parisians than amongst their compatriots when it came to furlough from the trenches in early 1918. The Bal Nègre dance hall, for example, at Montparnasse was a haunt for people from the French colonies of the Caribbean, and black American musicians with a New Orleans or Chicago sound found a responsive audience there. Alongside them would be those white people who thought it was in some way desirable to transgress bourgeois respectability in this way—or who just liked the music that they played. One observer looked at the audience and saw, 'mostly domestics, automobile drivers, office workers, musicians and soldiers', so it would seem to be the Parisian working classes driving this process of cross-cultural transfer.[39] The US music halls were still spatially segregated, with black audience members being sent to 'niggers' heaven' in the upper balconies. But bars in Paris might offer a tiny, transitory oasis, a space of integration, not segregation, in the modern city: white Parisians went to New Orleans; black soldiers experienced

de-segregation. It was an encounter which was to have profound consequences for Western culture.

By the mid-1920s, there was an indigenous jazz culture of some
sort, however 'whitified', in most big cities in France, Britain,
Germany, former Austria-Hungary, and even Russia. Double-sided
record pressings were invented in 1923, halving the price of recorded
music, and by 1926 there was a well-established network of record
shops in larger European cities—some specializing just in jazz, like
La Maison du Jazz and La Boîte à Musique in Paris. There was also
a large network of bars—legal and illegal—which provided the infrastructure for an encounter between white European urbanites and a
mysterious, liberating, exotic black 'other'. The most famous and
legitimate was the Casino de Paris on the rue Clichy (perhaps the
first 'English'-style music hall in Paris), which offered big shows of *la
musique nègre* from 1917. After the war, they continued with major hit
reviews like *Paris qui Danse, Cach' Ton Piano* and above all in 1920,
Paris qui Jazz.[40] These music hall shows spread the new sound to a
wide audience, but only within Paris, and one or two other large
cities where the shows would tour.

Less legitimately, dozens of jazz bars opened across Paris as the war
ended. Zelli's opened secretly in the rue Caumartin, and was constantly raided for one reason or another; Jed Kiley, an American,
opened the eponymous Kiley's, which was chased by the police from
one *arrondissement* to the other, with a bigger audience each time. Oda
Louise Smith, another American following the troops to Paris in the
First World War, opened Bricktop's, named after her red hair, where
she insisted that American customers would not be segregated from
either the black musicians they had come to hear, or the clients they
drank alongside. The Jockey, one of the first nightclubs in the world,
was extravagantly decorated with murals of cowboys and Indians.
Such was the phenomenal success of American-style jazz bars (though
the musicians rapidly became predominantly French) that the chief of
police for Paris, Jean Chiappe, attempted to close *all* of the bars in
Montparnasse in November 1927—an event of such importance that
it made the *New York Times*.[41]

This urban free-for-all was important, because it made a new sort
of rule-breaking very real and very conspicuous. Few of the bars paid
tax; many had no fire controls; most were unlicensed; and they all

suggested a challenge to a racial hierarchy which underpinned British and French imperialism. For if whites were 'learning' culture from blacks, then the logic of French and British foreign policy and national identity was implied to be a grotesque fraud, a foreign policy which was proceeding apace in the colonization of present-day Niger, Algeria, Zimbabwe, Uganda, and Kenya. As one Church of England canon was reported by *The Times* in 1919:

> it seemed to him to be a most degrading condition for any part of society to get into to encourage a dance so low, so demoralizing and of such low origin—the dance of low niggers in America—with every conceivable crude instrument, not to make music but to make noise. It was one symptom of a very grave disease which was infecting the country...[42]

Leyton Urban District Council in east London let their municipal hall for dancing, but banned jazz. The Walsall School Medical Officer, in the industrial sprawl of Birmingham, noted that children at school were 'no longer able to keep their feet still'. The *Daily Mail*, true to form, referred to the Charleston as being reminiscent of 'negro orgies'.[43]

* * *

Bars like these also sponsored a type of bodily movement which seemed to contemporaries to be massively destabilizing, threatening to allow sexuality and sexual freedom to explode unbridled in a syncopated dance ecstasy. In short, these spaces transformed Western culture by first transforming 'blackness' from either the colonial inferior or anthropological curiosity into the mainstream of musical culture, secondly revolutionizing the ways that Europeans understood their bodies, and thirdly transforming social relationships. They encouraged men and women to dance with the *whole* of their bodies: no longer did the man hold the woman in place, and steer her around the floor; no longer was dance organized round formal shapes, reels, wheels, and jigs in which the music is the background to a prestructured dance, as can be seen in Figure 3.2. Instead, women danced frequently with no one *at all* holding on to them, and men and women alike used their bodies to interpret the very fabric of the music in new and often illegal social spaces. Just as the music hall and cinema had seemed to constrain the body in orderly rows and restrained silence, this strange,

Figure 3.2 Dancing in Europe around 1900 was usually focused on pairs moving in a structured way through space, and often reserved for 'special occasions'—as here at Belle Vue Pleasure Gardens in Manchester in 1910. Fun it certainly was, but it was also about complex social rules, rather than raw sexuality or self-expression. The arrival of 'black' music in European cities in the 1910s transformed the way people understood their bodies, courtship, and race, and the venues became new worlds for experimentation and intergenerational segregation.

foreign 'jazz' offered total, introspective, unimpeded movement of legs, arms, head, body—and groin. It is a great shame that the history of dance is so tightly focused on performance dancing on stages, because the glimpses we can get into the new dance craze are tantalizing, and speak of a revolution in the ways people used their bodies and related to music.

The most potent symbol for this new, liberated body was Josephine Baker, the American dance sensation of the 1920s. Contrast the poses she strikes while dancing in Figure 3.3, with the 'order' present in Figure 3.2. Certainly, not everyone danced in the same extreme, stylized way as Baker after the war, and they always wore more clothes. But the way that Baker danced without being held or holding, the

Figure 3.3 Josephine Baker was an extreme example of what contemporaries called '*danse sauvage*' in the mid-1920s—and the racialized postures and costumes here may be distasteful to contemporary eyes. But jazz phenomena like Baker were part of a transformation of the ways people danced, related to their elders, moved their bodies, interpreted music, explored courtship, and understood race—a transformation effected in clubs, bars, and palais de danse across the continent between the wars.

ways she let the music shine through her movements, was emblematic of a profound revolution in attitudes towards social organization, courtship, music, ethnicity, and the body, which becomes conspicuous in comparison to Figure 3.2. She came to Paris in 1925, and appeared almost straight away in the most prestigious review theatre, the Théatre des Champs Elysées, on 2 October. She had already been a huge star on Broadway as a dancer and physical comedienne. In some ways, her reception reinforced racial stereotypes about culture and society: she performed the *danse sauvage*, the 'wild dance'—in fact, she created it as a craze—and appeared in grass skirts, draped in bananas. She was the wild, sexualized 'negro' other, the untameable, primeval, animal spirit, with staring 'minstrel' eyes and flailing, uncontrollable limbs. But she was also beautiful; her sexuality was linked with her 'animal appeal', it is true, but she was nonetheless sexual. That is to say, she was black and sexual, black and desirable, black and in public, black and in Paris. Her dancing used the whole of her body, taking the music as an inspiration for an emotion that was neither felt nor expressed in the cerebral, internal reflection inspired by 'good' music, but in the very fibres of her beautiful, sexual body.

While we may flinch today at the ways she was so crassly reduced to her ethnicity, at the time, she was seen as a radical challenge to the idea of a constrained, self-contained personality in general, and decorous womanhood in particular. She seemed to offer tremendous sexual, personal, and physical liberation. Everything about her embraced the physical and the primal, from the lyrics of the songs she performed (like *J'ai deux amours*) to the wild dancing to the barely-there costumes. She soon managed to capitalize on her domination of the Parisian music scene by 'legitimizing' herself, and taking the lead in Offenbach's opera, *La Créole*, again in the Théatre des Champs Elysées in 1934. Baker's type of dancing was profoundly influential across Europe: jazz clubs in France were generically called *hot clubs*, and in these bars, people did 'hot' dancing, where bodies were freed to interpret physical yearnings mediated by swinging, hot music.[44]

A combination of the chaotic, uncontrollable nature of *real* urban space, combined with the space-eradicating technologies of recorded music, made jazz, and the transformations it encompassed, unstoppable. By 1930, jazz had been 'whitified' (according to some interpretations), or 'enriched with the competing heritages of indigenous

European popular music' (according to others). In either case, European cities became capable of producing their own distinctive jazz styles and musicians, which transformed the ways that Europeans viewed their bodies—and perhaps more importantly, the ways they approached other people's. But to become really mainstream, the new music needed bigger spaces, and more of them, than cool bars in Paris. In short, it needed the dance hall.

The dance hall revolutionized culture in two ways. First, it segregated people not by class, nor by gender, but by generation, giving birth to the modern teenager. It invented an environment in which teenagers were totally separated from their elders, and consuming a culture unique to them and their generation, inaccessible to all others. That had never happened before. Secondly, it provided a space in which bodily movements and musical experience could be explored in a new and profound way, orienting courtship and self-expression in a more intimate, personal direction, by emphasizing one-to-one dancing, and eventually a personal interpretation of the dance moves.

Popular dancing was a feature of urbanites' lives before the dance-hall revolution, but outside Germany (where there was a nascent dance-hall culture from the 1900s) dancing tended either to be done at special occasions (such as weddings, May Day, or saints' days), or take place outside or at 'pleasure gardens', which tended to be on the outskirts of cities, like Belle Vue zoo and pleasure garden in Manchester, and which can be seen in Figure 3.2. Furthermore, in Paris in bourgeois society it was common to hold *bals* to raise money for charity. That is not to say that dancing was rare—many people got married, many children were christened, there were lots of charities. But it is to say that dancing was part of a well-established social ritual. Apart from in German cities, dancing was often not the end in itself of the get-together, but an important embodiment of another social function, and when it happened (in whatever context) it was often an expression of social organization, rather than a personal interpretation of the music. It is true that the Moulin Rouge remodelled itself in 1903 into a dance hall, but this was somewhat exceptional, and its clientele was almost entirely made up of domestic and foreign tourists. At 9 francs a time, it charged an entrance price higher than the daily wage of a well-paid, skilled Parisian worker.[45] Until the early 1900s, indoor dancing was largely about organizing groups of people into large 'teams', and manoeuvring them round the floor in formation—line, barn, folk, and Irish dancing are survivals of this. The music functioned as an underpinning to the social structures and relationships, which dance was there to reflect: dance was an expression of social organization, not of a personal relationship with either a romantic partner, or the music. Mancunians are not, and were not, noted for their orderliness, and at the turn of the last century, the dances at the pleasure garden at Belle Vue were regarded as very disordered. Yet contemporary illustrations from the dance there show very clear coordination and order, as can be seen in Figure 3.2.

Again, that is not to dismiss it: turning and turning and turning through a vast crowd at a waltz in Vienna or a ballroom in Manchester must have been a mesmerizing experience, as anyone who has been to a barn dance will tell you. But the function of the music was to enable this social relationship to happen—people did not freely or personally interpret it. Dancing was dominated by structures of reels, lines, quadrilles, and formations, and as such could happen between men and women, women and women, or men and men. It was neither about personal self-expression, nor musical interpretation nor sexual intimacy. As such, it was phenomenally difficult to organize in the most common places of urban sociability at the turn of the century: the street and courtyard were unsuitable, because they lacked music, and were often covered in the by-products of city life—food, water, waste, animal droppings (although very early street scenes shot for cinema do show children and young adults dancing madly around barrel organs that were parked outside factory gates). The bar or pub was unsuitable, because it lacked space—they were usually tiny. The dance hall revolutionized this.

The first two-person dances that focused on expressing the dynamics of the music, rather than expressing (as did the hugely fashionable waltz) a formal set of 'rules of engagement' between two people, emerged in the 1900s in the form of foxtrots and tangos from Latin America, and cakewalks and grizzly bears from North America. These dances were unusual before the Great War—primarily the preserve of the very, very rich in metropolitan cities like London and Paris, and even there, it was a rare thing indeed. The first clubs given over to dancing every night of the week opened for the very rich in London around 1913—the Lotus Club, Murray's, the 400 Club, as well as weekend dancing at the Carlton and Waldorf hotels. But they were all restaurants that cleared away furniture after dinner to cater for the new fashion in two-person, interpretative dancing, and there were very, very few of them. At the outbreak of the Great War, in London there were maybe five or ten such venues. None of them were spaces just for dancing, and all were very socially restrictive, the preserve of the upper classes.[46]

In German cities, the newest dances from America—the turkey trot, the grizzly bear, the cat step and the buck-buck—did get some play before the war, but also only in the most exclusive venues. There, the new style of dancing was also practised—called, in German, *Schiebtänze* and *Wackeltänze*, or 'shove dances' and 'wobble dances', because of the radically new ways they encouraged participants to relate to each other and use their bodies, some sense of which can be got from the extreme example of Josephine Baker in Figure 3.3, and from the German words themselves! The music was soon 'Germanified', and songs appeared celebrating this new world, about motorbikes, planes, bikes, cars, and curious racial differences. This remained, until the early twenties, the music of the well-to-do, but its impact in German-speaking Europe should not be underestimated. As one German dance teacher wrote just before the Great War:

> The great difference in the ways people dance today, from the ways they used to dance is this: people have become more *musical*. People no longer treat the dance in a planned-out, schematic way, but individu-alistically—people dance decidedly according to the music, and explore every nuance of the melody. So dancing in 1913 has become much more joyful than it once was.[47]

This too produced profound anxieties. Werner von Jolizza, a dance teacher from Vienna, perhaps fearing that his business would disap-pear if personal preference was to form the foundation of dance and physical music, reacted with a common concern of European elites by emphasizing its black origins—but also showing how Europeans had adapted it:

> This grotesque dance which comes from America, which places so much emphasis on originality at the expense of beauty, has aggressively and violently taken over in all the salons, and now occupies the whole of Europe. It is like a negro dance, and the main features of

the cakewalk are taken from the negro—his characteristic poses, while the lolloping gait and grotesque jumps of the negro have been replaced with modern dance steps.[48]

It is perhaps hard to understand today, but this is remarkably *un*-racist language for him to use in the time. We have some idea, albeit an exaggerated one, of the types of move he was describing in Figure 3.3. Writing in 1914, this was fairly tame. But Jolizza's description tells us two important things: this dance happened in salons, and not *Kneipen* or *Stuben* (bars, pubs), and the elite of Vienna were taking the cake-walk, and adding in their own 'modern dance steps'—by which he probably meant tango and foxtrot, which they may well have learnt with him. They were making these dances their own. They were inter-preting them themselves, on the basis of what they felt, how they responded to the music, and where they were.

Over the course of the war, in Paris, London, Berlin, and Vienna, this dancing became popularized—but little research has been done on this revolution, scholars instead focusing on 'high-brow' dancing in ballets and theatres. Suddenly, new spaces began to be made in British, French, and German cities where *only* dancing would take place; many such new spaces did not even serve alcohol. While dancing had been frequent during the war (again, historians do not yet know how fre-quent), very few buildings of any sort were put up in this period, because raw materials were directed into armament production. The first London dance halls, or palais de danse, just for the purpose of dancing, were built in London in 1919. The Hammersmith Palais de Danse opened on 28 October of that year, and charged between 3s. 6d. and 5s. entrance—it did not serve alcoholic drinks. Intended to cater for 2,000 dancers a night, some 7,000 waited outside for a ticket for the grand opening. The following year, the owners of the Hammersmith Palais opened a second in Birmingham, charging between 5s. and 7s.; dozens of cheaper ones, set up in any old hall, proliferated around it, charging only 1s. By the middle of the 1920s, there were about 11,000 dance halls and night clubs in British cities, and this was not just a city-centre phenomenon. Hulme, a poor, working-class area of Manchester, could boast eleven dance halls in 1926. There was a transformation in men dancing too—something helped by both the introduction of cheaper records and dance schools.

As the *Daily Mail* commented in February 1922, 'some hundreds of dance schools have reduced the shortage of dancing men. For every man who danced two years ago, eight or nine dance now. Freak steps...have gone out, and easy straightforward steps are the rule.' And *The Gramophone* highlighted in 1923, alongside news of the new double-sided record technology that halved the price of recorded music overnight, the British might be induced to dance as much as the Germans:

> Young folk have the opportunity to practise at home to music supplied, via the gramophone, by first class bands. Up to date and up to tempo, these records have killed the shyness that used to overtake the infrequent dancer on entering a ballroom. This country is following the continental lead, where everybody dances.[49]

The price of a record fell from about 2 shillings in 1922 for a single-sided recording, to around 6d. in 1925 for a two-sided pressing: a 75 per cent decline in cost for a 100 per cent increase of product. And by 1928, there were about 2.5 million gramophones in Britain—about the same number as legal wireless sets.

These venues were of such importance that they were even built before housing in the booming cities of the interwar years. In the vast growth of British cities into suburban estates of semi-detached housing, frequently the dance hall was constructed first, and the housing followed. They provided a space that linked the petty bourgeois suburbanite to the brightest of lights of the biggest of cities. One visitor to a new dance hall, built in the middle of nowhere outside London, but intended for the new suburbs ringing all of Britain's cities, wrote:

> it was a way of having a night on the town in the country, because however Arcadian the situation of the place might be, once you entered the doors you were back in Shaftesbury Avenue or Coventry Street [major entertainment districts in London's West End]. It gave you the feeling of one of those dreams in which you are in two places at once. You could sit in a Jermyn Street snack bar, and, through the window, fifty yards away, you saw the moonlit countryside.[50]

This feature of twentieth-century urban culture is important: being in two places at once. Very frequently, one of those places was America.[51]

The importance of the urban symbolism to this new cultural phenomenon is hard to underestimate. Since big-band music (though not quite jazz) started to be sold on records in Germany, the sleeves were emblazoned with (often fraudulent) claims to international glamour like, 'Recorded in London, Pressed in Berlin!' When genuine jazz bands emerged, their names often reflected this desire of the bands themselves to be seen or experienced as somehow urban, somehow strange and glamorous. The first distinctively jazz band in Germany formed in Berlin in 1920 and was called the Piccadilly Four Jazzband, emphasizing the exotic glamour of the capital of the victor nation for the new sound and its followers.[52] The focus of jazz songs was often the city and a celebration of its ambivalent qualities, like this Georges Millandy song, *Nuits de Montparnasse*:

> Montparnasse! Montparnasse!
> What are you hiding under your grimace?
> What nightmares and what remorse?
> Who knows whether the dead,
> Whose corpses you awaken,
> Might not raise up howling to the chords,
> Of jazz, under the gold of your fancy hotels?
> Montparnasse! Montparnasse![53]

Millandy was drawing on the notoriety of bars like the Bal Nègre, and opening its doors in a metaphorical way to less adventurous suburbanites—and even those rural communities that had gramophones. The spaces of the twentieth-century culturescape allowed people to be rooted in suburban Vienna, or Moscow, or Manchester, or Lyon, but open a door into London's West End, or Manhattan, or the Place de Pigalle, or Hollywood, or New Orleans. They allowed multiple identities and experiences to exist side by side, opening up the gap between 'life' and 'lifestyle'. These experiences might be the centre of some people's world, but simultaneously remain invisible to many more, as we will see in the chapter on sexuality, because they were shut away in the labyrinthine hideaways of the modern city. As one French historian has shown, jazz created 'New Orleans-sur-Seine'.[54] New cultural forms eliminated and erased locality, by making some very specific places—Montparnasse, Piccadilly, Manhattan—universal.

By the 1930s, dance music and big band dominated popular culture—especially for the young. New technologies like the radio bridged spaces with 'hot' music, which was the universal term across Europe for up-tempo or 'swing' music. Hot music erased the distance between cities and the images that people held in their head of them. Indeed, the term 'hot' was banned by the BBC in 1936 for being too suggestive.[55] Thus a young British person could exist in a bizarre triangle of real and imagined spaces: the living room of their home, listening to live 'hot' music on the BBC every night from 10.30 to midnight; the palais de danse, which would be open every night of the week, playing 'hot' music; and the mysterious imaginary places of London, Chicago, New York, and New Orleans where 'hot' dance really was 'hot', to which the BBC and palais de danse connected them.

Massive BBC hit shows, like *White Coons' Concert Party* or the *Kentucky Minstrels* transported listeners on a bizarre 'Tardis' ride through very specific real-and-imaginary environments, and placed teenagers and young adults in a universal community of listening strangers. 'Pirate' private radio broadcasts from Luxemburg, the Netherlands, Belgium, and France were initially intended for British audiences, but soon reached most of Europe from Glasgow to Marseilles, Bordeaux to Vienna, and promoted an even 'hotter' sound, allowing big band and swing to take off in a way that forced state broadcasters to follow.[56] One BBC listener, Beryl Heitland, complained in 1933 that 'the age of headphones is dead', and that it was now impossible to escape the all pervasive sound of 'hot' music. She opined:

> As things are, it is surely time that the official B.B.C. heard a Neighbours' Radio Concert in a big block of modern flats on a warm evening, or in a reasonably crowded street of suburban gardens.

She went on, setting a tone for the following ninety years:

> Now, are we all to be content to be plagued till midnight, night after night, by the thrum-thrum, and unutterably dreary whine and moan of the jazz band through walls and windows—because it pleases the proletariat?

And she concluded with the typical sarcasm of the offended moral majority offering plain common sense:

> Who will invent for us some device which will keep us sacrosanct from other people's choice in radio? Please tell us that, Messrs. B.B.C., and till then, marvel not that lovers of music and of a modicum of plain silence lift up their standard against the arch-fiend, noise.[57]

Far from destroying live music, recorded and broadcast music seems to have fuelled an explosion in the spaces of musical performance between the wars. While in Britain at the end of the Great War there were 4,000 premises licensed to perform music, by 1927 there were 7,600, and by 1938, 41,000.[58] That meant 41,000 environments with quite intense generational segregation, as music tastes diversified into rigid generational niches. It also meant environments in which people could meet, court, have sex, go home, and no one (older) was any the wiser. It is fair to say that in this respect, the development of the 'teenager' was as much about the development of teenage spaces, and the palais de danse above all, as any sort of human developmental processes.

It is well known that the Nazi cultural hierarchy loathed jazz for its 'primitive' rhythms and associations with 'racially inferior' African-Americans—in that, they shared the view of the Church of England canon, cited on p. 205. Many attempts were made to supplant or suppress it, but to little end: jazz music, like football, proved to be largely impregnable to the ambitions of the total state. All the major cities of the Reich—Vienna, Berlin, Munich, Hamburg—the Ruhr valley, and Saxon industrial conurbations had a flourishing network of underground (often, literally underground) bars where swing and hot were played. In Berlin, there were small clubs like the Quartier Latin, Sherbini, and the Ciro, owned by an Egyptian called Ahmed Moustafa. There were big venues, like the Haus Vaterland, the Wintergarten, the Scala, and the Delphi-Palast that put on large jazz-based reviews with a superficially 'whitified' play list. Some clubs, like Moka Efti, had two branches: one in the city centre, one in the suburbs. The success of suburban branches in big cities prompted some to gamble on opening in small towns, like the Rhythm Club in Königsberg, but they failed. This new culture really was only a big-city culture, and relied on big-city infrastructures, demographics, and geographies to support it.

While it is tempting to see National Socialism as something all-encompassing, the supreme dictatorship, this was far from the case—as the regular riots at football matches in Vienna attested. Much noise was made by the NSDAP about '*Negermusik*', and periodic attempts were made to close down swing bars and hot clubs, but generally the scene was tolerated—if for no other reason than that it was unstoppable. Stormtrooper Commander Count Wolf-Heinrich von Helldorf, the police commissioner for Berlin, absolutely loved the Quartier Latin club, and attended regularly. He was a particular fan of the half-Jewish singer there, Margot Friedländer, who allegedly regularly performed American songs both there and at the Orangerie and Patria. One night, she was picked up at the Quartier Latin by a man she called, 'a dashing colonel': it was Helldorf. With protection like that, jazz was in little danger.[59]

At the outbreak of war in September 1939, the regime tried to prohibit swing dancing, but it was still clearly happening. A Gestapo report from February 1940 notes from surveillance of the Kaiserhof Hotel in Antona, a working-class docks area of Hamburg:

> The swing dance was being executed in a completely hideous fashion... English music was played along with English vocals, while our soldiers are engaged in a battle against Britain.[60]

A month later, the Gestapo raided the Cuno-Haus on Rothenbaumchaussee in Hamburg city centre. Over forty agents were sent on the raid shortly before midnight, and found 408 'swing-boys and swing-girls'. Most were set free when it was realized that they were under eighteen, and more than half were actually members of the Hitler Youth. The prevalence of the dance culture, and the police's total incapacity either to understand or to control urban space made the task of policing this sort of activity hopeless and alienating.

The same happened at countless suburban bars—the Heinze, Trocadero, and Faun were next to be raided. The Hamburg Gestapo tried spectacular raids on big city-centre venues with a more up-market clientele, like the Alsterpavilion. But it failed, and in 1941 dancing was allowed three days a week. But by 1942, the Gestapo had concluded that even that exercise was pointless: every new raid (police and air) just drove the phenomenon further and further underground, and triggered a rise in more private, secretive activity: the ultimate horror scenario for a police state which wishes to see all. This is in fact what happened in Hamburg in the war, as cellars of private houses were turned into one-off clubs. Some became more permanent: the Persian Oromitchi Brothers and the Bellevue mirrored the cellar ceilings, scattered cushions, and swung the war away. Whether in Paris, Hamburg, or Berlin, jazz was unstoppable because the places it was played in were uncontrollable.[61] And the teenager or young adult had a place and identity of his or her own.

* * *

At the beginning of the twentieth century, there was another important space for experiencing a different world: the cinema. It did not segregate by generation, like the dance hall, but it offered a magical environment of glamour and darkness, as well as a window on the world—specifically, an *American* window on an *American* world. Alongside radio, dance, and pubs, and bars, the cinema helped define and almost encompass European culture between 1920 and 1960. But there is a major problem in the ways that we understand the history of the cinema. Most film scholars write about the content of films—and with justice: it is an important topic. It is this research which has revealed the consistent preference for American films—whatever the story— over indigenous 'product'. But there are only so many plot synopses one can read, and the obsession with the detailed content of films certainly was not shared by many cinemagoers. It is becoming increasingly clear that between the mid-1920s and the early 1950s, rather than going to 'see a film', people were 'going to the cinema'. It was the *place* of the cinema that was often more important than the content of the film; people went to the cinema in this period in the same way that they go to their living rooms today to watch the television.

Early cinema showings were mobile, temporary, noisy, and dangerous. At one of the first public showings of films in Europe, at a gala charity event attended by the great and the good in Paris in spring, 1897, 120 people—all rich, mostly women—went up in smoke in a wooden hall in the Faubourg St Honoré. Intended to raise money for Catholic charities to help the poor workers of Paris, the event nearly meant the instant end of cinema as either place, social event, or artistic form. The death of such luminaries as the Duchesse d'Alençon, French army generals, and the daughters of many ambassadors made for graphic journalistic output in the new, fully illustrated newspapers that dominated a newly literate market.[62] Despite setbacks like this, fairground operators remained undeterred and preserved the phenomenon until it had become safer.

Slowly, cinemas were constructed as places in their own right, in cities across Europe, but on a relatively small scale. Sometimes they were conversions of music halls; sometimes, as in Britain between about 1909 and 1914, they were built as small halls independent of other buildings. Around Manchester and Birmingham today (and many other British cities) they survive as dilapidated carpet warehouses, greengrocers, and charismatic churches, while some have been turned into up-market pubs. But it was during the war that film technology allowed the showing of longer features with fewer reel-changing intervals, which meant people could be charged more to see them, which legitimized more expensive structures to do so in, and it was in the 1920s that the environment of the filmhouse emerged, which permitted the take-off of cinema as a distinctive cultural form. But in order to become this, it needed its own space. From the minute the spectacular space of the 'movie palace' emerged in cities as a distinctive arena of cultural experience, first in French cities, then across urban Europe in the aftermath of the Great War, its potential for radical transformation of people's everyday lives was exploited. While ordinary cinema users have left little in the way of discussions of what they did, historians know it had a profound impact, above all from the near hysteria this sudden new space produced in the middle-class observers and self-appointed defenders of 'Culture with a capital C'. Reading the evidence they leave behind, but 'backwards', we can detect a huge change in people's behaviours—which prompted such anxiety.

Soon after Hamburg's first small, purpose-built cinema was opened in 1908, the Hamburg Teachers' Association formed their Society for the Friends of Patriotic Schooling and Childcare. Its first act was to form a committee of thirteen men and three women to investigate the new cinema, because the cinema offered young people a space which was dangerously free from supervision by suitable authority figures. It was dark, and so the people in it could not be observed; and it was fantastical and often 'American'. The teachers' early experiences of the cinema were not good: the films were 'moronic' and 'contrary', and the environment of the cinema was toxic. One teacher had to take to her bed for three days after her visit. Their conclusion was that:

> At the present time many cinematographic pictures (that is to say, living photographs) are substandard in execution, are dominated by the hateful, the mis-educative, and the morally endangering, and many cinema spaces do not meet even the lowest standards of hygiene. Visits to such presentations operate to undermine the civilising mission of the school.[63]

So, in May 1908, the city of Hamburg banned children from cinemas unless accompanied by their parents. In 1912, Cologne banned children from cinemas altogether, accompanied or unaccompanied, so radically polluting an experience they found it. Indeed, this type of moral panic associated with cinema and cities seemed to be universal.

While the concerns of the panic may seem exaggerated to us, the scale of panic did approximate to the scale of cultural revolution that was taking place. In the rapidly industrializing metropolis of Milan, the local newspaper, the *Corriere della Sera*, complained in 1910:

> Since the time of the Huns there has been no invasion more formidable than that of the cinematograph. The theatre, which is already under assault from the *café-concert*, now languishes under the blows of the cinematograph. Our great tradition of history, legend, poetry and the glories of our art are now all prey to the manipulators of the moving film and fifth-rate actors who celebrate on dim screens in darkened rooms this new triumph of vulgarity and the growing tyranny of bad taste.[64]

And in Britain, in 1912, the British Board of Film Classification was established to enforce rules on the presentation of sexuality, morality, and religion, although it was left up to local governments to allow or ban films in general.

On Easter Monday 1914, a public holiday, the local paper in Southampton, a large industrial port, sent out a reporter on what they knew would be a very slow news day. They asked him to characterize what people in the city were doing. Boat excursions were popular. Pubs without pianos were empty—pubs with them were bursting, and people were singing. The park was a 'seething mass of humanity', though strangely, the people were playing cricket and rounders and not football. There was a huge queue outside Brothers Beckett's Boxing Booth, where you could pay to watch your friends go a few rounds with a semi-professional boxer. Then he went to the 'various halls and palaces'—the two big music halls were the Palace and the Hippodrome. They were doing reasonable business. But the Philharmonic Hall had been bought in 1911 and converted into a cinema with *tip up seats*—the sign of a real cinema in 1914. There was standing room only, and a queue round the block. The Carlton Cinema was so full and so hot, he found it 'suffocating'. The Southampton Picture Palace he found 'heaving'. The cinema was conquering all—apart from drinking and singing. In the working-class industrial suburbs, the cinemas had put on special holiday shows. The Northern Picturedrome encouraged 'the jaded and worn-out worker to visit the *warm and cosy* picturehouse...where there is a special holiday programme that at once cheers one up and makes them forget their worries and their troubles for a few hours'.[65] Note the emphasis on 'warm and cosy', tied explicitly to attracting 'workers' whose houses may well have been no such thing.

The war revolutionized cinema and cinema-going—or at least, a revolution in cinema and cinema-going happened during the war. By 1917 in St Petersburg, there were 25 cinemas on the Nevskii Prospekt alone; there were 300 others in the wider city.[66] In Paris, there was a 'rationalization' of the industry: the first large, purpose-built cinema, built to be a spectacle in itself, was opened by Léon Gaumont in 1911 and seated 6,000—much, much bigger than anything else in Europe. A sense of the scale of French cinemas can be seen in Figure 3.4. Between the opening of the Palais Gaumont and 1918, half the cinemas in Paris closed, but the numbers of people seeing films rose: cinemas disappeared from back rooms of bars and *zincs*, and moved into converted theatres and music halls. After 1918, a distinctively French style of cinema architecture emerged, focused on what we, since the 1960s, have called Art Deco, after the 1925 Exposition Universelle des Arts Décoratifs; at the time, Art Deco was called Moderne. Cinemas came to dominate street frontages in northern, central, and eastern districts of Paris: that is to say, in the city centre and the industrial suburbs. Numbers of cinemas remained stable between 1918 and 1930, though the number of seats boomed. After 1930, talkies ushered in a new era: from 191 cinemas in 1930, there were 336 cinemas in Paris by 1940, with nearly a quarter of a million seats.[67]

Urbanites wanted to be in the space of the cinema, it seems, for several reasons. Cinemas were warm, while most urban Europeans' homes were cold. They were carpeted, when most Europeans' homes had floorboards, or stone or earth floors. They had flushing toilets and warm water, when most people went to the toilet in pots, and had to wash in cold water or use precious resources (coal) and vast amounts of personal energy (in terms of carrying water and coal) heating it up. In the very early cinema—from the late 1890s to about 1905—people milled around as they did in music halls, because many films were shown in music halls, circuses, fun fairs, and pubs. But from about

Figure 3.4 Cinemas, such as the Gaumont in Paris, shown here in 1943, cemented the idea of 'stillness' for millions of urban Europeans, a process which had begun in the music hall of the 1890s. The use of seating in fixed rows transformed culture in Europe: it turned friends away from each other in their leisure hours; it stilled their bodies; it meant that big business had big advantages in the production of culture; and it meant producers and consumers of culture were increasingly spatially segregated in a way they never had been before.

1905, large companies like Pathé and Gaumont in France raised capital to 'sedentarize' (as they put it) the public, 600 at a time, in prestigious city-centre static locations—and which can be seen in a later example in Figure 3.4. French companies and French cities led the way in Europe on this, from the opening of the Cinéma Monopole in Lyon in 1905, with Paris following a year later, and all large French cities having several by 1910. By 1914 in Lyon, all five of the first cinemas built on the most expensive boulevards were already closed, and French spectacular cinema building went suburban, heading out to the metal workers of Part-Dieu: in five years, cinema went from being a bourgeois spectacle to being the hang-out of the *ouvrier*.[68]

Rather than it being a unique destination with a specific goal in mind, it was the *environment* that people wanted to be in. As one Parisian bon viveur, a bourgeois eager to experience all the delights of the city, concluded in 1930:

When we behave like the man on the street and we go into some cinema or other, we suddenly seem to stop being 'professionals'. We don't judge a film so much as give ourselves over to the atmosphere of the auditorium. The other night, guided by change, I went into a big, glitzy cinema...the film being shown was part of some series, but there was no publicity to launch it.[69]

This 'lack of publicity' was fairly typical—many went to the cinema with no idea of what was to be shown, because they were giving themselves to the 'atmosphere of the auditorium', not a film. One teacher in Sheffield wrote in 1922:

Overcrowding at home, the promiscuous company of older workers, the intense and inescapable 'suggestion' of the life of the streets and the cinema, and, above all, the lack of 'higher' interests have produced [in the young worker] a sophistication and precocity which are none-the-less real for being, in many cases, cleverly concealed. They go to the Sheldon Picture Palace three or four times a week, and it is always to see the same picture, and if you say, 'Well, how did you like the picture?' they say, 'Eh, I didn't go for that'. They go parading at the back of the hall, and I think it must be meant for that...[70]

The space was what mattered, both at home and the picture palace, not the movie. One very serious French film magazine in the 1921 concluded:

Everyone knows that the cinema managers recently decided not to bother putting up the titles of the films they were going to show. Some managers have actually demanded the formal prohibition of sticking up the names of the films at the entrance to cinemas. Another boasts of getting fifteen hundred punters (children and dogs not counted) without a single one of them knowing what the films were, or what they were about, and they did not care either way. He concluded that it was the general public that you had to bring in, and specifically not those punters who come or don't come depending on whether there is some specific thing that pleases them.[71]

Bourgeois observers of this new cultural consumption were appalled at what they felt to be the profound passivity they saw in its consumers, who rarely bothered to distinguish between one film and another, and primarily consumed 'the ambience of the auditorium': it is a charge of passivity which is still widely levelled at such consumers of popular culture. Only a minority of cinemas ran 'first showings' of A-list films, where punctual attendance to catch the latest release was essential. Most showed either subsequent or ongoing releases of such films, or they showed films on other lists, which had no advertising promotion. These films ran in something like a loop and as part of a long 'programme', and while a particular blockbuster (like *Gone with the Wind* or *The Wizard of Oz*) might attract a punctual audience, frequently, people just turned up when they wanted to. As one leading film historian concludes:

> During the age of the movie palace in the 1910s and 1920s, the screening of the actual film was almost an afterthought for [cinema owners] intent on overwhelming their customers with elaborate architecture and interior furnishings, armies of attendants, stage shows, and mighty Wurlitzer organs…[Cinema] practices before the 1950s trained audiences to seek pleasure in the experience of film consumption rather than to rank the desirability of consuming any single narrative on a film-by-film basis.[72]

As one of the cinema-owners she studied said, 'We sell tickets to theaters, not to pictures.'

When local cinemas in Bolton, an industrial suburb north of Manchester, handed out questionnaires with the offer of a prize draw, asking why people came to the cinema, the answers were quick to come. Thomas Weatherill, nineteen years old, explained that, 'When you have spent a dull, dreary day in the spinning room, you want to see some open air life as you usually get in Western films.' Others expanded with more creativity and humour, like Arthur Harris, aged forty-three from 52 Alexander Road:

> I've filled in this form, I 'ope it's awreet,
> An I've put in mi name an't'number o't'street,
> Tho why yo should bother, blest if I know,
> It's a snug picture 'ouse—allus a good show.
> If yo' really ask me, I'd say 'bout a doubt [without a doubt],

Lets 'ave some more fun, that's better nor out [better than nothing],
T'world's ower full wi struggle an' strife,
Summat to laugh at suits me an me wife.
Why send in't form then? Well I allus bids [I always bid]
For any free tickets—an one o'them quids.[73]

The picture house for Thomas and Arthur was 'snug' and fun, a place
to enjoy perhaps a partner's company and enter into a fantasy world
for a brief period.

The wakeful darkness allowed an experience of silent privacy between
individuals used to living in very crowded dwellings which precluded
privacy, and it organized the people around them to look away at something else. While 'getting off' in pubs and bars was still common (and
indeed, would remain so!), people would often be drawn to look. But in
cinemas, most people would be looking at the screen: the physical layout insisted on it, as can be seen in Figure 3.4. The innovation of the
turn-of-the-century music hall in getting the working classes to sit still
by fixing them in ranks of rigid seating was extended here, and, in fact,
underpinned the development of the cinema. Moreover, within the
cinemas there would be spatial subdivisions: there would be stalls and
balconies, attracting different clienteles, and there were 'back rows' or
'lovers' rows', where seating might be provided in twin seats. This made
intimacy easier, as the arm-rest did not have to be negotiated to enable
physical contact. These were tucked away at the back of the stalls,
under the balcony, the darkest part of a cinema. Combined with thick
cigarette smoke, this meant that these seats were completely invisible to
the people in the balcony which overhung them, and not much clearer
to the rows of the stalls in front because of the deep shadow the balcony
cast. The striking art deco 1930s Odeon cinema in Woolwich in south-
east London where I grew up was still fitted with this 'facility' in the
1980s. Now, the same building is a charismatic church.

The environment inside a 1920s or 1930s cinema could be pretty
riotous. While people did not mill about in purpose-built cinemas in
the way that they had done in the pre-reform music hall, it seems
certain that the typical urban or suburban cinema was *not* a place of
reverential silence, especially before the arrival of sound around 1930.
Historical records are often silent around 'normality', as people rarely
bother to describe it. But one Parisian cinemagoer in 1922 described
a typical scene thus:

In any cinema auditorium there are spectators, or rather, *spectatrices* [female spectators] who read the text of the subtitles out loud. There's the woman who reads laboriously, so laboriously that the subtitle disappears before she's finished reading. There's the woman who reads very quickly, and who punctuates her reading with, 'There you go!', 'Well— did you see that?', 'No—please, come oooon!', all full of conviction. There is the woman who reads one word in two, or who thinks she is reading and says with authority—and oh, *what* authority—'Well what the hell is that supposed to mean?' There is the woman who…well, suffice it to be said, there are a lot of other women too.[74]

Then there were dogs, children, ice cream vendors, and a whole tribe of others. The *Picturegoer* as late as February 1947 complained of the impossibility of watching a film quietly: here there were commercial travellers snoring, there a group of women talking; children were playing and eating; people gave sarcastic or funny commentaries; while in the back rows there was some fairly rumbustious embracing going on. Disorder in cinemas seems to have been widespread before the war: in Bolton, in the north of Manchester, Fred Grundy, aged twenty-three, commented that, 'It is no use having a good picture at any cinema unless that cinema is qualified to have attendants to keep quiet rowdy people.' Another young man from the same suburb, Leo Greenhalgh, aged twenty-five, of 67 Arkwright Street, Bolton, commented, 'When my fiancée and I saw *For Valour*, the people behind us and around passed such comments that it wouldn't be at all nice to write.' Mrs Cotton, forty, of 155 Thickford Road, complained that, 'There is nothing more annoying than being disturbed by moving people, who always choose to move about when a tender love scene is on the screen.'[75] During the period of silent films, there was little cause to be silent at all in the audience, and people frequently talked throughout. In less salubrious cinemas which could not afford an accompanist, this was probably essential to the enjoyment of the film. In terms of what people did in it, the cinema before the late 1950s should be thought of as an environment much more like a contemporary living room, with people wandering about, talking, occasionally paying attention to the screen, cuddling, eating. It is an interesting historical coincidence that cinema audiences began to 'behave themselves' best as cinemas began to disappear, and the modern living room became a reality.

As for the possibilities of sexual liaison and privacy that the cinema offered, there seems to be little research. Part of the problem is that the experience seems to have been so universal, so much the focus of comedians' innuendos on Saturday night TV variety shows for so many years, that conclusions are perhaps too obvious. When the British National Museum of Film tried to explore people's experiences of talking pictures, they found that far from being universally appreciated as a site of enthusiastic sexual adventure, the sexual nature of the cinema could make some people very anxious. One woman from Leeds recalled a date in the early 1950s:

> I had accepted the date, looking forward to going out on my first kiss. The kiss happened. I was really looking forward to it and it had been the topic all day with my school mates. Being romantic, I expected it to be beautiful with orchestras playing. But everything fell flat. To start with, he had bad breath. He kissed me so hard, he hurt my lips and before I could take a breath his hand was straight up my skirt. I tried not to panic, but fighting him off was so horrible. I worked myself into such a state that I cried and wet my knickers...I felt the cinema was an isolated place, where help just wasn't available.[76]

For other women of the same generation, in the same city, the effect of the cinema was more liberating. Another woman recalled:

> One of the girls in our gang saw herself as the guardian of our morals, the keeper-in-check of the lad-mad ones of our number. Well, imagine our shock one night at the Ritz when after a gang of lads had sat up the back of us, bantering and chatting us up, we glanced along the line to see one lad's hand slipped inside her coat cradling her breast. The look on her face was totally inscrutable! Boy did we give her some stick after that![77]

For many men in the late 1930s and 1940s, that was precisely why they went. As one man recalled, he went to see *Wuthering Heights*, around 1939 or 1940—a strange choice of film for a single man, unless he hopes to meet romantically inclined women. He explained that:

> You went to meet girls, to experiment, and especially to shout things out. 'I'm coming, Cathy, I'm coming,' Heathcliffe cries out. 'That'll be a first', my mate shouts back![78]

For these cinemagoers, one did not go to the cinema solely to watch films. On the one hand, the importance of the experience of luxury, warmth, sexuality, and experimentation was crucial. On the other, it was a portal into a profoundly influential 'real-and-imaginary' place: America.

After the Second World War, the separation of cultural consumer from cultural producer, and cultural consumers from each other, were sealed in two spaces which have dominated the post-war culturescape more than any others: the living room and the nightclub/disco. The rise of the television in the years after 1950 transformed the ways that people constructed their 'window on the world'. Indoors became the primary source of information about outdoors: the private world became the arena for public life, as can be seen in Figure 3.5. Television turned the city inside out, in a sense. Most of the functions of culture to do with looking and listening had required, for thousands of years, that the individual left their homes in order to perform them. Another way of looking at the problem would be this: for thousands of years, most people's homes were so unpleasant, that the desire to leave them meant they had to invent something to do, and somewhere to do it, when they were 'out'. But slowly, from the 1950s to the present, two changes happened which turned this situation around, and made the home the focus of all life and experience for Europeans, rich and poor alike. First of all, the transmission of sound was coupled with the transmission of images: the miracle of radio and the miracle of cinema were brought together in one place: the living room. And secondly, 'home' became a more and more pleasant place for most European city dwellers. While most commentators have been keen to see the television as a malign agent, leading directly to 'the fall of public man',[79] they have overlooked the story of space and place involved in this process. The growth of the 'living room' as a warm, safe place, entrance to which is controlled by the people who own it, and which was quiet, well-lit, and packed with things to do, gave to the working and lower-middle classes a domestic world which the rich had been enjoying for two hundred years. There was a democratization of space as well as a democratization of taste.

There was a 'cult' of home in post-war Europe—although it is hard to see who or what specifically created it. Sociologist Christine Spigel has written about television in the 1950s in the USA, and the title of

Figure 3.5 Television transformed the geography of the city *and* the home in the 1950s and 1960s: it brought culture 'indoors', undermined the importance of the 'crowd' sensation, and changed the ways people viewed their homes. It 'atomized' the city, by reproducing the cinema, library, and dance hall in miniature, countless times over. It reconfigured the micro-geography of family life, so that relatives no longer sat facing each other, and no longer talked to each other for large chunks of their time at home. Instead, they faced in one direction—the layout of the cinema was brought into the living room. It was a revolution in family life.

her book is indicative of a profound change: *Make Room for Television.* She shows how the television came to be seen as an integral part of the ideal family in the post-war world, and can be seen in Britain in the early TV years in Figure 3.5. It had a physical presence in family space, even when it was not switched on, making it the only member of the family that was 'always there'. While father might go out to work, and the children might go to school or go to bed, or mother might attend a church event in the evening or busy herself in the kitchen, the television was always 'at home', and always demanded to be attended to. Furthermore, its content was designed to reinforce 'family' models. In truth, these models were relatively new, for it was only after the war that the norm of mother, father, and 2.2 children became anything close to a reality for most European urbanites. Geographer Paul Adams has emphasized that television is a *place*, not just a collection of programmes or a technological device, and it is the place that sits at the centre of our psychological world view and physical family lives.

The history of television as it is used or experienced in Europe has yet to be written, and we have only fragments of a picture, although strangely its impact is a media obsession in most Western societies. Obesity, family breakdown, delinquency, truancy, educational 'decline' (almost always a fiction), illiteracy, ignorance, voter apathy, and political change are almost always explained in part with some sort of reference to television, and the dis-integrative effects it has had. Most research on television, like most research on music, art, fiction, and cinema, is focused almost exclusively on the content of the broadcasts, rather than the use it was put to—a bit like understanding surgery through the molecular structure of the scalpel, rather than the procedures it performs.

But what is clear is that television fitted seamlessly into most people's lives. They were not shocked by it, or irritated by it, or even that amazed by it. Two economic historians published an intriguing study exploring the diffusion of the television set. They looked at all the electrical consumer goods that increasingly affluent Europeans could buy since the 1920s—vacuum cleaners, cookers, fridges, microwaves, washing machines, and so on. And they found that the devices which *took* time from people, which demanded from them an investment of time, like the radio and the television, diffused far more quickly and widely than those which *gave* time to people, like washing machines. In particular, those items which gave women time, like fridges (which freed them from daily shopping) or vacuums (which freed them from pulling up rugs) were much more slowly taken up than those technologies which *took* time.[80] What the study did not consider, though, was that in some ways a TV is a labour-saving device: it saves you the labour of going out to get culture just as much as a fridge saves you going out to buy food.

Initially, the TV as a thing could cause excitement, and actually be the focus of sociability. One woman in Britain described the acquisition of a set like this:

It was like going to a cinema in Aunty Betty's house, it was a room
about as big as this [her own living room]—just packed full of people.
The picture had a snowy effect. It wasn't very good.[81]

It is certain that TV sets were high on people's priorities—and they
were willing to make substantial sacrifices to attain them. In Milan in
1962, the city began to clear the vast self-built shanty towns that had
long surrounded it and housed workers from them (predominantly
low-paid industrial workers) in high-rise blocks in the suburb of
Comasina. They found that the most dense ownership of televisions
was amongst the poorest of the city's poor in these new environments—wealthier citizens had *fewer* television sets. Just eight years
after the introduction of broadcasting in Italy, 89.1 per cent of
Comasina's residents had a television—higher even than the number
of people with a boiler for hot water. And outside Italy's big cities,
barely 20 per cent had a television in 1962. Wealth was a reasonable
indicator of TV ownership, but geography was better. Poorer people
bought TVs before richer, and urban people before rural.[82]

It is possible to trace something of the impact of television through
the pictures in the women's magazines, home decoration magazines,
and newspapers. Here, presented in terms of décor and style, one
will also find depicted a revolution in family structure, effected by
space and technology. For the entire history of humanity up until
the 1950s, families faced each other in their own homes. From the
mid-1950s onwards, they stopped facing each other, and faced the
TV. These photographs show how the layout of living rooms changed
in the years between 1930 and 1970, and can be seen in Figure 3.5.
A veritable revolution in space occurred, which seems to have caused
a revolution in personal relationships. Photographs of the rooms
where people spent their time before the Second World War show
several distinctive features. In the poorer parts of Europe (Eastern
and Southern), and in the houses of the poor in Britain, western
Germany and northern France, they show a table at the heart of
family social life. People passed social time together facing each
other, quite close up. Poverty dictated that families were compressed
into one or two rooms. They ate like that, slept like that, played
games like that, talked like that, read like that, and listened to the
wireless like that.

In wealthier cities where richer skilled workers could afford a separate 'parlour', like the vast industrial conurbation that strings through the Ruhr valley, or Birmingham and London, there was a slightly different arrangement. In the 'back room', life would focus on the 'close encounter' of the table. But in the 'parlour' or 'front room', photographs show the first three-piece suites (bought through the new means of hire purchase, offered by department and chain stores—themselves new), situated in a circle around a fireplace (in Britain) or a tiled stove (in western Germany), with a wireless in the corner. While they were not as close to each other as around the table, people who knew each other and loved each other still organized their leisure—reading, talking, singing, playing games, listening to the wireless—*around* other people, and *facing* them.

But with the arrival of the television, the space of the living room completely changed its social orientation. Instead of looking at each other, people turned their gaze *away* from the people they loved towards a *thing* that they loved, for hours and hours every day. Historian Tim O'Sullivan is one of the few to try to understand the impact that the arrival of television had on people's everyday lives. First, the geography of the home began to change, as this respondent to an oral history project observed from the 1950s:

> I remember, you had to go into the front room to watch it, and in those days, the front room was really only used for 'best'—for special occasions. The television changed that.

Another British woman, recalling the mid-1950s, commented more on the impact on sociability within the family:

> In the evenings, it [the living room] became the television room...it was 'what's on tonight', and everything started to give way to television. It used to annoy me. You couldn't talk to people.[83]

Another of O'Sullivan's interviewees noted the way that it inverted people's experience of the town, and their priorities:

> Well it made a difference in that you could stay in and to begin with it was like not staying in because there was television to watch. It could be relaxing and it could send you to sleep. It was another option I suppose, and we worked out what was worth watching pretty quickly.[84]

The process across all European cities in the late 1950s was similar. In industrial Milan, there was a brief 'communal' phase of television watching, but by 1960 the television rooms in bars were largely deserted. For rich working-class families, the *salotto*, or parlour, ceased being 'for best', and became a TV-oriented room, and for the vast majority it sat in the kitchen-diner, playing through mealtimes by 1961. Chairs were arranged around the set, not around the table; different family members had established special places—and many acquired specific chairs for the watching of television. As one bar owner from a working-class suburb of Milan complained, 'They used to argue, play cards, sing and drink. I used to have a sore throat from talking and singing. Now they watch television.'[85] The photographs from the time, such as Figure 3.5, show that very often, people might even have their *backs* to each other: children, perhaps sitting on the floor in front of the settee or sofa or couch, would have their backs to their parents, an unthinkable arrangement for familial social time twenty years earlier. The settee or couch was itself something of a novelty. Two-seater settees had existed in the 1930s, but grew larger and became more common after the war, as salaries rapidly rose across Europe. Thus, people began to emulate the seating arrangement of the music hall and the cinema in their own living rooms: long rows of relatively static seating; long periods of stillness; an increasingly reverential interpersonal silence for the consumption of culture.

The profound revolution this spatial rearrangement has caused in the ways people relate to one another has still not fully worked itself out, as now televisions are often distributed throughout homes. This has meant that whatever residual sociability was left in this collective 'disregarding' is now lived out in a yet more atomized way with no sociability at all. And in those countries where urbanization was greatest, there were most television sets; and where there were least television sets, conventional family structures remained longest. By 1995, even the supposedly 'social' or collective experience of watching television reveals a further atomization. While in Britain, there were 1,433 televisions per 1,000 inhabitants, in Germany there were 944, and in France 895—this despite those countries being wealthier than Britain at that time. What this says about the spatial distribution of people *within* homes is hard to interpret with precision, but clearly, in Britain, more people are watching television alone. No one keeps more than one television in a room, so televisions must be cropping up in more and more rooms around the house. Even the living room, silent and ordered as it has become, seems to be less and less the focus of any sort of sociability. This is echoed by the consumption of radio culture in the car as a private space. The revolution that was begun in the 1890s, turning people away from each other for the consumption of culture, has been completed. The revolution has moved from the most spectacular spaces of city centres to the most intimate, private, and secret spaces of city suburbs.

* * *

Music underwent three major revolutions in the mid–late 1950s: one technological, one stylistic, and one spatial. The technological revolution meant that the 78rpm record was made redundant. It was heavy, brittle, difficult to make, expensive, had poor quality mono sound, and could not hold a large amount of music. While the 78rpm single could hold roughly five minutes of music, the 12-inch, 33⅓rpm long player could hold forty-five minutes. Although the technology was first introduced in 1948, the impact of it was not felt until the late 1950s, when stereo recording became possible and when artists began to realize that the whole record, both sides, had to be viewed as one *oeuvre* and the relationship of song to song was crucial. This made the album a larger, more coherent 'artistic' project than popular music in the technological age had been until then. The short record made popular music a music of fragments; the album made artists' outputs more substantial, more complete, more self-consciously whole. The modern 45-minute 'album' was born in the late 1950s, and remained the dominant musical form from 1960 until the early 2000s, when downloaded music meant that the artist once again lost all control over the sequence in which their music was played.

The stylistic revolution is one that has received most attention: rock'n'roll transformed the popular music market in the private sphere of the home in the same way that dance halls had done in the public sphere of the dance. It segmented music sales by generation, creating a highly fragmented set of markets and styles and tastes, which, with the new technology, was cheap enough for the first time to be purchased by young people on 7-inch and 12-inch records with money they might earn from Saturday and evening jobs, or from full-time work if they were over fifteen. Using the new electrically amplified guitars, rock'n'roll eliminated all the other instruments conventionally used in popular music apart from percussion, killing off the big band. Electro-amplification offered a stripped-down sound of vocalist, one or two electric guitars, and with both drums and bass guitar providing rhythm. Lyrics focused on the expression of sexual energy, and the beats and melodies stimulated a kind of dancing which did the same. Indeed, 'rock'n'roll' was just American slang for sex: 'You wanna rock'n'roll with me?' Initially, in both France and Britain, 'copycat' artists were rapidly produced by record companies, like Johnny Halliday and Cliff Richard, who worked to reproduce the 'rockabilly' white rock'n'roll sound which Elvis had made so prevalent. But within five years, Europe, and specifically, Britain and to an extent Germany, had begun to produce and consume an authentic sound, now called 'rock' or 'pop'—in France, it was called *le yé-yé*, due to the frequency of those lyrics in the songs.

But parallel to this live music phenomenon, another, perhaps more important, was developing. In the late 1950s, amplification technology made it possible to play recorded music *loud*, and this gave birth in Paris to the *discothèque*, the first of which was opened in the late 1930s, the early 1940s, the late 1940s, or the late 1950s, depending on one's definition of what a disco actually is. At any rate, it seems that it was in Paris that discos and nightclubs as we would currently recognize them came into existence. Some have claimed that the first disco was started at the bar La Discothèque on the rue Huchette during or before the war; it is certainly true that during the war, a ban on *musique nègre* was easily circumvented in the whole of occupied Europe by playing records on loudspeakers in cellar clubs, but this was regarded as a poor second to a live band playing *la musique hot*, rather than the ideal form of the music itself.[86]

In fact, the occupation of France boosted the listenership of jazz enormously, and promoted a reliance on records. In the early 1930s, some jazz purists founded the Hot Club de France in Paris, which played only 'non-whitified', 'authentic' jazz from the USA—in particular, Louis Armstrong. Four more Hot Clubs were opened before the war, but in the period between 1940 and 1944, some sixty-one Hot Clubs had opened—an enormous leisure chain, with several branches in all the major cities, again underlining the capacity of the spaces of the city to render irrelevant the ambitions of the totalitarian state. The chain was broken up in 1944, in part by the occupiers and Vichy, but realistically, no 'national' organization of any sort could survive the chaos in France of 1944. By liberation, thirty-seven had reopened. They presented a mixture of records and live music.

But even before this, by the very end of the 1930s, following the enormous success of *Je suis swing*, and *J'ai sauté la barrière, hop-la!*, the most freestyling, virtuoso jazz was widespread in French cities. *Je suis swing* contained the first use of the word *zazou*, a culture of sharp-dressing, baggy-suited, jazz-loving wide-boys and dilettantes which came to characterize a distinctively Parisian circumvention of the Occupiers' and Vichy morality. Their symbolic potency was recognized in the 1943 hit, *Ils sont zazous!* Their haunts were the Café Pam-Pam on the Champs Elysées, and the cafés in the university quarter around the Boul'Mich, emphasizing the upper-middle-class nature of the audience. One news report summed up the impact of a star like Johnny Hess, like this:

> The youth have all made him their idol. They cut out all the photos of him, they fight each other to get an autograph from him, and the great rallying cry of all the people under twenty is the famous, 'Zazou! Zazou!'[87]

However, it would not have been 'everyone' under twenty: it would have been only those who were in Paris, who were not working twelve-hour days, and who could access the old, baggy clothes that defined the *zazou* style. Bars like Dupont-Latin or Capoulade were where the identity became real, defined by sartorial style, musical preference and a lazy antipathy to occupation. But this marginal and oppositional nature was important, because it cemented an underground culture with a sophisticated infrastructure, linked directly to dance, *musique nègre*, and a specific generation—one that had been too young to surrender in 1940, but old enough to attend nightclubs in 1944, defining the style and consciousness of an urban generation. The focus was on recorded music—but this was still a compromise. In short, it produced a pop subculture.

In 1947 Paul Pacine opened Whiskey-a-Go-Go, something dangerously close to a disco, but with frequent live music, and with breaks in the playing of recorded music. It had garish décor and an elite clientele, and provided something of a blueprint. It played black US jazz and served trendy drinks, basing many of its cocktails on whisky, an exotic drink in France at the time, which inspired its tartan décor and which could be sold at a premium price. Soon, a chain of such 'clubs' was opened in several European cities. Not long after, Jean Castle opened Discothèque Chez Castle, but still there were breaks in the music, and live music was played. It was not really until 1960, when Pacine opened Chez Régine, managed by Régine Zylberberg, that the amplification was up to focusing just on recorded music, played non-stop. The recent introduction of stereo recording meant that it sounded good, too.

It was at Chez Régine that all the ingredients of the modern disco came together: Régine Zylberberg had started out as the toilet attendant at the first Whiskey-a-Go-Go, and ended up managing the new disco. It had all the garish, heavily stylized glamour of Whiskey-a-Go-Go, combined with an aggressive door policy which made it hard (and therefore desirable and socially distinctive) to get in, combined with non-stop recorded music, played partly to the request of guests, and partly according to the 'set' of a DJ, and at such a volume that chatting was difficult and non-stop dance inevitable. Of huge importance was the recent success of the twist, because it was a dance that did not need a partner, so any number of dancers could take part in any sort of configuration—males, females, mixed, small groups, large groups. Anyone could twist: the dance revolution was complete, moving from the predominantly social structure of dance before 1900, to personal interpretation of the music between two people between the wars, to personal interpretation on one's own by the century's halfway point.

For the first few weeks, Pacine made a horrific loss because of his door policy, but he was resolved to have a queue outside the club for most of the night even if it was totally empty inside. It paid off, and gave rise to one of the clearest spatial expressions of 'identity' in the modern city: the club. Olivier Coquelin took the concept to New York in 1960 with Le Club, which soon caught on with the Peppermint Lounge opening on West 45th Street in Manhattan. In Britain, the first London disco was La Discothèque in Wardour Street in Soho in London, which had all-black décor, red lighting, a gold entrance hall, and leopard-skin wallpaper in the toilets. It opened in 1962, but was slightly beaten to the prize of 'Britain's first disco' by The Place in 'downtown' Stoke-on-Trent, a heavy-industrial city in the north Midlands. The Place staked its radical credentials by being the first club to do away with seating around the dance floor; instead, double beds were provocatively set out.[88] It is a strange feature of British culture that many Northern and Midland industrial cities, some of modest size, have had a disproportionate impact on cultural life; it was in Wigan and Manchester in the late 1960s and 1970s, for example, that soul music was first widely popularized for a white, working-class audience in Europe.

Some dance-hall etiquette persisted into the 1960s, and the new clubs and discos, like the Ritz in Manchester, where Jimmy Saville first connected two turntables and mixed two records together uninterrupted creating the first segue, continued to emphasize partnered dancing. Saville's attempt to produce a seamless, 'total' music experience was crucial, because it allowed the DJ to create a 'set', which would lead a crowd through a set of ever more euphoric stages, before 'dropping' them down again to begin the 'build'. The segue broke forever the custom of 'asking for a dance', because in seamless music, dances never start or stop.

While clubs were designed to enable a para-sexual encounter amongst young people (para-sexual, because it was often the paraphernalia, accoutrements, and preludes to sex, rather than sex itself, that formed the focus of activity), they could also be potent arenas for discovering one's confidence. One observer attempted to characterize the behaviour of men in a disco in late 1960s suburban London:

> Scattered around the hall are clusters of boys in curious aggressive stances: heads thrust forward, backs arched like longbows, arms folded in front of their bodies. They will gaze at the girls but rarely ask them to dance. Occasionally, one will burst into rapid movement, then, dissatisfied, lope off to a new station on the floor. Simultaneously, three or four others will rise up like a flock of birds and follow him.[89]

Only with the disco revolution in the mid–late 1970s would it become completely normal to dance on one's own, despite the success of earlier 'novelty' dances like the twist. In modern club etiquette, one does not ask anyone to dance—a habit which persisted in dance halls in the 1960s, and which even remained for the final, slow dances in the

1970s and early 1980s. In the modern disco, one dances on one's own, and creates a display on the dance floor that is designed to attract the sexually interested. Conversation in the disco and post-disco age follows convincing and mutually acceptable dance displays, it does not precede it. In the interwar dance hall, talking enabled dancing; in the post-war disco, dancing enabled the talking.

The development of the 45rpm single, stereo recording, and strong sound amplification meant these 'discos' could be set up for very little money, and with a high degree of mobility, but in the early days (the 1960s) they followed a very simple format. There would be a bar, a dance floor, and usually an area for sitting down. In lots of ways, it would seem that these were a trivial, peripheral feature of the modern culturescape, but they were far from it, because of the type of very specific identity formation that these micro-spaces of the city—inhabited only between 10 p.m. and 2, 4, or 6 a.m., and often only once or twice a week—called into being. It was these quite transient, nocturnal, invisible places that enabled the subcultures to emerge which have defined many of the ways we see the world and ourselves in it in the late twentieth century, in terms of our age, ethnicity, class, gender, and sexuality. In particular, it is hard to imagine movements of gay or black equality existing without the spaces of the nightclubs; but more generally, they solidified the conception of 'young' people as a separate interest group or constituency with particular clarity.

It may seem peculiar to argue that subculture can define the mainstream, but it might help to think about it like this: subcultures exist on the edge of society—gay, black, radical, political, druggy, hippy, working-class, poor, punk—but if enough of them exist, then they can end up ringing the 'mainstream' culture like a horizon. It is by looking at the horizon, or the edges, that an observer locates him or herself in the landscape. Such clubs did not dominate in numerical terms in the urban landscape of the 1960s (where, for example, working men's clubs of some sort were common across Europe, offering a mix of music-hall acts and palais de danse atmospheres), but there were enough of them to cultivate a vibrant and noticeable subculture across a heavily urbanized society like Britain: Liverpool had the Iron Door, the Mardi Gras, and the Cavern; Manchester had the Oasis, the Three Coins, and the Twisted Wheel; Newcastle had the Guys and Dolls and Club-a-Go-Go; Cardiff had Disc-a-Go-Go. They marked

out the 'edge', but such a network of clubs is often seen by mainstream culture as a totality, as one coherent thing, threatening and
encircling, and they come to define the mainstream. Eventually,
through their conquest of space, risqué cultures can acquire a symbolic power which not only defines and characterize the lives of the
thousands who inhabit them, but the millions that observe and befriend
those people, or who borrow elements of their style in an ad hoc fashion. Furthermore, through their conquest of time, these peripheral
identities can come to dominate what it means to be 'nightlife' or
'Saturday', then while not immediately entering the mainstream, they
can help shape it. And if they can help shape the mainstream long
enough, eventually they will be absorbed into it.

So it was in nightclubs and discos in Paris and Cologne and London
and Manchester that gay men first began to associate with each other
in large numbers in a stable geographical way—through the emergence of a 'scene'. Through a network of bars, pubs, and clubs, gay
men and women became aware that they were a group of people with
something profoundly important to say about the world, and their
own place in it. David Robins and Philip Cohen were two left-wing
social workers in Islington, which was then a very poor inner-city
district of north London in the 1970s (it is now prosperous and fashionable, with the poverty neatly ghettoized). Seeking to challenge
some of the clichés of the liberal left's romanticizations of the working
class, they talked of how, in the early 1970s as youth workers, they
had witnessed the revolution on council estates which was enabled by
the club revolution in the city centre, and the types of brutal violence
that it had encountered in working-class cultures:

> One evening on the Wall by the Monmouth Estate, Tommy arrived
> looking like David Bowie, complete with make-up and streaked hair.
> Chorus of hoots, wolf whistles and jeers from the Wall. Then Mich,
> who used to be a close friend of Tommy's but is now more involved
> with his motor bike, starts to have a go at him. 'Where's your handbag,
> dearie? Going out with your fella then?'[90]

The club offered people like Tommy a place where they were 'normal' and 'in', where they could explore their identity—whatever it
was—on their own terms. It was because discos existed which could
survive on a very small scale and move from venue to venue with

portable P.A.s, enabling them to make money, that the daring theatricality and spectacular marketing of a man like Bowie could be transformed into a real act of personal politics in people's everyday lives. Provided they lived in a city.

In the early 1970s, even *The Sunday Times* noted how the disco culture was transforming urban life, noting that the second generation of West Indians in Britain were splitting apart culturally from their parents, and that the vehicle for this change was the nightclub. Crucially, these clubs were full of working-class white people too, enabling a horizontal cultural exchange across ethnic boundaries within the same generation. When this type of racial mixing was seen in public—for example, at school discos—it could cause scandal. For example, *The Sunday Times* had a special report in its new colour supplement on the dance culture of south London:

> There are two main ways of dancing: separately, several feet apart, cool, casual; or together, thighs between thighs, rocking gently, sometimes almost motionless, openly sexual. Both horrify some whites, particularly the second: 'It's disgusting,' cried a woman teacher at a school dance, 'They're masturbating in there!'[91]

Whether it was the sexuality of dancing to, say, David Bowie or T-Rex, or the miscegenation that bothered her most, it is hard to tell.

It was in the reggae and ska clubs of Brixton in London, Moss Side in Manchester, Toxteth in Liverpool, and Handsworth in Birmingham that the disparate identities of Britain's West Indian migrants shaped a *common* identity which eventually would come to dominate Britain's cultural mainstream. London clubs like The Roaring Twenties, Four Aces, 007, and Ram Jam were not, however, part of some indiscernible, inevitable 'trend' towards cultural exchange and racial toleration: someone had to open them, market them, pay rent on them, convince a brewery to supply them, get a music licence from magistrates, fill out tax returns. Newton Dunbar was a new Jamaican immigrant to London's East End in the 1960s, and was frustrated at not hearing music he liked, and being barred from many clubs because he was black. To challenge his exclusion from mainstream culture, he established the Four Aces at 12 Dalston Lane in Hackney. There, he played Desmond Dekker, Prince Buster, Jimmy Cliff, Percy Sledge, and Billy Ocean in the 1960s to black and white alike, before moving on to The Rudies, Bob Marley, and resident DJs like Sir Coxon, and even punk, like The Slits and The Sex Pistols, in the 1970s. His life was recently made into a film, *Legacy in the Dust: The Four Aces Story*, showing the ways a club might transform the status of an individual from 'outsider' to 'mainstream'. The important point here is that this process required individuals like Dunbar to commit to organizing a specific space—like the Four Aces—to draw in an urban crowd, and give them an identity.

Linton Kwesi Johnson is another Jamaican-born Briton who grew up in south London in the 1960s, and has come to be regarded as one of the best poets alive in English—one of the few living poets whose work is published as a Penguin Classic. But he started out doing 'dub reggae', a type of prototype rap in Britain, and wrote (or sang or spoke) in 1975, in his poem *Yout Scene*:

> last satdey
> I nevah deh pan no faam,
> so I decide fi tek a walk
> doun a Brixton
> an see wha gwaan.
>
> 'de bredrin dem stan-up
> outside a HIP CITY
> as usual, a look pretty;
> dem a laaf big laaf
> dem a talk dread talk
> dem a shuv and shuffle dem feat
> soakin in de sweet musical beat.
>
> but when nite come
> policeman run dem dung;
> beat dem dung a grung,
> kick dem ass,
> sen dem paas justice
> to prison walls of gloom.
>
> but di breddah dem a scank;
> dem naw rab bank;
> is pakit dem a pick
> an is woman dem a lick
> an is run dem a run when di wicked come.[92]

The city and music allowed a new culture to be formed—Johnson here shouting the significance of being out and about in a 'HIP CITY' as going out and having fun at the core of the experience of joy in modern culture, and organizing a resistance to the police who hassle them in public. The battle is not yet won, and racism still abounds, but an authentically 'white' British, or European, culture is now simply unimaginable thanks to the cultural work done in places like nightclubs, bars, and discos.

Even for a youth that was white, heterosexual, and 'free', the nightclub or disco had come, by the 1980s, to define identity for many—perhaps even most. In the 1990s sociologists and anthropologists (though not yet historians) began to focus on the environment of the nightclub. Having noted that most people under forty define their identities and the 'type' of person they are in terms of these urban environments, they have given substantial resources to investigating them—though it has proved far from easy. One such investigator was trying to interview one clubber, 'Bruce', about his experiences of music and dancing. Bruce responded by quoting Elvis Costello: 'Talking about music is like dancing about architecture'—an apposite comment on the difficulties of talking about lived culture in general.

But what seems clear is that dancing in these clubs at the century's close means sex, love, escape, and a 'high'—whether drug-induced or not. One clubber, Sim, said of his dancing:

> Oh yeah, you want to look horny, and I go off dancing on my own quite happily, and then part of it is just this display thing, part of it is just like, uh, a sort of martial arts sort of thing of control…and the other thing is you do get an amazing rush.

And in this rush, whether induced by alcohol, ecstasy, or the combination of pounding, racing beat and dance, identities, sub-identities and micro-identities are formed as the club is subdivided. With few words, an identity is formed:

> Mike said that we should start dancing in a circle because then we get more room, because usually you're like facing the front like a fucking tribe!

Another clubber, Luke, observed:

As a matter of fact, most of the time I move within a relatively small
area of a club. Every place in a club seems to attract a different type
of people, even in small clubs. Sometimes it even goes so far that I can
feel a little uncomfortable when being in the 'wrong' area. Not that I'm
afraid of anyone or anything, it's just that things don't seem to fit.[93]

Anyone familiar with club culture will know what he is talking about.
In Manchester, where I am writing this now, there are, just amongst
gay clubs, ones which focus on black customers and white people who
like R'n'B, rap, and hip-hop; ones which attract older people; there
are clubs with a strong ethnic mix, and ones with a weak one. There
are clubs for big and hairy people; younger people; people who like
the gym; people who like pop, 'indie', dance, folk, piano. There are
clubs which have a more working-class clientele and ones which have
a more middle-class clientele. And within these clubs, there are spaces
which sort of them out into yet smaller 'identifying' groups. And gay
people in Manchester can describe a man, characterize him, by saying
which sort of club he goes to, and where he would typically be found
dancing within it—'Strictly downstairs at Essential'; 'Always in the
experimental electro room at HomoElectric'.

This capacity for clubland to furnish an arena and an infrastructure
for the development of powerful subcultures was commented on right
at the birth of disco, in a seminal essay by cultural theorist Richard
Dyer. Writing in the troubled summer of 1979 for the magazine *Gay
Left*, he wrote an essay called 'In Defence of Disco', which justified the
phenomenon in the face of an angry, masculinist, and often violent
punk, rock, and punk-rock backlash—a backlash which the fears surrounding the AIDS catastrophe in the 1980s encouraged. But crucially, it was not the musical *product* of disco that he found
liberating—despite the cliché of some of the song titles (*I'm comin' out,
You make me feel mighty real, We are family, I will survive*). Most of these
were songs written by straight white men for black women to sing so
that large corporations could make money. There is no particular
reason why gay men should feel any real sense of affinity with straight
black women or large corporations. But on the dance floor, in a specific place at a specific time, the bodily experience of the song, and
the dancing and the sweat and the alcohol and the euphoria, they
were used as powerful agents of identity formation—and sexual
adventure, and fun. As Dyer himself concluded in 1979, along with
thousands of sweaty others, 'Disco can't change the world, make the

revolution. No art can do that and it is pointless expecting it to. But partly by opening up experience, partly by changing definitions, art, disco, can be used. To which one might risk adding the refrain—If it feels good, *use* it.'[94] It is the *use* of the nightclub which impresses so.

* * *

It is this culture—this urban culture—which has not only character-ized and documented the fundamental shifts in people's lives in Europe in the twentieth century, but produced them. Culture is not merely the place to look to see the *consequences* of change; there lie its agents too. Culture is not just the barometer of changes taking place else-where; it *is* those changes. The cultures of the music hall, the football ground, the jazz bar, the dance hall, the cinema, the living room, and the disco have driven and produced a revolution in people's lives in the twentieth century, and these cultures are geographically fixed. Culture does not float above us, but lives with us. The teenager, mod-ern sexuality, family life, sociability, capitalism—they have all been defined, produced, or enabled by music halls, football stadia, cinemas, palais de danse, living rooms, and nightclubs. Some of the most fun-damental social changes of the twentieth century have been effected, and made acceptable to us and comprehensible by us, because they have been so central to our cultural experiences. We can begin to appreciate the importance of these phenomena for shaping our view of the world, and forming our understanding of our place within it, by a process of subtraction.

Many people, of all sorts of social classes, have profited from the places of high culture—theatres, operas and, above all, museums and galleries. We know from the life narratives of many people how impor-tant wandering into a museum and seeing great art has been. But if we start a process of subtraction, we can see how important other, less studied, less subsidized spaces have been for the ways we represent the world to ourselves and to others. If one imagines the history of the twentieth century, but lived out in cities with no subsidized ballets or operas or art galleries, this history does not look radically different from the twentieth century that we have seen, however much specific individuals might have gained from them. Human sexuality would probably have developed in the same way; human sociability would probably have developed the same way. Our experience of life would have become just as divided by generation as it has become, and class and ethnicity would have become less relevant to the ways that people understood the world, and represented it to themselves and each other. The development of masculinity would have been unchanged, and the impact on the ways we have dealt with migration would have been negligible. The wonder of twentieth-century art, opera, classical music—glorious achievements as they undoubtedly were—changed the lives of very few people. 'Culture with a capital C' is, despite the aspirations and convictions of its practitioners, largely irrelevant to most humans' experience of the world. That is not to say it is bad, or 'equivalent' in quality to a rap song or swing played in a hot club; just less relevant to most living, breathing people, who must always be at the centre of history.

But let us now imagine a world without the capitalist revolution in the music hall and the cinema, and the new restraints on bodily movement and disposition that they introduced, the disconnect between audience and performer it set up, the 'industry' of show business that it established, and the fantasy of America that it promoted. If this were 'subtracted' from the twentieth century, its history would have had to have been unrecognizably changed. Imagine that we all talked to each other in cramped bars or our single-room dwellings in the evenings. Imagine we all moved around randomly during any sort of performance. Imagine you had spoken to every artist who had touched your heart with a song, and he or she had held your hand while he or she sang it. Imagine facing your family every evening for the whole evening. Imagine dancing according to rules and in social formation, instead of interpreting the music freely with your body. Imagine life as a 'teenager', with nowhere for teenagers to go separate from their parents. Imagine being in the 1930s and 1940s with no cinema—a war fought with no trips to the picture 'palace'—imagine the gags favoured by 1970s stand-up comedy, but stripped of the deviant, coded space of the 'back row of the cinema'. Imagine being a man without football. Imagine family life or political debate with no television. Imagine gay liberation and the experience of adolescence and young adulthood with no pop, no discos. There is little left. And this profound revolution in our bodies, manners, sex lives, identities, self-images, genders, and families happened without a single law being passed. It happened because of the evolution of the spaces and places of the modern city.

4

Sex and the City

It is a man's birthday in Berlin—his name is unknown. He is working class, poor, homosexual. He organizes a party in the private room of a *Kneipe*, or pub, in a working-class suburb. He invites all his friends, and his two heterosexual brothers are there. They eat typical German working-class food: potatoes done a variety of ways, Bockwurst, Swiss cheese. The landlord's son plays on the piano, and parodies the biggest names of show business with exaggerated gestures—especially Isadora Duncan. A drag queen happens to be in the front, in the public bar. She comes into the back, and the group asks her to perform her repertoire. Suddenly, a massive man comes in: a coal haulier from the canal boats, a real tough, covered in tattoos, a skinhead in a thick sweater, with 'that special mix of stockiness and agility which workers of that type' have. There is a moment of tension. Then he lets rip with a series of smutty songs in a broad Berlin accent, accompanied with gestures and *double entendres*, and the odd pirouette between verses. It has quite an effect—such that everyone clears the tables and chairs and begins dancing amidst great hilarity. Closing time arrives but goes unnoticed—and suddenly in the middle of the room the local policeman is standing, with all the dignity his office can muster. He grabs one of the people there round the waist—a gay musician—and begins a waltz. This is so sudden and dramatic, that the musician does not have time to resist, and they end up being (with the landlord's son and the coal haulier) the most honoured and in-demand dancers of the evening. The year? Around 1900.[1] We need to ask some questions about when, exactly, sexuality became 'open', and looking at the real spaces and places of the city can help us do that.

This chapter is about the changing role of sexual identity in people's ideas of themselves, and in the state's ideas of people. So it is a story of the state and the citizen, and the person and their self-regard.

'Sexuality' is a category that we view today as relatively 'fixed'. Outside the small community of historians, it is sometimes assumed that the past was a sexually conservative place—people talk of 'Victorian values', and assume that people did not know much about sex. This chapter will challenge that view, and show how the sexual melee of 1900 was tamed in the twentieth century, transforming the ways people viewed themselves and each other, and revolutionizing the relationship between the state and the citizen, and the state and people's bodies. In order to trace this story, I will focus on sexual activity and identity between men. This may seem wilfully controversial, but I am relying on this group for evidence for three main reasons.

First, while the history of 'homo'sexuality in the great academic libraries is thin compared to, say, the history of laws, politics, warfare, or medicine, the history of 'hetero'sexuality is close to non-existent.[2] On one of the largest global databases of historical research used by professional historians, there are 393 pieces of research with the word 'homosexual' in the summary. A similar search for 'heterosexual' revealed less than one hundred pieces of research—and many of these only mention 'heterosexuality' as something that homosexuality had to reject or overcome. It seems we know four times as much about the periphery, than the centre. There are many histories of masculinity, women, the family, and marriage—but none of these things is quite the same thing as sexuality in general, or heterosexuality in particular. So 'homo'-sexuality will have to stand as a yardstick for sexuality in general, not because I am trying to make some radical or controversial point, but because that is where most of the scholarship lies. And while 'gay' people may be a minority, they have a sense of self similar to any other person, and are individual citizens relating to big states, just like any other person.

The reason the scholarship on sexuality focuses more on 'homo' than 'hetero' is this. Men who have sex with men have been persecuted (generally incompetently and erratically) by both the police and the medical establishment, and the 'authorities' have called upon their 'patients' or 'criminals' to describe and narrate and discuss and explain their actions. These 'authorities' have written this down and put the evidence into archives. Heterosexuals have tended to be persecuted for their sexuality only when they have mingled it with money—and this poses a problem when thinking about sexuality, rather than sex. Sex is an act, but sexuality is a complex constellation of possibilities, habits, and beliefs. Few people identify with sex for money, whether prostitutes or their 'Johns'. I would still have included it here, though, if there were enough research to draw on; after all, the literature on prostitution in nineteenth-century cities is prolific.[3] But the interest in prostitution in Europe in the *twentieth* century is nothing like as detailed, and is far less concerned with the prostitute and her customer as people, and far more with them as symbols of reproductive politics.[4] Historians' interests in the twentieth century have focused far more on prostitution in the developing world on the one hand,[5] and 'discourses' about sex on the other.[6] What historians know about twentieth-century prostitution in Europe is minuscule by comparison. It is strange, but 'heterosexuality' rather drops off the historical radar in the twentieth century.

The nature of the documents does, though, mean a distortion in the record; one which it is important to recognize. Men who have sex with men often 'crop up' only when they are arrested or 'treated'—when they are 'bad' or when they are 'sick'. Thus, a word of warning is necessary: the men who have sex with men in this chapter might appear to be criminal deviants, intent on having sex in as many public spaces as possible, and often for cash. However, sexual activity in public was (and still is) a common feature of heterosexual behaviour—it is just that it rarely led to arrest. And while it was viewed as 'normal' in the twentieth century for men to treat women to meals, and for a woman to live on a man's salary, when two men did this, it was often classed as gravely immoral and such men might be charged with sodomy or gross indecency. This is important because 'normal' transactions in heterosexual behaviour were given a 'sexuality' when two men did it. Even today, 'parasexual' behaviour in public which is acceptable for heterosexuals (such as kissing, holding hands, petting, caressing hair) is more difficult to express for men who wish to have sex with men, than it is for men who have sex with women. So we need to be careful that we do not 'freakify' the behaviour of men who have sex with men.

Finally, this smaller sexual group can represent more than 'just' men who have sex with men. It is dangerous to assume that only gay people have sexuality—everyone has it (or, has come to have it), unstated as it may be—and this has been a profound revolution in the ways that we see ourselves. Men who have sex with men can stand as an index of so many things, not just the rights of the marginalized and persecuted.

The history of sexuality offers us more than 'just' the history of the bedroom. It offers us the history of the state, and its relationships to the citizen; the history of the body, and who owns it; the history of the law, its ambitions, effectiveness, and relevance to people's everyday lives; the history of medicine; it opens up the history of identity, masculinity, the family, childhood, and selfhood; it marks out the boundaries of privacy; it opens up the history of *space* and shows how suffused with sex it is.[7] And while the focus here is on men who chose to have sex with men, these issues affect everyone, young and old, male and female, 'normal' and 'abnormal'. A history of sexuality—*anyone's* sexuality— can help us understand how *everyone's* lives have changed—albeit with the 'corrupt' evidence of a one-sided archive.[8]

* * *

One major question that has troubled historians has been whether people before 1900 identified themselves with a 'sexuality' at all. It seems that 'self-identification' was heavily dependent on class: middle-class people by 1900 may just about have had a nebulous identifica-tion with a sexuality; working-class people seem to have had little 'political' identity with their sexuality. That is not at all to say that people did not have preferences for sexual partners of one sex, the other, or both: they did, and they firmly pursued these preferences. But it seems likely that very few people in 1900 made that an impor-tant part of how they saw themselves.

One influential doctor in Paris in the 1880s spoke for most doctors throughout Europe at the end of the nineteenth century when he presented a case of a type that was becoming more and more com-mon in doctors' surgeries:

> To start, here is the patient's own narrative of the bizarre phenomena that he experiences and that he associates with his so-called sensuality:
>
> 'My sensuality,' he says, 'manifested itself from the age of six by a violent desire to see boys of my age or men, naked....About the age of fifteen, puberty arrived; masturbating gave me even greater satisfac-tion...More than once I had an erection, an amorous convulsion, and seminal loss at the mere sight of a man's virile member....'
>
> The patient thus describes the characteristics of this irrepressible obsession of which he is fully aware.
>
> This sick person, what is he?[9]

This medical language, ending in the question, 'What is he?', was a genuine, open question at the end of the nineteenth century. The young Parisian being interviewed by the doctor described not his *sexu*-ality, but his *sens*uality. It was not part of his 'being' that he admired other men, but part of the way he sought to explore his senses. Jean-Martin Charcot—the doctor writing here—was convinced of the man's sickness, but sickness was better than crime. It was Charcot who opened the door to Freud, who studied alongside him at La Salpêtrière in the mid-1880s. And many in Europe classified homo-sexuality—or Uranism, unisexualité, inversion, and Urning, as the phenomenon was variously called at the time—as profoundly urban and modern and new.

What seems to have shocked doctors in the 1890s in particular was not the act itself—they recognized that people had been doing that since time immemorial, versed as all educated men at that time were in Greek culture. Instead, they were part of a cultural mainstream that fretted that cities so alienated mankind from 'his' natural self, so caught 'him' up in speed and technology, and so separated 'him' from the seasons and the earth and nature, that all sorts of moral and racial degenerations would follow, of which homosexuality was merely one. It was a commonplace of public debate around 1900 in Europe that cities corrupted mankind completely—racially, morally, economically, spiritually, psychologically, sexually. The widespread conviction on the part of Europe's urban elites that cities were causing a degeneration of the race was made starkly real for them in men who had sex with men almost above all things: 'inverts' and 'unisexuals' not only challenged the norms of Judaeo-Christian morality, but of necessity proposed a lifestyle completely detached from reproduction and therefore the pres-ervation of the race on the one hand, and the bourgeois family and the preservation of the social order on the other. One typical and hugely influential French doctor, Georges de Saint-Paul, collated a vast array of data on 'inversion' in the mid-1890s in French cities, because:

> These days, no one doubts that the number of degenerations, of cere-bral derailings—expressed by the tendencies towards suicide, phobias, etc—results in large part from the fact that in our nation the genital functions are often not accomplished as they should be. Therefore it is necessary, from the point of view of the vitality of the future of the race, to study the morbid causes, to discern the dangerous and evil

elements, among which must be ranked for an appreciable part the creature stricken with sexual perversion: the pervert, the feminiform born-invert.[10]

Thousands of doctors, journalists, preachers, imperialists, and scientists agreed. They said similar things about many forms of heterosexual practice too, being especially worried about the consequences of the female orgasm, female frigidity, male and female masturbation, oral sex, or any of the myriad features of sexual activity that people clearly regularly engaged in by their millions, but which did not fit the 'medical model' of healthy sex, focused on relieving male 'urges' and reproduction.[11] But at the end of the nineteenth century, and allied closely with the birth of psychology, psychoanalysis, and psychiatry, this slowly began to change.

Doctors and thinkers like Marc Raffalovich in Paris, Sigmund Freud in Vienna, Magnus Hirschfeld and Carl Friedrich Westphal in Berlin, and Edward Carpenter and Havelock Ellis in London, began to conclude for themselves what the habitués of the bar in Berlin were making clear in their everyday lives: a man who had sex with other men may still be 'masculine' and 'normal' in every other regard. As Raffalovich concluded in 1897, damning Saint-Paul's work but justifying the experiences of countless bars, factories, docks, and barracks that he had studied in Paris, Lyon, Lille, and Marseilles:

> It seems to me that that the fundamental error of his [Saint-Paul's] work is that he is driven to study inversion through books rather than an impartial and penetrating observation of life, and at more than one moment, personal scruples trouble the experimenter. [Saint-Paul's] imagined ideal of man comes to interrupt his science and science contradicts his ideal. Also, he is really far too sensitive to study sexuality; he writhes, he pushes himself, he defies himself, he knots himself up. All of a sudden that mysterious modesty that unisexuality imposes upon so many men strips him of his courage.[12]

We see here the idea emerging, not of sensuality, but *sexuality*: a part of a man's being. And the act of 'being' unisexual implies a level of masculine courage and self-discipline on the part of 'the' unisexual that many 'normal' doctors would fail to match.

Raffalovich's reports of the gay Paris underworld of the *fin de siècle* scandalized the French medical establishment. He estimated that there were 50,000–100,000 'upstanding and un-effeminate', which effectively meant 'middle class', homosexuals in Paris, in addition to the unknown thousands in the classes below. And it was not just in Paris that medical science was uncovering 'normal' homosexuals. In 1909, one Russian psychology textbook described two men in St Petersburg:

> They concluded a formal agreement between themselves, in which each swore faithfulness to the other to the grave, and they adopted the mutual appellations of man and wife. They occupied a single room and at night slept in one bed. As a ruse there were two beds in the room, and they went to bed separately for several minutes, and then the one who had to play the role of 'husband' in this revolting union came to his 'wife' and they would spend the night together.[13]

But when various people in St Petersburg were asked by doctors what or who they were, they refused to name themselves, rejecting all the epithets—catamites, woman-haters, *tetka* (faggot, poof, queer) or whatever. The closest that one noted Russian historian has been able to find are the occasional references to 'our own kind'—a sort of nameless self-definition. In London, too, men who had sex with men refused to be called 'Marjories' or 'Mary-Anns', but had little idea of a name for themselves. This seems to imply that people at that time did not identify strongly with their sexuality. This does not mean that everyone was engaged in a sexual free-for-all: people clearly had stable preferences for partners of a specific sex. But they did not place these sexual preferences at the heart of who they were.

This act of 'self-naming' is important, because it highlights significant questions about which facets of our lives we most closely identify as being at the heart of our 'selves', and the nature of our relationship to wider society. The Berlin doctor, Magnus Hirschfeld, emphasizes a sense of a nascent identity amongst middle-class gay men with two Christmas tales from turn-of-the-century Berlin, both of which seem to show that some middle-class people did, by the turn of the century, increasingly view themselves as being a sexual 'type', gay, or straight. The first example comes from the words one of his 'patients' wrote to him in a Christmas card:

> Glory be to God on high, and peace to all men on earth! When will people finally see that our Saviour did not come so that we should be shut out from his gracious, noble, merciful, all-encompassing love?[14]

This is controversial, because historians have been polarized around this word 'we'. 'We' implies an identity: a group of people claiming to be a recognizable group. Ask the men in the bar in Berlin in 1900, 'Who are you? What are you?', and their answers would probably have been, 'I am a man. I am a Berliner. I am a canalman/police-man. I am a Protestant. I am a German.' Few of them would have thought to say, 'I am an invert' or 'I am a homosexual', or 'we' must be free—because the men in the bar in Berlin in 1900 already were free. So 'naming' can be as much a part of constraining individual personalities and identities, as liberating them.

For middle-class men, though, the situation could be quite different. Drawing again from his Berlin casebook, one Christmas Eve at the very end of the nineteenth century, Hirschfeld was called to a young man who had previously confronted his well-to-do father with his sexuality; there had been a fight, and he had been beaten; he had left home. On 24 December, the young man had gone back to the family home and observed it, the lights shining in the cold night. He heard his brothers and sisters laughing, saw the warmth and love through the windows. The young man got drunk, returned to his flat, doused it in blood, paraffin, and ink; he destroyed all the furniture, ripped up all his books, and hacked at himself with pen knives. He was immedi-ately taken to the psychiatric ward of Berlin's famous hospital, the Charité. Hirschfeld concluded:

> I washed and dressed him on that Christmas morning, one wound after the other; he did not complain and said nothing, but the burning eyes spoke and the blood-drained lips spoke and every single wound spoke, of his deep sorrow and the high, holy mission of those who work for the freedom of homosexuals.[15]

Taking a tour of the spaces and places of the European city over the last century can help build a picture of human sexuality that is lived between these two extremes—the psychiatric ward and the exuberant bar.

Let us be clear about one thing, though: our Victorian forefathers were no prudes. 'Victorian values' and talk of the 'traditional family' by media commentators today invokes a mythical past, and focuses on doctors and moralists rather than what people actually did. To walk the streets of any major European city at the turn of the last century seemed to many at the time to be a hyper-sexualized experience, not a prudish one. Because rooms and homes were often so overcrowded and unpleasant in 1900, much life was lived outside them, and so the street in 1900 had many of the same political and personal functions then that the home has now. Just as people played, chatted, worked, and wandered the streets, they lived their sex lives there too. It seems from middle-class diarists that if you wanted sex in the Edwardian city, 'the street's the place to go'. For example, one very senior British diplomat, Roger Casement, wrote in his diary in 1909:

> At F. O. [Foreign Office] from 11.30 looking over papers until 5. Home to Lizzie and Louie and after dinner to Brompton Rd. and Albert (10/-) [10 shillings] X. [sex] In Park. Then M.[arble] Arch and fine type in Park but fled and home at 12.50. 15½ years Albert.[16]

Let us pause a moment and consider what is happening here, because it will be a useful 'index' to the general level of sexual adventure being undertaken in turn-of-the-century cities: a senior diplomat regularly goes and has sex with a variety of men, some paid for, some not, some who are not men at all but children, in parks, *twice* on a work evening, in public. This is almost unimaginable to us now. And while the sexual freedom of the late-nineteenth-century city, for working-class Berliner or middle-class Londoner, is very impressive in our more morally constrained time, the debate about the sexual knowingness of '15½ years Albert' is fraught and complex. Was Albert earning 10/- (about half a week's wages for an unskilled, casually employed workman) for something that he enjoyed, and that he would have liked to do anyway, or something that he was compelled to do because of poverty? To assume that teenagers do not have a sexuality and are not aware of how to use it to their own ends risks idealizing them in the face of much evidence to the contrary; to assume that teenagers have a sexuality of which they are in full control risks legitimizing abuses of power. Urban places and spaces around 1900 were the spectacular arenas in which this debate was lived out.

The diaries of other rich contemporaries in London, like the influential British economist John Maynard Keynes or the American author, Edward Prime Stevenson, show that this was fairly typical.[17] Keynes' diaries noted exactly whom he had sex with, and in what circumstances—and totted the encounters up each quarter. In 1911, one finds the heading, 'Lift boy of Vauxhall':

> I did in the end stroll out on Tuesday night and bring a boy back. He told me that there are many fewer this week because last week the police were active and locked two up.[18]

While the police seem to have been active, they were not so active that either Keynes or Casement or the lads involved seemed to think it necessary to curtail their activities.

Another diarist's entry from around this time shows cities were not secretly sexual, but overtly so. London literary critic John Addington Symonds was fighting desperately against his 'urges' when he came across a piece of graffiti on a wall of two penises ejaculating over each other, and daubed next to it the words, 'Prick to Prick—so sweet!' This seems to have acted in a liberating way for him, for he then 'yielded' to his 'urges':

> The wolf leaped out: my malaise of the moment was converted into a clairvoyant and tyrannical appetite for the thing which I rejected five months earlier in the alley by the barracks.[19]

One set of experiences in a street—an encounter with a soldier by the barracks—is transformed by another—seeing the 'free' graffiti. The graffiti raises a more interesting issue than the musings of the diarist: the man (or men) who made the graffiti was (or were) already fairly liberated, in the sense that they felt able to do what they did. They felt able, entitled, or obliged to commit a whole host of crimes (criminal damage, obscenity, soliciting, indecency) to state very publicly what they felt about their sexual lives. Furthermore, both the graffiti 'artist's' liberation, and Symonds' shift from 'self-control' to 'surrender', were experienced through an interaction mediated by the physical space of the street in a very physical sense: an experience with a soldier in an alley leads to feelings of guilt and repression; an experience of graffiti in a street removes that sense of repression (though not guilt). It seems that one way or another, the streets of London were drenched with sexual energy around 1900.

Navigating the sexual city at the end of the nineteenth century was enabled by a growing number of publications 'guiding' people in where they could find what, and this is evidence of a growing sense of sexual identities developed in urban environments. For example, a contemporary could have got hold of the notorious London gay-guide-cum-pornographic-novel, called *Sins of the Cities of the Plain*, which circulated in relatively large numbers in the 1880s when it was written, but especially in the 1890s. It was seemingly for sale in several places, including Charles Hirsch's Bookshop in Coventry Street, between Leicester Square and Piccadilly circus.[20] It was part pornographic novel, but also part guide and part instruction manual on how to go about finding, recognizing, picking up, and living with other men in and around central London and across social classes. Crucial was the technique of cruising and picking up in the area between Leicester Square and Piccadilly. It opens as the narrator encounters a character called John Saul, while hanging around Leicester Square looking in shop windows. Saul was almost certainly intended to speak with the voice of a real character, as someone of the same name crops up in legal records doing the same things in the same place. While a lot of this novel is pure pornography, some of the things that Saul says may be derived from the views of people like the real John Saul.

The unnamed author engages Saul to write the story of his life, which moves from the countryside, through the suburbs, to its ultimate fulfilment in the middle of London, finally getting a job with a chic merchant of bedclothes. There, he meets a former soldier in the Guards, who introduces Saul to the ways of the world—and which allows Saul to explain the sexual geography of both London and the human body in one and the same set of stories. The book moves between clubs, shops, streets, squares, private houses, and parks, setting out a geography of sexual adventure. It named the shops to stand outside in Piccadilly, it explained which balls at Haxell's Hotel in the Strand were the ones to go to, and The Star and Garter pub in Richmond, a wealthy London suburb, crops up frequently.

The writer spies Saul lurking in Leicester Square. He was 'dressed in tight-fitting clothes, which set off his Adonis-like figure to the best advantage, especially about what snobs call the fork of his trousers, where evidently he was favoured by nature by a very extraordinary development of the male appendage'. His 'sparkling blue eyes...spoke as plainly as possible to my senses, and told me that the handsome youth must indeed be one of the "Mary-Ann's" of London, who I had heard were often to be seen sauntering in the neighbourhood of Regent

Street or Haymarket on fine afternoons or evenings'. Thus the book
titillates the knowing reader, and educates the reader who may be new
to London, and interested in finding out about this side of themselves.
The author invites Saul for a glass of wine; 'he appeared to comprehend that there was business in my proposal, but seemed very diffident
about drinking in any public place'. So, they go to the narrator's chambers. This is important: Saul is happy to cruise in public, but if he is
going to take a middle-class gentleman, he wants to be able to relax.
Thus, the 'trick' could be as much about getting a privacy and luxury
that would not have been available to a working-class man around
1900, as money, sex, sexuality, or lust. The book, in the story of this
encounter, explains how to manage the 'public/private' divide.

Once back at the narrator's house, near Baker Street tube station,
the narrator asks Saul about his 'packet'—'Is it real or made up for
show?' The answer is interesting; in part pornographic titillation, it
also explains something important about the relationships that Saul
was forming. In the privacy of the narrator's rooms, Saul replies:

> 'As real as my face, sir, and a great deal prettier. Did you ever see a
> finer tosser in your life?' he replied, opening his trousers and exposing
> a tremendous prick, which was already in a half-standing state. 'It's my
> only fortune, sir; but it really provides for all I want, and often intro-
> duces me to the best of society, ladies as well as gentlemen. There isn't
> a girl about Leicester Square but what would like to have me for her
> man, but I did find it more to my interest not to waste my strength on
> women; the pederastic game pays so well, and is quite as enjoyable.
> I wouldn't have a woman unless I was well paid for it.'[21]

Saul is forthright about how sex can allow him to move between social
classes, and move between different sorts of space, public and private.
In Saul's 'ordinary' life as a shop-boy, he would never have been able
to afford a room of his own. And he enjoys the company of women,
but finds the company of men more rewarding and interesting—in
both senses of the words, it seems. So this exchange, intended as pornography, may well reveal some of the flexibility of people's sexual
behaviour too. Saul is happy to go with women, but he prefers men—
partly because they thrill him equally sexually, but partly because he
feels more financially stable because of it. Elsewhere in the book he
explains that he dislikes being called a 'Marjorie' by the girls that

fancy him, but who become angry when he rejects them. But he has no other name for himself.

Cruising, hooking up, and going home were not, though, new for men or women—something the anonymous author of *Sins of the Cities of the Plain* was keen to stress. But the attention that transgressive sexual behaviour attracted from doctors and legislators at the end of the late nineteenth century *was* new. As large, industrial, modern cities sprang up across Europe in the last thirty years of the nineteenth century, 'moralists' warned increasingly that the number of 'sodomites' was growing too, and that therefore the whole of western civilization was in peril. What strikes the historian reading texts from the last quarter of the nineteenth century is that it seems that suddenly sexual behaviour flourished into what one famous historian has called 'sexual anarchy'.[22] In October 1880, Jerome Caminada, Manchester's first superintendent of the CID, led a raid on a 'drag ball' being held in a meeting house just off York Street in Manchester city centre. The *Illustrated Police News*, which was a mass-market scandal sheet of the time, covering the most extravagant news from the crimes scenes of Britain (and further afield) led with this on their front page, with a picture of the police breaking in through the glass skylights in the roof, and abseiling down to arrest the attendees of the ball below. Some forty-seven men were arrested, of whom twenty-two were dressed as women.[23] This was a mass-circulation paper, and announced to everyone that there were regular drag balls in Manchester—and the response of the city's magistrates was merely to bind the men over to keep the peace. The *Illustrated Police News* framed the story in the context of 'outrage', but by doing so also advertised the flexibilities of the city far and wide, for late-nineteenth-century police forces and judiciaries were not much interested in crimes like this. The way that these stories—and there are many of them in tabloids across Europe's cities in the last twenty or so years of the nineteenth century—suddenly seem to erupt from nowhere would imply that they must have been relatively frequent, a regular feature of urban life, but one which only seldom attracted comment. Thus, for every ball or party or indiscretion that was reported on, there must have been countless others that did not make it to the light of day—if the moralizing of tabloids can be called the 'light of day'.

At the end of the nineteenth century, there was an explosion in 'expert knowledge', keen to pathologize people—especially poor people—and 'help' them to 'get better' by exercising control over them. A walk round a university campus today is to take a tour through the mental universe of the turn of the last century. History, criminology, sociology, psychology, economics, planning, architecture, anthropology—all these subjects solidified in Europe in the 1890s, and all of them analysed societies, and hierarchized society's members. They all produced knowledge, convinced that 'knowledge is power', in Francis Bacon's famous dictum—a style of thought explored more in Chapter 5. But this new class of experts was also convinced that knowledge, when applied by experts, could improve people. So they proposed building public toilets, public baths, parks, libraries, tram and tube networks, and gymnasia, as well as schools, hospitals, markets, abattoirs, and museums—a process which, from about 1890, European cities undertook with gusto. Many of these new, 'improving' spaces created by the rational state seem, in retrospect, almost designed to permit sexual anarchy (from the perspective of the moralist), and engineer sexual transgression.

It might sound like a vulgar, trashy cliché to start with public toilets and bathhouses, but they were crucial. These spaces had a clearly intended purpose: they were supposed to enable the state to 'improve' the citizen by ordering the citizen's body, teaching the citizen to control themselves, and cleaning the citizen's body. They were spaces of purity and self-improvement, and to visit the Müllersches Volksbad in Munich or the Victoria Baths in Manchester or the Turkish Bath in Jermyn Street, London was to see a palace of respectable cleanliness. Equally, when the Paris municipality started to erect cast-iron pissoirs on many street corners, or British, Russian and German cities began to construct expensive underground and above-ground toilet facilities, they hoped to teach their citizens self-control, dignity and hygiene. Toilets were intended to remove the 'obscenity' of seeing people defecate in the street—a fairly common occurrence in 1900 by all accounts. They were intended to be not just a sign and a symbol of a new type of civilized self-control, but a technology to enable it.

Yet by doing this, these spaces not only put the body at the centre of public debates about health, citizenship, respectability, and leisure by building them into the streetscape, but they legitimized nudity and semi-nudity in public, and provided spaces in the city where liaisons could take place. The pre-First World War 'sexual anarchy' was developed and facilitated by precisely the sorts of city spaces designed to overcome it. It is worth focusing on the mechanics of this a little, because they show up how the production of spaces is underpinned by a 'law of unintended consequences', and how individuals can resist attempts to regulate them in the minutiae of their everyday lives. Public toilets started to be built in earnest across Europe in the 1890s and, for men, mostly followed a similar design. In a men's toilet, on one side of a room there would be a urinal—that is to say, a space where a certain form of public genital display is not just possible, but actually demanded (for to stand at a urinal without one's penis in one's hand is actually 'weirder' than simply to get it out and hold it there). Often, above the urinal there would be a row of windows at high level (or in the ceiling, if underground). The true purpose of these was so that dirt on the tiled walls would be visible, and could be immediately scrubbed off—but also so that all could see what was being done. On the opposite side of the room would be a row of cubicles. On the one hand, these were to remove the feeling of vulnerability from pulling one's trousers down to defecate, and to *remove* the element of public nudity. However, a secondary effect of this was to couple a space of privacy adjacent to a space of enforced semi-nudity. For poorer men used to living in overcrowded houses, this called a whole new set of opportunities into being.

The same was true of the public bath which, by the 1900s, typically contained networks of steam rooms. Often, surrounding these rooms would be private areas where one could take a 'slipper bath' (in Western European cities), or have a massage and scrub (in Eastern European cities). Thus, these 'hygienic' and 'rational' installations became spaces where nudity and semi-nudity became not just legitimate, but necessary; and they were also spaces where privacy could be relatively easily secured. And even if people could not afford to take a cubicle at a public bath, the very fact that the steam rooms were full of steam meant that men could follow their desires there with less risk of 'intervention'—although some risk still persisted. The segregation of the sexes in public baths, designed to prevent 'abhorrent' sexual adventure between men and women, developed an entire physical infrastructure which promoted sexual adventure between men and men. While public toilets segregated the sexes, men and women could meet in similar ways in parks, cinemas, and pleasure gardens. Heterosexuals could meet just as easily and publicly—but measures taken to promote 'morality', by segregating the sexes, could also make homosexual encounters that much easier.

Bathhouses, shrines of purity and cleanliness, opened up a space where men (in particular) could socialize nude. Across the continent's cities, these spaces enabled the sudden, and widespread, facility for men to be naked with each other and, rather than being viewed as being deviants, be seen as macho brethren improving their bodies with the steam, and their social status by conversing with similarly virile specimens. Nowhere was this more true than in Russian cities. Commercial bathhouses had existed in Russian (and other Eastern European) cities since the seventeenth century, and had long been popularly associated with the 'possibilities' that they contained. But the impetus to hygienic reform stimulated the proliferation of these institutions, and a rapid decline in the price of entry. Palatial bathhouses were built that admitted men on a scale not previously seen, like the Sandunovskie Baths in Moscow. Work in the earlier, smaller, 'private' bathhouses was controlled by the *artel'*, a gang or group of buddies. Junior members (such as new immigrants from the country) would be expected to have sex with the customers for about 1 rouble, and the incomes of all the *artel'* would be pooled. As so often with sex and sexuality, both hetero and homo, sex was intertwined with status, power, and resources. In 1906, a novel was published in Russia by Mikhail Kuzmin called *Wings*, which opened up the culture of the bathhouse to public debate; but more importantly for the historian, this novel illustrates that there was widespread awareness that the bathhouse was a specific space where one could go to find sex.[24] When one historian began investigating sexual culture in Russia at the beginning of the twentieth century, he found that this novel marked a culmination of a twenty-year process of the formation of a subculture specific to gay men—a subculture put together in city spaces never intended to support it; indeed, these spaces were designed to suppress it.[25] And in 1930, a health inspector from London County Council was approached in the vapour room in the bathhouse under the Savoy hotel. One man 'exposed and stroked his person' and another 'partially clothed...beckoned with his finger, exposed his person and made suggestive gestures'. Men would then head off into the private bathing cubicles with each other.[26] And lists of such places were easy to get hold of—Baedecker's 1923 guide to London had a full price list of all the city's bathhouses, ranging from the cheap at Harrow Road to the upmarket under the Imperial hotel.

One of the responses to anxieties about racial degeneration across Europe was to emphasize sport to improve the physical 'stock' of the nation, and to construct gymnasia, swimming pools, sports tracks and playing fields upon which they could 'restore' their bodies— discussed in Chapter 3, pp. 187–200.[27] But the eternal law of spatial unintended consequences quickly moved into action. The cult of bodybuilding started to develop in the United States around 1900, and was promoted by strong-men in music hall and early cinema. It was in Germany that the cult of indoor sport—particularly gymnas- tics—had its most thorough penetration into urban culture, because athletics clubs had been an early cover for outlawed nationalist and socialist organizations dating back to the Napoleonic Wars, and con- tinued as such for German socialist groups which had been outlawed in the newly unified state (see Chapter 1, pp. 17–20). So they were deeply embedded in German ideas of masculinity and politics. They were especially popular amongst the working classes. As one con- temporary noted, 'the many athletic associations of the capital are composed mostly of unmarried workers between 18–25; many are locksmiths, smiths, and other iron workers'. He went on to provide a sketch of the values and culture of athletics clubs in turn-of-the- century Berlin, one which embodies familiar features of masculine culture today:

> Amongst these people, strength, danger and bravery are everything. For them, the fight between Russia and Japan is not really a fight, because there has been too much shooting, and not enough wrestling, stabbing and fist-fighting. We now enter an athletes' club which is often associated with homosexuals. In a neighbouring room there is a small bar. The small room is full of the smell of oil, metal and sweat, that particular smell that comes from metalworkers. On the floor lie bars, dumbbells and weights of 100 pounds and more. Next to them lies a mattress for wrestling. Eight or ten strong athletes are there, some in black trunks, with pallid bodies and tattooed arms and chest.[28]

The whole was presided over by a woman who ran the gym and collected the subs from the members—and made sure there were always cigarettes on hand! Bodybuilding was hugely popular—but not just for its aesthetic qualities: 'Many homosexuals join athletics clubs because when someone makes an affidavit against them under paragraph 175 of the criminal code [which outlawed homosexual activities] or tries to blackmail them under this paragraph, they had solid, loyal, unshockable men at hand, whose protection they could rely upon, and whose "proactive" friendship they could use to defend themselves.'[29] That is to say: they could call upon a reliable gang to beat up potential blackmailers. It is interesting here that these gyms that gay men were joining were not 'gay places'; rather, they were *masculine* places, and many of the gang would not be 'gay' (in our terms), but would beat up a blackmailer because their *masculine* mate was being threatened and it was their *masculine* duty to make sure a mate was always safe.

In London, the London County Council, convinced by the many 'scientific' treatises of the racial degeneration of urbanites, began to construct sport halls and boxing clubs themselves, and organized open ponds to be swimming areas, banning the wearing of clothing in them, and forcibly excluding women; i.e. they forced compulsory public nudity on these male-only ponds. Many of the new tennis courts and football and cricket pitches had to be booked in advance, which meant that once one had identified a few 'like minds', it was relatively easy to book a football pitch for what we today would call a 'gay' football team. Of course, as historians, we cannot know just how many such informal teams, clubs, or associations formed. But if we assume that gay men are no more stupid or disinclined to form a football team than straight ones, we would have to guess that there must have been a fair few. What we do know is that many of these places intended for the new, 'improving' sporting culture produced prosecutions for 'grossly indecent' behaviour in London.[30]

Such exchanges did not take place just in these places of 'bodily' improvement: new spaces of economic improvement could do the same. New urban transport technologies could provide the ideal forum for cruising between men and women and men and men before the Great War, a feature which still prevails today. In Berlin around 1910, one man explained to doctors how important cruising on public transport was to his sexual life. He draws our attention to the new spaces of public transport, where strangers would sit facing each other in disconnected silence—a type of encounter which was novel, invented for most in the last decade of the nineteenth century, and first decade of the twentieth. This opened up whole new possibilities for sexual flirting:

> My sexual wish is not to be the woman of the female impersonator, but rather my ideal would be, as a woman, to lead a genuinely physiological love life with a man. A gentleman who often stared at me in the tram plays in this instance a major role in my thoughts. His outward appearance fascinates me. He was built as I am, elegant as a former officer, his fine clothing fitting well, his beard neatly trimmed, his eyes, which were not overly large, filled with expression.[31]

This mixture of internal fantasy—about being a transvestite—coupled with the cruising of the daily commute on a tram in Berlin, merged to open up for this man a realization of an inner personal transformation, and a clearer orientation of his sexual desires:

> I confess openly that the world of unlimited possibilities that my imagination opened to me has something magical about it, which heterosexual intercourse could not at all have presented to me. (Just writing about this now makes my penis, which had been flaccid before, grow erect.) I imagine that no sexual behaviour with a man would disgust me. I have been told that some women like to suck a man's penis as if to wash it clean. I would willingly offer my mouth to suck my lover if he asked me.[32]

Accounts from Paris and London confirm that the new metros, underground, and trams made a panoply of new encounters possible because they legitimized both sitting and staring, as well as striking up a conversation with those that stared back. As one amateur London poet opined:

> When travelling home by 'bus or tram,
> I meet a hundred boys again,
> Behind them on the 'bus I ride,
> Or pace the platform by their side.[33]

It is important to remember what a different sort of *space* a tram, bus, or tube was in 1900. They were distinctively modern features of everyday life, only present in cities. Particularly on the undergrounds of Paris, Berlin, London, and Vienna, millions of people were organized for the first time to sit facing each other in silence as a central part of their everyday life. And on the small, cramped 'deep' London lines which started construction around the turn of the century, passengers sat in a long strip along the side of the carriage, which meant that they could observe not only people opposite, but by focusing on the reflections in the window, could see a long stretch of their neighbours too. A long stare could be followed by getting up and pursuing someone who stared back—male or female. Because the tunnels were dark, the reflective capacity of the glass was heightened in a way that overground travel did not do—although trams and buses did often preserve the 'facing rows' format, and for much of the year in Northern Europe (and often at night), the outside would be black enough to highlight the reflections. These spaces, where strangers had to sit silently staring at each other for protracted periods, often at the same time every day, had never existed before. They were almost designed for cruising.

Contemporaries were fully aware of the sexualized nature of modern cities—for both men and women. By 1908, one morality campaigner could map an entire twenty-four hours of gay *rendezvous* locations in St Petersburg—and, in doing so, made sure that anyone who did not know where these places were or what went on in them soon would do. The criticisms of 'moralists' were the best adverts for cruising grounds possible. It started at the dog exercise garden by the circus areas at the Champ de Mars, moved onto the Nevskii Prospekt, Café de Paris and Passazh (an arcade of shops) by the afternoon, before moving on to the Fontanka Embankments and the Tauride Gardens in the evening. Male prostitutes lined up outside the public toilets at Cinizelli Circus. For any men who wanted to experiment with this side of their personalities, moralists were keen to explain exactly how:

> In the summer the *tetki* ['poofs', 'queers'] gather almost daily in the Zoological Garden, but their assemblies are especially populous on Saturdays and Sundays, when soldiers come from their quarters and when officer cadets, regimental choirboys, cadets, grammar school pupils and apprentice boys have the day off. The soldiers of the Life Guard Mounted Regiment, cavalry guards, and both Urals and Ataman Cossacks come to the Zoological Garden solely for the purpose of earning a few 20-kopek pieces without any labour on their part. They

recognise all the *tetki*, and so a soldier, passing one of them, glances significantly at him and goes off in the direction of the toilet, checking to see whether the *tetka* is following him. If he does, then he pretends to see to his bodily functions and tries to show off his member. The *tetka* stands next to him and, if the member is really big, he feels it with his hand and pays the soldier 20 kopeks. In the course of an evening the *tetka* conducts several such probings and, having chosen a member to his taste, he sets off with the soldier to the nearest bathhouse, where he uses him in the anus, or conversely, the soldier uses the *tetka* that way, for which he would receive 3–5 roubles from him.[34]

If you did not know where and how to meet men who had sex with men before a 'moral' campaign like this, you certainly would after it. While the widespread use of parks by *all* sorts of people seeking privacy is easily demonstrated across urban Europe at this time (and observe the range of social classes present here, from apprentices up to the officer class), what really strikes historians is the role of soldiers.

In the late twentieth and early twenty-first centuries, it is hard to imagine soldiers being so relaxed about 'getting off' with other men. This is because we have come to associate 'masculinity' with 'hetero-sexuality' in a way much more restricted than one hundred years ago. But evidence from *every* large European city before about 1950 shows that many military men were relaxed about sex with other men, on certain conditions. Barracks commanders in Berlin and London regularly banned *all* of their men from going to certain parks and bars in rotation, as they shifted the 'problem' from one place to another; naval commanders in Toulon and Marseilles fought a con-stant campaign in this regard; Amsterdam military officials faced the same difficulties.[35] Why soldiers did this is a matter of some debate— a debate largely prompted by our own inabilities to conceive of sexu-ality in anything other than a binary system, which couples masculinity and heterosexuality on one side, with effeminacy and homosexuality on the other. But before about 1950, such a division just did not exist amongst working-class men (which is to say, most men); sexual part-ners and gender identity were not neatly aligned in this period. So apprentices, metalworkers, soldiers and other 'epitomes' of masculin-ity could choose to sleep with men for a variety of reasons while still preserving their masculine identities, which were of utmost impor-tance to them.

The evidence shows a wide range of thinking behind men's decisions to sleep with other men across the first half of the twentieth century. Some soldiers liked to see other worlds which would be closed to them with a girlfriend of their own class—getting taken to restaurants, receiving little gifts, going to museums, being able to have sex in private. These were the concerns raised by 'Saul', above on p. 257. As such, they enjoyed the pleasures of crossing class boundaries as well as sexual ones, and going out with a middle-class gay man might open up for them spaces of the city to which they would conventionally not have had access. For many working-class men, going with a middle-class man offered a sort of 'urban passport'. It was far easier for soldiers and sailors, and indeed any working-class man, to cross class boundaries by having sex with other men than with women—something to which many of them drew attention. It would be very hard for a working-class man even to meet a middle-class woman socially (although both had the option of hanging around in parks, pleasure gardens, museums, trams, and so on, and cruising there). Others liked the more 'masculine' associations of sleeping with a man, rather than a woman. There was a widespread emphasis on 'masculine' values in this period, which often privileged turning the profound love that men had for each other in many situations into a sort of sacred, 'Greek', physical love. Equally, the desire to be with another man could omit the cultural references and just emphasize a rejection of women and an elevation of masculinity and masculine friendship and company to a level so high that to love it was acceptable, even normal.[36] Others liked it because they felt that there was less risk of contracting a sexually-transmitted disease with a man (especially so compared to the military brothels), and no danger at all of getting him pregnant with all the difficulties that would entail.

But equally, they could end in a relationship. One leading historian of sexuality has pieced together the life of one Londoner, Cecil E., and it is worth quoting at length from his analysis of the evidence:

When Cecil E. joined the Welsh Guards in the 1920s, he quickly found that same-sex encounters were 'talked of in the barrack room'. Immersed in this milieu, Cecil was socialised into dominant forms of masculinity and sexual and cultural practice. Shortly after enlisting 'another Guardsman took him to London and introduced him to some people he called "soldiers' friends"'. Cecil learned of the possibilities of homo-sex; blackmail and theft; the sexual, social and commercial pleasures; and masculine status that it offered. Introduced to the sites where those opportunities could be found, he began to frequent Hyde Park regu-larly with other guardsmen, looking for queers. He received guidance in the conventions that should structure his interactions with other men: what he should—and should not—do, where and how he should do it. There was, he learned, an informal 'list of charges for the various grades of offence'—seven shillings for a casual encounter. Throughout, Cecil's investment in these practices was complex. He formed a rela-tionship with a clerk that lasted for two years, ending when Cecil blackmailed his partner, seeking the money to buy himself out [of his service in the Guards].[37]

So in this context, what started out as an expression of masculinity ended up in a relationship, which Cecil spectacularly mismanaged.

Frequently, money was exchanged—not much, often a token amount. This seemed to have served a few functions. Firstly, it got poor men a few marks, shillings, or francs extra—the same motive that a poor woman might have in going with a well-to-do man. But secondly, for some it made the transaction 'legitimate'. Amongst the elite regiments of the Guards in London, so long as the Guardsman was paid for it, it was generally expected that he would sleep with civilian men. Later, in the 1950s, sociologist Michael Schofield (writ-ing under the pseudonym Gordon Westwood) conducted a huge range of surveys of 'gay' men. One of his witnesses summed the situ-ation up neatly:

> One of my mates took me to the C—— [a bar] and told me I could make good money by playing around with queers. I was picked up the first night by a man and went back with him, but I didn't ask for money. I went to the C—— often and went back with many people but I never asked for anything. Then my mate found out I wasn't taking the money and he let on to my other friends and said I must be queer.[38]

Note that there was a distinction between 'sleeping with men' and 'being queer' for this man's barrack culture. The two were not at all the same thing. The exchange of money placed one on the 'mascu-line' side of the fence; this may have been important in preserving people's masculine identities, whether or not they preferred male

sexual partners. What is equally clear is that a lot of men were perfectly able to have sex with other men when, in the long term, they
might settle on a woman as a partner.

All of this indicates that having sex with other men did not imply
a collapse in the man's social status in the masculine culture of the
barracks, either in St Petersburg in the 1900s or London between the
wars and right up until the 1950s. Many of these encounters would
end in loving relationships—often ending when either the soldier got
married, or was posted away, or left the army. The payment would
continue throughout—not because the soldier did not love his partner, but because it legitimized the whole process. Even up to 1960,
one Lance Sergeant in London recalled:

> Some of us get quite fond of the blokes we see regularly...they're nice
> fellows...and interesting to listen to. As for the sex...some of the
> younger ones aren't bad looking...I've had some real thrills off
> them.[39]

Another soldier, 'Jim', exchanged letters with his civilian lover, John
Lehmann (called Jack), after Jim had got married. Jack described his
'friendship' with Jim, who 'treated my flat as another home and
relaxed happily on the sofa'. Jim wrote to Jack, 'I wish I was still seeing you Jack as you were the best friend I ever had...you were always
such a good friend to me...we had good times together Jack, and I
hope I shall see you some time.' One influential historian of sexuality
concludes that 'here casual sex shaded into an intimate and ongoing
relationship'.[40]

There was even a strange 'honour' amongst those soldiers who
used the relationship as an opportunity to rob what they were not
paid. One gay man interviewed in London in the 1950s reported:

> The Guardsman said, 'Are you going to give me your wallet, or are
> you going to be beaten up?' The Guardsman took the wallet, and
> handed me back five shillings and said, 'Come and have a drink.'
> When I protested he said, 'It's no use being upset by these things.
> You'll just have to get used to it.' We went for a drink and we talked
> about it. He said that even if I went to the police, he was twenty-one
> and I was over forty, so I wouldn't stand a chance.[41]

A situation like this resists all the conventional codings that an early
twenty-first century mind might instinctively bring to the situation.

The 'power' relationship of the older 'client' and younger 'prostitute' is very difficult to fix; the sexuality of the guardsman seems ambivalent; his attitude to gay men seems to be a mixture of abusive contempt and a roundabout sort of matter-of-fact respect. The fact that the man in question did actually agree to go for the drink with the guardsman also defies easy moral, ethical, or sexual categorization. Whichever way you cut it, soldiers across Europe—the epitome of masculine heterosexuality in many a modern cliché—and iron workers and coal hauliers all seem to have been relatively relaxed about who they slept with. Some slept with people of the same sex; some slept with people of the opposite sex; some slept with people of both sexes. This remained the case until the aftermath of the Second World War, when changing ideas about the family, but also changing layouts of the city, heightened the demand that people 'choose' what they were. This confusing (to us) set of sexual identities and practices can also be seen in the spatial organization of the city.

*   *   *

This began to change for the working classes between the wars. At the turn of the twentieth century, there were certainly places where people who chose to identify fully as an 'invert' or an 'Urning' could go and find others. There were places soldiers and sailors could go. There were 'gay' brothels that were fixed as such. But bars, restaurants, and dance halls tended not to be 'gay' in the modern sense—although a few 'exclusively gay' (rather than just bohemian or alternative) venues did exist. Other venues might be exclusively 'gay', but only on a specific night of the week—it became common for wealthier *tetki* to attend the Mariinskii Theatre, or the Palkin Restaurant at 47 Nevskii Prospekt on Wednesdays.[42] In several cities, there were masked balls which were held by hiring a venue, and spreading the word. But between the wars, looking at the evidence from cities, it seems that there were more bars aimed at gay people—this implies a crystallization of identity. It was estimated that there were twenty 'Urning' bars (an 'Urning' was a widespread technical term for homosexual men at the time) in Berlin in the 1920s, but far more common were 'mixed' venues, such as a specific beer-hall in suburban Munich, where gay men would gather by the hundred on Sunday afternoons; its name does not appear in the press, but contemporaries would have found it relatively easy to identify. Gradually, most European cities between the two world wars developed what we today would call a 'scene', a spatial expression of a new identity, marking out an important transition towards a new way of self-classification for working-class Europeans. This implies just as much the formation of specifically 'heterosexual' places too—and a key example of one of these would be the explosion of palais de danse, discussed in Chapter 3, p. 212. What is important about the 'scene' is the way that it shows us that space and identity are intertwined: there are no real identities that do not have territories or spaces or places in which they come to life and take shape.

One feature of sexuality in the first third of the twentieth century which is conspicuous, and which contradicts the clichés we might have of the past, is the absence of police intervention. This was particularly true before the First World War, although began to change between the wars. Across Europe, laws against homosexual acts (for men—women were generally more tightly policed as prostitutes than as lesbians) were tightened in the 1880s and 1890s, usually by broadening the definition of male–male sex crime from 'sodomy' to 'indecency' and, even more pernicious, 'procuring for an indecent act'. This was important, because it transformed the legal framework for men who had sex with men from being physical—sodomy is an offence of the body—to being social. New 'crimes', like 'procuring for an indecent act' or 'indecency', might include chatting someone up, or cruising them, or glancing at them in 'a funny way'.

This could have catastrophic effects, as Thomas B., a 23-year-old railway porter found in London in 1925. He had taken his mother to London to visit the British Empire Exhibition at Wembley, and her handbag broke, so he had put its contents in his pockets. Officers had been following him since he had been to the Tivoli Theatre, then to a Lyon's Corner House, then to a urinal on York Street. In their view, he 'accosted' several men. As this all happened with his mother nearby, the 'accosting' that took place must have been of the smiling and chatting kind. When he was arrested, they found a powder puff in his pockets—his mother's. Since the turn of the twentieth century, the law in Britain had been framed in so that the 'offence' moved from a physical act (sodomy) to more socially constructed 'crimes'—so that almost *anything* could stand as evidence for 'indecent acts'. In this case the powder puff was produced as evidence in court of his degeneracy and, on the strength of this evidence, he was convicted. Despite the fact that his MP and his Station Master attested in court to his 'exemplary character', the powder puff was accepted as evidence of Thomas B.'s 'importuning'—even though it was relatively common for men to use face powder then. *John Bull*, the polemical magazine that raised Thomas B.'s case with a wider public, itself carried front-page adverts for Clement and Johnson's Yadil Antiseptic Powder, which as well as being 'invaluable for the toilet and nursery' observed how 'men find it soothing after shaving'.[43]

And while this broader legislation in many European jurisdictions around 1900 did lead to a very small increase in prosecutions, overall one is struck by their small number before the war, and their growth thereafter.[44] Statistics for arrests and convictions for sodomy, intent to commit sodomy, and gross indecency with males for peacetime Edwardian London show surprising results. Sodomy arrests peaked at nine in 1904 and 1908, with convictions of five and two respectively; arrests for gross indecency peaked at forty-six in 1912 and 1914, with convictions of sixteen and twelve.[45] While this was pretty grizzly for the people arrested and convicted, it is clear that state persecution of men who had sex with men was fairly minimal, and that when they *were* persecuted, juries were not inclined to support the police in that persecution. Sodomy was difficult to prove without a confession; 'gross indecency' was easier, as it involved things like holding hands in public, kissing in a park, or having sex in a toilet. In Germany, the statistics tell a similar story. One historian has recently undertaken the daunting task of analysing the statistics on 'morality crimes' for the whole of Germany between 1882 and 1982, and has published some preliminary results. He has shown that the police prosecuted far more people for sex with a minor, pimping, prostitution, abortion, and rape than they ever did for homosexuality in this period up to 1933—a focus of police attention that many readers of this book would find reasonable, even if they might disagree with the details (and here it should be noted that abortion was not a clean, neat, medical affair at that time—it was brutal, bloody, and often very harmful).[46]

The First World War saw an almost total collapse in prosecutions against men for indecency across the whole of Europe, and a massive increase in the prosecution of women for sexual misdemeanours. This must be either because men stopped being 'indecent'—which seems

unlikely—or because the state in its various forms (police, local governments, law courts, superintendents of bathhouses, and so on) stopped
bothering to prosecute men for it. This could be either because state
resources were directed elsewhere, or because so many men's lives
became so focused on disorder (killing, filth, extended labour, death,
misery, disease), that singling out one form of disorder—like having sex
in toilets—seemed to contemporaries to be too bizarre to pursue. Much
more focus was placed on female sexuality, as heightened standards of
self-control or discipline were imposed on women to keep themselves
'pure' for the presumed return of men sacrificing everything at the
Front—a phenomenon discussed in Chapter 2, p. 123.

After the war, though, this 'free' attitude towards male sexual transgression was to change. Initially, in both Britain and Germany (the
states with the most reliable statistics), there was a massive decline in
prosecutions of every sort in the first few years of peace. Then there
was a surge in prosecutions for 'homosexual' offences—above all in
Weimar Germany, in 1926–7 and then again under the Nazis in
1937–9, and Britain in the late 1930s.[47] The popular myth of Weimar
Berlin (or Hamburg or Munich) might be of exuberant experimental
decadence, but both German and British society between the wars
were only erratically relaxed about sexual adventure, and were keen
to impose a sort of 'compensatory' sexual order on men and women,
gay and straight, to stifle the perceived disorder of both the war and
the 'anarchy' before it. The war had profoundly shaken European
understandings of masculinity: men's bodies were often mutilated,
their minds often fractured. Men were supposed to be heroes, yet in
both victor and defeated lands, the First World War was not a heroic
war: it was static, not mobile; it worked through impersonal mass killing, not man-to-man combat; it depended on technology, not character. Representations in film, art, and literature of masculinity and
manliness between the wars from the time, especially in cities, focus
on this chaos of sexuality and gender, and speak powerfully of this
confusion about what a man was, and what a man was for.[48] Thus in
the 1920s and 1930s, European states started to take a keener interest
in people's bodies, and what they did with them. People's bodies came
to be viewed as one of the most important interfaces between citizen
and state in this period, and the history of sexuality is particularly useful for showing this.

This was further complicated because the revolution in psychiatry and psychology between the wars wrestled with the fact that men came back from the war broken, babbling, and hysterical, while women held down jobs in the public sphere (as discussed in Chapter 2, pp. 119–22), or worked two service-sector jobs, to try to hold a family together and put food on the table. Before the war, it was thought that women were in some fundamental sense psychologically weak and emotionally labile: in short, they were 'hysterical', a uniquely female condition tied to their uterus. The war, in its grotesque way, 'freed' men to cry—by allowing so many of them to do little else. So in short, the war turned every conventional expectation of masculinity upside down, and distributed disorder and confusion throughout the socio-sexual order. Thus, it became an imperative from Glasgow to Milan, from Paris to Moscow, for 'the authorities' to restore 'proper' masculinity, and after the crises of demobilization between 1918 and about 1922 prosecutions rose sharply in Europe for *all* types of crime.[49]

But a tour through the *spaces* of European cities shows a different, but subtly complementary, story to the one of harsher laws and increased prosecutions, with different identities beginning to be formed. What a spatial history shows seems to be first and foremost the formation of *identities* around sexuality, and the start of an internal diversity to 'gay' culture which reflected the diversity of other cultural groups. We start to find middle-class gay bars, and working-class ones; we find bars with sailor theme nights; we find lesbian bars. We know this because in this period we start to see more sophisticated and open guidebooks emerging which explained to people exactly where they were and what they contained. Curt Moreck, a hugely popular and prolific German author between the wars, undertook one such guide to Berlin in 1931, his notorious *Guide to Immoral Berlin*. It starts by explaining what all readers would already have known: the street was the primary site for sexual adventure, whether gay, straight, or anything in between. It advised adventurers to walk the streets with their eyes and ears open, and that would be the shortest route to sexual adventure. The guidebook—readily available to visitors and inhabitants—then went on to explain where one could find all the trendy nightclubs, dancehalls, risqué bars, brothels, and above all the massive hit of this period, bars with phones on the tables, intended to speed up cruising and flirting. They sprung up everywhere, for flirting, fun and cruising, for both gay and straight. He explained where you could find cabarets, jazz, funfairs. And then he came to a chapter entitled, 'Pubs of Man-to-Man Eros'.

Estimating their number to be about eighty, reading the guide soon makes it clear that, contrasted to the spatial *instability* of sexual lives and the absence of a universal 'identity' as gay in the pre-war period, by the 1930s an identity was emerging. No longer associated with transient spaces such as toilets, parks, trams, bathhouses; or bars, pubs, and clubs in which homosexuality was an acceptable, but not defining, feature of existence on one or two nights a week, we see the emergence of a gay scene in Berlin—and it was this scene which drew so many middle-class Britons, like Christopher Isherwood and Stephen Spender, to the city. While before the war, observers noted that gay men would take women to gay balls along with their male 'cousin', by 1931 there were many bars which were actively excluding women. Of course, many 'straight' pubs and bars in European cities had effectively banned women for many years by making them so uncomfortable there, but this seems different. Then Moreck's guide explains that one has to divide up the bars of 'man-to-man Eros' in Berlin between *Schanklokalen*, ordinary bars with ordinary people in ordinary suburbs, and ones with a more up-market décor and a 'trendy' atmosphere and clientele, which might attract a crowd from right across the city.

The ordinary suburban bars, like the Bürgercasino on Friedrichsgracht, were old-fashioned and stolid. The Bürgercasino was very quiet, and in the backroom, someone tinkled on the piano while 'lads' (which can, in German, mean anyone from about fourteen to twenty-six; although most males would start their working lives at fourteen) leant on the counter supping beers and chuffing endless cigarettes. He describes the dress style of the people there—they wore pullovers, quite trendy in the late 1920s, and slightly American. It is a broadly middle-class and lower-middle-class bar—civil servants, salesmen, clerks. They dance, although there is not much room. More lively would be the Zentral-Diele, where on Saturdays it was always 'Sailors' Night'. Moreck observed that, 'Their uniforms are too blue and the faces not weathered enough; they have surely never set foot on a boat, other than a pedalo on the Wannsee.'[50] For a lively couples-oriented bar, one went to Voo-Doo in Skalitzerstraße; Café Nordstern was for dancing until three in the morning. More 'out there' nights could be had in the

Adonis-Diele in Alexandrinenstraße—where you could smoke drugs, find love of 'every sort', but should not imagine that it had anything to do with innocent youth. At the Zauberflöte in the Kommandanten-Straße, shown in Figure 4.1, a uniformed man guards the door. When you enter, it is straight on to the 'Frauen-Abteilung' (women's department), and up the stairs to the left to the Florida Saal, the 'Männer-Abteilung', where there was dancing and drinking. On the way up there was a secretive sign: BfM—Bund für Männer; the Association of Men, a human rights association campaigning for the repeal of Paragraph 175 forbidding same-sex love. Moreck uses the word 'Menschenrechte' to describe the BfM—*human* rights, and this is important. Frequently, rights for gay men (in particular) are not classified as *human* rights, but as something extra, as if there were human rights and then *gay* human rights.

Then he lists a row of bars near there that he found exceptionally noisy—he hears a lousy, but voluble rendition of Dietrich's smash hit, *Ich bin von Kopf bis Fuß auf Liebe eingestellt* ('From head to toe, I am made for love'), which still evokes the period today:

> Here, you are happy just to be a spectator, an observer. You can pay, stand up, and go. Nothing binds you to these places, and outside are night and stars and fresh air. From inside we hear, 'Ich bin von Kopf bis Fuß...'. Oh, poor love! They play you lousy love songs, and imprison you in musty bars![51]

Here he captures the empty, yet charged, fascinating, magnetic joy of clubland and evokes a world of freedom carved out in the city—a set of feelings familiar to any urban night owl today. No longer is the network one of toilets linked by streets punctuated by a beer-hall for 'Urnings' on a Sunday afternoon in Munich or a restaurant for 'like-minded gentlemen' on Wednesday evenings in St Petersburg. Here, in the Berlin nightlife, we have a self-identifying, stable emergent gay identity *with the full diversity of humanity within it*: there are couples, dancers, older and younger, fetishists, fun lovers, quiet talkers. And what of the opinion outside?

> But there is a tolerant 'Beyond'. This tolerance rests more on indifference than on understanding; it relies on the fundamental idea that each should be allowed to follow their own path of spiritual becoming, also in matters of love. The tolerant 'Beyond' loves from time to time to

Figure 4.1 The entrance to the 'Magic Flute' club, in Berlin, *c.*1931 by Christian Schad. The notices in German say, 'Men's Department' and 'Women's Department'. The Magic Flute was part of the growth of a 'scene' in European cities which became particularly conspicuous between the wars, in which bars 'just' for gay men and women emerged. These new bars underlined the impossibility of controlling urban space for the police and the state—as well as the usefulness of nooks and crannies to those seeking to challenge and define new identities. By the early 1930s in Berlin, there were possibly as many self-consciously 'gay' bars than at any time since.

break into the meeting places of 'inversion', to enjoy the wonderful drama that unfolds there. Then suddenly the bar is the in thing, and it becomes high class to hang out there.[52]

German is a more 'spiritual' language than English, and easy, common words in German can express cumbersome ideas in English, like 'spiritual becoming' or the 'Beyond', which have quasi-religious connotations when translated. In German, they are far more mundane words. But Moreck's guide establishes well that in Berlin, as in most cities, there was an attitude of 'live and let live'.

Similarly, in 1937, Routledge (one of Britain's oldest and most prestigious publishing houses) published *For Your Convenience: A learned dialogue instructive to all Londoners and London visitors*, anonymously written by Thomas Burke. It is written almost as a protracted comedic sketch, modelled, it would seem, on Rabelais. Two men, one an upper-crust British gent, the other a lower-middle-class self-made man, are sitting in an archetypal British gentleman's club in London. They have a squabble over the latest edition of *Sanitary World and Drainage Observer*, a journal which claims to discuss important advancements in the world of the toilet. The upper-crust gent observes, 'I had hoped from its title that it might tell one some of the things a man often wants to know.' He thought 'it would tell one what to do if one were walking through Wigmore Street after three cups of tea...'. 'I get you, sir', replies the self-made man.[53] Of course, after so much tea, one would need a toilet. There is a map of all the public toilets and nearby watering holes, shown in Figure 4.2, with points marking every possible site of encounter. One is struck by the huge range of places in central London, and the ease of referring to them—until one reads the list of options, which positively dwarfs the map.

For Your Convenience was itself a joke on the British term 'public conveniences', a polite euphemism for 'toilet'. The book then goes on, very humorously, to list in minute detail all the places one might hope to find 'relief'. One explains to the other:

> Places of that kind, which have no attendants, afford excellent rendez-vous to people who wish to meet out of doors and yet escape the eye of the Busy [policeman]...to exchange information out of earshot of their friends, or the observation of the Dicks [slang for detectives, and of course, penises].[54]

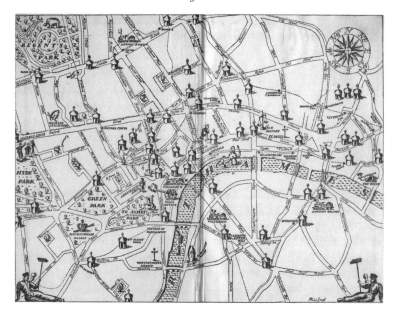

Figure 4.2 This map shows the various public toilets where men could meet other men for sexual liaisons in London in the 1930s, published in a book, *For Your Convenience*, in 1937. It shows how spaces which were designed for one purpose—the pursuit of hygiene, self-control and 'morality'—once created, could be 're-inscribed' with other functions: the inevitable 'law of unintended consequences', distributed through the city. It also gives a hint of the widespread, easily accessible nature of 'sexual adventure' in the city, and crushes any easy clichés of a past which was sexually 'neat' and well-ordered.

The widely available book is written as gag upon gag; information was exchanged about where to go, and how to get there without partners, lovers, wives, and girlfriends finding out. And 'the observation of Dicks' is something which is both the objective, and the great fear, of the public liaison. The detail is astonishing, ranging from:

> 'Why, sir, St Christopher's Place—that engaging little passage at the middle of [Wigmore Street], full of antique shops and second-hand book shops. In a cul-de-sac at the end of that passage, you would have found full service…'

They then go on to outline which department stores were good for 'a gentleman in need of relief', which churches, which streets, which office blocks (in the City, the financial district of London, 'go down King Street, and alongside the Guildhall, in a byway called Guildhall Buildings, a refuge will be found', as well as Transport House, the Prudential Insurance, and County Hall), which pubs ('Only a day or so ago, I was in a bar. The company were entirely men, and the staff were men...'), which working-class areas were particularly fruitful ('The great markets, too, are sure havens—Covent Garden; Smithfield; Billingsgate; The Borough vegetable market—indeed all the labour quarters'), the museums ('Cromwell Road [the museum quarter]—has any London explorer, do you know, reached its penetralia—discovered what lurks in its dusky curves west of the Natural History Museum...?'), bus depots, railway stations, theatres, lidos and ponds, barracks—and these were just scratching the surface: 'as for the concealed places, some of which have been named in our talk, they would make a list ten times as long...'[55] If we assume that for each place of homosexual encounter, there may have been five or ten or twenty or fifty of heterosexual, the vision of the sexual city we obtain is simply mind-boggling.

Given the scale of sexual adventure being undertaken, a vast amount of 'live and let live' must have been practised. This attitude of 'live and let live', though, blended into an attitude on the part of the authorities that 'there's nothing we can do to eradicate it completely, but occasionally we should try'. One of the chief problems facing the police in cities, though, was what might be called the 'spatial territoriality' of sexual lives, sexual identities: sex and sexual identity happened in many spaces, many places, but the police had legitimate presence in almost none of them. The bedroom was largely out of bounds for the police (for the time being—the British police in particular in the 1950s went to huge lengths to disrupt the private sex lives of the most discreet of gay men). Even penetrating the gay cultures of the semi-public spaces required the deployment of huge amounts of police resources. And when deployed, the police could not be sure that the world 'Beyond' would not, through its indifference, conclude that in fact, it had been a massive waste of time and energy.

The hotel industry between the wars was a key sector of employment for working-class gay people in European cities. Large hotels would house some of their staff—porters, sous chefs, and the like—in attic rooms. Employees were often required to double up in rooms, and thus working-class gay men could negotiate a space in the heart of cities in which they might live together legitimately. This is a good example of how urbanites can use the spaces of the city to meet their own objectives, whatever they may be. In London between the wars there was a thriving gay culture organized throughout the large network of hotel employees there; this meant that in a relatively concentrated area of central London, there were a large number of gay men, well networked, and who could afford to live (indeed, who were often required to live) in the city centre. As such, they could begin to organize spaces that were exclusively for their own use, which they themselves could control.

So in one case, a group of men organized a dance at the Holland Park Ballroom, which established an elaborate code to get in. This was largely planned by Austin C., who went by the name Lady Austin when he was hosting these evenings. In December 1932, Holland Park Ballroom was raided by thirty officers from F Division, the ball having been systematically infiltrated by undercover police officers. Sixty people were arrested, which resulted in thirty-three men and one woman being tried for keeping a disorderly house, and conspiring to corrupt public morals. Twenty-seven were convicted, with sentences of between three and twenty months' imprisonment. 'Keeping a disorderly house' is conventionally the charge for running a brothel—certainly *not* what was happening in the Holland Park Ballroom. So it seems that between wars the police and public prosecutors were quite willing to twist the law into uncomfortable shapes to make it 'fit', and in this case the jury went along with it.[56]

The judge at the Holland Park Ballroom trial, Ernest Wild, praised the police for opening up secret spaces in this way. It was by bringing this 'nest of sodomitical haunts' to light that these men could be prevented from 'making the metropolis another Sodom'.[57] In fact, often it was the *spatial* aspect of homosexuality that was the authorities' greatest fear—and the 'gay' man's greatest weapon. As the judge expounded again, 'one of the most disquieting features...is that most of you are connected with hotels, boarding establishments and restaurants, showing that these form a nucleus for this foul vice'.[58] For while sexuality could be legislated about in parliaments, or railed about in the press, or scientized in medical schools, it was in the spaces and places of Europe's cities that people would be able to organize their personalities and identities as they saw fit.

Both sex and identity are things that people *do* or *are*, not things that laws describe; and doing means doing it *somewhere*. In the raid on the Holland Park ballroom, we see how the ability to control space was at the heart of the project of self-assertion. The procedures used by 'gay' men (for at this time, a clearer identity was emerging) to establish spaces of freedom within the city were elaborate. Austin C. established a code to get in, and had to muster substantial resources to book and pay for the rooms, secure drink suppliers, organize bands and door staff. In much of this, he was assisted by entrepreneurs, who cared little whether the pound was pink or not. Seeing gay men as a 'market' rather than an 'identity' is something I will come back to at the end of the chapter. The men who put together what we would now call a 'club night' in Holland Park had previously been regulars at Selina H.'s Baker Street Dance Hall, which the police had been observing. Austin and John P. (a 22-year-old waiter) had organized it with Betty, a dance-hall manageress.

To get into such a space required a huge amount of police resource—and even transgression. PC Labbatt and PC Chopping were the undercover officers, and had to dress up like the defendants— one in 'drag'—and adopt their jargon. They had to go to the Mitre Tavern regularly in order to establish a 'cover', where many party-goers began their evening before heading off to Lady Austin's club night. At the Mitre, PC Labbatt had to flirt with the men, eventually getting one of them to give him the code for the door: 'say Betty sent you'. Then, at the Holland Park Ballroom, PC Labbatt played the queen to PC Chopping's 'king', as they danced together in the ball-room, 'collecting evidence'. PC Labbatt was later dancing with a man nicknamed 'the Bitch', who 'placed her (his) hands inside my trousers'. The Bitch asked PC Labbatt, 'Have you traded tonight?', 'trade' being gay slang for sex. PC Labbatt replied, 'Yes, twice, with my boyfriend', pointing to PC Chopping. This information about the level of com-plicity of the police in the 'immoral acts' they were trying to prevent, as well as the details of the entrapment, was all omitted from public accounts of the trial given by the press, presumably because newspa-per editors somehow intuited that if the public was fully informed about the ways the police had tried to subvert the spatial realm of tolerance that these men had shaped in the city, the police's spatial crime would have seemed worse than the men's sexual crime to a modern readership.

Even when such secret spaces were breached by the police, as at the Holland Park Ballroom, it did not produce a 'collapse' in the counter-cultural order prevailing inside. What it did was turn the ballroom into a battleground between two opposing views of what it meant to be a man, and more importantly, what it meant to be free. Indeed, Lady Austin even taunted the coppers during his arrest: Austin picked out the two spies who had been sent into the ball, and asked Inspector Francis (who led the bust on the ballroom) if they were, indeed, the 'bait'. Francis nodded. 'Fancy that—he is too nice. I could love him and rub his Jimmy for him for hours', taunted Austin. Francis cautioned him further. But rather than remain silent or cowed, Austin answered back:

> There is nothing wrong in that. You may think so but it is what we call real love man for man. You call us Nancies and bum boys...but before long, our cult will be allowed in this country.[59]

Others pursued the same strategy, either during arrest or in questioning. Charles C. told officers, 'There's nothing wrong in it. You would not understand.' William H. stated bluntly, 'The law can't tell me what I shall do with myself...if this boy likes to be my love, it's only a matter for us.' David M. told one policeman, who was approaching him:

> What? Are the bogies here? Surely in a free country we can do what we like? We know each other and are doing no harm....It's a pity these people don't understand our love. I am afraid a few will have to suffer yet before our ways are made legal.[60]

We should pause a moment and explore the significance of what these men were saying. Faced with brutality and persecution; having had their secret space subverted by spies; arrested, and facing humiliation and imprisonment, these working-class men, mostly employed in the hotel trade, were making a bold set of assertions.

First, they were taunting and humiliating the men who came to persecute them, showing substantial bravery and courage in doing so. Secondly, they were asserting what one historian has called a 'working-class queer citizenship': of those arrested, fifteen were waiters, eleven had other jobs in hotels, Thomas G. was a factory hand, and Thomas B. a shop assistant.[61] They were asserting their freedoms as citizens of Britain. This is important, because the usual emphasis on campaigning for legal reform as a barometer of human rights shifts attention away from the practical, day-to-day, embedded work that 'ordinary' people do, towards the concerns of the middle-class 'campaigner'. Human rights are neither won nor exercised in legislatures, but in places like the Holland Park Ballroom (or the buses of Montgomery, Alabama, or in the market places of colonial India). Thirdly, far from responding with a *personal* sense of self-pity or shame, these working-class men responded with a *collective* sense of pride, and a clear political pro-gramme which demanded that the individual have control over his or her own body and that the law must change to suit their demands, rather than their identities change to suit the law. Crucially, these men *identified* as gay; it had become a central part of who they were in terms of their personality, their attitudes to their bodies, and politics. In this light, this apparently peripheral event marks a courageous assertion in a century-long campaign for human rights for *all* humans, but while these men made universal claims, they only make sense in the very limited context of Holland Park Ballroom.

Even in the most persecutory of societies that showed a total com-mitment to supporting police control of every aspect of people's lives, clever use of space shows how unsusceptible to control it can some-times be; and the period between 1917 and the early 1950s produced the first—and most historians would argue, only—European regimes which have used large-scale violence as a sustained instrument of policy. Furthermore, the goal of Soviet and National Socialist policy was not to 'limit' the influence of those that did not conform to their ideals but to eliminate them from existence. However, when it came to sexual 'transgression' and urban space, their limits were soon exposed. In one case in St Petersburg in 1921, the Cheka (the first incarnation of the Soviet secret police) were observing a flat because they saw so many people going in and out of it. In particular, Red Army soldiers and Red Navy sailors were in attendance. Unable to permit such gatherings and assuming their only function could be to organize political subversion, they raided, only to find a wedding tak-ing place, with several men in wedding gowns marrying several men in uniform. The report observed:

a peaceful scene of family celebration, apparently a wedding, with a groom and a bride in a wedding dress, women in ball gowns, etc., whereupon the disarray which is always caused by the appearance of the organs of power was made more intense with the gradual revelation of the nature of those present. It turned out that all those, whether gentlemen or ladies, bride or groom, were men, and that the basis for these periodic parties was the homosexual desire to bring men together with men. The apartment where they gathered turned out to be a peculiar club or more exactly a den, for that type of perverted person.[62]

More frustratingly for the authorities, as they worked out in a radius from those attending the wedding in the apartment, many of the ninety-eight people arrested made 'cynical' or 'boastful' comments, suggesting a sense of pride and entitlement. The prosecution was vigorous in pursuing these men because they felt that this world beyond sight, running in networks invisible and inaccessible to the totalizing ambitions of the 'socialist society', could pose a profound, unknowable, unquantifiable threat. But the evidence also reveals a keenness to reach into the private spaces of the home—the 'den'—and move beyond the street in an attempt to intervene in people's lives. This ambition was widespread across urban Europe between the wars.

Importantly for Soviet thinkers, 'production' and 'reproduction' were inseparable socio-economic processes. Gay men—indeed, anyone who had sex merely for pleasure—excluded the possibility of producing a future worker untainted by tsarist, bourgeois norms. Therefore, they posed a massive threat to the credibility of the entire Soviet project at best, and a deliberate attempt to undermine the revolution at worst. But a criminologist, Orshanskii, in the 1920s found a vibrant homosexual subculture in what in 1924 came to be known as Leningrad—including sailors' doggerel, sung in the bars around the city's docks, such as:

> I knew a broadchested sailor
> With hands as hard as steel,
> His eyes sparkled through thick lashes
> Like a sky of enamel blue.
>
> [the sailor approaches]
> I shut my book—I didn't feel like reading,
> I knew he was looking at me...

He came and sat a little closer
As the blood pounded in my temples.

Soon I was in bed: and beside me
Lay my new master
Who alone fulfilled my desires
Who alone filled my consciousness.[63]

Worryingly for the authorities right through the 1920s, Orshanskii had studied many such couples, who lived perfectly 'ordinary' lives in the sense that one stayed at home, cooked, and cleaned, while the other went out and worked. And if Petrograd sailors were telling each other stories or singing songs about it, it must have been relatively common. Indeed, when historians have tried to explore the history of relationships, and in particular marriage, they have found that up until the 1950s, all sorts of relationships 'counted' as marriage to the people that were in them—and equally, Europe's urban working classes could dissolve their 'marriages' with just as little regard to the 'authorities'.[64] That is not to say that *everyone* enjoyed complete freedom in how they organized their private lives—they did not. But in the big cities of modern Europe, there have always been a very diverse range of options and habits surrounding marriage.

The USSR was slow to formulate explicit sexual rules, and homosexuality was persecuted haphazardly initially; later, under Stalin, more or less everything and everyone was persecuted with substantial resolve. Thus it is hard to say that men who had sex with men were any more viciously persecuted than men in general in the Moscow and St Petersburg of the 1930s. Certainly, under Stalin, such men *were* persecuted; but that did not make a man safe if he did not have sex with other men. But Lenin branded homosexuality (and feminism, and children's rights, and religious diversity) as a form of 'bourgeois separatism'; any 'rights' other than the rights of the proletariat were viewed in a unique way. They were constructed as a dangerous and deliberate self-indulgent individualistic diversion from the project of building socialism, although in the pre-Stalinist period (up to about 1930), they were not widely persecuted.[65]

After the Russian Revolution stabilized in the early 1920s, under the New Economic Policy, bathhouses, bars, and restaurants started to be leased out.[66] Under circumstances which allowed more private enterprise, 'gay' life could resume in Russian cities. However, anxious about *female* prostitution (about the most conspicuous form of 'capitalist exploitation' you could get, according to Marxist theory), public spaces were more rigorously policed than previously—all sorts of sexualities and uses of the body got caught up in sexual rules. But under the Five-Year Plans, the first of which began in 1928, the urban space which had been the cover of the 'gay' man became radically destabilized.[67] Millions of peasants migrated to the big cities, placing enormous stress on living conditions, and making privacy almost impossible within the 'home', such as it was for urban Russians. Average occupancy *per room* (not apartment or dwelling) in Moscow went from 2.71 per person per room in 1926 to 3.91 in 1940, making privacy ever harder to obtain. In Moscow, on the eve of the Second World War, only 6 per cent of families had an entire apartment to themselves; 40 per cent of families lived in one room inside an apartment; 24 per cent of families shared a room; 5 per cent lived in 'other utility spaces', like landings and cellars; and the remainder lived in barracks-like communal buildings.[68] Internal passports and identity documents were introduced from 1932, making free movement more and more risky (though not impossible). Secondly, the Gulag system grew, so men (and women, and children, and everybody in fact) who were arrested more than once for a whole range of petty crimes were sent for 're-education' as a productive citizen—i.e. a labour camp. By 1933 such a fate could befall anyone who was 'socially anomalous', according to Soviet medical literature—and when homosexual acts were criminalized in 1933–4, many gay men were sent, along with repeat offenders, prostitutes, 'work saboteurs', and millions of others into the Steppes of Siberia. Thus, there was an aggressive spatial separation in the form of the gap between the city and the Gulag which dissolved so many social formations in the 1930s USSR, whether peasant farm, heterosexual family, private space, or homosexual subculture. It is hard, though, to say that this was targeted specifically at gay men: so very many people were caught up in this nightmarish and arbitrary system, that anyone could get sucked into it. Finally, the development of a planned economy from 1928 onwards meant that private enterprise was effectively outlawed, and it became harder to establish any sort of space independent from the organs of the Soviet state.

Reversing the period of disinterest of sexual politics in USSR, in September 1933, Guenrikh Grigorievich Iagoda—soon to be made director of the secret police—initiated a plan to promote a wider persecution of gay men. Why is not known; historians have shown that when there was a sudden spike in the persecution of gay men in 1950s Britain, the motive was often not some 'moral panic' emanating from the centre, but the personal preoccupations and obsessions of ordinary police officers in police stations. Bigoted individuals in specific offices can drive the preoccupations of apparently inhuman, systematic, bureaucratic machines. What motivated local officers in the USSR remains closed to the historian. But in September 1933, Iagoda ordered a set of raids of 'salons, centres, dens, groups, and other organized formations of pederasts', and accused them of being proto-'spy rings'. He rounded up only 130 people, though, which implies either that there simply were not many people left *at all* by 1933 who were willing to meet in an unauthorized group, or that the operations were half-hearted or ineffective. Given the vast numbers of Soviet citizens hoovered up as spies in the early 1930s, this alternative explanation, and the one which seems more likely, indicates that even the NKVD (as the secret police was then branded) was simply not up to the task of finding such spaces. The scale of knowledge one needs to locate them in cities lies beyond even the most vicious of secret police organizations.

What really seems to have bothered Iagoda, though, was the *unknowability* of these people, and their 'haunts'. In correspondence to Stalin, he railed that 'The most active pederasts...had politically demoralized various social layers of young men, in part young workers, and even attempted to penetrate the army and navy.'[69] To the public at home and abroad, it was presented as protection against infiltration by foreigners, who were notoriously addicted to 'bourgeois decadence'. Whether the law could affect sexuality is hard to know—the NKVD files remain resolutely closed in Moscow, and furthermore, the frenzy of murder and death which characterized Soviet life in the 1930s and 1940s means it is difficult to identify the fate of individuals of any sort, given that years of loyal party service were as likely to get you a bullet in the head as not.

But the criminal archives from 'normal' criminal trials (rather than the 'political' offences singled out by the NKVD) show that the Boulevard Ring, which tightly circles central Moscow, in particular

remained a space where a highly coded, but public, sexuality could be
lived out. Bezborodov, a cook, and Gribov, a clerk, met in central
Moscow in the late 1930s. 'Wishing to drink alcohol, they visited the
flat of one Petr, by nickname "the Baroness", who kept an entire den
of homosexuals.' The police report makes homosexuals sound either
like harmless pets or dangerous lions. Trubnaia Square, Sretenskii
Boulevard, and Chistoprudnyi Boulevard also regularly cropped up in
the reports of psychiatrists as cruising areas. In the exquisite language
of police forces everywhere, in 1935 it was noted that Party-member
and Engineer, Aleyev, thirty-five, and Brodskii, a tram driver, twenty-
seven, 'met by chance on Sretenskii and other boulevards of the city
of Moscow with men-pederasts and entered into sexual intercourse
with them in toilets, apartments, and on the boulevards'. This makes
it clear that quite a substantial surveillance operation had been
mounted to follow these two around the city. But all the evidence
surviving indicates that the very structure of the city—the challenge of
the interplay between public and private spaces, or cruising and more
stable relationships—meant that people could carve out a life for
themselves. As one defendant noted, 'In 1936 in the apartment where
I lived, Afanas'ev, an artist of the ballet, moved in...He showed me
the places where pederasts meet: Nikitsii Boulevard and Trubnaia
Square.'[70] A profound friendship or a transient encounter could be
initiated and lived out by successfully navigating the public and private
spaces of the Soviet city.

There were, however, changes to the physical shape of the city in
Soviet Russia. In the 1930s, there was a widespread building programme of bathhouses, but their design changed. Rather than having
many small, steamy areas, and private rooms off the main halls, the
concept of privacy was abolished by communist planners and the
concept of collectivity emphasized. Lines of sight of intendents were
improved, and all remnants of the *artel'* culture of before the war,
discussed on p. 262, were designed out of the buildings. But the very
processes of urbanization had a strange effect. Huge works programmes in the city centre of Moscow, for example, disrupted many
of the conventional areas used by men to meet, forcing 'action' initially onto the Boulevard Ring in a more concentrated way—and
therefore more dangerous, from the point of view of paranoid Soviet
authorities. But while urbanization could disrupt established sexual

geographies, it could open up new ones just as well: the construction of the metro made people more mobile, and opened up dozens of other, more transient spaces, that could appear and disappear with the passing of a police van. Equally, new sights in the city centre, like the Hotel Moskva, attracted crowds of servicemen on leave, and anyone else who was curious about the new buildings. By the 1950s, the metro had opened up a huge range of potential meeting places.[71]

The great flaw and the great genius of the Soviet Union's terror regime was its apparent randomness. This meant that both enthusiastic conformity to, resistance to, and acquiescence to the ideological aspirations of the regime need not necessarily lead to a positive outcome for the individual. Thus, it made terror uniquely effective in destabilizing an individual's confidence in their own ability to chart a course through life—but it also made collaboration with the system equally thankless. This is in sharp contrast to the National Socialist terror apparatus, which grew rapidly from 1936 onwards. Within the territories of Germany, the NSDAP's domestic terror was far more tightly focused than the Soviet Union's, and drew substantially fewer people into its orbit. But from 1936, the party felt confident at last that it really did have a secure grip on power. More virulent anti-Semitic legislation emerged with a more systematic erosion of minorities' civil rights, as first Jews were stripped of their citizenship and disabled people sterilized (and 'disability' included all mental illness, deafness, alcoholism—it was a very wide definition), then Jews and gay men were increasingly persecuted. Then at the beginning of the war in the West, disabled people started to be murdered; by the end of 1941, and more importantly, the beginning of 1942, the mass murder of Jews was a central plank of the NSDAP's policy *outside* Germany, initially confined to the Eastern Front. Persecution against gay men spiked in the years 1936–40, when there was a sudden, eight-fold increase in prosecutions against gay men as the regime orientated itself towards war. In 1936 and 1937 there was a sustained set of raids on bars in large cities, as well as a set of show trials against Catholic priests and monks accused of homosexual practices.[72] During the 1936 Olympics, some gay bars were allowed to reopen and the police were told not to molest foreign travellers, but by and large men who were identified as gay had a bleak future. Many went into what Germans call '*innere Migration*', or 'inward migration'. This was the psychological technique by which most Germans who did not conform to the National Socialist 'ideal' managed to ignore or suppress those parts of themselves which remained moral, autonomous, and determined—but different. Those who could not or would not do this experienced first the penal justice system, followed by immediate internment in a camp—in this case, Sachsenhausen in January 1940, as one man from Vienna recalled after the war:

> When my name was called, I stepped forward, gave my name and mentioned paragraph 175. With the words, 'You filthy queer, get over here, you bum-fucker,' I received several kicks from behind and was kicked over to an SS sergeant in charge of my block. The first thing I got from him was a violent blow on my face that threw me to the ground...he brought his knee up hard into my groin that I doubled with pain. He grinned at me and said, 'That was your entrance fee, you filthy Viennese swine.'[73]

Most gay men caught up in this system died of starvation, disease, or beatings in the concentration-camp system—it is hard to know how many. But the persecution of minorities like Jews, disabled people, and gay men tells us a lot about the sudden expansion of the state's ambitions in the 1930s: from London to Berlin to Moscow, the range and vigour of intervention by the state into people's 'natures' was startling.

The war in general, however, led to widespread sexual chaos. Leaving to one side the most grotesque expression of sexuality in the war—the mass rapes and female humiliations that were perpetrated especially in the last year of the war, discussed in Chapter 2, p. 152—the chaos and death which marked the experience of war for most led to a riot of sexual adventure. It should be noted, though, that during the war the US armed forces for the first time began asking recruits if they were homosexual—a practice that would become more widespread after the war in other Western militaries. This marks out yet another important point in the transformation of Western attitudes to sexuality, and the shift from 'doing' to 'being'. Four thousand men were dismissed from the US armed forces during the war for this 'abnormality'; it is impossible to estimate how many more were expelled for the same reason but classified as 'neuropsychiatric' cases.[74] This was a taste of things to come as more and more people were being asked to define their sexuality for the first time, and relatively late in the century.

Most urban Europeans, however, could use the chaos of warfare to evade detection for all sorts of sexual adventure. Venereal disease in London almost doubled between 1939 and 1942, and these were just the official figures of those who remained in London long enough to seek treatment there. The throughput of troops on leave would mean that most would be back in their units by the time symptoms showed. The war itself could provoke sexual experimentation in London. Gerald Dougherty was at the Proms in the Albert Hall on 7 September 1940—the first night of the blitz. The programme was interrupted because German planes had been spotted approaching London. The city outside was pitch black due to the blackout, but as he emerged from the Hall, 'The sky was absolutely scarlet and the noise of the aeroplanes and the guns was everywhere.' His first instinct was to go home to his parents, knowing that they would be worried about him; but seeing the sky light up as his city was attacked, instead 'I thought I may die tonight—I'm going to see what it's [homosexuality] like.' He walked down a deserted Oxford Street to the Fitzroy pub, between Marylebone station and Oxford Circus tube:

> I thought I'm mad walking down Oxford Street because of all the glass windows which could have broken and killed me. Anyway I got to the Fitzroy and it was magic inside with lights and music and gaiety and I thought I'd rather die here than in the streets.

When he eventually left, he walked with another man to get a train at Charing Cross station. 'We ran dodging from door to door because the shrapnel from the guns was sparking on the pavement.' Of course, when they arrived at Charing Cross there were no trains running due to the bombing, so neither of them could get home. Gerald's companion, though, bundled Gerald into a first class compartment of an idle carriage:

> It was most exciting with the bombs dropping and the glass shattering and I thought this is the way to spend the first night of the blitz—in the arms of a barrow boy in a railway carriage.

About 350 people were killed that night in London, and 1,300 injured. In conditions like this, it is not hard to understand Quentin

Crisp's observation that the war turned London into a vast double bed.[75] While the war was of course miserable, the collapse in normality that it produced in cities produced extreme disorder in all forms of 'normal' sexual activity and identity for gay and straight, male and female, black and white. For the British in particular, this is significant, because in Britain there is a potent 'myth of the blitz' which evokes order, togetherness, uprightness, and a tight, authentic patriotic normality. Left out of these accounts are the looting, the strikes, the royal family being booed—the men having sex in railway carriages while bombs dropped—and the staggering rise in sexually transmitted diseases and illegitimate births. The story of the activities of one railway carriage stationary at Charing Cross can potently undermine the clichés of a more generic East End, of the sort that appeared for the US public's consumption in such propaganda films as *London Can Take It!*

* * *

The years after the war are, in many of the stories of 'progress' that we tell ourselves, about a civilized Europe 'rising from the ashes'. But they were marked by an extraordinary amount of sexual persecution which peaked at the end of the 1950s in Britain, and in the mid-1950s in Germany—although the tolerance of the urban population for sexual and emotional variety in the late 1940s was great. Even Paris, with its tradition (or perhaps, myth?) of sexual tolerance was caught up in this. Post-war France kept Vichy's laws on sex between men. A decree of 1946 declared that only people of 'good character' could work in the employ of the state, which gave licence to sack men who had sex with men, or unmarried women and men if they cohabited. A decree of 1949 by the Préfet of Paris outlawed men dancing with men, which shows us both that the Préfet was intolerant—but also that men dancing with men was so widespread (or perceived to be so widespread) that a law to deal with it did not look ridiculous. In July 1960, the National Assembly passed the Mirguet amendment which committed the French state to combating the '*fléau social*'—social scourge or plague or curse—of homosexuality, compared in this law to tuberculosis. This doubled the sentence for any act which 'outraged public morality' or took place between two members of the same sex.

Why this reaction against the sexual variety that pertained during the war happened is controversial and complex, and historians are left making 'best guesses'. The 'big picture' is that there was an attempt to 'put right' what had clearly gone so terribly, terribly wrong in Europe, and that the heterosexual 'family unit' was considered so 'right', so a-politically 'natural' and irreducible, that anything that did not fit into it was deemed to be wrong. In part, this is probably true. As Paul Mirguet, sponsor of the new, severe law in France, said in the National Assembly in July 1960:

> I do not think it is necessary to labour the point, because you are all aware of the seriousness of this plague of homosexuality, a plague which we have a duty to protect our children against. At the moment when our civilisation, dangerously minoritarian in a changing world, becomes so vulnerable, we must do everything in our power to combat anything which might diminish its prestige. In this domain, as in so many others, France must lead the way.[76]

On one reading, this is another example of a pompous Frenchman's obsession with the *prestige de la France*. But people were being gaoled for this: the prestige of France was a *heterosexual* prestige; homosexuality was a contagious disease which infected children. The furious postwar reaction to the well-established *practical* freedoms that cities seemed to provide in the first half of the century is still difficult to understand. Furthermore, the shift in focus on the part of many liberals from *practical* freedoms in *real* spaces to *theoretical* freedoms existing in law books also requires explanation, because at just the moment that gay men were being most systematically oppressed in Europe, some of them started to agitate most intensively for specific legal rights. In particular, in Germany there was no sudden corrective to the horrific persecution carried out by the NSDAP. And in Britain, random individual divisional commanders in major cities suddenly found themselves driven by a revulsion towards sexual non-conformity which went well beyond the low-level persecutory instincts of the fifty years before the war. In France, historians have yet to investigate the impact of the sudden increase in persecution against any form of sexual experimentation. As Guy Hocquenghem recalled of a meeting he attended of a new group, the Front Homosexuel d'Action Révolutionnaire, held in a backroom in Paris in 1971:

I arrived at a small room where there were about thirty people…
Everyone told their life story, their dreams, their desires, with whom,
how, and why they'd slept with the people they'd slept with. And how
they'd been living…[77]

And so many had been living in *fear*. The Front Homosexuel's first
declarations of their goals demanded rights for *all* forms of sexuality,
not just homosexuality, and tellingly proclaimed the enemy to be 'le
sexisme, le phallocratisme, et l'hétérofliquisme': sexism, phallocracy,
and heteropolicism—*flic* is derogatory French slang for police. Clearly,
these men and women were feeling the impact of police attempts to
disrupt their lives. The Front Homosexuel rapidly inspired branches
in other French cities, then Belgian and north Italian cities.

Organizing a 'moral' norm or a 'moral' hierarchy in a situation of
profound material devastation is so difficult that one is tempted to classify it as impossible. In Berlin, it was rendered even harder by the split
in police administration between 1945 and the construction of the Wall
in 1961. And yet the Federal Republic and Democratic Republic of
Germany both craved a restoration of some form of moral order and,
perhaps correctly, viewed it as a precondition for the re-establishment
of some form of 'civilization' in Germany.[78] This left open the question
of what sort of moral order should be created. With an impoverished
'repertoire' of order to draw on in Germany, the family emerged as a
key building block of a renewed morality. In particular, masculinity
was held up to particular scrutiny, because if what had happened to
Germany represented a defect, then it was a defect in men. Both parts
of Germany maintained the revised Paragraph 175 prohibiting homosexuality until the late 1960s and both took into account convictions in
the National Socialist period when prosecuting men. Cases such as
Otto N.'s were typical, lifted from the archives of the Department of
Youth Services, Berlin in 1951.

Otto N. was a 49-year-old cashier. One night, Otto picked up a
young man at the pissoirs near the Friedrichsstraße station. He entered
into discussion with the man, and made arrangements to have sex—
during which Otto checked to ensure that the boy had reached the
age of majority. Having assured himself that the lad was eighteen,
Otto agreed to pay him 5 East German marks—and they had sex.
Later the same night, they happened to meet at a local cinema, and
while there, they arranged another meeting—the relationship was

clearly moving beyond a 'simple' one of monetary exchange, and becoming something more complex. They left the Eastern Zone, and drove into the Western Zone, looking for a specific underground bar. Along the way, they both befriended a third man, and all three agreed to meet at Otto's house the next morning, after Otto's wife had gone to work. Eventually, his wife discovered what was happening, and he was brought before the Tiergarten District Court. Otto had a substantial record in both the Nazi period and after, and justified his actions on the basis that mutual masturbation was not illegal in the Eastern Zone. However, he had been arrested in the Western Zone, which, with all of its democratic commitments and greater civil rights, focused more on enforcing sexual norms for men and women, gay and straight, than the socialist East. In fact, the GDR had decided to reinstate the 1926 version of Paragraph 175 (requiring material proof that sex had happened), rather than the 1936 Nazi one, which required little more than a suspicion. West Germany kept the Nazi ordinance. Otto—and, apparently, his young male friend—did not realize that eighteen meant that in matters sexual the young man was still legally a minor. Their ignorance won Otto six months in prison.[79]

What distressed the authorities most, it seems, was that a visible homosexual subculture was beginning to reassert itself in Berlin. The physical chaos of the city was rendered more potent by the administrative and geopolitical chaos and the fact that the criminal police could not cross the demarcation line running through the centre of the city: men having sex with men enjoyed more freedom to move than did the police. The bombed-out city, though, provided a plethora of secret spaces and places where all sorts of 'mischief' could be enacted—captured so presciently by Graham Greene's screenplay and Carol Reed's direction of the classic *The Third Man*. Set in Vienna in 1949, it shows both literally and figuratively how the different layers of a large city could facilitate disorder, appearance, and disappearance for anyone with a mind to exploit it. It also shows how, without the capacity to *read* and *know* all the nooks and crannies of a city, the 'authorities' could be rendered fairly helpless fairly easily. The haunting music of *The Third Man* captures so convincingly the anxiety of the 'authorities' in a range of urban settings—the bomb site, the staircase, the bedroom, the police station, the advertising columns, the sewers—because they can palpably *know* and *sense* every manner of disorderly behaviour and disorderly agent, yet they can no more grasp its perpetrators in their hands than they can grasp the music with which the film evokes their presence. Thus again and again, bomb sites featured as crime scenes of sexual adventure in German police records. When Gerhard Z. and Karl-Heinz S. met in Friedrichsstraße station and ambled off together towards some bomb-damaged buildings, they were followed by two officers, S. and W., because the building 'was often used by homosexuals and callboys for unnatural sex'. But the nature of the site meant that Gerhard and Karl-Heinz realized they had been followed, and thus they could not be observed doing anything. Gerhard, it turned out, was married. Clearly, the 'flexible' approach to sexual identity and practice was still widely in evidence in Berlin in the late 1940s and early 1950s.

But also, people were increasingly distinguishing between acts in public and acts in private—a 'spatial' way of sorting morality, that means that the moralizer can separate morality from the person whom they have decided is the bearer of it. In Britain, Germany, and France, the public became increasingly hostile to police invasions of privacy, while maintaining—or developing—a heightened sense of moral 'order', for all forms of sexual relationship. Instead of moralizing about a person, one could increasingly moralize about a *place*. Horst K. picked up a hustler at the Savignyplatz station in December 1956. They went back to Horst's flat and had sex, whereupon the call boy demanded 50 marks from Horst, or he would destroy his apartment and beat him to a pulp. When Horst refused to give him all of the 50 marks, the hustler went to the police and placed a charge against Horst. Horst contested the charge and represented himself in court. The presiding judge took into account that Horst had cooperated with the police, and had confessed to the 'crime', and so did not give him a prison sentence, but a 100-mark fine. But most importantly, the judge declared that although an illicit act had taken place, it did *not* offend public morals because it took place in private.[80] This is important, because for privacy to emerge as a protection to people, the *spaces* in which privacy could be contained had to be created. And for the first time, in the late 1950s, such spaces *were* created in modern cities. Poor people could, for the first time, expect to have a home of their own. And within it, they might gradually develop a sense of entitlement to a bedroom, and the privatization of life could begin for ordinary Europeans.

Right up to the 1950s, the 'flexible' model of sexual behaviour amongst many working-class people outlined in the pre-war era prevailed. As one of the most influential historians of sexuality concluded, 'male identities and reputations did not depend on a sexuality defined by the anatomical sex of their sexual partners'—a concept almost impossible for us to grasp today.[81] This was true across the West—in New York, St Petersburg, Manchester, Paris, Vienna, Berlin, and London. But this flexibility was to be largely destroyed in the 1950s, across Europe—something which affected 'straight' as well as 'gay'— and a much more restrictive model of sexual behaviour was established. And its destruction impacted most strongly on the working class, who found the range of their sexual activities most heavily circumscribed. Several causes for this have been highlighted by historians. First of all, men who identified as gay began to politicize their position more vociferously, and this called for a crystallization of identity. While even in the early 1950s, it was common for soldiers in urban barracks in London to take male partners in a very open way (so long as some cash transaction was involved, however small and 'token'), by the late 1950s, gay men were increasingly insisting that men who had sex with men were not just *doing* something transgressive; they were, in their very core, *being* something transgressive. This 'requirement to identify' in order to produce a more 'theoretical' type of freedom has been one of the major factors in the second half of the twentieth century that has excluded many (although certainly not all) people from adopting an exploratory attitude to sexuality. But two parallel changes also seem to have had an impact—and these changes rely on the evolving shape of the city to understand: diversification *within* the 'gay scene' (as it came to be called), and a set of social changes that we might best sum up as 'suburbanization'.

After the war, there were vast changes in the ways that young men's lives were organized that took them out of the 'sexual anarchy', and into what one historian has called the 'heterosexual dictatorship'.[82] The world of work started later, and tended to involve many fewer transitory, mobile jobs—like errand boy, telegraph boy, portering, which took place in streets, entrance halls, front doors—that marked the time between fourteen, the school-leaving age, and seventeen or eighteen when an apprenticeship might be taken up. Men's work in youth shifted away from this more 'transactional', mobile employment. In 1931 in one London borough, Islington, 65 per cent of all males aged fourteen, and 44 per cent of all males aged sixteen and seventeen were engaged in this category of 'street', mobile work, including errand boys, shop boys, van boys, messengers and page boys, newspaper sellers, and hawkers. It was these jobs that embedded young males in the culture of the street, and all European cities had 'telegraph boy' scandals from, well, the invention of the telegraph until it was rendered largely obsolete in the 1950s by the more widespread use of the telephone and the extension of the school age across Europe to fifteen, then sixteen. Parallel to this, vast housing programmes across urban Europe shifted families out of city centres in huge numbers and put them in suburbs. This had several effects: it meant that young men were geographically removed from the 'downtown' areas, where sexual adventure for all was more of a possibility, and isolated in suburban homes and suburban schools. This meant that population densities decreased and social life became more segregated from workplaces, as people rapidly moved further away from them. The vast rings of 1960s housing around all large European cities represent the massive decanting of populations from city centres, and also a vast de-concentration of their numbers in any one physical space. It also meant that poorer people had *privacy* in their homes for the first time. Thus rather than living in a maelstrom of sex (hetero, homo, and every other sort), working in and through and about the streets, wedged at night into overcrowded rooms of multi-occupancy, which were themselves wedged into city centres of diverse function, from the 1950s sex could increasingly reliably happen 'behind closed doors'—a point noted by the Berlin judge above. This meant that sex for gay and straight alike could move out of the street and the park, and into the bedroom because, for the first time, it became reliable to assume that an adult might actually *have* a bedroom.

Nor was this transition from public to private left to chance. The 'right' to acquire one of the millions of flats built for social housing purposes in European cities from the 1950s onwards was explicitly linked, in every case, to conspicuous conformity to a relatively new, but romantically nostalgic vision of heterosexual normality: if young people got married, the state would reward them with their own home. If they had a child, the state would frequently *guarantee* them a home. Thus the system worked as a package: stay in school during the period of sexual awakening; sign up as rigidly and rigorously heterosexual, the younger the better, and you will be transported out of city centres, out of very crowded dwellings, and segregated into areas with little street culture of any sort (sexual or otherwise), little access to city centres, and in discrete housing units designed to engineer a very specific version of heterosexual existence: the modern, well-structured, birth-controlled family. Marriage ages for men tumbled across Europe.

In the new commercial venues like milk bars and coffee bars, young men would socialize with young women in ways they previously had not. Furthermore, these young men had money in their pockets which meant that they could afford to 'treat' each other and women, and had less desire, perhaps, to be 'treated' themselves. And this process of 'moving indoors' happened in the 'gay' world too; the rise in 'gay bars' in Paris and London meant that the 'chance' encounter, with its implied flexibility, was eliminated—or at least, radically reduced. 'Gay bars' require people to identify themselves as gay before they go in; but a 'bohemian' bar opens up encounters for everyone. Many 'mixed', 'gay-friendly' bars became de facto more heterosexual, as working-class men had more money to treat themselves, and the idea of a middle-class 'passport to the city' lost its relevance. And in the factory too, the introduction of women workers meant that previously homo-social environments became hetero-social; and, in the case of Britain, the winding down of national service from the late 1950s to 1963 removed another potent environment in which men were expected to form relationships with men only.

This 'lost world' was summed up in a hit novel of the 1950s, *The Heart in Exile* (1953). It was one of the first 'mass-market' novels in Britain to focus on gay characters—albeit rather two-dimensionally. But it brought to the fore of the public consciousness, in both Britain and America, a certain sort of 'gay imaginary world', inviting readers to enter the (distressed, sick, and immature) mind of a gay man. In it, one of the characters laments the lost world of the chaotic melee of the pre-war city centre in the new age of affluence:

> Boys accepted us because we were class...they liked us because, unlike women, we didn't cost them money...we made a fuss of them, which their girls didn't...Today they can afford women, and if they don't want women they have plenty of money for other amusements.[83]

But this imposition of physical order on the city—the insistence on 'indoor' work, 'indoor' leisure and 'indoor' living—had a flip side. This type of radical housing improvement left spaces behind, which could be filled by 'alternative' inhabitants—in Western European cities, primarily large numbers of migrants from Turkey, and the British and French Empires; in Eastern European cities from the countryside, as those societies re-emphasized industrial production and urban growth.

An area like Notting Hill in London became, in the 1950s, rapidly associated with two groups: West Indian men, and gay indigenous men. As one gay man, a migrant to London from 'the provinces' (viewed increasingly as a sort of 'gay Hades') said to a social investigator in the 1950s:

> I expect you know there is a huge homosexual kingdom just below the surface of ordinary life, with its own morals and code of behaviour. In Notting Hill Gate this kingdom within a kingdom seems to have come to the surface. That's why I live there. You would understand this better if you went to a homosexual party. You'd find there certain things were done and other things not. It is an entirely different code of behaviour to normal life. When I walk through Notting Hill Gate I feel I'm at a gigantic homosexual party.[84]

Such was the reach of this new form of 'ghetto' that even men who had been imprisoned because of their sexuality would be advised by prison counsellors to move to Notting Hill upon release:

> The After-Care people advised me to live in the metropolitan area where there were many homosexuals and where I'd be less noticeable. I now live in Notting Hill Gate, so no-one can accuse me of not taking their advice.[85]

The definition of 'ghettos' or 'scenes' was crucial in enabling a more stable gay subculture to emerge, because it allowed for there to be different *types* of gay man.

Clearly, such a system existed in Berlin in the late 1920s, but this was not the norm, and Berlin did not manage to repeat that level of diversity after the war. Far more important was Hamburg, which by 1959 could list twenty-nine 'gay' bars which actually identified as 'gay' in some stable sense. They were focused in the peripheries of the red-light district (something which would be common to other cities too, like Amsterdam and Manchester) where the police had already worked out the 'rules of a game' in a sort of semi-official set of negotiations with those who sought to detach themselves from the 'heterosexual-in-the-home'-ideal of the Bundesrepublik. So in Hamburg these bars were tightly focused in the areas of Sankt Pauli and Sankt Georg. Frankfurt and Berlin had about fourteen gay bars each, but other large German cities, like Munich, Cologne, Stuttgart, and Hanover still worked within the less defined, less 'identifying' framework of the pre-war model, with a greater emphasis on a more unstable 'outdoor' scene too. One historian has conducted an analysis of this 'scene' in large German cities in the 1950s and 1960s, and has demonstrated an interesting conclusion: once specifically 'gay' spaces were established as stable in identity, and safe from police threat, there followed a widespread disaggregation amongst gay men into 'types'—and four in particular dominated. They were the 'Tunte/Tante' ('queen'), the 'normal', the leatherman (or 'butch'), and the hustler. And out of contests and conflicts between these groups, as much as between 'gays' and 'straights', emerged a disputed imposition of 'identity'.[86] We may or may not agree with the 'typification' categories, but the construction of such powerful identities amongst gay men had important consequences. It was in the encounters *within* the spaces of the gay scene that many of the debates about establishing rights and identities were negotiated, rather than in relations with heterosexual people. The internal dynamics of the 'gay scene' were central to the types of identity that gay men formed, and many of the claims to 'rights' which emerged in the 1960s, 1970s, and 1980s were targeted as much at other gay men, as at the 'straight' community in which they lived.

The 'queeny' identity could well mark a rite of passage into the gay scene in many cultures, before and after the Second World War. Werner Landers was travelling to a Mardi Gras ball in 1946 as a sixteen year-old boy. This is important, as Mardi Gras is a big festival in Germany (above all in big Catholic cities, like Cologne where it is called 'Karneval', and Munich, where it is called 'Fasching'), and provides an opportunity for people to dress up as the opposite of what they are, and behave inappropriately or outrageously for a fixed period of time after which they would be expected to re-adopt 'normal' roles. Thus, men could go out as women for the period (it should be noted, some cities had an extraordinarily long period of 'Karneval', stretching from 'Three Kings' Day' on 6 January, until Shrove Tuesday, up to six weeks later). Thus they had an important role in allowing sexual adventurers to go out and about unmolested, dressed how they wanted. On the train, Landers' friend declared that from that day on, he would be known as 'Natascha', and asked Landers what he would be called. 'As of today,' he said, 'I am called Therese and I come from the country.' It was a name that he kept for the rest of his life, and marked his entry into the gay scene. It signified an assertion that he defined for himself who he was, and how he should be addressed. However, the widespread adoption of a feminized persona could form an increasingly negative image of homosexuality for those who wished to emphasize the claims on 'normality' that some gay men wished to invoke. These conflicts were described in occasional debates in print but, more significantly, lived out—and a myriad of encounters forever lost to the historian, which nonetheless were crucial.

As one German 'normal' gay man wrote in a popular magazine at the time, *Der Kreis*, in 1955: 'the strictest war is to be declared against fairy behaviour [*Tantentum*], for it is this above all that brings us opposition and—there is nothing more irritating!—makes us ridiculous'.[87] This 'war' within an emerging gay identity would be fought through the use of bars, as differing groups attempted to define the parameters not just of what was acceptable, but what was normal. Many gay men in the 1950s—and up to the present day—find their first experiences of gay bars are of the most conspicuous or 'notorious' bars, and that in these bars, the 'queeny' type can dominate, which some men can experience as an affront to their masculine ideals of themselves. It is hard for the historian to capture these 'everyday' exchanges, but new techniques in oral history are gradually making them more available. For example, in the northern German naval city of Kiel, there was only one 'gay' bar—a bar just for people identifying as gay. It was called the Bunte Kuh—the Colourful Cow. There, in the mid-1950s, Peter M. met Uwe, and they went back to Uwe's flat. Peter viewed himself as 'masculine', and an important part of his identity was that he was the penetrative partner in sex. However, Uwe convinced Peter to let himself be penetrated which he found painful. However, the next day, Peter could not stop thinking about Uwe, so went back to the Bunte Kuh that night to see if he was there. In a period where private telephones were rare, it is important to understand that for most people, specific places were required for *any* relationship to evolve, gay or straight. It was largely impossible for most Europeans to 'swap numbers'—they could just revisit a place. When Peter returned to the Bunte Kuh, a 'Tunte' (queen) called Maria shouted across the bar, 'Where did you leave your husband?!' Maria beckoned Peter over, saying, 'Hello, *meine Kleine* [my little girl]', which irritated him. 'Even if she [*sic*] acts like a woman, she doesn't have to lay all this effeminacy on me.' Peter remonstrated that he objected to being called by female words (in German, referring to someone in a female way is more possible than in English). Maria laughed riotously, and shouted out, 'The world is simply set up in this manner: He who sticks it in is the man, and he who gets it is the woman! Do you see? And everyone here knows that Uwe is always the one who sticks it in. No hole is safe with him.' With a look of feigned curiosity on his face, Maria inquired, 'Or did things turn out differently with you?'[88] In the 'war' that has since raged about what a gay man 'is', confrontations of this type have been frequent, and the emergent identities amongst gay men have been constituted in dozens of 'Colourful Cows' in dozens of ways in dozens of cities. Out of these conflicts *between* gay men, identities were crystallized, and the foundations for an organized political presence to campaign for gay rights could emerge in many Western European cities in the 1970s. Similarly, contests about what a straight man or woman 'is' have also raged—but sadly, escaped the gaze of the historian. But this exposes the complexity of the dynamic of sexual identities: they were not fought out solely with 'opposites'; the most bitter conflicts have often been within groups of people clumsily labelled 'the same'.

This is not to say that Germany was a liberal haven: a profound sense of 'moral panic' after the 'hoodlum riots' of 1956 and 1957, the real threat of communism from the East, the sacred position of the family as an antidote to the moral corruption of National Socialism, and an inability to make sense of the recent past as any sort of 'progress', meant a tense sociopolitical landscape in which strong homophobic voices were common. Gay men were even pursued for 'care costs' for their own imprisonment under National Socialism. One Berlin man, who had been imprisoned between 1936–9, was prosecuted to pay 350 marks in 'care costs'—which he agreed to pay, finally to get the (now democratic) German state off his back.[89] Contemporaries tended to conceive of the 'threat' of homosexuality in

terms of spaces and international politics: Catholic civil servant
Richard Gatzweiler's *The Third Sex: The criminality of homosexuality* of
1951 denounced a 'party of inverts' and 'Moscow's new guard' who
were busy in Germany building a network of 'clubs and sects' and
thereby creating a 'state within a state'. 'What should one do', he
asked, 'with a tree that bears no fruit?' The geopolitical map of Europe
was superimposed onto the socio-sexual map of the West German gay
scene. Thus, the state should destroy these 'nests' without mercy—the
same vocabulary used by the NKVD in Moscow and St Petersburg in
1934.[90] The statistics in Germany show, though, a rapid decline in
morality prosecutions after the mid-1950s, and a huge proliferation in
specifically 'gay' spaces in all of *West* Germany's major cities. Crucially,
in the case of Gatzweiler, a tiny organization of 'friends' in Berlin used
this moment of attack to crystallize an identity and attempt to use the
instruments of the legal state to challenge their persecutors. The Berlin
Association for the Reform of the Sex Laws—which no one had heard
of—leapt to prominence by launching a civil prosecution of Gatzweiler,
for 'incitement to murder'. The tiny association of friends became a
coherent civil rights movement at that moment.

But it was in Britain that the persecution of gay men reached its
post-war apotheosis in the 1950s. Between the end of the First World
War and the mid-1950s, 2,467 prosecutions for some sort of sexual
misconduct between men were brought in London. Thirty-three of
these were for offences which took place 'in private', but twenty-six of
those followed complaints of non-consensual sex (or to give it its
proper term, rape), and so would seem to be justified on any moral
scale, liberal or conservative. Presumably, one would hope that the
police would prosecute all non-consensual sex. Thus between 1918
and about 1954, 'only' nine prosecutions followed consensual sex in
private—a disaster for those caught, but a small number. But in the
later 1950s, British cities, uniquely in Europe, experienced an unpre-
dictable and inexplicable 'reign of terror' by organs of the state against
gay men which focused for the first time explicitly on penetrating and
politicizing the home and exposing it as a site of dangerous deviation.
From the late 1940s, there was an upswing in a rabid campaign
against gay men's private spaces, which historians have struggled to
explain. Some have emphasized orders from the centre and the arrival
in office of a new Conservative government and the obsessions of a

particular Home Secretary; another has emphasized the inconsistency with which the persecution took place, leading him to conclude that the culture of individual police stations, divisional commands, and groups of police officers was the defining factor.

With each arrest came the sifting of the men's private papers and then the arrest of the writers of love letters. Thus, a chance arrest in a raid on a bar could lead to a cascade of catastrophe for dozens of men—jobs lost, families destroyed, suicides, imprisonment. Sexuality could build a bridge for the state between the public toilet and the private bedroom. New spaces recently acquired, this time new bedrooms, living rooms, and flats, thus seemed to some to present an unquantifiable threat from an unquantifiable number of locations. The rate of change was extraordinary. The Bow Street magistrates' court (in central London, so in an area where many sexual adventurers converged) averaged about 25 prosecutions a year for 'homosexual' offences between the wars, soaring to an average of 200 or so afterwards. Greenwich magistrates' court in industrial south-east London went from a mighty zero prosecutions in 1917 to eight a year after the Second World War; Lambeth in south-central London, from one to sixteen; Marlborough Street in West London went from sixteen to ninety-nine; West London magistrates' court leapt from two to one hundred per annum; Clerkenwell, in the East End, from two to twenty-five per annum.[91]

It was a level of persecution which drew in elites and 'ordinary' citizens alike: the Labour MP for Paddington North, a working-class part of west London, was arrested twice for 'importuning' (i.e. chatting up another man), and fined in January 1953 for visiting a toilet too frequently while out drinking in the West End.[92]

Public revulsion at this frenzy of witch hunts was, however, extensive. Even the Church of England queried 'the validity of the right of the state to take cognisance of immoral private actions between adult male homosexuals'.[93] The Conservative Home Secretary in the early 1950s, Sir David Maxwell Fyfe, told the House of Commons with some pride that while in 1938, the police had prosecuted had 138 'unnatural offences', 822 'attempts' at 'unnatural offences' (including importuning), by 1952 there were 607 prosecutions for the former, and 3,087 prosecutions for the latter. This breathtaking extension of the state's powers into the private life of the citizen was justified on the grounds that:

One element in dealing with this matter is the protective element in punishment because homosexuals in general are exhibitionists and proselytisers, and a danger to others, especially the young.[94]

But some, inside and outside the establishment, started to worry about the extension of the power of the state like this; if gay people were left unprotected, and in particular, if they were persecuted for activities in private, then an Englishman's home was very much *not* his castle, and the police and the Conservative administration were proposing a radical extension to the scope and nature of the British state. It was a type of transformation which even Conservative MPs could not countenance. One, Sir Robert Boothby, commented that there was a 'homosexual underground' in most of our big cities, which was a constant menace to youth, but that:

The sporadic campaigns of the police against it, often accompanied by methods of great dubiety, do nothing towards its eradication. On the contrary, they simply intensify the squalor by which it is surrounding and widen the area in which the underground flourishes.[95]

Boothby concluded that homosexuality was awful, and young people needed to be protected, but that the police risked alienating the public—and had failed to understand the nature of modern cities: they are, in matters like this, unpoliceable. Driving a 'problem' underground was the ultimate nightmare for the modern, surveilling state because it made the phenomenon invisible—and therefore all the more potent.

Especially following the arrest of many members of 'society' in London, several committees were set up to enquire about how best to treat homosexuals in prison. But eventually, public revulsion at the vigorous expansion of the state in this field so extreme that in 1957 the Conservative government commissioned Sir John Wolfenden to conduct a wide-ranging enquiry into sexual 'crime'—primarily, prostitution and homosexuality.[96] A notable exception to this was the medical profession, whose professional body, the British Medical Association, conducted a review of the matter which concluded, 'The proper use of sex, the primary purpose of which is creative, is related to the individual's responsibility to himself and the nation.'[97] The BMA were very happy to promote the idea that sex was really about the state or nation. The British state was being, in the middle of the 1950s, humiliated by the total penetration of the highest ranks of the civil service by the Soviet intelligence services, and several of the ring, which included Burgess, Blunt, and Maclean, were gay. Perhaps this helps explain how such a link between sexuality and the state could be sustained with such vigour. It does not explain, though, the energetic prosecutions of gay men in large cities prior to this discovery.

The Wolfenden Committee soon focused on homosexuality, proposing a set of reforms leading to legalization in 1967. Contemporary sociological investigators were baffled by the sudden leap in persecution too and, in the context of Wolfenden's enquiry, many studies were done of 'the' homosexual by sociologists and doctors. Most of the medical studies concluded that homosexuality was, indeed, a pathology, the result of various factors, ranging from immaturity to poor relationships with mothers, to generalized degeneration and weakness. But they also acknowledged that it was 'incurable', part of someone's 'nature', rather than a crime against it. But sociologists offered a different perspective. Most influential was Michael Schofield and the evidence he collected on the everyday lives of gay men. He put together the life stories of many gay men in a way which highlights the viciousness of the state's sudden interventions in their lives.

In one cohort of men he interviewed, eight of them were sent to prison for their first 'offence' in private. In each case, the police set up networks of emotional entrapment so that they could make the move between the public space, to which they did have legitimate access, and the private space which the men might have believed accorded them some protection from a suddenly arbitrary and hostile state. Stories like these were common:

> My friend was picked up for being drunk and disorderly. The police tried to pin a job on him. They kept him there all night and in the end he confessed about us, so as to explain where he had been the night he was supposed to have done the robbery....My friend got 18 months but I got four years. The judge said I was the corrupter. [Four years; first offence; in private]

Another man was arrested at work after his workmates informed on him:

> After he had been at work a few weeks, we had a conversation about sex and love and he told me he'd been around with several men. Then it started to be quite a regular thing with us, usually at night after we'd

been left to lock up. We grew very fond of each other and I think other
people must have seen it. At any rate tongues began to wag. After three
years the police suddenly appeared at night when we were alone in the
workshop. I heard later that they kept a watch on it several nights... On
the night they came, they looked around but they didn't see nothing.
But they followed Jim home and took him to the station. He was kept
there a long time and in the end he gave the whole game away... [Seven
years; first offence; in private]

It is interesting here that for three years, these men had a fulfilling
relationship using their workplace after lock-up as a 'private space',
complementing its public nature during the day. The police would
even pursue men who had been the victims of sexual assault in hospital, hoping to build up a 'chain':

We sucked each other off and then the next thing I know he was trying
to choke me. I went out for the count. When I woke up he was standing over me fully dressed and then helped take me to the hospital.
I was in a terrible mess. My jaw was mashed. I think he must have
stamped on my face. I was in hospital for two months. I had to have
an operation on my face. The police kept coming to see me, asking
who'd done it. They even came to the rest-home where I went next.
Just about then another man was caught and at the police station he
admitted having sex with me. I gave in then and told them everything.
[Four years; first offence; in private][98]

Frequently, the police would lie and say that if a man confessed, he
would get off lightly, or that if he gave the names of all the gay men
he knew, they would let him off—it was the same tactic used by the
secret police in the Soviet Union. But the inevitable consequence was
a harsh sentence, plus the arrest of all the men he had named:

At the police station I was shown letters I had written to this man.
They were quite harmless, although a few phrases could be interpreted
to mean that we'd had sex. The policeman told me that they did not
want me, and it was in my own interests to tell them about the other
man. They would move heaven and earth to see that I didn't get into
trouble. So after a lot of persuasion and some strong arm methods,
I signed a statement admitting sex three times. [Seven months; first
offence; in private][99]

Eventually, the scale of state violence against these men shocked the
government, and the public more widely, into a change of attitude.

What particularly appalled people throughout Britain was the sense that the state should see into private space like this. The discoveries of the Wolfenden Committee, and sociologists like Schofield, placed this 'secret' policing firmly in the public domain. Furthermore, both this sociological research *and* the steady stream of prosecutions showed that gay men were not predatory perverts: there were gay teachers, engineers, bricklayers, clerks, company directors, and engine drivers cropping up in both academic enquiries and salacious tabloid news reports. The frenzy of police oppression showed that 'they' were not just a few 'pansies' in the theatre, and that there was no connection between homosexuality and paedophilia. Stories like this matter, both in their own terms for recognizing the horrific tragedy for the people involved, but also for the wider history of the modern West. Tales like these, and sentences like these, would not be out of place in Eastern Europe, and while such excesses were always on a vaster scale there, these histories should challenge us to do two things. First of all, we need to re-evaluate the meaningfulness of British self-perceptions of being the 'home of liberty', of a uniquely British, uniquely liberal national trajectory. But they should also disrupt radically the clichés of a century of progress: Europe did not move from darkness to light over the twentieth century in matters sexual, but from light to darkness, and then slowly back out again.

But this attitude of change was engendered most conspicuously not in a change of attitude towards 'gay' men—that, if anything, hardened in the 1960s and 1970s as fewer and fewer men had the free-flowing experience characteristic of the pre-war working-class world, when sex with men was a more everyday experience. What changed was a public attitude in Britain towards *space*, and who should be allowed access to it. Widespread revulsion at homosexuality was expressed, often more virulently. But the idea emerged that 'if they're not ramming it down my throat', and 'if it happens behind *closed doors*', this made the activity—and the identity—permissible, although still undesirable. When sociologist Michael Schofield tried to summarize his survey evidence of heterosexual men, he found that they oscillated between two general opinions, often simultaneously:

It sickens me. It's nauseating. Something should be done about it. What, I don't know.

[If I met one] I'd give him a punch between the eyes and then run like hell.

And:

I wouldn't lock them up. What good does that do? It's a defect, you see. The best thing is to tell them: 'We'll leave you alone providing you behave yourself, *keep out of public sight*, and don't go making a nuisance of yourself.'

We should have moved out of the times of Oscar Wilde by now. Mind you, I don't think homosexuals should have special rights. But *if they keep it hidden*, one has no cause to object, especially as I'm told that in some cases it's not curable.

I can't see anything against it *if they do it in private*. We've all got kinks of some sort. Live and let live, I say.[100]

Of fifty heterosexual men that Schofield interviewed in the early 1960s, thirty-five felt that it should be decriminalized, but with a *spatial* caveat: homosexual love must remain hidden. Hand-holding, kissing, and all the 'paraphernalia' of modern public displays of *hetero*-sexuality would be prohibited in public. Homosexuality was morally acceptable if spatially encapsulated.

Yet gay men have been reluctant to accept this demand for privacy. As such, they have been at the fore of late-twentieth-century attempts to push back the attempts by the state to regulate private lives. In most European cities, gay men have staked out particular zones upon which they have focused their demands for equality. But this has been double-edged, because the agents of the establishment of these areas have been, very often, corporations and rich individuals who have seen gay men not as a sexuality, but as a market. Such areas of concentrated asser-tions of equality can be found in most European cities, like Manchester's Canal Street, shown in Figure 4.3, and the process was similar through-out: businesses would open in 'run down' areas of town where rents were cheaper, and city councils would promote this as a way of 'regen-erating' difficult areas. This is all well and good, but it has little to do with sexuality, and more to do with managing property values and making money. That does not make it 'bad'—but it does mean that it is not directly connected to the idea of sexuality, and sometimes, they turn 'sexuality' into a sort of neatly packaged 'spectacle' or 'vibe' for visitors, rather than a type of identity or activity itself.

Figure 4.3 Canal Street, Manchester, England. By the 1990s, gay subcultures had 'turned the city inside out': rather than gay bars being spread secretively throughout the city, the fusion of sexuality with capitalism (and often, urban regeneration projects) started to produce 'gay villages' in European cities (or ghettoes to their critics). On the one hand these spaces demonstrate people taking control of the city streets to assert themselves without fear; on the other, they have aligned gay men more and more into a very homogenizing set of ideas about an appropriate 'lifestyle'—styles of clothes, types of politics, trends in music, and ideas of body image.

Typical was the Marais, in Paris. Up until the 1980s, gay bars in Paris clustered around the rue Sainte-Anne, near the Opéra Garnier. It was an invisible, secretive 'scene' of locked doors, and needed a deep knowledge of the city in order to operate. But in 1978, a bar called Le Village opened across town in the Marais, and it transformed the nature of being gay in the city. It was at street level, it was open during the day, it had windows. It was both obvious and, at the same time, paraded a more conspicuous 'respectability'. It was decorous—'normal'. With Le Village as a kernel, a gay 'quarter' grew up around it, in which gay men (typically) asserted their right to 'be', to 'be' visible, to 'be' respectable—but all in the context of conspicuous consumption. As one sociologist noted in the late 1980s, the acquisition of this space in the city was felt to be equivalent to a special sort of freedom:

> From Le Village to the Duplex, from the Piano Zinc to Le Central, the gay quarter set itself up in the 1980s... Today we have attained a new level with boutiques, nightclubs, a bookstore, postcard shops, sex shops, restaurants, bars, clothing stores (as well as laundromats), and recently a pharmacy waving the gay flag that was inaugurated by 'the entire community'. Paris could at last have the honour of joining the other modern capitalist capitals with its gay neighbourhood.[101]

The 'capitalist' element is crucial, because land prices in the Marais prohibit all but the wealthiest business people establishing there, and the bar Velvet shown in Manchester in Figure 4.3 is a multi-million pound design extravaganza: no 'ordinary' person could open bars here any more. Some have seen a sad loss in this commercialized, sanitized sexuality, mourning the departure of an urban sense of chaos with all the possibilities it contained, and its replacement with a commercial, capitalist, sanitized, 'Disnified' normality.

While one contemporary noted that this 'colonization' of the city meant that, 'Homosexuality has come out of the shadow and from the domain of the not-talked-about', others were more critical. One observer found that this new, Americanized, sanitized sexuality was obsessed with 'lifestyle', not life, and concluded that it was based on the neglect 'of those that did not fit in, or who were outside this nocturnal effervescence. Gay pride was nothing more than a commercial carnival.' Another, Frédéric Martel, concluded:

In the 1980s a veritable gay 'citizen' was born. He lived in Paris, ate his breakfast while listening to [the gay radio station] Fréquence gaie, worked in a gay establishment (there were over a hundred of them in Paris already), and informed himself by reading *Gai Pied*...In the evening he would have dinner in a restaurant in the Marais and then dance until dawn at the Palace or the Broad...[It was] the beginning of the era of the body, a cultish narcissistic wave that continued to develop through countless gyms and saunas. The new gay had arrived with string bikini and leather jacket. The queen and the sissy were gone.[102]

The freedom to take the city, to be open and public within it, had been won—but at the cost of homogenization, and the enforcement of strict hierarchies *within* gay culture, just as repressive for those on the wrong end of them because their bodies or their 'gayness' did not conform to the public, capitalist, boutique ideal.

Frequently, the 1960s are represented as a 'turning point' in the assertion of individual rights. And indeed, inasmuch as rights on paper are relevant to lives as they are lived, the average individual would possess more of them after the 1960s than before. But 'rights' in their legal sense are strange things, often curiously detached from lived reality. Just as the acquisition of 'rights' by black people in the American South, or Serfs in Russia, both in the 1860s, could often lead to a worsening in the quality of everyday life for an individual, so the birth of the 'rights' culture, coupled with the redesign of cities in the 1950s and 1960s, made people fix their sexual colours to the mast ever more rigidly. I am not advocating a return to the world of blackmail or unpunished violence towards 'effeminate' men (whether they were gay or not) that clearly existed, and clearly still exists, merely a recognition that history works in 'swings and roundabouts', not clear stories with happy endings.

It is also important to recall that potent phrase used to characterize the sexual landscape at the century's opening: 'sexual anarchy'. It was an anarchy that allowed (or was unable to prevent) all sorts of sexual adventure, men with men, women with men. But it was also unable or unwilling to prevent sex with children or rape (let alone rape within marriage, which it did not even recognize). While these problems are also with us today, on balance we have established a framework for dealing with them that is infinitely better resourced than in 1900. But it is worth pointing out that looking at the *where* of the history of sexuality—which is also the history of the body, the state, the individual, the law, medicine, and so many other things—there is no straight line from darkness to light. The sexual world of European cities for the first fifty years of the last century was clearly one which emphasized, on a tour through its spaces and places, a vast amount of diversity and freedom, often relatively unmolested by the police (but with catastrophic consequences when they roused themselves into action), and unconstrained by a sexual reductionism that insists that one fundamentally 'is' one thing or the other, and that one must declare it, and thereafter stand by it. It is, in fact, the second half of the century that impresses for its order and systematization of the individual, as even in the moment of clearest liberation, the new-found freedoms of the city have served merely to put people into a 'more stately closet'.[103]

5

Building Utopia: How Cities Shaped our Lives and our Minds

'Town planning' is a concept that seems today to sum up irrelevance, boredom, and small-mindedness. As an idea, it is slightly more viva-cious in German—*Städtebau,* or 'city building'—and more intellectually convincing in the French *urbanisme.* But in English, it sounds decep-tively anodyne. It speaks of conflicts over sheds and regulations on drainage. In an age where one would hesitate to build a porch without consulting an array of administrators, bureaucrats, and technicians, it would seem perhaps fatuous to assert that planning represents, perhaps more than anything else, the genius of the twentieth century. 'Planning' in this chapter will stand for the whole panoply of schemes and projects that proposed total solutions to humanity's problems. Planning deserves this exalted position as the 'genius' of the twentieth century because it is both the means and the end of the last one hundred years of European civilization, intellectual endeavour, and state formation: the end is order, perfect knowledge of the citizenry by the state, everything in its place. The means is ordering, sorting, examining, relocating, reposi-tioning. And most large plans to perfect the world can trace their roots back to a revolution in the ways people thought about cities around the turn of the last century: the city was the first object of planning, and possibly the last remaining one too.

'Planning' as a concept leads something of a double life. Most Europeans have a folk memory of unplanned worlds, and the horrors they contained. And today, we have potent examples of planless worlds in Somalia, Congo, and Afghanistan. Drawing on this folk memory and living examples, on the one hand, planning as a way of thinking and behaving represents the elimination of typhoid, tubercu-losis, scarlet fever, polio, nits, lice, and typhus; the birth of privacy in bedrooms and living rooms; the achievement of a dry home with central heating and hot water; parks; literacy for all, and education for girls in particular. In a word, in this part of our understanding of the world, planning is 'progress'.

But there is a darker side. Planning is also the self-same logic that underpins the Holocaust and the Ukrainian famine in the 1930s and 1940s, the Great Leap Forward, the Cultural Revolution, and the Khmer Rouge in the 1960s and 1970s, and the European Union's calamitous Common Agricultural Policy right up to the present day.[1] Planning embodies the recognition by the state and its angry citizens that 'something must be done' about disease, incest, cold, damp, alienation, loneliness, overcrowding, pollution, coal dust, noise, and exploitative landlords. And yet it also stands as a byword for the failures of the state, for the elimination of personality, for the stripping back of autonomy, for greyness and ugliness and soullessness; in short, for inhumanity. Mention it, and one scribbles a cursive shorthand for the despoliation of our cities. The plan stands for the infantilization of the citizen in the liberal democracy, and the oppression of the citizen in the communist East. Planning is the twentieth century's triumph and tragedy, the poison and the antidote mixed together. Planning, as a way of thinking and behaving, represents the paradox of progress and the genius of the twentieth century.

'Planning' in the sense that it is being used here is relatively new. People have always laid out cities; they have always had a sense of what makes them beautiful, and thought about how best to express the social order inherent *in* them, in the fabric *of* them. But the idea that there should be a cadre of experts that should glance into every realm of the citizen's life, from their workplace to their bedroom, and reorganize each space and place in the service of an ideal vision of universal wholesomeness is a new one.

The great city-builders of the ancient world from Babylon to Athens to Rome and of the medieval world in Sienna or Lincoln; and the Baroque designs of Pope Sixtus V in Rome and Christopher Wren in London had a breathtaking capacity to create an aesthetic order. One cannot visit any Continental European city from Barcelona in the west to Moscow in the east, and not be struck by the tremendous, rigid uniformity on show. Often, designers of cities managed to link this aesthetic order to a social or a religious order, and express both beautifully: Sixtus' Baroque expression of resurgent papal power, or Haussmann and Napoléon III's neo-Renaissance vision of a bourgeois Paris in the mid–late nineteenth century, are masterpieces in this regard. But they did not aim at producing a *total* world, a *total* experience, or a *total* human being, touching on every aspect of human life. They were not intended simultaneously to produce ideal gender relations, exterminate disease, enhance economic activity, facilitate transport, engineer the ideal family life, prevent pollution, eliminate class conflict, define the qualities of childhood, resolve women's status in society, and facilitate industrial development *all at the same time*. Such a totalizing ambition could only emerge in the late nineteenth century, in the wake of Darwin's work.

It may seem strange to relate the origins of modern planning to a mid-nineteenth-century biology book. Charles Darwin published *The Origin of Species* in 1859, and in it he proposed an intimate and total relationship between the organism and the environment. Every minuscule variation of environment that he observed in his slow trip down the coast of Argentina, up along Chile, and across to the Galapagos Islands, revealed a minute and perfect adaptation in the body or behaviour of each organism he encountered, engineered perfectly (though, crucially, randomly) to respond to the most subtle environmental change. Such a trip taken today would leave a naturalist with little or no meaningful data, for it was only by travelling at the painfully slow speed at which wind propels a ship (or leaves it to drift for a few days, allowing the ship's naturalist long periods ashore) that Darwin could observe the tiny details that emerged with changing landscapes; a present-day naturalist in a car or a plane would see enormous jumps in flora, fauna, and geology, and be unable to link them.

Darwin's work did not inspire people overnight to prohibit cellar dwellings or lime houses in order to kill typhus mites, or become anxious that a casual disregard for the welfare of the poor might endanger the whole of society—and they were doing many of these things by 1859 anyway. But it did stimulate the rich and the educated to begin to view the poor in the same way that they viewed their prize horses and best cattle: as breeds to be improved. 'People' turned into 'stock'. In most of Europe, Darwinian thought (more usually, its various twisted, bastardized offshoots, like eugenics) arrived at the same time as rapid, mass urbanization, and so it seemed that a new hellish field of environmental exploration and experimentation had opened up imperatively before them.

While Darwin's specific message and conclusions were revolutionary, by the end of the nineteenth century, his methods were not. The key to Darwin's thinking was the systematic collection and analysis of data through fieldwork, and by the end of the nineteenth century the basic foundations of a systematic understanding of the human world were established. The rules of empirical sociology, anthropology, economics, history, psychology, and criminology were all crystallized in the last twenty years of the Victorian period, and vast amounts of data were collected to try to understand the human condition in its totality. This was complemented by a profound faith that the human condition *could* be comprehended in its totality if enough data were collected. Moral or religious categories in the understanding of human affairs, like 'good' and 'evil', were challenged by new social ones like 'privileged' and 'deprived'. As Riff jeeringly shouts to Officer Krupke in *West Side Story*, having been sent to a 'shrink' to cure his antisocial behaviour, 'Hey! I'm depraved, on account I'm deprived!' Each of these areas of enquiry were established as university disciplines and vigorously began systematizing data about humans, how they lived, and what made them flourish—or fail.

Much of this data was flawed, and then (corrupt as it was) refracted through the distorting lenses of upper-middle-class, white-heterosexual, healthy male culture, the 'gatekeeper' of the new knowledge. When rich, upper-middle-class men saw that the human world was not as they wished it to be (not like them, and their lives), they set about deploying their knowledge to try to produce perfection: the black should be made white; the feminine should be made masculine; the homosexual should be made heterosexual; the loud should be made quiet; the chaotic should be made orderly; the proletarian should be made bourgeois; the riotous should be made decorous. What took place standing should take place sitting; what took place outdoors should take place indoors; fluids ejected in public should be ejected only in private. Many such reformers fitted the cliché of the brutal, angry, racially obsessed, woman-hating, conservative, homophobic, greedy imperialist; but most did not. Most of the people who collected the data about humanity, and tentatively suggested applying conclusions drawn from it, were humane, liberal, well-meaning people, determined to try to alleviate the soul-destroying misery that seemed to characterize life for so many in Europe's cities, and who modelled the prosperous order of their own lives as the best way to achieve this. But in doing so, they opened up a Pandora's Box of death, disease, and destruction, while simultaneously showing the way to happiness and prosperity.

It is important to understand what contemporaries saw when they went into cities and tried to describe them, for the true potential horror of the poorest parts of London or Glasgow or Moscow or Berlin or Vienna or Paris would have appeared to an observer in 1900 in the same way that the slums of Rio de Janeiro or Bombay do to us now. They would have seemed just as distant, though they were very nearby. Fatal and debilitating diseases were widespread. Housing was so overcrowded for many that meaningful talk of incest or child abuse was hard to sustain, for if children worked at twelve it was hard to define them properly as children. If they slept six to a bed with friends, relatives, neighbours, and lodgers, the 'sorting' of people into 'family/not family', 'too young for sex/old enough', 'children at home/adults at work' was a hopeless task. Proceedings against 'abusers' were frequent across the continent (although often, the abusers themselves were little more than children), and show how the dynamics of residential space might exacerbate the problems of poverty.

Such cases were popular stories in newspapers, like this one from the *Berliner Lokalanzeiger* of 8 March 1908. 'Worker K' lived in one room plus kitchen with his two children, eleven and eight. He rented the room also to two '*Schlafburschen*'—'lads who slept over'. The two lads and the two children slept in one room, while 'Worker K' and his wife slept in the kitchen. The eleven-year-old child was eventually diagnosed with a 'hateful' (i.e. sexually transmitted) disease, found to be also present on Andreas Wojciechowsky, one of the boys renting the room during the day while the parents were out. Wojciechowsky was sentenced to 1¼ years in prison.[2] Such stories were common, and the 'shame' of overcrowded housing was often a euphemism for abuse or sexual misconduct of some kind—the German word for the 'disgrace' (*Schande*) of the housing situation is related to that used to describe child abusers (*Kinderschänder*). However, Wojciechowsky's age is unspecified, and he is described as a '*Bursche*'—a lad—and his sentence was not particularly long by today's standards.

Engineering spaces that would define and facilitate the life of just one family, on its own, to the exclusion of others, was an idea that would have seemed unrealistic to most working-class people in the 1890s, who often lived more than one family to a room, or three families to a flat, or several families to a landing, or twenty families to a toilet. Separating out by governmental command factories and homes, so that noxious gases, particulates from soot, and fires could be so significantly reduced that they would not constitute the background activity of most citizens' lives was often regarded as an idea so dictatorially dangerous, requiring such vast and regular intervention and *re*-intervention into citizens' lives (especially rich, factory-owning citizens' lives) that it was unthinkable. But around 1900, people did slowly start to imagine just such a world. People began to propose that by changing the environment of cities, the poor could be made healthy, strong, content, and docile. Central to this revolution was a new understanding of the physical and emotional implications of being a poor urbanite.

Early interventions in the urban environment often focused on combating disease, because while the poor could be contained and ignored (or shot, when they can no longer be contained, as in the Paris Commune in 1871 or in Moscow in 1905), their microbes and their viruses cannot. Many of the early attempts to get the state involved in understanding people and society, and in intervening in economics and social life, came out of the desire to fight epidemic diseases—most conspicuously, Asiatic cholera in the 1830s and 1840s. By 1900, in most of 'industrialized' Europe, most of the major water-borne diseases had been eliminated. While nineteenth-century civic leaders were rarely, if ever, interested in regulating the minute details of their citizens' private lives, they were interested in preventing them getting cholera—not least because infected poor people can so easily lead to infected rich people, especially with a highly communicable disease like cholera.

Asiatic cholera arrived in urban Europe in a devastating wave in 1830–2, and by the end of the century it was felt that the provision of clean water and the removal of foul had largely eliminated it in Western Europe (it persisted in parts of Russia until the 1930s). Historically, though, it can be something of an invisible disease because it lacks an appealing narrative structure—there is no resolution to the story, no time for redemption. Cholera offered novelist, journalist, report compiler, and reader a few agonizing hours covered in diarrhoea and vomit, slowly turning blue and going deaf, then either a prompt recovery or a heart attack. It killed half the people who contracted it, with little or no way of predicting who was vulnerable.

Cholera is not a literary disease. It is hard to find heroism, dignity, or any sort of Damascene experience of redemptive love in that sort of volume of faeces or vomit. Tuberculosis is lingering, one fades in and out of it, the loss is slow and protracted—tuberculosis, deadly as it was, is the charming disease of Baz Luhrman's film, *Moulin Rouge*. Cholera was not like this, and it is important to understand what a disease like cholera implied, because most of us have become so estranged from deadly epidemics like this. Western Europe's last great outbreak of the disease was very late in the nineteenth century. At 3 a.m. on 15 August 1892, Dr Hugo Simon of Altona, a suburb of Hamburg, was called to the house of a building worker, Sahling, a man so poor he does not merit a first name in the records. Sahling had been working on the outlets of a sewer into a foetid ditch, the Kleiner Grasbrook—the rather bucolic sounding 'Little Grassy Brook'. Sahling had collapsed on the way home from work, and proceeded to smother himself and Dr Simon in large amounts of vomit and diarrhoea. Victims would typically expel 25 per cent of their body weight by this method in a few hours, and expulsion was so violent that no one within a few metres was safe. If we assume that Sahling was a strapping man of fifteen stone (210 lbs), then he would rapidly have expelled over three stone (45 lbs) of vomit and faeces. Dr Simon diagnosed cholera. His superior, city medical officer Dr Wallichs, overruled his diagnosis, believing Dr Simon had blackballed his membership of the prestigious and exclusive Hamburg Doctors' Club. The last great cholera epidemic of Western Europe had begun.[3]

An enormous debate erupted on the cause of the disease, with samples of Sahling's, and the second victim's (another builder called Köhler) stools being sent all across Germany. Sahling and Köhler were unlikely to have travelled much in their own lifetime, but in death, they went to every corner of the Reich. Rod-like bacilli were found; but no one could ascertain where they were from. Ground water, tap water, food, 'intemperate living', and animals were all debated as the source, but nothing conclusive could be decided. For a *fin de siècle* scientist to find bacilli, they had to be present in huge quantities, not floating randomly

in sewage, or hiding under the fingernail of a loved one.[4] But the conclusions that were reached universally, both in Hamburg, and across
the medical and scientific communities in the institutes and universities of cities across Europe, was that the very fabric and structure and
form of cities needed to be *fundamentally* grasped, revised, and improved
in order to prevent visible disease like cholera, but also immorality and
disorder, which the new sciences of psychiatry and psychology were
happy to classify as sicknesses. The only institution capable of grasping
the totality of the city was the state—either in its local or national
form—and the great mission of intellectual endeavour was to devise a
system—or plan—of how to go about it.

Contemporaries had good reason for their obsession with environment and locality. Death was linked to poverty which was linked to
the environment, and they knew it. As Parisian Dr Vallin claimed,
'Without being a mystic, a well-informed hygienist is able to say,
"Show me your home, and I will show you which diseases threaten
you." '[5] Environment was everything—the sudden acquisition of evidence from 'fieldwork' in the 1890s complemented the Darwinian
emphasis on the environment which emerged in the 1860s and 1870s.
The administrators of Paris, for example, suddenly became interested
in collecting data about citizens and housing in new and dynamic
ways in the 1890s—a pattern that was repeated in many cities across
Europe in that decade.[6] In the rich arrondissements of Paris in 1901—
like Elysée and Opéra—experts calculated that the death rate from
tuberculosis was 119 and 186 per 100,000 inhabitants per annum
respectively. But in the cramped central Marais, just a short walk from
the Elysée and Opéra, it was 484, and in the north and east of the
city, in Montmartre, Buttes Chaumont and Ménilmontant, it was 443,
487, or a staggering 581. That means that in 1901, in Ménilmontant,
1 in every 172 people died of TB *every year*. While the statistics for
water-borne diseases like cholera plummeted with expert intervention
in the environment, the statistics for TB mortality in Paris did not
change between 1865 and 1930, related as they were to poverty and
environment.[7] In 1906 the city council proposed totally destroying the
environments associated with TB, and by 1919, seventeen *'ilôts insalu-
bres'* had been destroyed—entire areas of the city demolished, in the
name of health and purity, and private property had been overridden
in the cause of environmental improvement.

In the industrial German city of Mannheim, a local manufacturer, Carl Frendenberg, visited the homes of 300 people who had died of TB around 1900. What he found was profoundly shocking: 42 per cent of the dead lived more than three to a room; 34 per cent, two to three per room; 23 per cent, one per room.[8] He could not resist the conclusion: environment and disease were totally interdependent. Overcrowding caused death; death caused poverty; poverty was a financial burden on the state and produced citizens who (a) could not fight for it, (b) probably would not want to, and (c) required expensive social security. In the big cities of France in 1906—Paris, Marseilles, Lille, Rheims, Bordeaux, Lyon—over half of all families lived in only one room.[9] The mathematics of misery were terrifying. In Glasgow, where more than half the family units lived in one room, the chief medical officer for health, Dr Chalmers, crunched his statistics, and found that if there were four or more rooms in a family's dwelling, the death rate was 10 per thousand per annum for the inhabitants. If there were three, it was 13; if there were two, 17; if there was only one, the death rate was 20.14.[10] One was twice as likely to die in a small dwelling as in a big one. So joining together data like this (at, for example, the first International Housing Conference in 1889, or the first Congress on Sanitary Improvement and Salubrity in 1895), the evidence was compelling: where you lived and in what you lived determined not just how you lived, but *whether* you lived at all. Something had to be done; that something required a plan.

This process of intervention, treating, directing, and organizing the city was based on knowledge—the steady acquisition by the state of information and data about citizens. Sometimes this knowledge was acquired 'by accident' in the pursuit of other goals—states engaged in warfare started to measure and assess their young men; journalists keen to find the most poignant human-interest stories casually exposed child prostitution, before moving on to the next emotional exposé. Sometimes the state deliberately set out to acquire knowledge, systematically trying to understand the people the state was there to govern. States did this to varying degrees. In Britain, France, and Germany, the state, especially in its local form of urban government, harvested breathtaking amounts of data about its citizens. In Russia, no one bothered to collect meaningful statistics on poverty and disease systematically.

The poor, too, had come to their own conclusions about the cities in which they lived. The secret police in Hamburg overheard some workers talking in a pub in the 1890s, saying:

> Three workers were overheard to make the following remarks: that the building type of the larger flats has really got out of hand in the last few years, even though the owners can see the damage it causes. There are always more and more of those sorts of palaces being built, in which no-one can ever live given the current employment conditions. They [the three workers] want to build different flats, namely housing designed to suit the circumstances of the working classes, and as near as possible to the city. The current workers' housing lies an hour-and-a-half or two hours from their workshops, and if one wants to live there more cheaply, one has to pay for the horse omnibus. If one does not want to do that, one has to take a beautiful house in the Steinstraße or Niedernstraße palaces, which are popularly referred to as 'hell on earth', and which are notorious for cholera.[11]

From information like this, states began to worry that they would be unable to preserve themselves, so disaffected were many citizens, so miserable their lives. No statistic could capture the distress felt by the district inspector of the 16th Bezirk (Untere Au) of Munich, who reported to his superiors—apparently unprompted—in July 1909 that sometimes he felt unable to go on with his job, so great was the suffering which he had to confront every day. He wrote:

> The awful suffering of the housing emergency has been growing—insofar as I can tell—for some time on a terrible scale. Hardly a day has gone by since November in which families have not come to me after days of desperate searching. Families are daily broken up, and compelled to live in stables and under bridges with up to ten children, sleeping on the floor in the hay amongst the horse droppings. Another man whose wife is dead is forced to live in a cellar with no light or heating with his six children, and he is about to be evicted from what I hesitate to call this 'dwelling'. He is preparing to move to a lumber yard and sleep under the planks, and hopes to be allowed to make himself a shack. At any rate, it is so urgently to be wished that even these people of low worth should be given accommodation which matches their worth as people.[12]

I have searched in the archives, but cannot find his superiors' response. But in that year, the city fathers of Munich trebled their commitment to house-building. In Vienna, there were riots throughout 1911, as people clamoured for warmth, for privacy, for quiet, for cleanliness, for dignity, for dryness; and in the winter of 1911–12, the mayor and aldermen of Munich were so shocked by the homelessness and the bitter winter that they opened council buildings for sleeping—tram sheds, electricity stations, wagon depots, some schools. Across the continent, in city after city, political and moral and social and family order was imperilled by an incapacity to manage the urban environment in a way which did not so regularly and so systematically kill its inhabitants.

The renewed vigour with which states counted and measured from the 1890s was often linked tightly to geopolitical goals: empires were being formed by the USA, Japan, Britain, Belgium, Germany, the Netherlands, and France at a rapid rate and on a huge scale, and contemporaries drew a straight line between the dark spaces of the city and the open spaces of the African savannah and the dense jungles of Indochina. When the British state became embroiled in the Boer War, it had to take on large numbers of new young soldiers who volunteered to serve the Empire. It had to measure them, assess their strength and size, their literacy, their capacity to follow instructions in order to achieve a goal. The state found what dozens of concerned amateur social investigators had found in the 1890s: the poor of Britain were a 'degenerate race', and should be classified with the same language (not quite at, but near, the same point on the scale) as the non-white colonized peoples they would encounter after the Boer 'problem' had been dealt with.

In 1899 in Manchester, 11,000 men of appropriate age and marital status volunteered to fight in the Boer war. 8,000 of them were rejected as unfit at first glance; 2,000 were felt to be fit enough to join the militia, but not the army. Only 1,000—less than 10 per cent—of the men actually made it into the army. The rest were too weak, crippled, small, or ill to do so.[13] Major General Sir Jan Hamilton wrote of the Manchester Regiment after the siege of Ladysmith:

> I cannot but think that it is the fault of someone that these brave and stubborn lads were not at least an inch or two taller and bigger around the chest, and altogether of a more robust and powerful build.[14]

This phrase, 'the fault of someone', is important—it shows the rich and the powerful, the 'establishment', suddenly taking an interest in the health of the 'race' or the 'stock'. It represents the dawn of a certain type of consciousness in a much larger number of people than previously. Poverty was not a shock or a surprise, but as the state's ambitions in empire grew, the limitations that poverty imposed on the state's capacity to act increasingly came to be seen as a problem.

The conclusions that were drawn across the continent were on the one hand terrifyingly Darwinian, and on the other socially progressive—the two logics went hand in hand. Liberals in Britain like Thomas Horsfall and Charles Masterman promoted the message tirelessly of a 'degeneration of the race', a threat to the Empire from within, and the danger of racial, moral, social, and political collapse. And the blame was laid directly at the door of the urban environment. Manchester Liberal and housing-reform campaigner Thomas Horsfall wrote in terms which directly linked biology to human behaviour to morality to control to the environment:

> The causes of the degeneration which goes on in our large towns, and of the high death rate of many of those towns are obvious. The main cause is not overcrowding of dwellings, though that is a very marked and serious evil, not excessive drinking, nor licentiousness, nor betting,...nor the cutting off of light by smoke,...nor the lack of physical exercise, though each of those...would by itself almost suffice to cause the *ruin of the race*....The chief cause of evil is that the towns lack the pleasantness which is the most important condition of cheerfulness, hopefulness, physical and mental health and strength and moral well-being. This cause and its effect on physical and moral well-being have been most tersely and yet fully indicated by Mr Justice Day, who speaking of drinking to excess, said: 'IT IS THE SHORTEST WAY OUT OF MANCHESTER.'[15]

The cause of degeneration was *not* socio-economic according to Horsfall: it was environmental. Elsewhere, he elaborated on the decline of the race, and linked the city to foreign policy directly:

> Unless we at once begin to protect the health of our people by making the towns in which most of them now live, more wholesome for body and mind, we may as well hand over our colonies, our whole influence in the world to Germany without undergoing all the trouble of a struggle in which we condemn ourselves to certain failure.[16]

It is important to remember that in his own time, Horsfall was a man of the left—and others on the left agreed with him.

Charles Masterman, a British Liberal and campaigner for National Insurance to provide support to the unemployed, disabled, and elderly, wrote perhaps the archetype of this sort of analysis—*The Heart of Empire: Discussions of problems of modern city life in England*—in 1901. He drew a direct line between the failure to produce pleasant cities and the entire geopolitical project of the British state of the time. A dingy alley in Glasgow or Birmingham might produce imperial fragility in Bengal or Rhodesia. In another of his hugely popular works, *From the Abyss* (written in 1902, the abyss being the secret spaces and places of London), he wrote:

> Our streets have suddenly become congested with a weird and uncanny people. They have poured in as dense black masses from the eastern railways. They have streamed across the bridges from the marshes and desolate places across the river. They have been hurried up in incredible tubes sunk in the bowels of the earth, emerging like rats from a drain, blinking in the sunshine.[17]

It sounds almost like a war, or an invasion—but it was the typical language of urban exploration in turn-of-the-century Europe. It sounds, in fact, like the language used in Conrad's damning critique of imperialism, *Heart of Darkness*, which appeared first as a series in 1899, and was published as a novel in 1902—and Marlow, Conrad's narrator, is speaking on a boat in the Thames estuary by London, which he also calls a 'dark place'. Such language presented an unknown terrain of mystery and misery—and proposed a big, imperial state to colonize and order it. And the reason that I have chosen all of these examples from Britain, despite there being thousands more from France, Germany, and Austria-Hungary, is that it is too easy to think that this sort of visceral concern for 'racial purity' and 'fighting vigour' is something foreign and illiberal—specifically German. It was not. It was universal, and as likely, if not more likely, to be found in liberal Britain as liberal Germany at the turn of the twentieth century.[18]

Across the continent, there was an obsession with racial degeneration in cities, versus an upright, racially pure, mythologized 'peasant stock', which was in no way a particular preoccupation of conservatives or those on the right. It was liberals and progressives who, again and again and again, predicted the demise either of the whole of Europe, or of their particular corner of it, if the environment was not turned from chaos into order.[19] Britain was, by a long reach, the wealthiest nation in Europe in 1900—and yet even in London, contemporary social investigators like Charles Booth calculated that 30.7 per cent of the population existed on *less* than subsistence wages, unable to feed, house, and clean themselves, no matter how hard they tried.[20] Contemporary popular debates about this process in cities crossed national and linguistic boundaries, and books like Tomàs Masaryk's *Suicide and the Meaning of Civilisation* and Max Nordau's *Degeneration* in Austria-Hungary, Gustave le Bon's *The Crowd: A study of the popular mind* in France, and Julius Langbehn's *Rembrandt as Educator* in Germany, all presented an urban world in political, economic, psychological, and racial decline—and they sold in their millions across Europe, being translated and republished many times. This was not a peripheral debate—this was the territory on which social reform, foreign affairs, the 'woman question', revolution and political order, and all manner of other topics were negotiated. The city was a corrupt, unnatural environment and could only produce collective and individual ill-health.

Knowledge like this, combined with a profound fear of what sort of terrifying revolutions or diseases or weaknesses which might debilitate the entire state in the future conflict which so many assumed would purify Europe, provided a powerful impetus to act. At the end of the nineteenth century, most European cities were only just triumphantly celebrating the prohibition of the private mass slaughter of animals for food in backyards, and the arbitrary disposal of their carcasses. They were too preoccupied with trying to acquire the tram networks, the water supply, and the gas industry from their private owners to worry overly about systematically planning their transport systems (although in the 1890s, London, Paris, Vienna, and Berlin started to plan underground railways as a system). But to understand the thinking of a planner in this period when planning was invented is to gaze into the heart of the twentieth-century state—if it had a heart. It is to understand the fears and hopes, the dreams, and nightmares of this impersonal entity which has woven itself into every aspect of twentieth-century life.

Around the turn of the century, attempts to solve urban social problems were hampered by several features, the most debilitating of which was the lack of any intellectual framework or one, coherent system to comprehend the variety of problems. So many intellectual pieces of the jigsaw were missing, right across the continent. First, while many viewed cities as sites of civil disorder, many people were naively unconvinced of the danger that cities posed to the *whole* political order. This meant that they did not regard pacifying the people wedged into the continent's hovels as an imperative—a belief that would be corrected with vigour in 1917 and 1918. They sometimes felt that the threat of democratic socialism could be dismissed and should not be indulged, or that troops were more effective than housing in avoiding chaos. People seriously believed, without a grain of cynicism, that to build the poor houses would be to engage in a fundamental moral hazard: one would have to take property from those who had it, and one would have to give it to those who 'had not earned it', thereby undermining the whole natural order of the world. The German Federation of Builders, a group one might think would profit from a state-sponsored construction boom, wrote to every city council in Germany in 1901, stating:

> Numerous voices, almost exclusively from the laity, scream 'housing emergency'. But the deployment of state or city money would be an attack on the private life of the citizen. Experiences in Berlin and Spandau [a suburb of Berlin], where there was a particularly conspicuous temporary lack of small dwellings in early 1901, have shown that in most cases, the problem came down to the ill will of the homeless, in that they would not undertake to occupy a home.[21]

They cited the example of some gas workers in Berlin who had found new 'accommodation' within four hours of bailiffs ejecting them from their dwellings. Thus, they concluded, there was no fundamental problem with housing. The quality of the accommodation they found may well have been like the dwelling the district inspector in Munich found, cited on p. 326. While the poor occasionally rioted—and to serious effect in Moscow and St Petersburg in 1905, threatening a major revolution—the newly formed socialist parties of the 1900s did not seem to pose a sufficient threat to merit seriously challenging the status quo—and even if they did, no left-wing party had a coherent approach to what to do with the city. There seemed better ways of containing political disorder—through violence, for example—than urban reform.

The second big reason why people could not conceive of a solution to the 'problem' of cities was that the dominant political ideology of the late nineteenth century was liberalism, which was anchored in a firm belief that the state should interfere as little as possible in the private life of the individual. The market, most liberals believed, was the optimum mechanism for securing personal freedom, and most city councils were gerrymandered to ensure majority liberal representation. Many liberals argued that landlords should not be forced to build in a certain way or rent at a certain price because that would mean the state interfering in private property, and thereby threatening individual liberty; citizens should bear the primary responsibility for housing themselves, as they knew best how to do this, and doing so would fix them to the path of self-improvement; the best person to decide where to build a factory was the person who had invested their resources in doing so, not a university-trained civil servant who would most likely have focused on the Greek classics for his education. This viewpoint was not 'cruel' or 'selfish'; it represented the conclusions of the best contemporary thinking and imagining on the practicalities of managing public life. But it also shows that 'just' building more or better or cheaper houses was not a question of will. Anyone who proposed changing the urban environment also had to propose transforming the relationship of the citizen to the state, and the displacement of the major tenets of political orthodoxy—a deeply radical proposition.

Finally, the biggest obstacle to any sort of comprehensive reform of the urban environment was that no one had much clear or credible idea of what to do with a dirty, diseased city as a whole in order to fix it, even if they had got past obstacles one and two. The vision to tackle the economics, the politics, the role of the state, a description of family life, transportation, and the million and one details of daily life that make life in a city bearable were simply lacking. That is, until the publication in 1898 of a profoundly revolutionary text: *To-Morrow: A peaceful path to real reform*, written by Ebenezer Howard—called, in subsequent reprints, *Garden Cities of Tomorrow*. In this book, for better or for worse, lies the genesis of the idea that the city can be perfected, in order to produce a happy, just, and above all orderly society.

Howard was a peculiar figure; his day job was as a stenographer for *Hansard*, the verbatim record of proceedings of the Houses of Parliament. He had no formal training in architecture, hygiene, urban design (in fact, no one at this stage had a formal training in urban design). He was not a sociologist, nor a criminologist, nor a geographer, nor a transport engineer, nor a psychologist—in short, he was not part of the explosion of 'human sciences' in the 1890s. Yet Howard's work proposed a solution to contemporary problems of breathtaking vision—and also, of severe limitations. He proposed that the family was the central unit of society, from which all else flowed; thus, the main goal of policy was to single the family out, and clean it up. The family needed to be isolated and defined, and this needed new spatial designs of cities because, in the melee of the modern city, it was impossible to isolate the ideal family—mother, father and a 'rational' number of children—from lodgers, relatives, strangers, and so on.

He argued that both the free market and communism distorted human nature, and so a hybrid form—a 'third way'—needed to be evolved if 'a peaceful path to reform' was to be followed, and a series of violent revolutions avoided. He concurred with most contemporaries that the countryside and the earth and the green was the source of racial strength, of loyalty, of the true nature of the Englishman, indeed of every man—but that the countryside was boring, incapable of art, science, architecture, and technological achievement. The city could manage these things, but was dirty, diseased, and riven by conflict between rich and poor, liable to erupt into dramatic violence if ignored. Neither the city nor the country could represent the 'full plan and purpose of nature'. The city was deeply problematic:

> Its social opportunities and its places of amusement are very alluring, but excessive hours of toil, distance from work, and the 'isolation of crowds' tend greatly to reduce the value of these good things. The well-lit streets are a great attraction, especially in winter, but the sunlight is being more and more shut out, while the air is so vitiated that the fine public buildings, like the sparrows, rapidly become covered in soot, and the very statues are in despair. Palatial edifices and fearful slums are the strange, complementary features of modern cities.[22]

He expressed this 'trichotomy' in a potent visual form, which can be seen in Figure 5.1 (top). He proposed a universal solution, that would resolve *all* social problems, but which was based on rational environmental revision, rather than the traditional plea of utopians or religious devotees—'being good to one another'. The solution to human problems would lie in creating a balanced environment, not in the love of a redemptive God, nor in Christian selflessness, nor in a Hobbesian total authority, and this was the revolutionary nature of his proposal:

> There are in reality not only, as is so constantly assumed, two alternatives—town life and country life—but a third alternative, in which all the advantages of the most energetic and active town life, with all the beauty and delight of the country, may be secured in perfect combination; and the certainty of being able to live this life will be the magnet

THE THREE MAGNETS.

TOWN.
Closing out of Nature. Social Opportunity.
Isolation of Crowds. Places of Amusement.
Distance from Work. High Money Wages.
High Rents & Prices. Chances of Employment.
Excessive Hours. Army of Unemployed.
Fogs & Droughts. Costly Drainage.
Foul Air. Murky Sky. Well-lit Streets.
Slums & Gin Palaces. Palatial Edifices.

COUNTRY.
Lack of Society. Beauty of Nature.
Hands out of work. Land lying idle.
Trespassers beware. Wood, Meadow, Forest.
Long Hours. Low Wages. Fresh Air. Low Rents.
Lack of Drainage. Abundance of Water.
Lack of Amusement. Bright Sunshine.
No Public Spirit. Need for Reform.
Crowded Dwellings. Deserted Villages.

THE PEOPLE
WHERE WILL THEY GO?

TOWN-COUNTRY.
Beauty of Nature. Social Opportunity.
Fields and Parks of Easy Access.
Low Rents, High Wages.
Low Rates, Plenty to do.
Low Prices, No Sweating.
Field for Enterprise, Flow of Capital.
Pure Air and Water. Good Drainage.
Bright Homes & Gardens, No Smoke, No Slums.
Freedom. Co-operation.

WARD AND CENTRE
GARDEN - CITY

N.B.
A DIAGRAM ONLY.
PLAN MUST DEPEND UPON
SITE SELECTED.

GRAND AVENUE

BOULEVARD COLUMBUS

CENTRAL PARK

LARGE FARMS

DAIRY FARMS

ALLOTMENTS

SCALE
0   110   220   440 YDS = ¼ MILE

which will produce the effect for which we are all striving—the spontaneous movement of the people from our crowded cities to the bosom of our kindly mother earth, at once the source of life, of happiness, of wealth and of power.[23]

As a solution, he proposed a totally new environment directed from top to bottom by a benign rationalism: the garden city. His definition of the problem, and his design for solving it, are shown in Figure 5.1, and have proved the blueprint for cities for a hundred years now.

The garden city would be a community (or rather, network of communities) of 32,000 souls, explained in all its parts in the lower part of Figure 5.1. Experts would plan it so that it contained 'good' (bourgeois, folksy) architecture, inhabited by the 'right' sort, in the 'right' balance, in the 'right' place. Things in the 'wrong' place would be prohibited— the garden city would require a gardener, and the gardener would sort out the fruiting plants from the weeds; nourish one, eliminate the other. Industries would be selected according to expert guidance on economic balance, and would be situated so that they did not pollute nearby dwellings but could still be accessible by railways for goods transportation and workers by foot—a suggested schema is provided in Figure 5.1 (bottom). There would be total social unity, with all the friction-points of class conflict eliminated. The working class and the middle class would live in close proximity, and the middle class would function as a didactic example of temperate living and the self-contained, isolated bourgeois family to the workers. There would be neither pubs nor gambling outlets; entertainment would be 'rational', and the city would be oriented around theatres, libraries, and art galleries. There would be no conflict

---

Figure 5.1 *Garden Cities of Tomorrow*: top, Ebenezer Howard's definition of the 'problem'; bottom, his schematic diagram of how to solve *all* of the problems in one go. Howard was one of several intellectuals who gripped the European public's attention when talking about the city around 1900. In these diagrams, he represents the benefits and problems of urbanization and the advantages and disadvantages of rural living in the top two 'magnets'; then he proposes a total plan to reconcile all problems—economic, social, cultural, educational, care of the disabled, transport, health—in the bottom magnet and the plan for a town of 32,000 (bottom). This totalizing human vision came to dominate European thinking on every problem across the century.

between agriculture and industry, for all would be engaged in agricultural production on their allotments. There would be total environmental control, governing population density and, *crucially*, the functions and activities of every aspect of everyday life—where one slept, what one saw, the routes one took to work. The one feature which could have made all this happen, and happen quickly, Howard did not propose: a vigorous, interventionist, all-powerful, directive state.

Given the scale of the problems, this sort of romantic solution was never going to be enough in the years before the Great War. It was hopelessly naive, partly because it located the solution to society's problems in a fictional past, not a pragmatic future. The construction of garden cities was a voluntarist project, springing from man's 'goodness' and 'reason', coupled with some ineffective economic trickery that aimed to show how this could pay its way under capitalism. Furthermore, this 'ideal city' was somewhere else—it was elsewhere, nowhere. It did not suggest how to intervene in an extant chaos. Most problematic of all, the garden city obsessives could not effectively address the role of the state; they could not find a way of drawing a line that would pass through the Cabinet, Parliament, council chambers, front gardens, kitchens, and bedrooms in one continuous dynamic swoop. So at the beginning of the twentieth century across Europe contemporaries knew there was a terrible problem with their cities, thanks to new forms of social investigation and journalism; they knew what they wanted to create, through the work of Howard and the dozens of 'planners' that followed his lead. But they did not know how to make these dreams reality without destroying the foundations of the liberal state which they hoped to bolster.

* * *

The Great War was not primarily a war of the cities. While starving cities did actually bring about the victory of the Western allies, as discussed in Chapter 1, cities were not the main targets for enemy action, and despite the odd raid on London or Paris, the technology simply did not exist to assault them directly (although some cities in north-east France were extensively shelled). Gotha bi-plane bombers and Zeppelins were so big, so slow, and so flammable, that a competent, well-prepared defence with a machine gun—or simply a rifle— could eliminate them quickly and easy.

As every big city in Central and Eastern Europe erupted into political violence, at the heart of that violence was the demand for higher quality housing for the demobilizing soldiers—housing that did not kill, as investigators in Paris, Mannheim, and Glasgow had found it to do. City administrators across the continent were terrified of the effect that returning soldiers might pose—the mayor of Munich wrote in a top-secret memo of the 'terrifying spectre' of returning troops six months before the war's end. They were right to be afraid, for the angry men who returned from the war rapidly married and started families, and demanded high-quality housing as a condition for supporting the political order. They demanded, then, a revision to the urban environment, and brought a political impetus to a theoretical problem.

More important than high-quality housing might be the right to be housed at all, for surrounding Paris, Milan, Cologne, Vienna, St Petersburg, Berlin, Moscow, and Hamburg, and dozens of other large European cities, were large rings of what contemporaries called 'wild settlements' or 'wild colonies'—*wilde Siedlungen* and *colonies sauvages*. So profound was the collapse of *every form* of order—moral, administrative, gender, economic, social, political—east of France that millions of urban inhabitants in the defeated lands left the city as it was currently constituted, and went to live on its peripheries, building shacks and attempting to farm the ground. This process of shanty-town construction confirmed the worst fears of bourgeois Europe: every manner of diabolic disorder might come out of a neglected, invisible urban environment. Progressives felt licensed to intervene deeply into previously unknown and remote aspects of everyday life to prevent physical disease, psychological disorder, and family breakdown; conservatives felt emboldened to prise open the private lives of the poor—how they washed, where they ate, with whom they slept every night—to inspection and reconfiguration, in the quest to preserve social order and a governable society. A remarkable intellectual unity that was to last until the mid-1970s across Europe, democratic and dictatorial, was formed around the idea of the plan, developed by experts outside the formal political process, and the obligations of the state to enact it.

Solutions across industrialized, urbanized Europe had many things in common in the 1920s, despite the apparent contradictions between British conservatives, German social democrats, and Russian Bolsheviks. Surprisingly perhaps, Soviet planners and British property speculators,

German city councils and French parliaments, and Austrian architects generally agreed on one thing: the city in its current material form was corrupt, unhealthy, immoral, dangerous, and fundamentally problematic and so should be largely either destroyed and rebuilt or abandoned and rebuilt elsewhere, and in totally innovative ways in order to force a citizenry into new forms of behaviour. It is often assumed that the 1960s was the age of violence to the inherited patterns of our cities. However, the idea that there was nothing of value in the nineteenth-century inheritance was developed around 1900, and put into effect in the 1920s and 1930s. The 1960s was the last gasp of a way of viewing the world—the plan—which had dominated for forty years.

In the *immediate* aftermath of the First World War in Central and Eastern Europe, housing was far from planned. Even in Paris, capital of a supposedly 'victor' nation, the number of night shelters for the homeless had jumped from 700 in 1911 to 1,792 in 1921, and France and Britain had by far the happiest exit from the war.[24] Further east, the situation was even more chaotic: around the big cities of the defeated and destroyed empires sprung up vast, chaotic settlements as people returned to the land on millions of smallholdings, dwelling in belts of shacks around St Petersburg, Moscow, Vienna, Budapest, Warsaw, Berlin, Düsseldorf, and Munich. Food could not be bought, nor building materials procured, so as armies collapsed, garrisons and barracks were raided for planks, corrugated iron, wire, and nails, and parks and fields and city edges were dug over, a physical process in the material world that underlined in the urban fabric the total transformation of political authority and habits of social deference. Vienna in particular 'returned to the land'; its function in the vast Austro-Hungarian Empire was to administer it, but Austria is a tiny country with next to no agricultural lands. So the armies of bourgeois civil servants with nothing to administer, and nothing to manufacture and sell to the grain regions of Hungary, Romania, and Bulgaria had to head to the urban periphery, and build huts, plant turnips, and hope for the best.[25]

In 'Red' Vienna and the new Soviet Union the initial response to the new order was to leave the existing, nineteenth-century buildings where they were, and reorder the people according to a planned assessment of an ideal set of minimums and maximums for a rationally perfected existence. In the USSR the policy was called 'compression': the bourgeoisie would be 'compressed' to the same population densities as the urban poor, and overcrowded proletarian families moved into the rooms that were freed up. The problem seems to have been that either the workers became too chummy with the bourgeoisie with whom they were compressed, being seduced by their devious ways, or they were so stupid (or desperate for food or unaware of the true value of plumbing) that they wrecked their new dwellings, selling off all the copper and lead they could find, and burning wooden fixtures and fittings—even the floorboards in some instances.

The voices of 'ordinary people' are hard for historians to come by in the USSR, partly because their opinions were not valued, and partly because during the revolution, civil war, New Economic Policy and the Five-Year Plans, there was too much chaos to collect them. But one memo inside the Moscow Soviet in May 1919 observed that:

> The policy of placing workers or groups of workers in dwellings in which the bourgeoisie have been 'compressed' has not always achieved its purpose, for the workers thus separated have been exposed to the danger of moral corruption by the bourgeoisie. The results have been no better in houses occupied solely by workers, owing to the unsatisfactory management of these buildings and the fuel shortage.[26]

It is significant that this report views the relationships between different social groups in terms of contamination and corruption, caused by the 'misplacement' of people in the urban landscape. It is the same language as used in reports about cholera or TB. Another Moscow City Council report of May 1922 was a little bit more forthcoming on the failures of the proletariat and highlighted the level of the assault on conventional customs of everyday life that revolutionary city life proposed—and the vengeful response that elicited:

> The measures of so-called 'compression' sweep away all consideration for the individual customs and characteristics of different sections of the population. In many cases its consequences have been disastrous, for the new tenants, being ignorant of the use of the appliances placed at their disposal, have employed them in such a manner that the whole dwelling has soon been completely ruined and can no longer be used.... Everyone lives in constant fear of...being driven out of a well-equipped dwelling. This has extinguished love of home and the desire to protect it from dilapidation.... The new tenants installed by decree are, to say the least, indifferent to the dwelling assigned to them by the authorities.[27]

The city council in Moscow here set out the parameters of the most extreme problems that 'cities by decree' have faced right across the twentieth century, as they have tried to replace 'customs and characteristics' with systems and methods. But for each failure of housing planning policy the solution has always been the same: what was wrong was *not* the idea of cities by decree per se, or the idea of placement and the control of the state, but insufficient expertise, control, and intervention. People required better 'installation by decree'. The plan was never wrong; it was simply not good enough, and required a better plan to correct it.

In Germany, large settlements were planned on housing estates across the country, designed to produce a total environment which would engineer the 'new human'. As soon as the country had recovered from the crippling financial crises in which it found itself after the war, city after city set about building thousands of dwellings a year, each painstakingly designed to force people to live in a certain way. Where women were expected to be nurturing, social, and maternal, the kitchens were merged with the living rooms; where women were supposed to be rational, professional, and industrious, the kitchens were hived off into minute workstations which forced women to work alone on domestic chores. In some cities, like Frankfurt, heating and laundry were centralized and everyone was forced to pay for it—causing substantial resistance, as 'taking in' washing was a standard source of income for working-class women, allowing them to work but stay at home. When money was tight, traditionally, women organized their families to sleep together to save on coke and coal, and central heating made that impossible too. There were no walls for dressers to be stood against, no mantels for knick-knacks, and no poles for lace curtains. These were not accidental by-products of sloppy planning, spilling over into the micro-aspects of every day life: planners deliberately wanted to force women to live a certain way; they wanted to stop families bundling together in the same bed; they wanted to eliminate lice in clothing, and the habit of keeping girls off school on wash day. They proactively and publicly loathed the decorative instincts of the working classes and their taste in 'ornaments', and sought to remove all possibility for them to use them.

Grete Schütte-Lihotzky was one of the leading architects of the time, working in both Vienna and Frankfurt. She despised the 'wasteful' practice of having a 'parlour for best', which was the aspiration of prosperous working-class families from Milan to Manchester. She felt it they were crass imitations of the rooms of the rich: 'We progressive architects campaigned against this false, inauthentic, cold "display"', she recalled in her memoirs. She insisted on specialized fitted kitchens with all the furniture built in, which can be seen in Figure 5.2, and the labels on the storage containers already specified, so that housewives would be stimulated to buy the 'right' foodstuffs in the 'right' quantities. Schütte-Lihotzky was a great woman, a formidable architect, and an effective underground fighter against Nazism in Vienna when that evil day came, but when she came up with her plans, she modelled them as being '*by* women, *for* women'. But the women did not like her middle-class model of family life, separated from their traditional kitchen-dining-living-rooms. And they were loath to get rid of their doilies and ornaments, which they had worked so hard to obtain, and displayed with substantial pride. The guiding question for her and her team was, 'How can we overcome...the irrational and the primitive?' That view of the 'planned for', that they are irrational and primitive, pervades all the 'rational' discussions about the world that have underpinned the great projects of the twentieth century, good and bad.[28] The goal of the kitchen in Figure 5.2 was to make women's domestic labour easier; but it also isolated them from their families while they worked (traditionally, kitchens were social rooms not just work rooms), extended the state's reach into people's everyday lives, and removed choices from women about how they laid out their homes.

In Frankfurt, under the direction of Ernst May and Grete Schütte-Lihotzky, they installed central laundries, so that girls would not be kept off school to help with the washing—which housewives hated, not because they did not want their children to go to school, but because many working-class women took in clothes to wash as a way of earning money from their own homes. But if *everyone* on the estate had to pay the laundry fees to the housing association, an important form of income was planned out of some of these women's lives by a middle-class woman who did not do her own laundry, and

Figure 5.2 Kitchen in social housing, Frankfurt-am-Main, *c*.1926. Between the wars, planners and governments resolved to intervene more deeply and profoundly in the minutiae of people's lives—right down to how women did their housework and interacted with the family. But they often lacked a tool to get them into these 'private' spaces. Social housing was invented, in part, to be that tool. This kitchen was designed to change women's lives: lessen their domestic workload (and so make them less likely to want to leave the house), separate them from their families while they worked (turning women's domestic work into something more like men's paid work), and direct them in an appropriate diet—by pre-labelling all the drawers on the right-hand side with 'appropriate' products.

an often unaffordable expense planned into the lives of their neighbours, in the name of their daughters' liberation.[29] Planning had
already started to overlook its most fundamental law: that of unintended consequences.

It was in the USSR, though, that this idea of building from scratch
to produce a total, rational society took deepest hold. Russia lacked
a widespread urban, industrial base; Marx decreed that the revolution of the proletariat must come from industrialized cities. Russia
tragically did not fit the plan. Either the plan would have to be
changed, or Russia would. After Lenin's death in 1924, his 'New
Economic Policy' continued to allow some forms of private enterprise. But eventually, the Bolshevik leadership concluded that the
plan according to Marx must be right, and Russia must be wrong, its
people 'primitive' and 'irrational'. So under the Five-Year Plans starting in 1928, Stalin, and the team of ideologically convinced bureaucrats around him, decided to reshape an entire world. They would
create an urban nation, in which even agriculture would be driven
by the principles of industrial modernity. In the existing cities of
Petrograd (soon to be renamed Leningrad), Volgograd (soon to be
renamed Stalingrad), Moscow, Kiev, and several others, vast exten-
sions were planned. But where there were no cities or only small
villages, hyperurbanization was the order of the day, and new cities
sprung up across the former tsarist agricultural horizons, focused on
producing coal, steel, electricity and, above all, ideologically appropriate, orderly, obedient proletarians.

It is important to understand this idea that the plan is both the
means and the end of much twentieth-century endeavour. Every
powerful elite throughout history has been interested in producing
order, compliance and greater wealth and power for themselves. But
for the ideologues of the revolution in the USSR, the plan was a
quasi-spiritual thing. In the production of it, all the rational knowledge of the sciences of society opened up by Marx, Engels, and
Lenin would be brought to bear, exterminating the bourgeois intellectual corruptions of habit, convention, tradition, religion—and even
beauty. It was in the devising of the plan that society developed the
intellectual framework to replace everything that went before. Central
too was the process of the execution of the plan, for it was in this (far
more than the completion of it) that the true objectives of the plan

would be met: the reform of the individual. The modern plan is as much the end as the means. The great problem that preoccupied Stalin, Lenin, and Trotsky was this: socialism was the result of the actions of the proletariat; Russia had a tiny proletariat, and millions of peasants. How, then, would the society be made to fit the theory? It was in the construction labour of making cities, then the diversion of that labour into the new industrial activities planned in those cities, that socialism would be brought into existence. The proletarian would be created by his or her engagement in the process of making the planned environment; the proletarian would be preserved by thereafter existing in the perfectly rational, socialist environment he or she had created. Every aspect of the plan, from drawing it up, through executing it, to living in the planned environment, would produce true socialism.

The revolution broke Moscow as a city. *New York Times* correspondent Walter Duranty described its inhabitants in 1921 wearing garments 'sewn together from blankets and curtains or even carpets'. Shops were boarded up, 'but in most cases the boards had been torn away for fuel and you saw empty windows or no windows at all, just holes, like missing teeth'.[30] The solution Lenin had to adopt was to re-allow capitalism, through the New Economic Policy—an ideological compromise to overcome the limitations of the weak Soviet state in the early 1920s. But this did not produce a socialist environment, a socialist economy, or a socialist humanity. But under the first Five-Year Plan of 1928, Moscow was completely recast: it became a city-region, and the phase of hyperurbanization began. One historian of Moscow has emphasized that the city—both physically and intellectually—became one, vast 'factory of plans', and the minutiae of Moscow's development obsessed Stalin more almost than any other aspect of government, for Moscow was a metaphor for all Soviet society, all politics, and all humanity.[31] And at the heart of this was the 'metro'. As one historian of the USSR has concluded, the metro was the 'church of Soviet civilisation'.[32]

In this context, a project like the construction of the Moscow Metro could take on an enormous significance throughout the 1930s. It was typical of thousands of projects in the USSR, but also had a symbolic significance that made it the archetype of *all* the projects. The decision to build was taken in June 1931 and the first line, the Red Line, was opened just four years later. The planning for, and construction of, the Metro was not merely an urban infrastructure policy: it served foreign policy, economic, social policy, aesthetic, and cultural objectives. It was not just a 'train line', but the physical embodiment of everything the USSR was trying to achieve.[33] As one worker, Pavel Sizikov, wrote in a 1935 memoir, *I Grew Up with the Metro*:

> While I worked on the Metro, I could not forget for one moment my cultural growth. While on the shift, I worked down the tunnel, then I went to the workers' educational institute and studied. I haven't finished my studies yet, but I've been to the University of the Metro, and that taught me a lot. Now I can work under any conditions![34]

Contrived as it may seem, such opinions often seem to have been expressed. Construction projects and rational plans were not there to help the Soviet project; in many ways, they *were* the Soviet project.

And the conditions on the metro were so harsh that he probably could have worked under any conditions after that hellish experience—and in that respect, the experience made him a subservient, obedient worker, the ideal Soviet citizen, the 'new man'. Some 40,000 people were working on it at any one time, and the process was explicitly intended to serve as a 'Forge for new humans'. As one party apparatchik in 1934 wrote:

> So it is completely natural that the construction of the underground railway is not just a technical display, but rather a great big human machine which produces not only a material value or worth, but the reshaping of the human; a forty-thousand-headed collective in a whirlpool of production, and which serves as a forge for the creation of a new humanity. This construction site lifts our technology to new levels, and likewise, lifts our human activity to new levels.[35]

This elevation and education was in a very literal way not some dreamy, figurative architects' metaphor. Peasant farmers were turned into industrial labourers, often acquiring vast amounts of rational technical knowledge on the way, if they became brigade leaders or shock workers; even literacy had to be acquired in order to follow engineering briefs, work routines, and canteen menus on the metro project, and thousands of others imitating it—a skill most Russians did not have in 1931.

But existing cities, practically important as they were, still were suspect in some ways to Soviet ideologues—although they were equally suspect to Howard, who proposed starting anew with a rational plan some thirty years earlier. They were full of churches, apartment blocks, opera houses, and department stores—the physical paraphernalia of the nineteenth-century bourgeois urban paradigm. There were pre-revolutionary microscopic habits of everyday life: the pre-revolutionary walk to work; the pre-revolutionary insignia on the letter boxes; the pre-revolutionary fairgrounds of frivolous enjoyment of rare leisure hours. A total faith in the power of environmental determinism required a total faith in the capacity to create a totally new environment, and the archetypal expression of this was Magnitogorsk. The city of Magnitogorsk, on the farthest fringes of Europe in the foothills of the Ural Mountains, was begun in 1929, and rapidly grew to an experimental city of hundreds of thousands of miners and steelworkers. And in this environment, criminals were mixed too, as the faith in the capacity of labour and a purely socialist environment was so profound that every form of social deviance would disappear through proletarianization. The penal colony was re-branded a 're-education centre' in socialist labour and socialist living, and as a result of this belief in the reforming power of labour, early 'legitimate' settlers had to endure constant criminality. In Magnitogorsk, bedrooms were abolished, and people slept in communal barracks with a 'reading corner' in each one; bourgeois individualism was a thing of the past—and so was privacy. Revolutionaries knew how they themselves had used privacy and the secret spaces of the city, and were determined to ensure that only perpetual comradely surveillance was acceptable. Kitchens were centralized, so women could enjoy the same leisure as their husbands; bars were not built, so as to prevent alcoholism, and cinemas only showed educational films rather than Hollywood fantasy. Everyone worked either in construction or in the vast steel plants erected throughout the sprawling new city. The plants were laid out to optimize production. It was a spectacular disaster.[36]

People built mud huts willy-nilly rather than sleep in dormitories, and in the dormitories they built walls or hung curtains to obtain privacy and separation. In particular, brothels, bars, and distilleries required the construction of dozens of huts 'off plan'—a typical example of which can be seen in Figure 5.3 (bottom). The canteens were undersupplied with food, so people had to cook *and* farm for themselves to get extra food *and* contribute to the 'collective canteen' that theoretically supplied all their needs; the failure of the plan in this regard produced the precise opposite of its intentions. Collective provision *caused* an increase in private farming. The technocratic plant managers quickly tired of living in proletarian equality surrounded by sewage slurry and industrial effluent, and built separate zones for themselves to live in, ending the brief experiment in the abolition of the class Apartheid which characterizes the modern capitalist city. The criminals in the 're-education' brigades overran the settlement and had to be rounded up and deported, yet again. People changed job and dwelling whenever a slightly better opportunity came up, so never invested in where they lived nor stayed around to offer the plant a return on any training they received. Illicit drinking dens appeared everywhere, and in a city with no 'districts', red-light and entertainment districts rapidly emerged.

In the USSR in 1929, there simply was not sufficient technical expertise on hand to design a steel plant from scratch, as the technocrats and owners of the previous steel plants had largely fled the country, or been murdered, so all the various parts of it were built in the wrong place. There was an attempt to buy in German expertise, and Ernst May, director of planning in Frankfurt, was hired to take charge—but little attention was given to his insufficiently ideological approach. The scale of the project was breathtaking—as can be seen in Figure 5.3 (top), which shows just part of the vast iron works constructed in virgin territory. Local engineers, planners, and labour brigades built roads before sewers; pipes before reservoirs; and free-flowing sewage in open ditches dropped into the river upstream of where 'clean' water was taken out of it downstream. They put in toilets in buildings where they had forgotten to build sewers underneath them. The city was mired in mud and disease and misery. But it was *very* compliant; utter environmental degradation and instability situated every detail of everyday life in the full capriciousness of 'rational ideology', made everyone dependent on the party and the technocrats and the plan for the hope of getting out of the mess that the party and the technocrats and the plan had got them into. The ultimate cycle of modern dependency had been created in absolute, total, perfect circularity. The total state produced a total environment which produced total failure, the only hope for the resolution of which was a yet bigger

state, and firmer, more productive interventions in the environment. As a popular song in Magnitogorsk ran:

> To the left? To the right?
> Socialist city, where will you be?
> Your designs have been drifting,
> Two years without an answer!'[37]

Meanwhile, by 1937, the director of the project, Avraamii Zaveniagin, was living in a house that cost 250,000 roubles, and his wife shopped in an exclusive perfume shop in the new city centre.[38] For the poor, all sense of self and identity was lost—precisely the goal of the planners: 'You'd come home, searching and searching,' explained one barracks resident, 'but all the barracks were identical and you couldn't find yours.'[39] All personal, ethnic, and national identities were lost, and as the city stabilized, people identified with their class, their labour skills, and a particular shop of the vast metallurgical complex. In that respect, the plan succeeded completely in producing a new human.[40]

In France and Britain, the future was not socialized and rational, but privatized and individual: but the plan was no less systematic, no less thorough. Capitalism is just as capable of producing rigid, inescapable systems as communism. The state in France promoted the construction of suburbs—or rather, promoted the use of the built environment to break up the upper echelons of the working class, convert them into good bourgeois citizens, discourage them from socializing after work, and encourage them to breed. One historian has begun to challenge at last the clichéd, romanticized vision of Paris that

---

Figure 5.3 The Soviet new town of Magnitogorsk, early 1930s. The planners of the USSR wanted to urbanize and industrialize their agricultural country, and 'the plan' was the way to do that. The ideal of the plan can be seen in the image of the vast new iron and steel plants being erected in Magnitogorsk, which would transform peasants into proletarians. But the reality of 'total plans' is that no human mind can comprehend the messy complexity of humanity well enough to devise one complete solution to it, and the result was often inhuman suffering, and a certain form of chaos. As can be seen in the lower picture, people sent to live in this high-tech city of the future quickly resorted to building mud huts with turf roofs on makeshift streets with no paving, rather than live in the dormitories the planners had conceived of.

dominates both academic history, and popular consciousness. The suburbs of Paris experienced extraordinary growth in the 1920s and 1930s, constantly expelling transient armies of *zoniers*, or shanty-town dwellers, to the ever more distant peripheries. The view from these shanty-towns was distressing, as one French senator observed in 1928: 'From the threshold of their pitiful houses surrounded by cesspools, thousands of families can see on the horizon the silhouette of one of the most sumptuous cities in the world.'[41]

This landscape of pity merged into a landscape of danger for a bourgeois establishment obsessed with the idea of a *ceinture rouge*—a red belt of political menace, encompassing the industrial zones to the north and east of the city.[42] As one of the leaders of the first organization intended to plan Paris noted, 'Multitudes of communists have surrounded Paris with the famous red belt, and, more fearsome than the French realize, bands of foreign proletarians in the shallows of the *banlieues* are forming an army ready to riot.' The product of this pity and anxiety were two laws in 1928, the *loi* Loucheur and the *loi* Sarraut, which regulated the parcelling of land, its function, and enacted massive subsidies for middle-class and upper-working-class families to build their own suburban villa. As Senator Chastenet noted, 'We'll combat the communists by making property owners out of them.'[43]

Sixty thousand suburban villas were to be immediately constructed, far from pubs, far from factories, rendering traditional models of after-work socializing and extended family life impossible. One leading historian of Paris has concluded that, by the end of the 1930s, 'the progressive reformers who acquired political power from the state conceived of Paris as homogeneous, abstract and regulated space'—a perspective that hid the processes of social and political reproduction, the means whereby social rules preserve themselves, and political power repels its threats. Poincaré pestered the interior minister that 'the Paris region requires more than ever a plan limited to its current population, because if the Parisian population grows, it will result in grave social danger, and the situation will become irreparable'.[44] But grow it did; the suburbs grew by over a million people in twenty years. And yet no more revolutions; class dispersal and a sort of suburban familial solitary confinement worked.

But the real 'home' of the suburb, rolled out by free-market consumer capitalism, and sanctioned at every turn by the state, was

Britain. Every substantial city in the UK is surrounded by a vast swathe of 1920s and 1930s housing, and the surface area of many British cities doubled in these two decades, while the urban populations of this most urbanized of countries climbed only slowly. Between 1900 and 1920, the urban acreage of Britain increased by 10 per cent; between 1930 and 1940, it increased by 50 per cent. In the twenty years between the wars, in England and Wales city councils built 1,200,000 homes, and private enterprise created another 3,000,000. The idea of Britain in the 1930s as utterly economically inactive, gripped everywhere by depression and universal misery, is a popular myth, given the lie by the very fabric of our cities. While unemployment and poverty between the wars were a terrible blight on the lives of millions, they were by no means representative of the 'typical' experience, and should not characterize the economic state of Britain. The 'north–south' divide was not a product of uncaring Thatcherism in the 1980s: its geography was well established by 1930. Even in 1933, in the depths of the recession, private enterprise constructed 288,000 homes—double the figure of any subsequent or previous yearly record. The number of houses in Greater London doubled in twenty years.[45] To put this into context: in the year to September 2009, characterized by another major recession, there have been 26,120 social housing units constructed, and 107,710 private homes built in the UK. Even in the boom years of the mid-2000s, say in 2006, there were only 18,460 social homes and 144,940 private dwellings brought to completion.[46] The interwar years marked a building extravaganza in Britain, the scale of which becomes apparent in Figure 5.4.

The layout of these houses, and the massive economic infrastructures that supported them—from building societies to furniture shop hire-purchase schemes, to massive borrowing to build underground and overground railways—resembled only very superficially the paradigms evolved by the garden-city movement, as can be seen by comparing Figure 5.4 with Howard's theoretical masterplan at the bottom of Figure 5.1. The superficial affinities are striking. But these were not garden cities with *integrated* functions, balancing work, play, commerce, agriculture and manufacture all in one site, but garden *suburbs* with *segregated* functions; and the plans of capitalist investors in suburban estates and the large social housing projects put into effect were sanctioned by the Tudor Walters Report in 1918 on 'Homes fit for heroes',

Figure 5.4 This aerial photograph of Bellingham from around 1930, a social housing estate in south-east London, shows the vast scale of what the state was trying to achieve in Britain between the wars (and the extensive influence of Ebenezer Howard, whose detailed plans in Figure 5.1 seem to be reproduced here). The scale of social housing provision in British cities was something that many Europeans—even in the USSR—could only dream of. The scale of social building, in terms of quantity of housing units, build quality, internal space, gardens, parks, schools, and health centres was at a level that the British have never achieved since.

largely drafted by Ebenezer Howard's disciple, Raymond Unwin. The 'standard-plan' house, with two large and one small bedroom, an indoor bathroom, a galley kitchen, a living/dining room, and a parlour for best, is one of the most common, and perhaps the most popular, housing types in Britain to this day: the 'interwar semi'.

It is important to understand what contemporaries were up against. City officials rapaciously gathered data on how people lived, and the pictures the data painted were miserable indeed. Liverpool was a typical British city in this regard. When a team of investigators from the University of Liverpool investigated the wards around them in 1929, they discovered a world of filth, with no privacy, a highly destructive incapacity to be alone. One dwelling, a nine-roomed house, was absolutely typical of how the poorest half of urban Europe lived at the time, and the microgeography of one dwelling could tell so much about a whole urban system; and this example comes from Britain, the richest country in Europe at the time, and one with relatively progressive welfare provision. The house had nine rooms, including cellars. In each room in the house, numbered 1–9, there were:

1. A Corporation lamplighter, earning 50s. [shillings] 9d. [pence] [about £127 in 2010], with a wife and three small children. Rent 8s.
2. A ship's fireman unemployed for a year. Benefit exhausted and gets 29s. [29 shillings = about £73 in 2010] relief. Has three children surviving out of nine. The eldest boy is 15 but has had no work since leaving school. Rent 9s [9 shillings = about £23 in 2010].
3. A separated wife drawing 17s. allowance. A son in the army allows 7s. a week. The rent is 9s., and she has three dependent children.
4. An unemployed ship's fireman drawing 17s. benefit. His wife makes 25s. as a bag sewer. Rent 6s. for one basement room.
5. An unemployed ship's fireman drawing 18s. benefit; wife makes 37s. 6d. as a rag-sorter. One child. Rent 10s. for one room.
6. A tailor's presser, aged 24, unemployed for 2½ years, wife of 19 and a one-year-old child. Benefit exhausted, draws 13s. relief. Pay 6s. 6d. rent for one room.
7. A war widow, unemployed cotton-picker, but gets 26s. 8d. pension and 5s. orphan's pension for son of ten. Daughter of 19 earns 24s. in a jam works. Rent 8s. for one room.
8. A young married couple, both 22, with a three-months-old baby. Husband describes himself as 'casual labourer', but has apparently never even had an hour's insurable employment, as he has never possessed an unemployment insurance card. They live on 22s. relief out of which they pay 5s. rent.
9. Man and wife, both rag and bone dealers, make 20s. between them. Pay 4s. 6d. rent.

Nine families share one yard and one lavatory. Seven of them share one tap, the other two having taps of their own.[47]

About thirty people lived in this home, all of them more than one person to a room. They had one toilet. The environment must have been saturated with grief and anger, and drenched with indignity as they struggled to cook, clean, wash, and sleep.

But the city of Liverpool responded with real dynamism and vigour: between 1919 and 1929, it moved over 80,000 people out of the over-crowded city centre to new housing estates on the periphery—almost 10 per cent of the population—with a further 15,000 municipal dwellings constructed in the established urban districts. Then, in the 1930s, they moved another 60,000 out.[48] Across the country, these developments resembled the one in Figure 5.4. Financial innovation in the form of new, flexible mortgages, combined with a relaxed attitude to urban expansion and a commitment to subsidize social housing, produced millions of the most popular, successful housing units in Britain. And this process happened in every large city in Britain: a visual sense of the scale of such projects can be seen in the aerial photograph of Bellingham in London (Figure 5.4).

Social housing and private housing followed the same styles and layouts, for the first time bringing toilets, electricity, and bathrooms indoors for all—or for all who could afford the private housing, and for the 'respectable' working classes judged worthy of the social housing. The inter-war legislation stipulated that no more than twelve homes be built per acre—a spacious disposition. These endless miles of suburban semis, of Tudorbethan semi-detached houses of sunrise windows and sunrise gates have been the butt of vicious scorn since the moment of their inception. Figure 5.5 shows perhaps the archetype of all these dwellings, built in Petts Wood in south-east London (the residents always say 'Kent') by a speculative builder, Noel Reese, in the 1920s and 1930s. General de Gaulle would live there, at 41 Birchwood Road, for part of the Second World War, joining the bank managers and insurance underwriters on the train to London in the morning.

Intellectual after intellectual has heaped angry vitriol on these structures, these environments, and the people who lived there. They have been labelled 'petty', 'tasteless', and 'individualistic'; the people in them are sometimes caricatured as 'racist', 'uncultured', and 'alienated'. For Clough Williams-Ellis (architect of the fantastical Portmeirion, background to cult TV series *The Prisoner*) in 1928 they were 'mean, perky little houses that surely none but mean and petty little souls should inhabit with satisfaction'.[49] He published a book in 1929 called *England and the Octopus*—the octopus being the suburb, strangling true Englishness. This was followed nine years later by *England and the Beast*—the beast was the bungalow. He opined:

> Take any square mile you like of sub-urban Black Country or of the industrial North or Midlands...It is difficult to believe that the houses

Figure 5.5 House in St George's Road, Petts Wood, south-east London, *c.*1928. British and French cities saw an extraordinary growth in suburban development between the wars, driven by an alliance of capitalist property developers, innovation in financial products, lower middle- and middle-class aspirations, and a state keen to dissolve the densely populated city with all its political, economic, health, and crime 'problems'. While not all French and British suburban expansion was this grand in style, both cultures exploited a hodgepodge of popular traditional vernacular motifs to produce homes which, in both countries, are still highly sought-after today.

have been deliberately placed just *so* by thinking social animals—an untutored and charitable Martian would surely deride the idea and suggest the more likely theory that the buildings had been caught by some tidy-minded wizard playing unauthorised blind-man's-buff in a bit of no-man's-land, and has been punished for their skittishness by being petrified on the instant, just wherever they happened to stand.[50]

Osbert Lancaster, cartoonist for the *Daily Express*, classified them as the 'slums of the future'—though many of his readers would have lived in them, or aspired to do so. George Orwell thought they were 'semi-detached torture chambers', and in a 1940 textbook on town planning, they were labelled a 'vast new prison'.[51] But as every investigation into them that has ever been done has found, by and large the people there were and are *happy*. These environments—which are unquestionably more dispersed and isolating than crowded city-centre living—represent for an overwhelming majority of Britons the ideal home in the ideal environment.[52] Yet 'experts' in taste are obsessed with pathologizing this joy, and current politics, especially on the right in whose constituencies these existing suburbs usually lie, is obsessed with preserving a 'green belt', thus perpetuating the current housing difficulties Britain faces by strangling the free supply of land and planning permission that underpinned this enormous construction boom.

On council housing estates the general model in the bourgeois planners' heads was that the working class generally constituted a tightly knit, sociable corps of salt-of-the-earth types, and that their intense sociability should be replicated as far as possible in new housing. At the heart of most such estates were institutions like community centres and libraries, which were supposed to provide the spatial facilitation of 'community' that courtyards, back alleys, shared toilets, pubs, bookmakers, and factory canteens had done, but without their negative effects (like alcoholism or socialism). There was an idea that 'community' was something which would 'erupt' from social housing, if planned in a 'garden suburb' way, giving expression to an innate working-class joy in bonding—bonding with each other, and bonding with the land. This turned out not to be the case.

On the Becontree Estate in Dagenham, near the new giant Ford factory, in 1942, observations of the behaviour of the tenants vis-à-vis the community centre found that there were five approaches people took:

1) Those who take a great deal of interest, spend a lot of time here and do a lot to help. These are mostly older people.
2) People who also spend a lot of time here but come for what they can get out of it. These are mostly younger people.
3) Those who come once or twice a week for a particular activity.
4) Those who come occasionally—perhaps for a special lecture.
5) Those who keep as far away from us as they can, perhaps because we've got a bad name as far as they're concerned.[53]

Of the five groups, the fifth was by far the largest. But people did befriend each other on these estates—just not in the formal, rational, 'improving' way that planners hoped. Planners generally wanted people to socialize around events like informative slide shows about volcanoes, Mayan art, and healthy nutrition. But they did not. As on Becontree estate, people steered well clear of community centres.

On the Watling estate in London (4,000 houses built around the new Burnt Oak tube station), this resident's recollection was typical:

> When I moved in here, there wasn't a house along this road that I couldn't go into and have a cup of tea. And there's not a house that they wouldn't come into me...Everybody knew everybody, and everybody's house was open to everybody.[54]

The difficulty with this evidence is that it comes from oral history. That does not automatically make it doubtful; but personal testimony about the past is heavily shaped by contemporary anxieties and clichés developed in the present. The past is *nearly always* described as friendlier, safer, more respectful in current media representations, even when every other type of evidence may indicate that it was not.

Other oral history evidence from the huge Roehampton estate in London, and the biggest of them all, Wythenshawe in Manchester, shows the keenness with which the upper working class took up the bourgeois model of the inward-looking, self-contained home, luxuriating in a privacy never before available to them. 'My mother wouldn't have *anybody* in', recalled one woman from Roehampton. 'She wouldn't make *anybody* a cup of tea...We didn't entertain. There was enough with family and relatives.' Another confirmed, 'It was very reserved. It wasn't like the East End.'[55] And historians of the vast Wythenshawe estate in Manchester were forced to conclude that the skilled working-class tenants there enjoyed a seclusion that was 'explicitly contrasted with, and preferred to, the old tighter-knit communities of the inner city'.[56] Designed to produce an organic community which was interested in self-improving lectures and slide shows, not pubs and chatter, rational planners of the state and capitalistic planners of the free market accidentally generated one of the most successful forms of housing and residential spatial organizations yet devised, for reasons that have appalled them, and cultural commentators, ever since. The period between the wars marked out the establishment of 'the plan' as the best way to organize any social or political project, a prestige which planning would maintain despite the human costs of the Five-Year

Plans in the USSR and the plan for the Final Solution of the Jewish Question in Europe.

*   *   *

The Second World War transformed the material structure of our cities in revolutionary ways. While all Europe's cities had expanded enormously in the interwar period, the aerial bombardment of cities opened up the possibility of—in fact, compelled—the redesign of city centres *after* the war. But the war itself was not without its plans, although very little building took place. These plans show how deeply the idea of a total environmental solution to every human problem had penetrated the European mind.

Łódź is—and was—a large industrial city in Poland. One architectural historian has called it 'Poland's Manchester'.[57] In February 1940, shortly after its occupation by the Wehrmacht but long before the decision to murder the Jews, the National Socialist administrators in Poland decided that all the Jews of the city and the surrounding areas should no longer be randomly distributed through the environment, but should be zoned, just as a factory or a school would be zoned. According to National Socialist 'science', Jews required classification, relocation, definition, in order to meet the 'best' standards of racial, political, and social knowledge that they felt they had acquired. The first stage was to reclassify Łódź (pronounced similarly to 'wodge'), giving it a new name: Litzmannstadt. It was incorporated into Germany; it ceased to be in Poland, occupied or otherwise. This happened relatively quickly after the invasion in November 1939. The local governor, Friedrich Übelhör, was interested in making the local population manageable. He had little idea of what was actually to become of the Jews, but knew that something would be done with them—he probably suspected deportation—perhaps, bizarrely, to Madagascar. There were about 230,000 Jews in Łódź, in a population approaching a million. Lacking direction from Berlin, Übelhör, and his provincial superior, Greiser, developed, almost instinctively it seems, a plan to 'contain' the Jews in order to 'manage' them.[58] The 'habit' of planning was instinctive, automatic, irresistible.

Concentrating the Jews into a smaller space, a 'ghetto', would make them manageable, and free up accommodation for Poles (as Slavs, they rated almost as low as Jews in the National Socialist classification of the world; but there were more of them, so they posed more of a threat, and they would be required as farm and factory labourers in the extended Reich). The area planned for the ghetto was declared unsafe in January as it was 'full of infectious diseases'—much the same logic that was used to legitimize early interventions in the urban environment that led to social housing between the wars, but with different moral underpinnings. The French state, in particular, declared zones of Paris and Lyon to be 'islands of insalubrity', in order to give the state total planning control there. Thus the Christian Polish population was cleared from the area destined to be the Ghetto, marking out a pattern of moving populations around to solve problems that had been present in the French plans to defuse communism by building suburbs, or Soviet plans to build new cities to remove the habits of bourgeois life ingrained in the old ones. In February, Jews were instructed to move into the newly cleared area instantly. In April, a fence was put round the Jewish zone. In May, the ghetto was sealed. All of this, it should be noted, was done without instruction from the SS, and well before the 'Final Solution' was thought of.

Many Jews initially welcomed the sealing of the ghetto—it meant an end to the beatings and humiliations by Poles and Germans, as they were no longer allowed in. A bizarre figure, Mordechai Chaim Rumkowski nominated himself (or was selected by the Nazis—no one is quite sure) to be president of the council of elders; he began to mint money and print postage stamps with his face on, and set up teams to deal with human waste—there was no sewer system in this part of Łódź. There was no food—the Nazis insisted that the ghetto pay for its food. So Rumkowski negotiated food for labour; if the Germans delivered food and raw materials, the Jews would process them into goods. Rumkowski's tight supervision of food resources to the 'most needy' (or most compliant) quickly gave him absolute power in this urban prison for a quarter of a million. The Germans began cramming more Jews in; then they sent Gypsies. Rumkowski and his supporters militated against the gypsies, regarding them as an under-race of brigands, arsonists, and thieves.

In the summer of 1941, Germany attacked the USSR, and the first phase of the genocide took place in that context: it was frenzied, gun-toting, and caught up Slavs as well as Jews. It had yet to morph into the 'Final Solution to the Jewish Problem'. But soon, what was chaotic took on the form of a plan: the first experiments in planned, systematic, industrial mass murder (a difficult category, because machine-gunning a village is also industrial mass murder) were begun at the end of December 1941, and the death-camp network of systematic, industrial death was planned in detail, being announced within the Nazi party elite in January 1942. When the request came in December 1941 to supply 20,000 to the first death camp at Chelmno, fifty miles away, the first to be sent by Rumkowski were the Gypsies. Thereafter, regular requests for thousands for extermination were received. Rumkowski could not refuse them. The demands for murder victims came piecemeal. It could be none at all, if Chelmno was busy with other train-loads of people being integrated into the plan for solving the 'problem' of racial infestation. Or, as on 22 February 1942, it could be a demand for 32,000, who were duly delivered over the next six weeks. In June, 1944, with the Eastern Front collapsing and the Red Army advancing, Himmler ordered the complete liquidation of all the Jews in Łódź. The very 'urban' nature of the Polish part of the genocide is intimated in Figure 5.6. When the Red Army liberated Łódź (although few experienced the Red Army as 'liberation'), 877 Jews remained from the total of 255,000 sent to live there. Or, in fact, sent to die there. After the initial chaos of the war on the Eastern Front, this rapidly became part of a careful, methodical plan. Primarily, though, death in Łódź was a slow death, a patient battle with hunger, disease, cold, and overwork.

Ethno-musicologists have explored the rich cultural life of music, songs, revues, and such like that was produced in these conditions. The songs are sometimes emotional, sometimes bitter, sometimes domestic, sometimes loving—they are the songs of everyday life, from cultures where singing was central to living. They tell us, though, that there was a profound awareness of the 'logical' and 'planned' nature of what was going on, even amongst children. Hunger, death, and cold dominate, along with hope for salvation—by the British, by the Americans, by the Russians—and by the creation of a state in Palestine. But something that permeates many of them is the sense of a *plan*, of the harsh evil that 'logic' and 'science' can sometimes conspire to produce. Sang one Yiddish song, 'The notorious ghetto, / It

Figure 5.6 The liquidation of the Krakow ghetto, 1943. The Nazis' 'Final Solution to the Jewish Question', and the Five-Year Plans in the USSR, are not equivalent to 'town planning' in terms of intent or effect, but they both derive from the same intellectual starting point which crystallized in thinking about cities in the early twentieth century: one can use *total* environmental control, alongside a *total* state, to achieve a *total*, and perfect, transformation in human societies. In both the management of the ghettoes in Poland, and the designs of the death camps, the procedures, assumptions and methods pursued by the NSDAP were indistinguishable from, and often overlapped entirely with, town planning practice.

runs like clockwork, / Everything is in order, / No unemployment.'[59] Some children put together rhymes, like this one which was heard on a street corner:

> Rumkowski Chaim,
> He gives us water,
> He gives us pepper,
> He gives us poison.
> He made a ghetto
> With a diet.
> He made a ghetto

By the metre—
And he claims
That he is right.[60]

This sense that 'everything is in order', that social problems like unemployment could be eliminated by a yet-more-rigid order, that one can
make a world 'by the metre' and therefore 'be right', is at the heart
of what it means to plan a city, and at the heart of what it means to
create a ghetto. Rumkowski's tragedy was that he placed himself personally at the heart of this ordering process. He had little choice, it is
true; but he aggrandized himself by enthusiastically embracing the
plan for the city of Łódź—a microcosm of the plan for all the Jews.
Work them until they die; and if they do not die swiftly through work,
kill them anyway.

To assert a link between something as banal as regulations about
indoor toilets and fire walls and something as horrific as the Holocaust
may seem tendentious, perhaps grotesquely disrespectful to the many
millions murdered. To draw a line between the benign Housing and
Town Planning Act, passed in Britain in 1909 and intended to stop
polluting factories being built cheek by jowl with primary schools, and
the experiments of Mengele on living twins in Auschwitz-Birkenau, or
the painful suffering at Łódź, would seem at first glance a devastating
dismissal of evil and suffering, or a grotesque misrepresentation of
British health campaigners' desperate attempts to alleviate human suffering. But two of the late twentieth century's leading thinkers, Hannah
Arendt and Zygmunt Bauman, whose works have influenced the study
of the humanities through every department in every university, from
philosophy to politics, sociology to literature, have drawn this parallel,
and they have drawn it in interesting ways.

Hannah Arendt's work on the nature of the Holocaust has impacted
on twentieth-century intellectual life because of the bold nature of the
argument that she made about the nature of evil, and particularly the
nature of evil on the sorts of scale that we have seen so repeatedly in
the twentieth century. In 1960, Mossad (the Israeli secret service)
tracked down Adolf Eichmann, the main transport coordinator for the
'Final Solution of the Jewish Question'. They kidnapped him in
Argentina, brought him to Israel, and tried him for crimes against
humanity—crimes which he had enthusiastically facilitated. He was

hanged. Arendt went to Israel from America (she had been born in Germany, but fled to Paris in 1933, then to America in 1940, because she was herself Jewish and feared Nazi violence). What struck her most observing the trial was what she called 'the banality of evil'. Eichmann was not particularly anti-Semitic in the context of his time, nor was he psychologically unbalanced. He had been responsible for Viennese Jews wanting to emigrate before the war, and had been courteous in his face-to-face dealings with them, although he vigorously promoted the expropriation of their property. Every psychiatric report suggested that Eichmann was intelligent, well read (he was aware of Immanuel Kant's arguments about ethics), loving, and friendly. One of the six psychiatrists who evaluated him was heard to exclaim that he is 'more normal, at any rate, than I am having examined him'.[61] He spoke in the *Amtssprache*, or official jargon, of his everyday life, and was a loving family man. This led Arendt to propose something quite radical about huge evil.

For evil to work on a grand scale, she suggested, it must be embedded in the everyday world. It must be normal, almost unnoticeable, quotidian. It must *not* be politically charged or controversial—otherwise, someone would stand up and shout, as Zola stood up and shouted at the persecutors of Dreyfus, 'J'accuse!' Furthermore, when someone shouts, 'J'accuse!', if the action being opposed is strange, bizarre, exceptional, or outside the parameters of normality, thousands of others will hear the call, and act to prevent the abnormal thing happening. Eichmann was what highlighted this to her: he was the arch-bureaucrat. When Eichmann found out about the plans to murder European Jewry, he did not shout out 'J'accuse!' Instead, he organized the transport infrastructure to facilitate it. He was initially responsible for administering Jewish emigration to Palestine; he went on to become an exemplary railway coordinator, organizing the various railways of the occupied territories to transport Jews to the labour and death camps. He never ran berserk through a ghetto with a machine gun; he filled out timetabling chits. His acts of murder were carbon-copy requisition forms. His evil consisted not in a personal perversion facing inwards into his own heart of darkness, but in his system, his logic, his bureaucracy, his expertise, facing outward into the norms and forms of everyday life. Thus, evil on a grand scale like the Holocaust, or the Ukrainian Famine, or the Cultural Revolution in China, or the Common Agricultural Policy in modern Europe, must be deeply rooted in the *normal* assumptions of a society. They might be extreme forms of that normality, but normal they must be. Big evil must be routine, not conspicuous. A good man (and Arendt usually referred to 'man' and 'men', never to 'people' or 'women') may do an evil thing; but usually another good man will reproach him for it. But if the evil thing is banal enough, no one will reproach him for it. She also proposed a banality of good; Danish administrators proactively opposed the deportation of Jews by deliberately obstructing bureaucratic decision taking, while French administrators helped it with gusto.[62] Big evil and big good are *everyday*, and not spectacularly heroic or diabolic. In this focus on the everyday, the mundane, and the banal, she drew attention to the idea that planning is not just a twentieth-century *activity*, but a twentieth-century *mentality*. It is the normal way of doing things. Ultimately, Arendt concluded, the devil was an idealist.[63]

Zygmunt Bauman is a British sociologist of Polish origin, who fled to Britain to escape the anti-Semitism of the post-war communist government in Poland. He built on this observation of the rooted, unspectacular, everyday-ness of really vast evil and explored sociologically where that root might be in the case of the Holocaust, and by extension, any really vast, murderous evil. Bauman has shown how the logic of the Holocaust was not a uniquely German form of normalized malevolence. Those who have developed his terrifying theory have begun to show how the potential for this sort of evil is a pervasive potential feature of *all* modern systems—a similar logic underpinned British colonialism (the British were semi-enslaving large parts of the population of Zimbabwe in the name of civilization while the Nazis were stripping Jews of their civil rights in the 1930s; the US and Sweden were compulsorily sterilizing disabled people at the same time as the Nazis). Bauman argued that the Holocaust was ultimately a rational act, not an irrational one.

He explained it through the metaphor of 'the gardening state'. The modern state (in its myriad forms—social workers, nutritionists, teachers, doctors, planners, waste-disposal managers, tourist boards, heritage organizations, fire-protection officers, art galleries—the list is almost endless) is like a gardener; the country is like the garden and the population is like the plants and the animals of the garden, to be classified into 'useful', 'beautiful', 'pests', and 'weeds'. The gardener designs his (always his) ideal garden in his head, based on what he knows about plants, their beauty and usefulness, and the particular terrain that he gardens—whether it is hot or cold, windy or sheltered, with clay soil or sandy. He deploys the best, most scientific knowledge of plant habits, nutrition, ecology, climate, geology. He nurtures, feeds, and waters the plants he likes. Occasionally he prunes them 'for their own good'. He moves them to where he wants them—where they will 'flourish'. They may breed, but only under supervision. If they breed too freely, only their strongest offspring will be allowed to succeed: crops will be 'thinned'. They will be trained along walls and up wires, according to the gardener's ideal of beauty, and to make it easier for him to pick their fruit and see their flowers. The 'weeds', on the other hand, will be uprooted, burnt, and destroyed systematically, week on week, so that the 'good plants' may flourish. He will spray with chemicals and lay traps to destroy pests, so that almost everything that is not a desirable plant or complementary animal will be exterminated totally. Expressed in these terms, gardening is a hobby that produces beauty and order, as well as good things to eat; but if the state is the gardener, and the weeds are still being burnt, and the weeds are people, the conclusions become more problematic.[64] Rational, purposive plans were, for Bauman, part of an apparatus for the 'social production of moral indifference'.[65]

The Holocaust, for Bauman, as for Arendt before him, was not an anomalous return to an atavistic, primordial barbarism—which is how, frustratingly, it is so often portrayed in television programmes or in newspapers, and even sometimes in university curricula. Rather, it was the 'logical', 'neutral', 'rational' outcome of the modern process of collecting information about humans dating from the late nineteenth century, and the development of comprehensive, totalizing plans for acting on it which emerged through city planning around 1900. One of the most uncomfortable conclusions of this argument is that genocides are not 'nationally unique', but a part of a wider Western culture in which we all share. The 'garden city' movement was suggesting—indeed, demanding—an all-seeing, systematizing, categorizing, arranging, sorting gardener. Garden-city enthusiasts modelled the world as a garden, and exploited the metaphor of husbanding a population.

While town planners themselves tend to be benign folk, passionate about eliminating (that word is a violent word) poverty, and exterminating (again, a murderous word) disease, and fighting (violence again) incest, the *system* which they pursue—and the assumptions that they make about the 'correct' order of things, the 'appropriate' place for things, and the 'suitable' arrangements of everyday life—are actually the same as those which underpin all large plans, whether the Holocaust or the elimination of polio. Indeed, the benign language of 'warfare' on poverty and disease and incest provided an explicit foundation for the language and ideologies of all sorts of oppressive projects in the twentieth century.

The Holocaust for Bauman (and most scholars now agree with him) was not an exceptional glitch in modern morality, but the logical conclusion of modern morality—a morality which is as British, French, American, and Russian as it is German. The racial ideas of 'improving the stock' in early town planning, as well as the bureaucratic, totalizing, uniform, mundane, day-to-day means of doing so, root *the habits of thought* (though *not* the intention) of the twentieth century's terrifyingly frequent mass murders in the ways planners think. The 'planning mentality'—collect data, identify a problem, design a total solution to 'correct' the problem, employ all the means at the state's disposal to implement it, manage it with experts, exclude the voices of the people with the 'problem'—dominated the twentieth century until the 1980s, when in Britain and America, Reagan and Thatcher rejected the idea of the plan as having been a disaster, in *all* its forms—although the sudden withdrawal of 'gardening services' by the state in the 1980s often caused more problems than it solved, as the urban fabric of any northern American or British city can show. Furthermore, in Eastern Europe the planning mentality collapsed with communism around 1990, and in China, the plan was allowed to wither on the vine from the early 1980s to allow for a measure of chaotic capitalism. In the wake of formal plans followed a no-less restrictive, no-less rigid, far more global, and much more decentralized free-market capitalism, without even the promise of democratic accountability. Often equated with 'freedom', particularly in Anglo-American discourse, capitalism functions to a logic at least as rigid as any other form of plan, and is far more totalizing in its ambitions. The 'concentration camp' and the 'housing estate' both try to produce a total environment to manage human beings in order to eliminate undesirable traits, neutralize dangers and improve the well-being of all. The shopping mall produces a total environment, up to and including artificially managed air supply, for the pursuit of profit.

Of course, this is not to say that planners should be equated with Nazis on a scale of evil, or that the people that live on housing estates should be equated with concentration camp inmates on a scale of suffering. And to say that the Holocaust was banal is not, according to most scholars, to dismiss it, or put it on the level of a soap opera or fixing the office photocopier. Just the reverse. The tragedy of the Holocaust is that it was neither the first, nor the last, systematic, wholesale mass murder in order to produce a 'rationally' defined, wholesome, healthy, ordered, pure world. In the twentieth century such behaviour was something close to a habit.

Yet immediately after the war, planning was not seen that way. The excesses of collectivization in the USSR and the mass murders caused by the Nazis in Germany were generally greeted with an eerie, anxious silence in the 1950s and 1960s. The Holocaust received little public discussion for two decades after the war. Inasmuch as the mass murders of the USSR and Germany were discussed, they were typically associated with *ir*rationalism, not rationalism; with psychotic individuals like Stalin and Hitler, rather than rather pleasant administrators like Eichmann. Immediately after the war, scholars and the wider public wrote of 'Hitlerism' and 'Stalinism', rather than universal problems of modernity, or big systems. Thus the solution to disorder and destruction and irrationality seemed to be order, construction, and rationality. The cities that came out of the war would be *hyper*-rational; indeed, they probably needed to be. No private-sector economy could rebuild what had to be rebuilt in post-war Europe, and states cannot build for the individual. States must act either systematically or not at all.

And they acted on a vast scale. The nature of the problem is well illustrated in Figure 5.7: the destruction of urban fabric in the war was truly exceptional, and one cannot help but contrast the image of central Hamburg here with the prosperous city that one could see just twenty years after the war. The scale of change almost defies belief. The thirty years from the end of the war mark the triumph of the modern, rational state—sometimes, as with the provision of universal

Figure 5.7 A woman and child walk through the streets of Hamburg after the 'Firestorm' of July, 1943. The British carry deep scars from their aerial bombardment in the Blitz; while no aerial bombardment is 'easier' to endure than any other, the staggering scale of destruction in German, Polish, and Soviet cities is difficult to comprehend fully. Women and children were prime-movers in managing this urban chaos, both during the war and the slow process of reconstruction during the repatriation of men in 1945–6. They were, however, rapidly excluded from this role, and encouraged to return to 'womanly' functions. With so many Continental cities in this state, the question about the future of cities was truly 'open' for the first time.

health care, in a benign and very public way; at others, as with the Common Agricultural Policy, in a more sinister and hidden way. In both the Soviet East of Europe and the social markets of the West, economies were redesigned. Instead of the market functioning as the regulatory mechanism, the state stepped in and deployed vast armies of economists, engineers, sociologists, educationalists, architects, planners, and medics to produce a total social–cultural–physical environment to make war unthinkable and to correct the 'injustices' of the past. To approach any European city by car, train, or plane is to see the results of an attempt at total environmental control, total social reform. The view down from a plane will show large, neat, rational industrial estates and city centres of office blocks and pedestrianized entertainment zones, separating once and for all the lives of work and the lives of leisure of millions. Look out of the car window or the train, and one cannot but be amazed at the vast tonnage of concrete that surrounds one. From Barcelona and Marseilles; through Paris, London, Birmingham, and Glasgow; stretching across Hamburg and Berlin to Warsaw, St Petersburg, and Moscow, the power of the social state made real cannot but impress the visitor arriving in any metropolis. And this uniform geography also highlights the weakness of using nation states to organize modern history—in terms of the history 'of Britain' or the history 'of Poland'—because many of the features which dominated everyday life of Europeans in the twentieth century were common to almost all cities, and national and regional identities merely inflected the debate rather than defined it.

The Attlee government in Britain came to power with an absolute commitment to end the 'chaos' of the market; there would be a plan for everything, and everything would have a plan.[66] In France, all national reconstruction after the war was explicitly seen as an offshoot of town planning, and the Ministry of Reconstruction and Urbanism sought to reshape a society to be successfully modern. In West Germany, as in East, piecing together devastated cities was the central priority of government. In the USSR, the focus in Stalin's last years was on spectacular showpiece city-centre developments; but, as he ailed from the late 1940s, planners in the Soviet Union realized that the total society required total housing if people were to offer even minimal collaboration with the state's objectives. Once the Soviet government gave up mass murder as a central policy tool, mass housing was the only possible replacement for securing compliance. We can get a sense of what was expected from post-war planners by focusing on a typical example that just happened to be democratic: France.

In France in 1946, the new Ministry of Reconstruction and Urbanism surveyed the problem facing them with a comprehensive report into the country's cities. France had 14,000,000 housing units. Forty-eight per cent lacked running water; 80 per cent did not have a toilet; 95 per cent did not have a shower or a bath.[67] 'Our common desire', declared Raoul Dautry, first minister for reconstruction and urbanism, 'is to make a new France.'[68] The new France would be built according to plan; and Dautry is an excellent example of the irrelevance of much party politics to the juggernaut of the state. He served, or tried to serve, in every sort of French government from the 1920s to the 1950s—the political expression of the state's power was like the froth on the waves. The logic of the rational plan was the underlying tide or current.[69] The first thing that the new ministry did was construct an experimental station of sixty innovative units; they moved 200 people into them; and they studied how this new form of life would impact on the French family. The new world was to be a vast social laboratory, and humans, and the societies they made up, were to be the guinea pigs. They wanted designs which would make life easier for women so that they would breed more, and would be less inclined to leave the house for any reason (specifically, because housework was so burdensome). The goal was clear: 'douze millions de bébés'.

It is important to understand the potency of the vision that the total plan produced, for while planning itself was 'rational', the drive to make it the heart of every aspect of the state was an emotional one. As Eugène Claudius-Petit, a young communist and minister for urbanism after Dautry from 1948, wrote in an appeal to architects and planners:

> After the night of oppression, the daylight casts an even harsher glare over the wounds of our used-up society, over the ugliness and rot of our suburbs and company towns, over the tomb-like darkness of our slums, over the filth of our factories and their anachronism. We understand very well now why France does not have enough children, and why the few that she has include far too many suffering from tuberculosis and rickets....Surely we are not going to, as we did in 1918, rebuild the same little houses along the same little streets? We are not going to sacrifice to the spirit of the old décor the possibilities of man's liberation that a new décor can bring us?...We are not going to rest on our laurels like a dying country?...What would the world think of a France that would preserve its slums in order to preserve its picturesque qualities, that would 'recommence its past'?...France owes it to herself, in order to regain her true grandeur, to give the world the style of our society.[70]

It is worth pausing a moment to unpick what is being said here, because this impassioned plea could stand for the intellectual ambitions of the European intelligentsia in every large European city east of Spain.

First of all, every aspect of society from the past was bad—it was used-up, ugly, rotten, anachronistic—out of time. This was a typical belief across Europe in 1945—and probably a reasonable one, given what the continent had just undergone. The City of Manchester's plan of 1945 concurred, showing a picture of nineteenth-century housing with the caption, 'No hope'.[71] Secondly, the reason that there were social problems—in the particular case of France, the obsession was with birth rates and insufficiently broody (and breedy) women, but more widely TB and rickets—was that the environment was degraded. Note the profound faith in the environment to resolve behavioural 'problems' (women's broodiness), as well as physical ones (tuberculosis or rickets). Thirdly, the way something looked was not trivial or peripheral: the way something looked—its décor—touched man in the heart of his very being, and *freed* him—whether he liked it or not. Architects are obsessed with this idea; it is, perhaps, the best explanation of their persistent and unique obsession with the colour grey: they view it as a rational, liberating colour. More widely, attacking frills, froth, ornaments, trinkets, knick-knacks, doilies, net curtains, and the like was seen as a potent way of grasping the inner life of the individual in its most intimate places, and *policing* it. It grabbed the proletarian's irrationality, religion, superstition, conservatism, and dusted it away with a clean line and a broad, uncurtained window, offering clear sunlight—and supervision—directly into the heart of the secret spaces of the home. Finally, this was not a regional vision, confined to one estate here and there—nor even just a national one, but a universal one. It was a global redemption: France's mission in urbanism was 'to the world'.

This new way of living was to represent a world civilization, the birth of a new society in which disease and warfare and social conflict would not be suppressed through force, but would be designed out. They would become irrelevant—museum pieces of corrupt environments, like the skeletons of dinosaurs wiped out by environmental change. It is hard, therefore, to talk of nationally specific ways of planning environments, for in fact by the end of the 1950s it was hard to tell from a schematic masterplan, with its relocated factories, its health centres, new schools, laundries, absent churches and pubs, its new living and shopping environments, whether one was in Birmingham, Marseilles, Lyon, Hamburg, Berlin, Milan, Leningrad, or Moscow.

They were not designs for a specific place, but for a universal human-ity. Tuberculosis was the same everywhere, so the cure would have to be too. The scale may vary, but the principles were the same, whether democratic or communist—though with estates like Thamesmead in south-east London, Motherwell in Glasgow, Les Minguettes in Lyon, or Sarcelles in Paris, all with populations of above 70,000, the scale was suitably Soviet. In West German cities, the number of square metres per dwelling (about 62) did not substantially diverge from those in Eastern Europe until the late sixties, so similar was the approach in these two superficially most different of states. For the first twenty years of reconstruction, if a historian is presented merely with the plan of the urban project, it would be hard for them to tell which polity had dreamt it up.

But these were not totally inhuman projects, and many benefited, something we can begin to grasp in an image like that shown in Figure 5.8 of a shanty town in north-west Paris. The cranes in the background are building the *grands ensembles* of Nanterre, which are often condemned now as 'inhuman' but which were surely better than living in shacks in the mud. Even in the Soviet Union's ever-increas-ing urban centres, there was room for humanity as people were put 'in their place' in the post-Stalin era. One councillor from the Sverdlovskii district of Moscow in 1959 intervened to mitigate the rational logic of the process:

> Emergency repairs had to be done to the flats on two floors of a house in my electoral ward. So tenants in these apartments began to be evicted into 'resettlement points'. It suddenly transpired that several residents turned down the rooms made available to them, opposing even a temporary stay in them....I learned...that Shuvalova had just had a heart attack and Gurevich had lost 60% of her sight. I took a look at the resettlement point and discovered that the temporary hous-ing was...at the top of a steep stairway. I went to the ward's housing directorate and tried to prove to them that the problem was not with any quirkiness on the tenants' part but with the new housing's unsuit-ability for them...As a result of this, the ill women received better lodging in another resettlement point.[72]

This assumption that the people or entities (companies, schools, churches, pubs, factories) being moved were 'quirky' if they did not

Figure 5.8 In our rush to condemn the 'mistakes' of the 1960s town planners, we forget what they were up against. This *bidonville*, or shanty town, was in north-west Paris in 1969—the large cranes in the background are building the social housing projects of Nanterre to rehouse the 10,000 souls living in these particular huts. Such slums surrounded large French and Italian cities into the 1970s, and Spanish and Portuguese ones until the 1990s—Barcelona struggled to eliminate them all by the time of the Olympics in 1992. Given the options, high-rise looked good and was quick and cheap. We are not so many steps away from Nairobi, Calcutta, or Rio de Janeiro, and we need to be a bit more forgiving of our forebears' passion to alleviate suffering.

recognize the pathway to rational progress was widespread, and this councillor's tale from Moscow could have been told anywhere in Europe in the reconstruction years.

It is tempting to heroize this 'quirkiness', but in fact, it was often a self-absorbed attachment to place that could cause obstacles to much-needed improvement. Planners were always amazed at how much 'a pig could love its sty'. Romanticizing the foetid, diseased, filthy cities of the war-torn Europe as the folksy environment of chirpy, salt-of-the-earth types is a dangerous game. Many wanted desperately to get out. As one British soldier commented on his dream home during the war, home to him meant 'Leisure, quiet, privacy, courtesy, relative luxury and comfort, forgetfulness of the army and all idiocy and petty oppression, muddle, hurry and noise and squalor and discomfort, anxiety and worry.' This was the opposite of his wartime experience—but also of most homes in Britain's metropolises during peacetime. For another woman in London, she declared it was 'the antithesis of a billet'.[73] Very few dwellings in Europe provided this in 1945: infestation, overcrowding, noise, damp, cold, and lack of sanitation were typical features of housing right across urban Europe. Investigating Ship Street, a typical street of 1950s Liverpool, researchers found:

> Frequently, several rooms in a house are out of use owing to damp, the ceiling having collapsed and caused general disrepair. Few houses have electric light. Most have gas, though one or two still use oil lamps. Most, too, have only cold water taps. In one case, water has to be brought from a tap in the yard.

And in Manchester, in the census of 1951, 41 per cent of Manchester families had no access to a bath, and 44 per cent did not have either their own toilet or stove; ten years later, in 1961, 25 per cent still did not have a bath, and 20 per cent had no hot water.[74] We romanticize the 'salt-of-the-earth' 'community' of 'yesteryear' at our peril. Europe's cities up to the mid-twentieth century were grisly places to live.

In Britain, two young sociologists in the 1950s and 1960s were eager to test the hypothesis that this wholesale resettlement had destroyed the 'genuine' communities of the older, denser cities. They looked at the area of Dagenham, east of London, which had been scheduled as an area of substantial industrial and residential development. There they found—to widespread surprise—that resettlement had been a boon to most families, and that while family structure had changed, it had not dissolved. Extended families were still common, embedded in a rich social life, and residents were enormously happy with their new world, by and large. They relished the new employment opportunities in skilled labour that became available to them, because planners had put car plants near their houses. They loved the smoke-free living and having more space and more privacy. They were keen to leave behind the close-knit social relations of the East End, because they found them oppressive and invasive.[75] Contrary to every subsequent myth and cliché developed from *c.*1967 (when wholesale planning in Britain started to decline) onwards, the people in new housing estates were, by and large, happy and saw themselves as embedded in a rich, stable, integrated community.

In Britain, there were three major features of planning practice after the war. The first was the obsession of British planners with destruction. Staggering quantities of nineteenth-century housing were demolished, probably rightly: they were mostly fetid, unwholesome 'slums', not the charming cottage dwellings of upright yeoman stock that they sometimes appear in the popular imagination. This process of destruction continues apace; it is striking that middle-class campaigners trying to prevent this demolition are not keen in living in the houses being destroyed. They are keen that working-class people live in them. But also huge amounts of industrial infrastructure (including *every single tram line in the country*) were destroyed—France behaved similarly with tramlines, but left its old apartment blocks intact. Around nearly every city centre of a large conurbation in Britain, the visitor will find a ring a mile or two wide of near-total destruction of the Victorian city. This contrasts directly with Berlin and Hamburg and Warsaw, where the level of devastation meant that everything that could be saved, patched up or repaired, was. On the continent, bricks were cleaned, dressed, and put back where they had been as a matter of urgency, and mass demolition did not take place.

While the French, along with the British, expressed their faith in 'Motopia', ripping up all their tramlines too, urban demolition exercises like the one around Montparnasse station in Paris were rare, and the French did not demolish with the same zeal—because in the 1940s and 1950s, Britain was by a long margin the richest state in Europe and could afford greater extravagance.[76] The next British departure from the norm was that, for the first ten years after the war, both the Labour and the Conservative administrations focused on the construction of houses, as well as flats. Ideologically, they felt that British people must be bonded to the soil, and they were influenced by the garden-city movement which situated bourgeois family life in a home separate from other homes, and ringed by green. This changed in 1957, when the Conservative government linked subsidy to height of building directly, rewarding councils that built high-rises disproportionately. Thirdly, also drawing on the garden-city tradition, the Labour administration signalled its despair at existing cities and committed to building 'new towns' in the New Towns Act of 1946, though this policy has been strongly promoted by both Labour and Conservative administrations since.[77] Much maligned as bland and boring, these new towns have generally succeeded—some more than others. Most have become comfortable commuter dormitories, like Stevenage and Crawley near London, or Warrington between Manchester and Liverpool. Others have fully succeeded in their objectives of creating economically autonomous communities—like Milton Keynes, started in 1967, and now with a population of 200,000, most of whom work in the area. German and French cities too developed these *villes dortoires* (dormitory towns) and *Trabantenstädte* (satellite towns)—Cergy Pontoise just outside Paris, Neu-Harlaching outside Munich are typical huge examples.

Sometimes, rarely, new towns failed horribly. Economic planners and new-town planners decreed that Corby in Britain's East Midlands would become a centre of the steel industry, a rationally organized exemplary production environment, in which the conventional labour conflicts of unionized metal production would be eliminated through perfectly balanced social and domestic organization. Thousands of Glaswegian steelworkers were resettled 300 miles south to this Midlands new town (the people there still speak with a bizarre hybrid accent). This new harmony did not happen; labour relations in Britain never became 'socially democratic' as in Germany, and the steel industry retreated and migrated first to Japan and Korea, and now to Brazil, China, and India, and the steel works in Corby were gradually wound down from 1975 onwards—again, not part of 'Thatcher's' revolution, but organized by a Labour administration as part of yet another plan to 'rationalize' the steel industry to five coastal sites. Rancour, bitterness, and unemployment could pervade such experimental communities just as in the old—although this was far from typical. But by the end of the 1950s, under the socially committed Conservative administration of Harold Macmillan, tower blocks were the order of the day, and housing subsidies increased with the height of buildings. The vast experimental blocks of Park Hill, towering over the cliffs at the heart of Sheffield, and the massive settlements in the towers on stilts in Roehampton in south-west London begun in the mid-1950s led to a wave of buildings in the sky—in Birmingham alone, over 450 high-rises in ten years.[78]

It was in the mid-1950s that building began in earnest in France—and it was building upwards, in tower blocks, around the edges of France's great cities. One of the difficulties in collecting research on this sort of planning exercise is that culturally, these experiments are almost invariably narrated in stories as unmitigated failures. One French historian has noted that any discussion of post-war planning which deviates from the established view that it was a '*vaste erreur collective*' is just smothered instantly, or dismissed.[79] It was surely not a *vaste erreur collective* to move people from the *bidonville* in the foreground of Figure 5.8 to the warm, dry, plumbed, heated high-rises being constructed in the background. It is viewed as a disaster in British cities too, and while Britain had few shanty towns, it had many people billeted in substandard mass-produced shacks, many more in houses with earth floors, and millions without hot water. French and Italian big cities were surrounded by shanty towns until the end of the 1960s—and Spanish and Portuguese ones were until the late 1980s. It is something we have conveniently forgotten—that this 'terrible' high-rise housing often replaced shacks, or two families to a room. In the East of Europe, these vast plans took on a particular ideological significance which, unlike in the West, was publicly stated. Such developments embodied the aspirations of the new regimes in Eastern Europe—new too in the USSR, after the death of Stalin in 1953. They were the physical form of a collective endeavour, conspicuously concrete expressions of an ideological obsession. In their materials they are technological; in their aesthetics they have no relationship with the past; in their methods of production they required vast teams working together, and rendered the private builder and the speculative landlord redundant. They did this in France and Britain too, though the French and the British were more ready to gloss over the details.

Figure 5.9 The Jam's songs are often hymns to the big city, as on this seminal pop album from 1977. Yet even here the equivalence is asserted of the
'modern world' with carefully selected shots of motorway flyovers and concrete high-rises, devoid of trees and greenery, people, and facilities. Most
social housing projects do not look like this, yet such photographs are repeatedly selected to produce an atmosphere of bleak despair. It certainly does not
reflect either The Jam's origins in the prosperous suburbs of London, or the
reality of social housing. But we have yet to find a language of 'happy' social
housing.

A central problem here is that the ways we approach this massive environmental experiment have been conditioned by a set of problematic cultural values. The media that trumpeted the construction of social housing in general, and high-rises in particular, between 1945 and 1970 has trumpeted their failure ceaselessly ever since. In Figure 5.9, showing the cover to The Jam's seminal hymn of praise to urban life, *This is the Modern World*, the 'modern world' in question is desolate and concrete, when our cities have never had so many green spaces in them. Even the modern city's fans have portrayed it as grey and lifeless, signing up to a lazy shorthand that marks out social housing as a place of decline and negativity. One sociologist has examined the ways that newspapers have reported housing estates, and found that journalists have produced a constant metaphor of *universal* social breakdown, reported from *anomalous* environmental conditions.[80] She found that while most housing estates are full of greenery, this is never shown—instead, the press focuses on grey, barren areas for their photo shoots. Most housing estates do actually have windows with glass in; these too are seldom shown.[81] She noted how novelists and film-makers and government reports described the planned environments of the modern city— this one is a journalist's report on the vast estate of Les Minguettes in Lyon:

> Les Minguettes became the archetypal dormitory city…a jungle in the town. It was 1981. The large estate was in a bad way. The signs had been visible for a while. Not a day without a letterbox being torn out, lifts wantonly damaged, abusive graffiti, rubbish bins emptied out of windows, complaints about rampant and aggressive delinquency. Bands of disturbed youths stood out against the enclosed sky-line, spasmodically burning large cars, emblems of a civilisation to which they had no key. The police response was tense, then tough. The worst nightmare had become reality—a cycle of violence, repression, violence—which would never resolve anything…[82]

What is important, as history foreshortens into the present, is that we look at the language being used here. Partly, this is the language of the nineteenth-century colonial explorer—the language of the jungle, full of wild beasts to be tamed and surly, uncivilized natives. The language of colonization and military conflict is used throughout. Alternatively, it is a constrained world, with an audience of journalists and experts looking on, like paying visitors to a mental institution: a sort of eighteenth-century asylum—sympathetic, but secretly enjoying the sense of shock and daring, generating a slight frisson at the dramatic disorder. And what about the police here? Are they people with hopes and fears of their own, or merely part of some typical recipe in a trite social tragedy? The problem is that there are no news reports on the factories that worked, the projects that succeeded, the lives well-lived in this new model world. There are no headlines saying, 'Milton Keynes a Desirable Place to Live'.

Cumbernauld, just outside Glasgow, was architecturally the most experimental of British new towns, but recently had some of its city centre demolished. Images of distressed concrete megaliths abounded, but the headline, 'Cumbernauld: Lower than Average Unemployment and Higher than Average School Attainment for Forty Years' has yet to be written, true as it is. The successes have faded into invisibility, and only the failures have been reported. We have lost a way of talking intelligently about plans.

Did 'the plan' fail? Did, for example, high rise housing fail? The answer must be 'no' in both cases. High-rise housing is successful in many cities across Europe—even British ones, where they have come in for especial criticism. Some certainly failed, but the difference between success and failure was often things like having a regular repainting schedule, or running late-night bus services—not planning issues, but management issues. They highlight the failure of the state, in its local and national forms, and the failure of the residents to organize effectively—not the failure of planning or architecture. And low-rise housing fails just as much as high-rise, though is bathed less frequently in media hysteria. In both the 1970s and the 2000s the British state has spent billions of pounds trying to put right the problems of low-rise housing, both socially and privately owned. Paris, Vienna, St Petersburg, Glasgow, and Berlin are all dominated by nineteenth-century tenement blocks that work fine when properly cared for, and at five, six, or seven storeys, they are effectively 'high-rise'. There is no law of sociology that says that the eighth, ninth, or tenth floor is the one that causes the problems.

There are, however, laws of sociology, criminology, psychology, economics, and physics that say that if you clump together vast numbers of very poor people, under-invest in their schools, neglect their health care, watch idly as their jobs move abroad, proactively de-skill them, adopt ineffective drugs policies, send all the most hap-less citizens and vulnerable immigrants to live with them, ignore the development of ethnic and religious ghettoes, fail to link them to the rest of the city with good public transport, demonize their young people as predatory morons, police them with a policy that alter-nates between desertion and oppression, and abandon their build-ings to physical decay and dilapidation, then you will soon see a 'failing' environment.

But these are not flaws of the buildings, or the plans, or the plan-ners—flawed as many of these genuinely were. Planners did not close the steel mills of Sheffield, or the shipyards of Hamburg, or the Lada factories in Moscow, or the garment workshops of Paris. And con-versely, there are no grand Georgian or Victorian terraces in London, however fine, that can survive zero maintenance for thirty years—as the riots in Notting Hill in the 1950s and Brixton in the 1980s dem-onstrated. There are no graceful Haussmann-esque apartment blocks in Paris or Vienna or Berlin that magically resist the ingress of water and insect infestation after decades of neglect, as the surveys of dwell-ings in the reunited Berlin of the 1990s showed. There are no charm-ing workers' terraces in Manchester, nor cramped apartments in the Quartier Latin or Prenzlauerberg, that somehow have achieved bring-ing toilets indoors by themselves. When I lived in Paris in the early 1990s, the lady above me in the Marais had to empty her pot in the communal toilet on the landing, and when my family moved to a house in the 1970s in south-east London, it had an outside toilet; our neighbour kept hers until she died. There are no blocks of flats any-where, be they ever so charming, that become fireproof by some organic process of gradual, evolutionary transformation. Sociologists have shown that in estate after estate across Europe since the 1960s, the media characterization of social housing's failures (many of which are fictional) has been a driving force in producing *dis*investment in these environments, allowing planners to be blamed for voters' and taxpayers' and politicians' decisions not to construct the promised rail connections, and allowing the poor to be blamed for the effects of globalization by the people holding precisely the stock-market pension funds that incessantly drive capital to the poorest corners of the world where environmental regulations are weakest, workers' rights least defended, and profit margins highest.

Above all, across urban Europe, between 1980 and 1990, 'the plan' underwent a transformation. States stopped investing in the plan, stopped building and maintaining; but they did not replace it with anything else. The plan, for all its problems, was replaced with the market, and markets are very erratic at delivering socially desirable objectives. Crucially, across the West, *social* housing became *emergency* housing. Up until the late 1970s in Britain and France, housing was apportioned in order to produce balanced communities. Housing officers would ensure that housing estates had a spread of 'types' of tenant: old and young, wealthy (plumbers and teachers) and poorer (casual labourers and unemployed). In 1977 in Britain, this changed, and the then-Labour government, facing a fiscal crisis, decreed that housing was to be given strictly to the neediest. From 1977 onwards, being a plumber or a teacher would *dis*qualify someone from social housing, and teenage motherhood or unemployment would qualify someone for social housing. As the 1970s Labour government col- lapsed amongst industrial crisis and fiscal incompetence, it gave up on building, gave up on planning, and social housing became 'antisocial', about crisis and disaster and neediness and inability to cope, for both the state and its tenants. German, Dutch, Belgian, and French gov- ernments followed suit in the 1980s.

Planners should look back and see a lot to be ashamed of. They sometimes acted in haste, with too little thought for the cultural and social aspirations of the people they planned for. In fact, they usually despised those cultural and social aspirations. Planners were (and are) often convinced arrogantly of their rightness, and of the deep stupidity— even evil—of the planned-for. They built motorways through poor areas, physically dividing communities forever, while turning rich dis- tricts into conservation areas and preventing further development in them. They often resettled the poor from city centres to lonely colo- nies of poverty on the far-flung city edges. They built inflexible shop- ping centres that only chain stores could afford, and left derelict high streets that small businesses once occupied. They banned street mar- kets because they were untidy and 'unhygienic', making it harder and harder for an individual to start a business. They planned-out alcohol consumption, as if the absence of bars and pubs would mean the absence of alcohol and alcoholism, rather than merely the replace- ment of socially supervised drinking with private, secretive drinking.

They deliberately put miles between where people lived, where they played, and where they worked—and although they designed express trains to link them, many democratic societies failed to build them (in Paris, the metro stops where the fashionable, nineteenth-century Haussmannian boulevards stop; much of the 'success' of French mass transport is myth). And too often, the underlying dehumanizing mentality of all planning, and the ways it strips individuals of the responsibility and ability to manage their own destinies, has been simply brushed aside.

In new estates, planners single-mindedly stripped out almost every shop, café, locally owned workshop, and craftsman that they could find, extinguishing nearly all indigenous economic activity in vast swathes of our cities, leaving functionless 'green space' (S.L.O.A.P.—'space left over after planning'—as it is called) as a casual, ill-thought-through substitute for quality parks and gardens. Planners made, and continue to make, claims about what they could achieve that were far too bold, far too unrealistic, and they had little conception not only of their own limitations but those of their political masters, be they governments or electorates. They built in rigidity to their designs, not flexibility, using concrete instead of brick. And they also overlooked the occasional wilful stupidity and fecklessness of a tiny minority of the people for whom they built, frequently omitting to factor in the law of unintended consequences. Planners too often overlooked the texture, randomness, and mess of the everyday joyful experience of being alive in a city—the chance encounter; the sense of enclosure; the afternoons spent in the pub; passing a bar and hearing a new band playing, perhaps the next big thing, perhaps not. And for every failure of the past, there is a planning office somewhere—everywhere?—that is still making the same arrogant, inhuman assumptions. Since 2009 the City of Liverpool has spent billions of pounds developing the 'L1 shopping experience', which inevitably can only be afforded by chain stores (thereby excluding all local people from, say, setting up a stall and starting a business), and which, with its open-air escalators and shopping 'units' will also one day be too inflexible for whatever the next phase of consumer capitalism brings, and which the city will have to rebuild again at its own expense.

But the planners—for all their short-sightedness—had a clear view of some things. They understood well the role of damp and smoke in pneumonia, tuberculosis, diphtheria, and whooping cough. They knew that gloomy, dark interiors make gloomy, dark lives, and that carrying water and coal to wash made lives gloomier still. They knew that cold and insect infestation caused infant deaths, asthma, eczema, and a host of other debilitating diseases of childhood and old age. They knew that overcrowding made the elimination of incest and child-abuse harder because it bundled together six or seven family members, strangers, lodgers, and visitors in the same bedroom, the same bath situated in the shared living room, the same bed. They knew because, as upright sons (and they were almost all sons) of the middle class, they had lived well and that having a 'room of one's own', in Virginia Woolf's famous phrase, could transform the interior life of the individual. They knew that they liked privacy and that maybe the poor would enjoy it too. They knew that washing clothes by hand once a week was back-breaking work for women, that it disrupted girls' education and that laundries might alleviate this. They knew that schlepping coal was dispiriting work and that gas or electric central heating could banish it forever. They knew that living in shanty towns on the edge of cities, shabby cellars, or attics in the heart of them excluded citizens from the wealth, aspirations, and values of the shared experience of society. All these problems they fixed, *in spite* of the return of mass unemployment, the failure to build the transport links, the evacuation of a police presence, and disinvestment in schools and technical training. Historical amnesia has meant that these successes are hard to talk about, but they tell us powerfully that we *can* shape the environment if we choose to. Almost all of Europe's cities are now democratic: if their residents choose to do something, they can do it.

6

Epilogue: The Way We Live Now?

Cities have revolutionized every aspect of Europe's history over the last century or so. And cities are not an abstraction: they are an aggregation of real times and real places, sometimes similar, sometimes unique. They have given the personnel, the ideologies, and the mechanisms of political change; they have been the arena of women's struggle to transform their place in the world, and the means of achieving that transformation, as well as inhibiting it; urban spaces and places have transformed the ways we represent the world to ourselves and each other, and defined the ways we see ourselves; they have provided the infrastructure for a total transformation in the ways we see our bodies and sexualities; and they have furnished us with the guiding ideas and intellectual frameworks, embedding them in every aspect of our lives.

Cities are so important to who we are, the ways that we live, and the nature of our society that one would assume that we would love them out of a principle of self-respect. They are so much a part of us, where we have come from and where we are going that, surely, we would value them. After all, we love our nations and our religions, and these contribute so much less to the fabric, texture, and assumptions of everyday life in modern Europe than our cities, with their factories, housing estates, night clubs, offices, universities, and shopping centres.

This may seem like a controversial statement, so natural has it become to see ourselves and each other through a national lens, developed in the nineteenth century. But compare the lives of a nineteen-year-old lad wanting to be a mechanic in a super-estate of the 1960s and 1970s, like Neuperlach in Munich, Les Minguettes in Lyon, or Thamesmead in London, and they will have a lot in common. Their lives will be lived out in a similar environment; they will share similar cultures; their working lives will be similar; their sexualities will develop in similar ways. But contrast these young men's lives with their supposedly 'national' brothers farming sheep in the hills of Thuringia, the Midi-Pyrénées, or the Yorkshire Moors: there will be some overlap, but you will find vast differences in their patterns of sociability, their politics, their environments, and their working lives. It is unlikely that there are many rap bands and nightclubs in the countryside, but you would probably find both on most large housing estates. It is unlikely that there are many railway lines, factories, or non-white people in the countryside, but very likely that all three will be found on the estate. So it would seem that the lads growing up on the housing estates have more in common with each other, across national boundaries, than they do with their 'brothers' in the same country, but who live in the countryside—perhaps only a few miles away. But because we cannot quite embrace our urban selves, we often behave as if it were not so.

In fact, we barely recognize our urban selves, let alone love or value them. Some people do explicitly celebrate the city: occasionally, a tourist board will say something positive about the experiences there. More often, young people will fête an 'urban vibe' and seek out a big city to live in. And for many people seeking to escape the oppressive weight of the classic monoliths of power, like class, sexuality, gender, ethnicity, and poverty, cities have long seemed to hold the promise of freedom—to make money, become invisible, escape, build a new life, be someone. But perhaps more often, our cities, and our urban selves, are a source of shame. Instead of shouting from the rooftops, 'our cities are us; we are urban', they are used as a symbol of coded discussions about race, community, nature, and culture. While occasionally we see 'urban' being used to denote 'cool' and 'sophisticated', 'liberal' and 'progressive', 'free' and 'adventurous', too often our cities, over the last hundred years, have been used as a shorthand for our defects, our failures, and our disappointments. When it comes to our cities, we have the self-esteem of a battered wife, and the sense of self of a troubled schizophrenic. It is uncomfortable for us to reflect on our awkwardness with cities; we think of them with the nostalgia and bitterness we might reserve for a great love, now lost. But such reflection is important for the future—not because we can 'learn lessons from the past' (history offers us no lessons ready to be lifted unmodified into the present: history has no useful answers, but many useful questions), but because they help us to face reality with confidence, rather than anxiety. It is worth spending some time exploring just how pervasive and insidious these impressions can be, because they are striking in their consistency across the century: we may think we have left the past behind, but in many ways, it is with us still.

At the start of the twentieth century, it was commonplace to view in cities a particular and new form of racial problem. This process had begun in Britain in the 1840s and 1850s, as the first country to urbanize. Observers' descriptions of the Irish in particular, and the working classes in general, emphasized their alien, inferior qualities and their 'need' to be colonized, civilized, and scrubbed up. But it was in the years either side of 1900 that this view came to be stabilized and extended. In the 1890s and 1900s, cities were often seen as terrifying racial melting pots, sucking in noble peasants with *genuine* culture, *genuine* sexualities, *genuine* families, having lived in *authentic* buildings, on *authentic* national soil, and grinding these 'honest' types into racially debased, culturally impoverished examples of family breakdown and racial catastrophe. Max Nordau, one of the great European pessimist philosophers of the 1890s, concluded of France that:

> The peasant population, and a part of the working classes and the bourgeoisie, are sound. I assert only the decay of the rich inhabitants of great cities and the leading classes. It is they who have discovered *fin-de-siècle*, and it is to them also that *fin-de-race* applies.[1]

He defined 'degeneration' as the 'morbid deviation from an original type'—the 'original' being national, pure, agricultural. His book was a European sensation, and chimed with many others on a similar theme. Cities crystallized that modern deviation from the original, genuine, and authentic that promised to destroy civilization in general, and individuals and nations in particular. And *fin de siècle* attitudes implied the *fin de race*. In so much thinking around 1900 a specifically urban 'degeneracy' was responsible for women's rights, anarchism and socialism, much liberalism, smoking, drinking, drug addiction, a soulless quest for an impertinent and rational explanation for everything, and many other calumnies.

Nor was this viewpoint confined to, or even most typical of, 'dangerous' or 'extremist' foreigners. In 'liberal' Britain opinions were also firm. Mainstream medical practitioners would frequently argue for a sort of 'culling' of the poor. One, C. T. Ewart, a doctor in an asylum, argued of the urban poor in 1910:

Nothing is more wasteful than this army of degenerates who, when they are not living at the cost of the taxpayer in workhouses or prisons, are wandering at large, idling, pilfering, injuring property, and polluting the stream of national health by throwing into it human rubbish, in the shape of lunatics, idiots and criminals.[2]

While Karl Pearson, Professor of Eugenics at University College, London, and government advisor on mental health, concluded in 1914 that, 'just as the Kaffir and the Negro have failed to produce a culture comparable to that of the white man':

it is to parentage itself that the patriot who would work for racial progress must turn in the first place, if he would achieve a greater success than the environmentalists with a century of social reform have hitherto been able to claim.[3]

The problem is, Pearson was arguing, racial: improving slums will not help. It is important to note that people like Ewart and Pearson were not at the radical extremes of British life, but at the heart of the mainstream. They were men who *cared*. And it is important to note, too, their Britishness: it is not just crackpot foreigners that are obsessed with race, while we bumble liberally and progressively through history. While to a 'modern' reader, the views of a Nordau or a Pearson or a Ewart seem appalling, they have the benefit of at least being frank when it comes to race. We have now evolved a subtler way of having similar discussions. Instead of seeing pure peasants destroyed by migration to cities, we see pure white citizens (or at least, their 'way of life' or their 'values') at risk from non-white migrants from poor countries, often encouraged to come to our cities to do jobs the indigenous population was unwilling to do. We see our 'indigenous' cultures at risk from a threatening 'other'. We talk of 'floods', 'saturation', and—in Britain in particular—'our crowded island'. But racialized anxieties are found across Europe today.

In May 2010 in Novara, a small city of 100,000 people in northern Italy, a woman was fined €500 for wearing a Muslim veil over her face. In Belgium and France there are active discussions about whether to ban them in public too, while France has already banned headscarves for women in schools and universities, and in Britain the UK Independence Party has suggested doing the same.[4] In November 2009, Swiss voters banned the construction of minarets in Swiss cities in a referendum—though not spires—prohibiting the expression of just one religion in the cityscape.[5]

For a sustained period in late 2005, almost all large French cities showed extreme violent disorder in which the 'forces of order' were engaged in sustained violent conflict with people often dismissed as 'scum' in official discourse, but simply as 'Beurs' or '*les blacks*' in many bars and cafés. Even when the rioting protagonists were white, they were often lumped together into the 'failures' of black people fully to integrate into true French republican values. The French interior minister, later president, Nicolas Sarkozy, described the two black boys whose death sparked the widespread and sustained disorder as 'delinquent scum', and declared a state of emergency. On 9 November 2005, Sarkozy issued an executive order to deport all non-French nationals found guilty of rioting, even if their presence in France was legitimate. The French media was confirmed in its view that there was a deficit of 'Frenchness' and '*citoyenneté*'—'citizenlike' behaviour—in vast tracts of urban France.[6] That many of the rioters were white, and that many of them were third-generation 'migrants' (and therefore not migrants at all, but products of true, modern, progressive France) got lost in the widespread view that cities—and particularly the vast zones of poverty and exclusion that the French call *banlieues* (and which in France are on the outskirts of cities, but in British and American usage correspond to the ways we describe 'inner cities' or 'estates' or 'projects')—were full of a dangerous, foreign, deviant, ungrateful 'other'. The French establishment viewed the riots not as the extreme anomaly that they were, but as an example of a fairly typical type of urban failure, Sarkozy declaring: 'Violence in French *banlieues* is a daily fact of life. Since the beginning of the year [2005] stones have been thrown at 9,000 police cars and each night 20 to 40 cars are torched.'[7] However, he neglected to mention that, over the previous five months, fifty-two non-white people, thirty-three of whom were children, had died in Paris in three separate building fires in overcrowded, dilapidated apartment blocks and hostels, housing mostly non-white people, some of which had been long since declared unfit for human habitation. This caused little in the way of outrage. To paraphrase Wilde, 'To lose one black life in a fire may be regarded as misfortune; to lose fifty-two in three fires looks like carelessness.'[8]

In Britain, as in France, there have been frequent examples of urban violence in the last thirty years, often dismissed as 'race' riots—the most recent were in 2001 in northern industrial cities and suburbs; there were serious conflicts in the summers of 1991 and 1992; and violence in British cities in the early and mid-1980s was frequent. In January of 1975, *The Sunday Times* noted that in London, 80 per cent of the offenders in street robbery were black, while 85 per cent of victims were white. How they collected these statistics is unclear, but a basic knowledge of social statistics would alert the wise to their unlikely veracity. In May of 1975, when sentencing five black men for street robbery, Judge Gwyn Morris opined:

> These attacks have become a monotonous feature in the suburbs of Brixton and Clapham, areas which within memory were peaceful, safe and agreeable places to live in. But immigration resettlement, which has occurred over the past 25 years, has radically transformed that environment.[9]

This language on the part of the wealthy and the powerful is important, because there is a difference between a 'race' riot, in which race is the problem or issue, and a 'racism' riot, in which racism is the problem or issue. And the judge here focused on race and migration, just as many around 1900 did, but overlooked the decline in public services, the oil price spike, and the collapse of British industrial employment as causes. Poor black and Asian men do not get up in the morning and have a problem with their *own* race; nor do they get up in the morning and have a problem with people of a *different* race; and that means the problem is not 'race'. What bothers them, and what often provides the spark for violence, is rac*ism*. And when people have bothered to ask rioters what bothers them, as in, for example, the Scarman Report after the Brixton riots, the answer from both black and white has generally been a constellation of 'ineffective policing, poverty, exclusion, hopelessness, lousy education, the export of jobs we can do, and the import of migrant labour we can't compete with'. Very often, poor white voices are excluded from the retelling of these stories. If the response to poverty, exclusion, hopelessness etc. is violence, it is not a 'race riot', but a poverty, class, and exclusion riot, with rac*ism* as its spark.

Generally, we heroize people who confront racism and poverty, but only if they do it in 'nice' and 'decorous' ways. The rioters in Brixton in London, Toxteth in Liverpool, Moss Side in Manchester, and Handsworth in Birmingham in 1981 were not heroized. The last major outburst of urban violence in Britain, in 2001, was sparked by the organization of the extremist, racist British National Party in suburbs of northern English cities with a large Muslim population of South Asian origin.[10] If more Europeans had responded to racist demagoguery with angry, violent rage in the last century, the world would have been a better, not a worse, place. I do not wish to suggest casually that rioters in these contexts are, or were, heroes: but it is important to recognize the ways that urban environments, like 'estates' and 'projects', inner cities and *banlieues, Vorstädte,* and *Großsiedlungen* are often used to represent a danger and a moral corruptitude that is, on closer inspection, very, very profoundly 'coloured'.

Our ancestors in 1900 worried about 'degeneration' and racial 'corruption', but that is also what they called it. We use bits of the city to do the same intellectual dirty work as words which we no longer find acceptable. 'Racism' is increasingly excluded from 'respectable' discourse, and it is not 'done' to condemn the poor—but 'geographism' is perfectly fine. We code the problem as geographical, or economic, or environmental, but at the heart the problem is colour and money and the form it takes is urban. Until we love our cities, and stop discriminating against those parts which are dodgy, dangerous, down at heel, trashy, or whatever, we will not love each other as people, because our cities are the physical form of the relationships we hope to create. Study after study in the USA (studies which are slowly being replicated in Britain, France, and the Netherlands) have shown that 'white flight' is a common response both to attempts to tackle racism, and to growing civil rights and integration on the part of nonwhite citizens. White people who can, often just move somewhere else where there are few, or ideally, no non-white people. 'Good' neighbourhoods are typically 'white' neighbourhoods.

But what is really striking is that in a century of sustained migration, the people in cities who have been migrants themselves (and in some sense, every urban resident was relatively recently a migrant from somewhere), and who live in areas characterized by migration, there is so much tolerance and integration. It largely goes unnoticed, and uncommented upon—it does not make easy journalism, and challenges many of the clichés about cities and modern life. When it is

commented upon, it is sometimes viewed as a sort of 'contribution' to
white people's quality of life—the addition of Punjabi, Bangladeshi,
Turkish, Greek, Algerian, Moroccan, Vietnamese, Chinese, and
Caribbean foods symbolizing the 'contribution they make', as if one
had to contribute nice food to be a valid and valuable human being
(and based on that criterion, some might say that the indigenous
British have little stake in the island). But far more impressive than the
conflict, and far more substantive than the 'decorative' aspects of ethnic diversity, is the overwhelming readiness of people in areas of high
migration to adapt, involve, integrate, marry, and work things out. If
migration is a genuine evil or threat, then we would have to conclude
that 'ordinary people' (whether indigenous, migrant, or children of
migrants) have dealt with it remarkably well given the scale of migration over the last century in general, and the last half of it in particular. There are moments of tension and crisis; there are persistent
injustices and problems. But contrast every day of 'racial' conflict with
the tens of thousands of days of patience and equanimity and resolve
and live-and-let-live, and it is clear that we all have a lot to learn from
these parts of our cities. These 'estates' and *banlieues* are not the worst
of us, but in some ways the best. Far from viewing our cities as dangerous swamps, ready to wash away the foundations of our society, we
should be celebrating their breathtaking capacity to absorb, change,
and just get on with things.

And this issue of relationships and 'getting on with things' is another
one that we pathologize in cities on a very fundamental level. It is not
just that 'group x' and 'group y' do not get along; it is often assumed
that the city fundamentally corrodes *every* form of real community and
fulfilling human relationship altogether. At the beginning of the century, philosophers and scholars worried that the city was ultimately an
agent of disintegration of human relationships and atomization of the
human psyche. One, a founder of the modern discipline of sociology,
spoke for many when he concluded in 1903 that the city produced so
much psychological stimulation, so many people in one place, so much
invisible control (in the form of railway schedules, water authorities,
school boards, traffic lights, and so on), and so much outer chaos, that
the only possible response was a complete reorientation of the human
psyche. The psyche was compelled, he argued, to become blasé in all
social relations, and exhibit an almost hostile wariness. He concluded:

For the reciprocal reserve and indifference and the intellectual life conditions of large circles are never felt more strongly by the individual in their impact upon his independence than in the thickest crowd of the big city. This is because the bodily proximity and narrowness of space makes the mental distance only the more visible.[11]

And this reserve and indifference occurred according to some ineluctable demographic tipping point in urban life: 'All this forms the transition to the individualization of mental and psychic traits which the city occasions in proportion to its size.'[12] Georg Simmel's conclusions above are still widely cited in the humanities today.

But when historians have explored the ways that social relationships were formed in cities at the time that Simmel was writing around 1900, they have struggled to detect the alienation that so preoccupied him and his contemporaries. They find Parisian cafés that were so intimate that the same café might enable husband and wife to meet, and from which many of the regulars at the café would appear as witnesses at the wedding.[13] When German-speaking historians from the 1960s on have tried to investigate life in the rapidly growing cities of the 1890s and 1900s, their training in Marxism (in Austria, West Germany, and East Germany) led them to seek capitalist alienation everywhere. But what they found, from Hamburg to Vienna, from Berlin to Cologne, and from Düsseldorf to Leipzig, was a fully worked-out *Arbeiterkultur*, or workers' culture, with its own songs, bars, sports, morality, family systems, and welfare and support structures. These cultures were tightly focused on particular works, factories, city blocks, and apartment buildings and were tightly knit and profoundly intimate. Economically alienated these workers may have been, but their lives were embedded in a rich, textural terrain of highly personal intimacies and enmities.[14] In Southwark in south-central London, patterns of neighbourhood integration were so deep and profound that religious practices and beliefs might be particular to certain streets or extended family networks. People there exchanged a rich brew of knowledge and belief in all sorts of things around 1900, ranging from the use of dragons' blood as a love potion, to how to read cinders to predict death, to the significance of the way cutlery fell if you dropped it on the floor. One folklore investigator in south London concluded in 1907, having explored beliefs about protective amulets and lucky charms, that far from abandoning a deep, embedded sense of community and relationships in cities, these belief systems were far richer than in the countryside:

> It is a common idea that few traces of folk beliefs can be found in great cities but my experience is that, at any rate for the seeker after amulets, there is no better hunting ground than the hawkers' hand barrows in the poorest parts of our slums of such dense aggregations of people as London, Rome or Naples.[15]

It seems that most middle-class observers around 1900 saw breakdown, dissolution, and isolation—but such a picture would not have been painted by the inhabitants. When people have looked for dense, rich networks of villages, kinship, loyalties, fashions, beliefs, habits, and relationships in big cities, they have always found them. It is just that very few middle-class people looked—or look.

This belief in the atomized, lonely nature of urban life is not confined to academic study, but occurs in many forms of cultural expression. Many have striven to capture this sense of loneliness and desolation in the city. Eugene Atget's many images of Paris, like Figure 6.1 from 1907, evoke for us a familiar cliché of the sudden awareness of desolate loneliness, surrounded by the city which, paradoxically, contains so many millions of souls. As Marlene Dietrich sang in one of her big hits in 1933, *Allein in einer großen Stadt*:

> You live in a big city,
> And yet you're so alone.
> The man you yearn for,
> Is nowhere to be found.
> You don't know him,
> But you know somehow all about him,
> And you live in angst,
> That he'll pass you by.

The British rock band The Jam echoed this portrait of a landscape of despair on the cusp of the 1980s, and also preserved the sense of ambivalence towards the modern world in their hit, 'Down in a Tube Station at Midnight':

> And I'm down in the tube station at midnight,
> I fumble for change—and pull out the Queen,
> Smiling, beguiling.
> I put in the money and pull out a plum.
> Behind me,

Figure 6.1 Many artists, like Eugène Atget here in the rue de Cléry in Paris in 1907, were quick to use new media to develop images of the city as a lonely or desolate environment—a theme already mentioned. Others in the early twentieth century, like Georg Grosz (on the front cover of this book) went to the other extreme, characterizing them as chaotic, overwhelming, and conflictual. In doing so, they set up a vocabulary for describing cities which it is proving very difficult to enlarge.

Whispers in the shadows—gruff blazing voices,
Hating, waiting,
'Hey boy' they shout—'have you got any money?'
And I said—'I've a little money and a take away curry,
I'm on my way home to my wife.
She'll be lining up the cutlery,
You know she's expecting me
Polishing the glasses and pulling out the cork'…

I first felt a fist, and then a kick.
I could now smell their breath,
They smelt of pubs and Wormwood Scrubs [a famous
London prison],
And too many right wing meetings.
My life swam around me.
It took a look and drowned me in its own existence.
The smell of brown leather,
It blended in with the weather,
It filled my eyes, ears, nose and mouth,
It blocked all my senses,
Couldn't see, hear, speak any longer…

Though strangely, in the mouth of Paul Weller, The Jam's insightful lyricist and lead singer, such is the enthusiasm for all things urban that even this cry of violent despair sounds slightly festive. These anxieties of alienation and breakdown and despair are widespread—although rarely expressed with the joy of The Jam. On the one hand, we know that we are surrounded by people but, on the other, we are profoundly anxious that some ancient organic 'bond' of community has been dissolved by the thing that most defines us.

Print and broadcast media have relentlessly promoted just one vision of urban life: a decayed, almost apocalyptic one—typified by the type of reporting seen in Figure 6.2. Here, the basic ingredients are all present: an older woman is attacked by a younger man; the newspaper invokes public opinion to obscure the origins of its agenda, and dress them up with democratic credentials by reporting on 'how you would tackle the thugs' and emphasizing that more police (and so heightened control) should come before higher pensions (so poverty reduction). Compare this image to Figure 5.9 and the Jam lyrics above, and it is clear that both supporters *and* critics of the city are all working from a remarkably restricted vocabulary.

British political debate in the period prior to the 2010 election came to be dominated—or perhaps, haunted—by an alliterative phrase that has come to sum up our defective urbanized lives, and our true, national selves: 'broken Britain'. The phenomenon of 'broken Britain' is easily mocked, but it does tell us something important about the unquestioned assumptions frequently used to frame the world. 'Broken Britain' is not classless, or placeless. It turns out on closer inspection that the Britain that is broken is usually urban. One report in a leading conservative newspaper, which could stand for thousands of other such reports, describes the basic character type—aesthetically vulgar, sexually incontinent, aurally challenging, spiritually void:

> Deana —— sits at her kitchen table, fingering a heart-shaped pendant that hangs on a heavy silver chain around her neck. At 44, she has five children. Those children have three different fathers. 'When I married

Figure 6.2 Britain's 'streets of fear', evoked regularly in popular newspaper headlines—here from Britain's leading tabloid, *The Sun*, in 1978. And in the sub-headline, 'Police before Pensions', the desire to control is placed before the desire to eliminate poverty. It is difficult—close to impossible—to report on cities and urban spaces, *except* in this catastrophizing way. This general 'shape' to the urban story remains stubborn and immovable, but does not represent the 'typical' day on the 'typical' street. © The Sun/nisyndication.com

my first husband and had my first child, I thought it was for life,' she says, her voice jagged from years of smoking and hollow from decades of disappointment.[16]

Proceeding apace, such stories usually expand from the person to the place, and this one is no exception, leaping straight to both the specific and the general: 'estates like Monks Hill in Croydon [south London], where Deana lives'.

Such reports, such characters, work from a hackneyed, stunted vocabulary of urban storytelling that relies on a certain type of 'nod-and-a-wink' complicity on the part of the reader. 'Deana' is a cliché, but one that is remarkably widespread. What gets lost in the cliché is that Deana clearly tried to live up to the 'traditional' ideal (although most historical research on marriage and relationships indicates that it was the 1950s and 1960s that were the anomalies, and that before and after this period, relationships were often, but not always, flexible and negotiated[17]): she got married in order to have children, and resolved initially that that marriage was for life. This aspect (the conservatism of many poor people) is seldom focused on, because it disrupts the story of helplessness and lack of self-control that is more often told. The 'shorthand' of Deana's type emerged in the 'human-interest story' which characterized the 'new journalism' of the 1890s and 1900s, and its basic ingredients have remained unchanged ever since.

The shorthand is not even dependent on national context or political outlook. While Deana appeared in a British, conservatively inclined newspaper, a French socialist newspaper, *l'Humanité*, could describe the world in similar terms—as with most fundamental underlying assumptions about the world in the democratic West, there is no simplistic cleft between left and right. One headline in 2006 ran, 'In Aix[-en-Provence], Whole Areas Lack Community Spirit' (what the French call, *citoyenneté*). The sub-headline summed up the crisis of the world, and fixed it to a place:

> *Banlieue.* Unemployment, Racism, Discrimination, Death. That is the picture painted by a recent inquiry into young people on estates in difficulty in the city.[18]

The concerned state in its report also concurred. Everywhere, a lack of community. The Germans, as they are wont to do, have a whole word for these problem areas: *Brennpunktviertel*—'crucible suburbs', 'clashing quarters', 'intensive areas'. And in Germany, the mass-market daily, *Die Bild*, laments the lyrics of the 'darkskinned rapper' (their opening-line description of him), Samy Deluxe, which describe modern Hamburg as a 'nightmare'.[19] The more up-market paper, the *Hamburger Abendblatt*, summed up the future: 'Fat, Weak, Sick: The Problems of the Youth of Today'.[20]

Describing 'community', or measuring it, or quantifying it, is a tricky business. There is certainly a lot that is disruptive to community if the community is poor, has bad schools, struggles to find housing, or is isolated from good, cheap public transport. But these are not qualities of the community itself, nor of the people who live in it. What will strike anyone who knows areas that are characterized by poverty, bad schools, poor housing, and so on, is that the people who live there often know more people more intimately than in more prosperous areas. The members of political parties who knock on doors at election time, the church organizers, the agents of the state (like police officers and social workers), will often remark openly that the people they talk to in places like Monks Hill or the *banlieues* of Aix or the suburbs of Hamburg are remarkably embedded in networks of informal employment, informal childcare, romantic relationships, patronage and obligation, family connections across generations, and patterns of sociability.

In Manchester, where I am writing this now, most houses have back alleys behind them, which the city has been gating off one by one to improve security (these were once used as the main entrances to traditional working-class housing). Looking at these alleyways, it is easy to spot the ones in 'poor' areas, versus the ones in 'gentrified' or wealthy areas: the ones in 'poor' areas typically have been set out with tubs containing bedding plants and wooden furniture to enable people to sit down, and the walls are often painted, as can be seen in the left-hand image in Figure 6.3. The gentrified ones, such as that on the right, remain sterile, stark, and lifeless. The number of alleyways in poorer areas that are decorated like this is breathtaking; and so, in its own way, is the number in rich areas. The space of the city is telling a remarkable story—one which completely contradicts the limited vocabulary of apocalypse. If we look for community in these traditional working-class neighbourhoods, rather than its absence, we will find it in all its imperfect, abundant glory. This is not to romanticize 'salt-of-the-earth' types, and paint a Panglossian picture of poverty, but it is to

Figure 6.3 Northern British cities have suffered terrible socio-economic change over the last forty years, and are characterized by back alleys. In poorer suburbs of Manchester, as in Longsight above, people often decorate their back alleys and furnish them with potted plants. In wealthier areas, like Chorlton-cum-Hardy opposite, they have not. Yet areas like Longsight are assumed to lack cohesion, community, and a sense of shared purpose, while communities like Chorlton are often fêted for their well-integrated nature. But if we read the space separate from the clichés, we read a different story.

Figure 6.3 *Continued*

recognize that community and inter-human connectivity has not been a universal casualty of modernity or urbanization.

It seems that middle-class observers, from Simmel in 1903 to the *Daily Telegraph*, *Die Bild*, and *l'Humanité* in the 2000s, project middle-class experiences of a more detached, mobile, disconnected lifestyle onto poor people, but in them it becomes a pathology. There are other voices, though. The leading contemporary French sociologist in the world, Loïc Wacquant, is a specialist in such housing estates. Writing about the 'Cité de Quatre Mille' (the 'Estate of Four Thousand') in La Corneuve in Paris, he observed that it has a reputation as a no-go area, full of crime, deprivation, and depravity, characterized by outsiders as a sort of 'urban purgatory'. So he went to investigate it. He found that it was true that young men did regularly engage in vandalism and street fighting, that scuffles were frequent, relationships with the authorities tense, and physical violence in social intercourse widespread—all more so than in comparison to middle-class neighbourhoods. But he also found that:

> Nonetheless, it is quite safe to walk about in the Quatre Mille, including after nightfall, where one can go about freely in and around the buildings as they attract and harbour much public life. In the park...one can spot families out for picnics in springtime, joggers and cyclists in action, a game of pick-up soccer on a makeshift field, children flying kites and couples walking their dogs. People who work in the vicinity routinely cross [the estate] to reach the adjacent regional transit station, which is packed with commuters going to and from Paris at rush hours. Those holding jobs inside the Quatre Mille express exasperation and disbelief at the idea that their place of employment would put them in any kind of jeopardy...The permanent presence of residents and especially the young in the squares, play areas and streets that connect the slabs to one another helps to reassure the visitor.[21]

It is unlikely to reassure the middle-class visitor, however. Young people playing is only slightly more anxiety-inducing in the bourgeois urban lexicon than the nightmare of young people 'hanging about'.

There has been a truly remarkable change in urbanization in Europe even in the second half of the twentieth century—and cities now account for about 80 per cent of Europeans' living environments. Conventional definitions of 'city' versus 'country' have become harder to sustain, as huge stretches of settlement merge almost into one vast, extended sprawl, like the 'central belt' between Glasgow and Edinburgh in Scotland; the 'M60 corridor' linking Liverpool, Warrington, Manchester, Huddersfield, Leeds–Bradford–Sheffield, and Hull in northern England; the London and Paris regions; much of Belgium and the Netherlands; or the Ruhr Valley in Germany. In France in 1955, about 55 per cent of people lived in urbanized areas; now it is about 76 per cent. In Germany in 1955, about 64 per cent of people lived in urbanized areas; now it is about 75 per cent. In Britain in 1955, 77 per cent lived in cities, while now about 90 per cent do. Russia has moved from about 50 per cent in the middle of the century, to about 75 per cent now.[22] In this context, given how much social discord there was in Europe's past, both recent and distant, I am not struck by how *little* we like each other, but how much. Given the quantity of us crammed into small spaces, the number of people clamouring for resources in ever greater spatial concentration, it is breathtaking that we have become so peaceable, so amiable, so tolerant. Looking back into Europe's past, I see a world, not of well-integrated individuals befriending people they like and ignoring the people they do not, but a frequently brutal struggle for existence often hampered by selfishness, fatigue, poverty, and intolerance.

Ours is not a golden age of friendship and integration—there are many people who are isolated and lonely, and golden ages do not exist (except as sticks for moralists to beat us with). But even notwithstanding the catastrophes of the former Yugoslavia, and the heated intolerances of Belfast and (London)Derry, we do seem, in our urban worlds, to be much more relaxed about each other. But we should not let this blind us to the real moments of human interaction in the past: the gay men dancing in a bar in Berlin, and the policeman joining in; the women refusing to stay at home in wartime Vienna; the commitment of the citizens of Liverpool to build spacious, sturdy homes for the working- and lower-middle classes; the friendships made in workshops that might lead some to form the Labour party in Bradford and Leeds, or the SPD in Berlin or Hamburg; the friendships, acquaintances, and bonds between black and white that led jazz to flourish in underground bars in Paris in the years after the First World War; the abiding male friendships made on the football terraces of Moscow, Milan, or Manchester. Cities can no doubt be alienating and lonely, but few places are more literally lonely than the countryside—and it is there that suicide rates, the ultimate human statement of despair, are highest today.[23] It might seem drastic to revert to suicide as an explanation of people's connectedness, because it overlooks the nuances of emotional interaction. But suicide rates are important because they are more or less the only statistics about people's emotional states that are widely available, universally comparable, and collected in the same way in all Western (and most developing) countries. They show that now, in our supposedly debased, alienated, atomized world, suicide in cities is less common than suicide in the countryside.

In part these anxieties about race and alienation are a reflection of a more general discomfort at the whole modernizing process. At the beginning of the century across Europe, there was, intellectually speaking, a sharp intake of breath when beholding the mighty transformation already underway. One response to that transformation was to look forward to an era of progress, reason, and perfection—this was the faith of most of the planners, the doctors, and the sociologists of the 1900s and the 1920s. But others looked back. Russian intellectuals lamented the turning away from the old ways and the old Church—an anguished cry also heard loudly and clearly amongst the Catholic elites of Munich, Vienna, Warsaw, Lyon, Paris, Bilbao, and Barcelona. In some ways, this look backwards was built in—literally *built in*—to the modern transformations being wrought in the rapidly growing nineteenth-century metropolises of Europe. Munich and Manchester built neo-Gothic town halls; London and Budapest built neo-Gothic parliaments. And all Continental European cities built mile after mile of neo-Renaissance street frontage. But this stylistic look backwards, this borrowing of superficial historical styles, was not nostalgic. Rather, faced with a vast quantity of new buildings, new building technologies, and new building functions (from railway stations to public baths to parliaments to department stores), architects and engineers plucked styles from the past almost at will. Occasionally, they might claim a deeper significance for them—but by and large, they just borrowed from a canon in a relatively unselfconscious way.

But in the 1890s and 1900s this began to change. Outside Paris, Hamburg, Munich, St Petersburg, and Vienna, artists' colonies were set up to gain access to the 'true' forms of nature.[24] The National Trust was set up in Britain to preserve the past; in Germany, the 'Homeland League' (Bund Heimatschutz) was a hugely popular vehicle for campaigning for the preservation of 'traditional' architecture, and its resurrection in the contemporary period.[25] Further afield, in the USA, the 'wilderness' was rapidly transformed in these two decades from being something which had to be conquered through internal colonization to something which had to be cherished and preserved in national parks; the indigenous peoples of the USA went from being a problem and a threat to be expelled from the 'wilderness' to being objects of anthropological curiosity to be preserved in reservations. And as the Parisians built their metro, a shrine to modernity combining electricity, engineering, the big state, and the rational plan, they furnished it in the natural, plant-like forms that have come to characterize it. Hector

Guimard's sinuous organic shapes adorning the entrances to many Paris metro stations, with their green paint, symbolize the gateways to these ultra-urban, ultra-modern places in many guides to Paris, but the dissonance of their green, organic forms to the technological, industrial, infrastructural monster below is remarkable.

Relatively quickly in the 1890s, the models of the past in novels and art and architecture and music became hugely self-conscious—just as did its rejection in Modernism. The past ceased being an innocuous way to adorn the present, a benign catalogue of tropes and motifs to be perused at will, and became increasingly seen as a way of smothering the present—by both people keen to look back, and keen to look forward. People started to look to the pre-modern world, not as a curious and engaging point in time, but as a variety of salvation. Of course, people had looked to the past to make comments about the present before: Gibbon's Roman Empire existed to comment on eighteenth-century Britain, and Thomas Carlyle and John Ruskin's medieval worlds were invoked to imply the poverty of their own nineteenth-century one. But at the end of the century, a certain form of polarization took place between those who viewed the past as a disaster to be extirpated from every aspect of life and those who viewed the present in the same light.

One enormously influential writer on the Continent, Camillo Sitte, who shaped many of his contemporaries' thinking about how cities should look, commented:

> The modern city planner has become poverty-stricken as far as art is concerned. He can produce only dreary rows of houses and tiresome blocks to put beside the wealth of the past. We are confused and disturbed because our cities fall so short of artistic merit. In seeking sensible solutions we are bewildered when, on every occasion, block plans are brought out for technical discussion as though the problem were purely mechanical in its nature.... We are perfectly aware of the great difference between our modern uniform plazas and the ancient public squares which we can enjoy.... On the other hand we are charmed by the picturesque appearance of old cities. We simply overlook the methods that were used to obtain the varied artistic impressions they make.... Modern systems! That, indeed, is the appropriate term! We set up rigid *systems*, and then grow fearful of deviating from them by as much as a hair's breadth. Suppression, or sacrifice to system, of every ingenious touch that might give real joy of living is truly the mark of our times.[26]

In this world view, the past was a model to aspire to, not a set of styles to borrow from. It was a whole system which, if understood correctly, and applied with vigour, could fix the modern world. For many (though not, it should be noted, for Sitte) the past became a rule, a force for discipline, instead of a free choice of styles from a historical palette.[27] Across the continent, similar voices were heard. In Britain, the Arts and Crafts movement advocated a return to hand-made objects to end alienation of worker from worker, worker from employer, worker from consumer, and worker from product. At the same time, the Salvation Army set up colonies around London to redeem lost young boys and girls by engaging them with the 'wholesome' English soil and very, very hard labour (frequently, before sending them to Australia and New Zealand).[28] The idea was that if boys and girls were removed from 'the wasteland', as T. S. Eliot would come to call the modern world in his epoch-defining poem of the same name of 1922, and sent to the real land, they would be in some sense restored. As Eliot wrote in *The Waste Land*, 'In the mountains, there you feel free', while modern urban life was characterized by an encounter with commuters on London Bridge:

> Unreal city.
> Under the brown fog of a winter dawn,
> A crowd flowed over London Bridge, so many,
> I had not thought death had undone so many.
> Sighs, short and infrequent, were exhaled,
> And each man fixed his eyes before his feet.[29]

The countryside was uplifting; the city, downcast. The countryside was free; the city imprisoned in routine, its inhabitants barely able to breathe.

This complex set of fantasies about the countryside and the past is still with us—but we no longer have the courage to call it what it is. In Britain, we consume many TV programmes that sell the ideal that the city, though it defines who and what we are, is somehow dangerous and should be left behind. Shows like *Build a New Life in the Country*, *Relocation, Relocation, Relocation/Location, Location, Location*, *My Dream Farm*, *The Great Italian Escape*, and *Escape to the Sun* all follow a similar line: the cities in which we live are unwholesome, problematic, risky—especially for children. The country is full of 'villages' with a 'real sense of community', they seem to suggest. But when people on these shows move to the country, it is not usually to farm, or live with nature (and when it is, as on *My Dream Farm*, city types rapidly realize that rural life is grindingly hard). Far from it. In fact, what they want are easy commutes to shops, theatres, bars, highly paid urban jobs, leisure facilities, rapid transit systems, schools, and universities. The brief for one of the most recent episodes of *Location, Location, Location* at the time of writing, in which two estate agents help a family find a home on a budget of £1,075,000, is: 'They'd like lots of amenities nearby…but are looking for a rural feel.'[30] It also needs to be within a short commute of the centre of London. This echoes exactly the contradictory pulls of modern culture that Ebenezer Howard defined in *Garden Cities of Tomorrow*, and shown in image 5.1 on p. 334. What they want, in fact, 'just happens' to be every distinctive feature of the modern city, but without poor people or black people, or a keen sense of social responsibility to solve, rather than flee from, perceived problems. It is never stated explicitly—it is 'entirely fortuitous' that these features arise. But the trend is to produce a fantasy world, where we are unable to read community and belonging and integration in cities—and unable to detect their absence in semi-rural commuter dormitories. It will shock some to hear a preference for 'nice' areas and 'nice' people implicitly criticized as having, in part, tones of racial and class politics, but this phenomenon has been exceptionally widely studied. One major database of academic research alone identified 1,132 articles in English on the topic; Amazon suggests 1,641 books in English that cover it.[31] Sociologists call it 'white flight', and it works with a rigid, ineluctable, predictable logic.[32] Yet because of the emotionally charged nature of the underlying arguments, it is a difficult one for people to bear, or associate with themselves. It is one of the most well-supported conclusions of modern academic investigation, yet few have heard of it, and fewer still are willing to see themselves in it—perhaps understandably.

Nor is this quasi-rural fantasy found only in Britain, despite the readiness of the British to bemoan their own nostalgia—and for others to bemoan it for us, when we cannot find the time. The French have a vibrant culture of 'white flight' of their own, and similar dynamics are emerging in Germany too.[33] And the penetration of this anti-urban, anti-modern habit of thought can reveal itself in the most surprising of everyday places. In France, walk into a supermarket, and approach the chiller cabinet: you will be entering a fantasy world. The cheeses will be wrapped in gingham-printed waxproof paper, and placed in little wooden boxes, both of which speak of small batches, grandma's farm, hand production. France claims to be a culture of many cheeses, but most of the cheeses that people can easily buy are now produced by vast agro-industrial concerns. The *image* is of a restorative, 'national' countryside, artisans, nature, *la vieille France*: the *reality* is rapidly increasing milk yields, intensive farming, industrial processing, careful branding, declining dairy-cow life expectancy, rapidly growing obesity, and a jealous management of European Union farm subsidies. The suggestion is 'olde worlde', as if these cheeses were not produced by vast agro-industrial combines like Danone, Nestlé, Parmalat, and Kraft. And while the British often berate themselves for their slightly kitsch tastes in cottage-esque architecture, in cities from Lisbon to Warsaw, from Lille to Milan, you will see rings of brand new nostalgic housing—steeply pitched roofs, imitation historical detailing—built in suburbs which speak, indirectly, of a past when people belonged, people bonded, people knew each other. The acres of cottage-esque homes—often now constructed by vast corporate construction concerns from high-tech aggregates, fibres, and compounds—that surround cities in Britain, France, Germany, and Italy speak of an unwillingness to recognize that the world has changed.

In some ways, this does not matter. If people are happy living in olde worlde architecture, it costs nobody anything, and the tireless sanctimony of out-and-out Modernists about how these dwellings are a crime against taste seems like a crass imposition. While so many people entertain a fantasy about a 'new life in the country', they also show a remarkable ease with many aspects of technology and modernity. They have embraced air flight, complex pharmaceuticals, innovative surgery, and broadband communications without much anxiety. But the question has to be about the ways that the olde worlde fantasy *does* do damage: especially, the ways in which it promotes segregation and the neglect of poverty and the poor. It is not even just a question of money: many communities and nations have invested vast sums in utterly modern systems, like the National Health Service in Britain, the Trains à Grand Vitesse in France, the RER express railway in Paris, and the swift renovation of the east of the newly reunified Germany. These have all been technological, rational, modern, expensive, and well supported. And they have delivered. If we could commit to loving our cities the way we love our health-care systems or transport infrastructures, what could we not achieve?

Whether it be anxieties about race, human contact, or modernity itself, one is struck by the readiness of our urban forefathers around 1900 to speak as they found. When they worried about race, they used a language of race. When they worried about social atomization and community failure, they wrote and sang about that. When they did not like modern life in general, they condemned modern life in general. It may seem, from the portrait I have painted here, that this generally negative vision can stand as typical for the *fin de siècle*—the nineteenth-century one, that is. While a quick survey of European culture around 1900 will throw up many conspicuous examples of an ugly, brutal pessimism, there are in fact far more examples of an almost unbounded faith in the future, and an excitement about getting there. Historians have tended to focus on the pessimism and despair because it seems to offer clues to our sinister selves, and ties in to 'what happened next'—the mass killing of the Marne, the Holocaust, the Five-Year Plans, the Eastern Front, the 'great' dictators. Misery sells, in history books as in contemporary news media. But the unbridled exuberance that many in 1900 had about the future is far easier to find, in newspaper reports, political speeches, trade union meetings, sermons, books, and public debate. And it is this that we seem to lack today. We have preserved in a debased, coded form, so many of the anxieties that could be found in 1900, and both lost the courage to call these fears by their proper names *and* given up on the hope and the sense that the human will, individual and collective, can transform the world. And those people left in our democratic societies who *do* believe this, our politicians, are the most universally derided of all.

Does any of this matter? If cities made us and if they help to define our politics; our modes of thought; the organization of our states and our environments; the ways we experience our lives as sexual beings, or as women and as men; the ways we represent the world to ourselves and ourselves to the world, then this emotional paralysis surrounding cities matters greatly. We are like an individual with no self-esteem; a mind with no sense of ourselves and reality. If we cannot face the world as it really is, and our history as it really was, then we cannot celebrate that which is good about us, nor can we fix that which needs to be fixed. And it also means we will waste a lot of money fixing things that 'ain't broke', and ignoring a lot of broken things in serious need of repair. And we have much to be proud of about ourselves and our cities: they are far more impressive for their social cohesion than their division, for their rich patchworks of communities and networks than for their loneliness and alienation, for their health than their sickness, for their wealth than their poverty, and for their tolerance and liberality than for their ethnic conflict and confrontation.

But we also have much that needs to be 'fixed'—readers will have their own agendas; it is not my intention to define other people's social, cultural, economic, and political priorities. However, if we keep on viewing our problems, whatever we define them to be, as located in the 'nation', or in the 'economy', or in 'society', or in the 'banks' or the 'markets, or in 'politics' or 'culture', we will overlook the basic law of geography and history that has underpinned this book. We need to turn to our streets and our houses, our trams and our night-clubs, our planning offices and our shopping centres, our factories and alleyways, our offices and bars and pubs if we are to see ourselves clearly, celebrate our true identities proudly, and cure our many faults effectively. We cannot walk away from these things, and 'escape to the country'. We must learn to love our true selves. We must learn to love our cities.

Notes

Introduction

1. Mitchell, 1962: 19, 20, 22, 24–5.
2. Mitchell, 1978: 12–14.
3. Habermas, 1989.
4. For two good examples, see Mazower 2008, Hobsbawm 1995.
5. For some good examples, see Weber 1976, Figes 1997, Bosworth 2006.
6. For example, Kershaw 2001; Bullock 1990; Montefiore 2004, 2008; Service, 2009; Williams, 1997.
7. For example, Langhamer, 2000; Reese, 2006; Sandbrook, 2007, 2008.
8. For example Niall Ferguson, 2008; Richard Evans, 2004, 2006, 2009.
9. Soja, 1989: 4–5, 11–16.
10. Williams, 1958: 312, 327.

Chapter 1

1. Certeau, 1988: 1–14, 91–110; Foucault, 1990: 91–101.
2. Hall, 1976.
3. Mitchell, 1978: 11–13.
4. Berger, 2000.
5. Hall, 1974.
6. Berger, 2005: 292.
7. Blewett, 2006.
8. Lynch, 1998: 58–9.
9. Howell, 1983; Wright et al., 1997; Moore, 2001.
10. Howell, 1983: 340.
11. Ibid.: 334.
12. Stuart, 1999.
13. Leo XIII, 1891.
14. Ibid.
15. Ibid.
16. Wistrich, 1983.
17. Geehr, 1990; Boyer 1974.
18. Boyer, 1995: 80–1.
19. Maderthaner et al., 1999: 145–75.
20. Boyer, 1995: 55–6.
21. Dong-Woon Kim, 1995.
22. There was a widespread phenomenon of rural factories in Russia in this period, in the Central Industrial Region.
23. Brower, 1982; Murphy, 2005: 11; Johnson: 11–27.
24. Smith, 1985: 27.
25. Ibid.: 8–11.
26. Lawrence et al., 1992: Table 1.
27. Smith, 1985: 30.
28. Bassin, 1992: 7–8.
29. Haimson, 2000; Herrlinger, 2004; Brym, 1995.
30. Smith, 1985: 50.
31. Surh, 1981.

32. Petrov, 2000.
33. Murphy, 2005: 15–26.
34. Bater, 1976.
35. Read, 1996: 61–143.
36. Mandel, 1983; Johnson, 1979: 120–54.
37. Mandel, 1984: 246.
38. Ibid.: 246.
39. Bookchin, 1998: 29–38.
40. Mandel, 1984: 407.
41. Bosworth's *Mussolini's Italy* (London, 2006), is an excellent exploration of the haphazard nature of fascism's early years, and a great read.
42. Doumanis, 2001: 131–55.
43. Valli, 2000: 141.
44. Bell, 1984: 7.
45. Ibid.
46. Sonnessa, 2005.
47. Ibid.: 192.
48. With the exception, perhaps, of particles or rays of light, and other quantum phenomena. The NSDAP was not, however, a quantum phenomenon.
49. McElligott, 1997: 167.
50. Ibid.: 183.
51. Ibid.: 187–8.
52. Ibid.: 184.
53. Hoffmann, 1991.
54. O'Mahony, 2003: 138.
55. Hoffman, 1991.
56. O'Mahoney, 2003: 144.
57. Jenks, 2000: 703.
58. Colton, 1996; Neutatz, 2003; Kettering, 2000.
59. McElligott, 1997: 220–7.
60. Noakes et al., 1985: 545.
61. Sandvoß, 2007: 118.
62. Ibid.: 120.
63. Parry, 1998.
64. Jankowski, 2002.
65. Millman, 1993; Passmore, 2005.
66. Jenkins, 2006.
67. Soucy, 1981.
68. Jenkins, 2006.
69. Galera, 2002.
70. Jenkins, 2006; Soucy, 1999, 2005.
71. Ozouf, 1966; Dobry, 1989.
72. Passmore, 1995.
73. Tartakowksy, 1986.
74. For an introductory survey of global power relations in this context, see Reynolds, 2002.
75. Macreedy, 2001; Backer, 1984.
76. For a survey of the literature, see Leffler, 1999.
77. Steege, 2005: 419.
78. Murphy et al., 1997: 19.

79. Ibid.: 53–4.
80. Ibid.: 69.
81. Cromeens, 2007: Appendices A and C.
82. FDGB (Freier Deutscher Gewerkschaftsbund), 16.6.1953.
83. All the evidence in this paragraph comes from FDGB, 16.6.1953.
84. *The Times*, 17 June 1953.
85. FDGB, 17.6.1953.
86. Operativstab PdVP Berlin, 17.6.09.
87. CIA: III-3: Comment on the East Berlin Uprising, 17 June 1953 (Mori No. 144301), 18.6.1953; III-4: Closing of Berlin Borders, 18 June 1953 (Mori No. 144211), 18.6.1953.
88. Pringle, 2004.
89. Knight, 1993.
90. Kramer, 1999: Parts 1–3; Baras, 1975.
91. Granville, 2002, 2003: 265.
92. Machcewicz, 1997.
93. Persak, 2006.
94. Rainer, 1997.
95. This, and the detail of the sections that follow, are derived from the account in United Nations, *Report of the Special Committee of the United Nations on the Problem of Hungary*, General Assembly Official Records: Eleventh Session, Supplement No. 18 (A/3592), New York, 1957.
96. Freedman, 2002; Gearson, 2002; Schake, 2002.
97. Ostermann, 1996.
98. Ross, 2002: 468.
99. Ibid.: 473.
100. Harrison, 2002.
101. Maddrell, 2005.
102. Murphy et al., 1997: 343–6.
103. Maddrell, 2005.
104. Bouscaren, 1949: 61.
105. Most studies take a 'political science' approach, which tends to view phenomena as somewhat abstract and transnational, for example Kersbergen, 1995; Kalyvas, 1996. See Kaiser, 2004 for a historian's take on the 'problem' of the scholarship on Christian Democracy.
106. Carnevalli, 2000: 249.
107. With some exceptions, such as Carnevalli, 2000; Scrivano, 2005.
108. Rioux, 1969: 42.
109. Ibid.: 37. This section closely follows the narrative that Rioux establishes, and all citations are drawn from it.
110. Ibid.: 37.
111. Ibid.: 53.
112. Seidman, 2001: 258.
113. Ibid.: 271.
114. Berstein, 1994.
115. Bracke, 2003; Ouimet, 2003; Kramer 1998; Mastny, 2005.
116. Bloom, 2006: 46.
117. Ibid.: 49.
118. Wacquant, 2006; Dikeç, 2006; Donzelot, 2006; Balibar, 2007.
119. Joyce, 2003.

Chapter 2

1. William Shakespeare, *As You Like It*, Act II Scene 7.
2. Malone, 2002: 285.
3. Engel, 1994: 122.
4. Outstanding, readable explanations of 'a woman's place' and its significance for the history of Europe in the mid–late nineteenth century can be found in Nead, 2000; Walkowitz, 1992; Corbin, 1990; Engel, 1994; Marcus, 1999; Thompson, 2000.
5. Mitchell, 1978: 4, 396–400.
6. Bush, 2002.
7. Tilly and Scott, 1975: 40, 1978; Tilly, 1979.
8. Mitchell, 1962: 60.
9. Land, 1980: 61.
10. The positions are characterized by two classic studies: Hartmann, 1981; Humphries, 1977.
11. Land, 1980: 61.
12. Heimann, 1923.
13. Frader, 1998.
14. Engel, 1994: 222; Frader, 1998, throughout; Showalter, 1992; Tosh, 1999, 2005a, 2005b; Hunt, 2004; Healey, 2004; Davis, 2000; Benenson, 1993.
15. Satre, 1982. Price conversions using the economic conversions for retail price inflation at <www.measuringworth.com>, accessed 6 June 2010.
16. Satre, 1982: 12–13.
17. Ibid.: 13.
18. Karl Marx and Friedrich Engels, 2002 [1848].
19. Riedi, 2000.
20. Koonz, 1976.
21. Evans, 1976; Joannou, 2005; Faraut, 2003; Aitken, 2007.
22. Blum, 1990; Bellasai, 2005.
23. Caws, 2001: 512–3.
24. Mosse, 1990; Adamson, 1992.
25. Wilkinson, 1998: 101; Tosh, 1994, 1999; Kessel, 2003.
26. Wishnia, 1995.
27. Accampo, 2003; Wishnia, 1995; Tomlinson, 1985; Koven et al., 1990.
28. Bavel, 2007; Cook, 2007; Szreter et al., 2003; McMillan: 163.
29. Mitchell, 1978: Table A3.
30. McLaren, 1977; Bavel, 2007; Cook, 2007; Szreter et al., 2003.
31. Szreter, Nye, and Poppel, 2003.
32. McMillan, 1999: 171.
33. McRandle et al., 2006: 676–7.
34. The discrepancy between life expectancy at birth, and life expectancy at fifteen, is because the first five years of life represent particularly high levels of mortality, dragging down averages; Szreter and Mooney, 1998.
35. Grayzel, 1999.
36. Blackwell, 2001: 141.
37. Ibid.: 142, 147, 156.
38. Vining and Hacker, 2001.
39. Healy, 2004: 42.
40. Ibid.: 95.
41. This was a feature well established by the late nineteenth century; see Nead, 2000, or Thompson, 2000.

42. Healy, 2004: 92.
43. Ibid.: 94.
44. Ibid.: 95–6.
45. Ibid.: 96.
46. Brader, 2005.
47. Ibid.
48. Wilson, 1991.
49. Wende, 1999, my translation.
50. Peterson, 1977: 99.
51. Davis, 2000: 76–92.
52. Ibid.: 76–92, 106.
53. Engel, 1997. This article also provides an excellent survey of such disorders in Moscow and Petrograd throughout the war.
54. Healy, 2004: 95–6.
55. Mitchell, 1978: 60.
56. Mitchell, 1962: 62–3.
57. Mitchell, 1978: 60.
58. Todd, 2003: 296.
59. Ibid.: 306.
60. Moutet, 1987.
61. Downs, 1990.
62. Todd, 2003: 306.
63. Green, 1997: 274.
64. Mitchell, 1978: 12–13.
65. Goldman, 2002: 5–69; Koenker, 1995.
66. Markevich, 2005.
67. Clements, 1991: 270.
68. Evans, 1981.
69. Vallin et al., 2002: 262.
70. Engel, 2004: 176.
71. Guenther, 2004: 55–6; Scott, 2006.
72. Gronberg, 1998: 23.
73. Ibid.: 24.
74. Todd, 2004: 139.
75. Gronberg, 1998.
76. Benninghaus, 2000: 50.
77. Ibid.: 51.
78. McIvor, 2001; Summerfield, 1998a, 1998b.
79. Summerfield and Peniston-Bird, 2000.
80. Krylova, 2004.
81. Summerfield, 1998b.
82. McIvor, 2001: 196.
83. Sladen, 2005; Calder, 1992; Smith, 2000.
84. Werrell, 1986: 708–9.
85. Friedrich, 2008: 50; Werrell, 1986: 708–9.
86. Friedrich, 2008: 58;
87. Lowe, 2007: 297; Diefendorf, 1993: 11.
88. Addison and Crang, 2006: 1.
89. Hewitt, 1994.
90. Haynes, 2003: 309.
91. Bidlack, 2000: 109.

92. Ritzel, 1998: 296.
93. Heineman, 1996.
94. Harsch, 1993: 34.
95. Höhn, 1993: 64–6.
96. Ibid.: 64–6.
97. Diefendorf, 1993: 15.
98. Ibid.: 22.
99. Moore, 2005: 661–5.
100. Virgili, 2002: 137.
101. Mark, 2005: 137.
102. Ibid.: 137.
103. Ibid.: 149.
104. Anonymous, 2003: 53.
105. Auslander, 2005: 253.
106. Ibid.: 256.
107. Bucher, 2006: 66.
108. Ibid.: 117.
109. Ibid.: 147.
110. Cited in Giles, 2004: 40.
111. Willmott et al., 1957: 32.
112. Höhn, 1993: 70.
113. Harsch, 1993: 36–7.
114. Ibid.
115. Willmott et al., 149.
116. Langhamer, 2005: 341.
117. Casey and Martens, 2007.
118. Willmott et al., 1957: 121–30.
119. Langhamer, 2004: 49.
120. Carter, 1997.
121. Reid, 2002, 2005.
122. Scott, 2006: 2–7.
123. Buckley and Fawcett, 2002: 123.
124. Grotum, 1994.
125. Poiger, 1996: 594–5.
126. Dupâquier, 1979.
127. This section is taken from August, 2009: 83 ff.
128. Council of Mortgage Lenders, 2001.
129. Ibid.
130. Office of National Statistics, 2009a.
131. Amnesty International, 2005.
132. Myhill et al., 2002; Amnesty International/ICM, 2005.

Chapter 3

1. Nott, 2002: 39.
2. Williams and Chambers, 1997, <http://www.robbiewilliams.com/discography/singles/angels>.
3. *The Scotsman*, 10 March 2005.
4. Comments attached to the song at <http://www.youtube.com/watch?v=LF8unwxh Nho&feature=PlayList&p=CAE6798866C713BE&index=0> (accessed 14 Oct. 2007) confirm that many people are currently playing this at funerals of close family members.

5. Chambers, 1985: 3.
6. Sassoon, 2006: 1336–7.
7. Faulk, 2004: 82.
8. Ibid.: 82.
9. Bailey, 1986.
10. Höher, 1986.
11. Rearick, 1985: 91–3.
12. Rearick, 1988.
13. Abrams, 1992: 92–108.
14. Rearick, 1985: 92 ff.
15. Faulk, 2004: 159.
16. Abrams, 1992: 22.
17. Veitch, 1985: 366.
18. Ibid.: 369.
19. Korr, 1978.
20. Baker, 1981.
21. Korr, 1978: 226.
22. James Scott in Edelman, 2002: 1454.
23. See for example, Lenz, 2006 and Kennedy et al., 2006.
24. Gehrmann, 1989.
25. Marschik, 1999: 219.
26. Ibid.: 225.
27. Ibid.: 226.
28. Dunning et al., 1988.
29. Edelman, 2002: 1451.
30. Murray, 1984: 144–64.
31. Edelman, 2002: 1460–4.
32. Austin, 1966; Baldwin, 1981.
33. Ritzel, 2001: 164.
34. Krasner, 1995.
35. Riis, 1986.
36. Lange, 1996: 16.
37. Hustwitt, 1983.
38. Cited in Baxendale, 1995: 137.
39. Jackson, 2003: 41.
40. Ibid.: 72.
41. Rearick, 1997: 63.
42. Hustwitt, 1983: 12–13.
43. Ibid.
44. Berliner, 2004.
45. Rearick, 1985: 95.
46. Nott, 2002: 150; Hylton, 1926.
47. Ritzel, 2001: 167–81.
48. Ibid.: 182.
49. Nott, 2002: 156–9; Hustwitt, 1983.
50. Nott, 2002: 161.
51. Baxendale, 1995.
52. Lange, 1996: 18–23.
53. Jackson, 2003: 62–3.
54. Tournès, 1999.
55. Nott, 2002: 89.
56. Briggs, 1995; Pickering, 2008.

57. Letters to the Editor, *Musical Times*, September 1933.
58. Nott, 2002: 116.
59. Kater, 1992: 152.
60. Ibid.: 153.
61. Ibid.
62. *Le Petit Journal*, 10 May 1897.
63. Müller, 2001: 69.
64. Sassoon, 2006: 847.
65. Hammond, 2006: 18–22.
66. Jahn, 1995: 154.
67. Davray-Piekolek, 1994: 11–16.
68. Chaplain, 2003.
69. Lefcourt, 2004: 105.
70. McKibbin, 2000: 187.
71. Lefcourt, 2004: 105–6.
72. Hark, 2002: 3–8.
73. Richards and Sheridan, 1987: 47, 61.
74. Lefcourt, 2004: 109.
75. Richards and Sheridan, 1987: 48–9, 74.
76. Harding and Lewis, 1993: 17.
77. Ibid.
78. Ibid.: 25.
79. Sennett, 1977.
80. Bowden and Offer, 1994.
81. O'Sullivan, 1991: 164.
82. Foot, 1999: 146.
83. O'Sullivan, 1991: 167.
84. Ibid.
85. Foot, 1999b: 384–7.
86. James, 2003: 14.
87. Tournès, 1999: 61–72.
88. James, 2003: 14–18.
89. Chambers, 1985: 41.
90. Cited in Chambers, 1985: 81.
91. Ibid.: 150.
92. Johnson, 2006: 3.
93. Malbon, 1999: 85, 88.
94. Kooijman, 2005: 265.

Chapter 4

1. Hirschfeld, 1905: 28–9.
2. Herzog, 2006: 78. See also Halperin, 1989.
3. A good starting point is the work of Judith Walkowitz (1980, 1982), but the number of major monographs on the topic in the nineteenth century is vast, and new ones are published each year. Major city and university libraries will have many that are readily available.
4. The poverty of the scholarship on twentieth-century European prostitutes and their customers as people is discussed substantively in the long introduction to Harris (2010) which is also an excellent, readable attempt to do something about it.

5. Again, the literature on prostitution in the developing world is vast, but Jeffreys (2009) or Ballantyne et al. (2005) are good places to start.

6. For examples of the importance of 'discourse' in the writing of histories of sexuality, see amongst many others Naiman, 1997; Carleton, 2005; Fenemore, 2009; Cook, 2003b.

7. Mosse 1985, 1996; Berliner, 2004; Dean 2000; Hall, 1996; Sonn, 2005; Arnade et al., 2002; Hubbard, 1999, 2001; Rose, 1998; Giles, 1992.

8. Carter, 2005; Spector, 2007; Erber et al., 1999.

9. Rosario, 1996: 146.

10. Ibid.: 160–1.

11. Because late-nineteenth-century doctors proscribed so many forms of sexual activity that were clearly a major part of so many people's lives, there is a rich literature on this which cannot be referenced here, but to start: Moore et al., 2010 (frigidity); Laqueur, 2003 (masturbation); Maines, 1999 (the female orgasm).

12. Rosario, 1996: 164.

13. Healey, 2001b: 43.

14. Hirschfeld, 1905: 32–3.

15. Ibid.: 34.

16. Lewis, 2005: 368.

17. Ibid.

18. Moggridge, 1992: 214.

19. Kaplan, 1999: 280.

20. Cook, 2003a: 36.

21. Kaplan, 2005: 260.

22. Showalter, 1992.

23. *Illustrated Police News*, 9 Oct. 1880.

24. Malmstad, 2000.

25. Healey, 2001: 246.

26. Houlbrook, 2005: 99.

27. Somerville, 1994.

28. Hirschfeld, 1905: 53–4.

29. Ibid.

30. Cook, 2003b: 35.

31. Hill, 2005: 325.

32. Ibid.

33. Cook, 2008: 26.

34. Healey, 2001: 249.

35. Rifkin 1993: 137–71; Hekma, 1991.

36. Hancock, 1998; Bruns, 2005; Luft, 2003; Williams, 2001; Fout, 1992.

37. Houlbrook, 2005: 181–2.

38. Westwood, 1960: 155.

39. Cook, 2003b: 359–60.

40. Ibid.: 360.

41. Westwood, 1960: 151.

42. Healey, 2001: 248.

43. Houlbrook, 2007.

44. Cocks, 2003; Hekma, 1991; Saurer, 1997; Peniston, 1998.

45. Cook, 2003b: Appendix 2.

46. Dickinson, 2007.

47. Houlbrook, 2005: 33; Dickenson, 2007; Waite, 1998.

48. Whitford, 1997; Lewis, 1971; McCloskey, 1997; Rowe, 2003.

49. Dickinson, 2007: 9.
50. Moreck, 1931: 136.
51. Ibid.: 142.
52. Ibid.: 149.
53. Pry, 1937: 2–3.
54. Ibid.: 9–10.
55. Ibid.: 24, 40, 70.
56. This section is derived from Houlbrook, 2002.
57. Ibid.: 32.
58. Ibid.: 38.
59. Ibid.: 35.
60. Ibid.: 35.
61. Houlbrook 2002: 244–5.
62. Healey, 1997: 91.
63. Ibid.: 93.
64. For example, see: Klein, 2005; White, 1986: 134–60; Haine, 1996; Sohn, 1995; Bajohr, 2003; Abrams, 1993.
65. Healey, 2002: 353, 367.
66. This section is based on Healey, 2002: 361 ff.
67. For an excellent survey on how Soviet life was further 'destabilised' in the 1930s, and the distinctions between city and country in general in this period, see Fitzpatrick, 1999.
68. Sosnovy, 1959.
69. Healey, 1997: 97.
70. Ibid.: 362–5.
71. Ibid.: 215–6.
72. Dickinson, 2007: 221; Giles, 2005; Micheler, 2002.
73. Miller, 2006: 202.
74. Jivani, 1997: 58.
75. Ibid.: 56–7.
76. *Journal officiel de l'Assemblée Nationale*, 1960, p. 1981.
77. Miller, 2006: 363.
78. Timm, 1998; Evans, 2003; Herzog, 2005.
79. Evans, 2003: 606.
80. Ibid.: 631.
81. Chauncey, 1994: 97.
82. Higgins, 1996.
83. Houlbrook, 2005: 190; Houlbrook and Waters, 2006.
84. Westwood, 1960: 181.
85. Ibid.
86. Whisnant, 2006.
87. Ibid.: 380.
88. Ibid.: 382.
89. Pretzel, 2002: 288.
90. Whisnant, 2006: 231; Pretzel, 2002: 305–7.
91. Houlbrook, 2005: Appendix 1.
92. *Manchester Guardian*, 26 Jan. 1953.
93. Ibid., 5 Dec. 1953.
94. Ibid., 4 Dec. 1953.
95. Ibid., 29 Apr. 1954.
96. Mort, 1999.

97. *Manchester Guardian*, 16 Dec. 1955.
98. Schofield, 1965: 18–19.
99. Westwood [Schofield], 1960: 137.
100. Schofield, 1965: 139–40.
101. Gunther, 2004: 332.
102. Ibid.
103. Ibid.

Chapter 5

1. De Wit et al., 1987; Koester et al., 1990; Sampson et al., 1977; Feld, 1979; Boardman, 2003; Robinson et al., 2002.
2. Südekum, *c*.1909: 41–2.
3. Evans, 1990: 285–8.
4. Ogawa, 2000; Gilbert, 2000; Sarasin, 2004.
5. Shapiro, 1985: 137.
6. Fijalkow, 1998.
7. Shapiro, 1985: 82.
8. Horsfall, 1905: 187–8.
9. Power, 1993: 35.
10. International Labour Office, 1924: 72.
11. Evans, 1989: 65–6.
12. Bezirks-Inspektor des 16. Stadtbezirkes an den Magistrat der Königlichen Haupt- und Residenzstadt München, 8 July 1909. Stadtarchiv München-Wohnungsamt-23.
13. Horsfall, 1905: 19; Heggie, 2008.
14. Horsfall, 1905: 21.
15. Ibid..
16. Harrison, 1991: 298.
17. Driver, 2001: 195–6.
18. Numbers and Stenhouse, 1999; Weikart, 2002, 2006; Brantlinger, 1985, 2003; Kaye, 1986; Claeys, 2000; Pick, 1989; Kushner, 1989.
19. Pick, 1989; G. Jones, 1980; Burrow, 2000; Solomon, 1988; Weikart, 2006.
20. Rodger, 2000.
21. Innungs-Verband Deutscher Baugewerksmeister an die Staats- und Städtischen Behörden in Deutschland. Eingabe betreffend die Beschaffung billiger gesunder Arbeiterwohnungen, 30 August 1901. Stadtarchiv München-Wohnungsamt-23.
22. Howard in LeGates et al., 2003: 347.
23. Ibid.
24. International Labour Office, 1924: 114.
25. Blau, 1999; Weihsmann, 1980; Langewiesche, 1979; Gruber, 1991.
26. International Labour Office, 1924: 456.
27. Ibid.: 459.
28. Schütte-Lihotzky, 2004: 145–63.
29. Jerram, 2006, 2007b; Schütte-Lihotzky, 2004: 145–63.
30. Colton, 1996: 154.
31. Ibid.: 215, 249–356.
32. Jenks, 2000.
33. Ryklin, 2003.
34. Neutatz, 2003: 42.
35. Ibid.: 43.

36. Kotkin, 1995: 106–45.
37. Ibid.: 114.
38. Ibid.: 127.
39. Ibid.: 136.
40. Ibid.: 198–237.
41. Wakeman, 2004: 119.
42. Stovall, 1998.
43. Wakeman, 2004: 119.
44. Ibid.: 126–7.
45. Swenarton, 2002: 267.
46. Office of National Statistics, 2009b.
47. Jones et al., 1930: 517.
48. Ibid.: 511; McKenna, 1991: 173.
49. Barker, 2009: 59.
50. Ibid.: 62.
51. Swenarton, 2002: 278.
52. Willmott and Young, 1957; Clapson, 1998; McKibbin, 1998; Whitehand et al., 1997, 1999; Olechnowicz, 1997; Oliver et al., 1981.
53. Olechnowicz, 1997: 191.
54. Bayliss, 2003: 382.
55. Ibid.: 383.
56. Hughes and Hunt, 1992: 88.
57. Poplawska and Muthesius, 1986.
58. Kershaw, 1992; Dobroszycki, 1984; Adelson and Lapides, 1989; Hilberg, 1980; Browning, 1986. The literature on the 'Final Solution', or Holocaust, or Shoah, is vast, and competent studies of it can be found in all public and academic libraries, so I have taken the liberty here of stepping back from referencing this fully, citing only the texts I have relied on for this section. A full bibliography of the history of the ghettos can be found on the United States Holocaust Memorial Museum's library website.
59. Flam, 1992: 73.
60. Ibid.: 43.
61. Arendt, 1994: 25.
62. Ibid *passim.*
63. Ibid.: 42.
64. Bauman, 1988, 1989, 1991. The 1988 article is the clearest exposition of the problem, and a good introduction to the 'gardening state'.
65. Bauman, 1988: 485.
66. Chick, 1998.
67. Rudolph, 2004: 483.
68. Ibid.: 484.
69. Baudouï, 1987.
70. Rudolph, 2004: 486.
71. City of Manchester, 1945: plate 1.
72. Colton, 1996: 403.
73. Langhamer, 2005: 343.
74. Ibid.: 344–5.
75. Willmott and Young, 1957.
76. Picon-Lefebvre, 2003.
77. Simmonds, 2001; Clapson, 1998; Meller, 1997.

78. Jones, 2005.
79. Fourcaut, 2004: 198.
80. Power, 1999: 114.
81. Ibid.: 157.
82. Ibid.: 119.

Epilogue

1. Nordau, 1895: 2.
2. Stone, 2001: 405.
3. Ibid.: 409.
4. <http://www.guardian.co.uk/world/2010/apr/22/belgium-burqa-ban>, accessed 1 May 2010; <http://www.guardian.co.uk/world/2010/may/05/woman-fined-burqa-italy>, accessed 5 May 2010.
5. <http://news.bbc.co.uk/1/hi/8385069.stm>, accessed 1 May 2010.
6. Ossman and Terrio, 2006.
7. Haddad and Balz, 2006: 25.
8. <http://www.afrik.com/article8764.html/>, accessed 3 June 2010.
9. *Sunday Times*, 5 Jan. 1975; *Guardian*, 16 May 1975.
10. Alexander, 2004; Poynting, 2007.
11. Simmel, 1997: 181.
12. Ibid.: 183.
13. Haine, 1996.
14. The literature on *Arbeiterkultur* and *Arbeitermilieu* is vast, but a good introductory survey can be found in Kaschuba, 1990; and, in English, Abrams, 1992.
15. Williams, 1999: 63.
16. *The Daily Telegraph*, 12 July 2009. They use her real name but, as she is not a figure of fun, it was not appropriate to do it then, and it is not appropriate to do it now.
17. Good places to capture the sometimes flexible nature of relationships would be Haine, 1996; White, 1986; Klein, 2005.
18. *L'Humanité*, 2 Mar. 2006.
19. *Die Bild[zeitung]*, 1 Aug. 2008, <http://www.bild.de/BILD/hamburg/leute/2008 /08/01/city-talk-samy-deluxe/darum-hilft-er-sozial-schwachen-kindern.html>, accessed 5 June 2010.
20. *Hamburger Abendblatt*, 18 May 2007, <http://www.abendblatt.de/politik/deutschland/ article859740/Dick-schwach-krank-Die-Probleme-der-Jugend.html>, accessed 5 June 2010.
21. Wacquant, 2008: 206.
22. United Nations Department of Economic and Social Affairs, Population Division, 2009; Mulligan et al., 2005.
23. Middleton et al., 2003; Hirsch, 2006.
24. Lübbren, 2001.
25. Gaze, 1988; Lekan, 2004.
26. Sitte, 1979: 53, 59.
27. For a classic example of how the past moved from being a joyful, open thing, to being used as a stick to beat people with, see Porter, 2001.
28. Morris, 1890; Rider Haggard, 1905; Marsh, 1982; Meacham, 1998.
29. Eliot 2005 (1922): ll. 17, 60–5.

30. <http://www.channel4.com/4homes/on-tv/location-location-location/episode-information/location-surrey-10-05-13_p_1.html>, accessed 15 May 2010.
31. A search on JSTOR for the term 'white flight', <http://www.jstor.org>, 1 June 2010; search on <http://www.Amazon.co.uk> for the term 'white flight' in the category 'Society, Politics and Philosophy', 1 June 2010.
32. The literature on 'white flight' is vast, and is growing rapidly. A good starting point is Avila, 2004.
33. Wacquant, 2008.

Bibliography

Abel, Richard (1998), *The Ciné Goes to Town: French cinema, 1896–1914*, London.

Abrams, Lynn (1992), *Workers' Culture in Imperial Germany: Leisure and recreation in the Rhineland and Westphalia*, London.

—— (1993), 'Concubinage, cohabitation and the law: Class and gender relations in nineteenth-century Germany', *Gender and History* 1, 81–100.

Accampo, Elinor (2003), 'The gendered nature of contraception in France: Neo-Malthusianism, 1900–1920', *Journal of Interdisciplinary History* 2, 235–62.

Adams, Annmarie (1996), *Architecture in the Family Way: Doctors, houses, and women, 1870–1900*, London.

Adamson, Walter (1992), 'The language of opposition in early twentieth-century Italy: Rhetorical continuities between prewar Florentine avant-gardism and Mussolini's fascism', *Journal of Modern History* 1, 22–51.

Addison, Paul and Jeremy Crang (eds.) (2006), *Firestorm: The bombing of Dresden, 1945*, London.

Adelson, Alan and Robert Lapides (1989), *Łódź Ghetto: Inside a community under siege*, London.

Aitken, Jo (2007), ' "The horrors of matrimony among the masses": Feminist representations of wife beating in England and Australia', *Journal of Women's History* 4, 107–31.

Alexander, Claire (2004), 'Imagining the Asian gang: Ethnicity, masculinity and youth after "the riots" ', *Critical Social Policy* 4, 526–49.

Allen, Thomas (2005), 'Clockwork nation: Modern time, perfectionism and American identity in Catharine Beecher and Henry Thoreau', *Journal of American Studies* 1, 65–86.

Altrichter, Helmut (2003), ' "Living the revolution". Stadt und Stadtplanung in Stalins Rußland' in W. Hardtwig (ed.), *Utopie und politische Herrschaft im Europa der Zwischenkriegszeit*, Munich, 77–96.

Altrock, Uwe and Harald Bodenschatz (eds.) (2003), *Städtebau im Schatten Stalins: die internationale Suche nach der sozialistischen Stadt in der Sowjetunion, 1929–1935*, Berlin.

Amnesty International/ICM (2005), *Sexual Assault Research: Summary report*, London.

Arendt, Hannah (1994), *Eichmann in Jerusalem: A report on the banality of evil*, London [1963].

Arnade, Peter, Martha Howell, and Walter Simons (2002), 'Fertile spaces: The productivity of urban space in Northern Europe', *Journal of Interdisciplinary History* 4, 515–48.

Attwood, Lynne (ed.) (1993), *Red Women and the Silver Screen: Women and cinema in the Soviet Union*, London.

August, Andrew (2009), 'Gender and 1960s youth culture: The Rolling Stones and the new woman', *Contemporary British History* 1, 79–100.

Auslander, Leora (2005), 'Coming home? Jews in postwar Paris', *Journal of Contemporary History* 2, 237–59.

Austin, Gerlyn (1966), 'The advent of the negro actor on the legitimate stage in America', *Journal of Negro Education* 3.

Ayers, Pat (2004), 'Work, culture and gender: The making of masculinities in post-war Liverpool', *Labour History Review* 2, 153–67.

Bachmann, Michael (ed.) (2000), *Fritz Lang's* Metropolis*: Cinematic visions of technology and fear*, New York.

Backer, John (1984), 'From Morgenthau to Marshall Plan' in Robert Wolfe (ed.), *Americans as Proconsuls: United States military government in Germany and Japan, 1944–52*, Carbondale, IL, 155–65.

Bailey, Peter (ed.) (1986), *Music Hall: The business of pleasure*, Milton Keynes.

—— (1998), *Popular Culture and Performance in the Victorian City*, Cambridge.

Bajohr, Stefan (2003), 'Partnerinnenwahl im Braunschweiger Arbeitermilieu, 1900–1933', *Jahrbuch für Forschungen zur Geschichte der Arbeiterbewegung* 3, 83–98.

Baker, William (1981), 'William Webb Ellis and the origins of rugby football: The life and death of a Victorian myth', *Albion* 2, 117–30.

Balderston, Theo (2002), *Economics and Politics in the Weimar Republic*, Cambridge.

Baldwin, Brooke (1981), 'The cakewalk: A study in stereotype and reality', *Journal of Social History* 2, 205–18.

Balibar, Étienne (2007), 'Uprisings in the *Banlieus*', *Constellations* 1, 47–71.

Ballantyne, Tony and Antoinette Burton (2005), *Bodies in Contact: Rethinking colonial encounters in world history*, Durham, NC.

Baras, Victor (1975), 'Beria's fall and Ulbricht's survival', *Soviet Studies* 3, 381–95.

Bard, Christine (ed.) (1999), *Un Siècle d'antifeminisme*, Paris.

Barker, Paul (2009), *The Freedoms of Suburbia*, London.

Bassin, Mark (1992), 'Geographical determinism in fin-de-siècle Marxism: Georgii Plekhanov and the environmental basis of Russian history', *Annals of the Association of American Geographers* 1, 3–22.

Bater, James (1976), *St Petersburg: Industrialisation and change*, London.

Baudouï, Rémi (1987), 'Raoul Dautry, la conscience du social', *Vingtième Siècle* 15, 45–58.

Bauman, Zygmunt (1988), 'Sociology after the Holocaust', *British Journal of Sociology* 4, 469–97.

—— (1989), *Modernity and the Holocaust*, Cambridge.

—— (1991), *Modernity and Ambivalence*, Oxford.

Bavel, Jan van (2007), 'The decline of illegitimacy and the control of marital fertility during the demographic transition: Testing the innovation-diffusion hypothesis using cohort fertility data from a Belgian town, 1850–1910', *Historical Social Research* 2, 42–67.

Baxendale, John (1995), '"…into another kind of life in which anything might happen…" Popular music and modernity, 1910–1930', *Popular Music* 2, 137–54.

Bayliss, Darrin (2001) 'Revisiting the cottage council estates: England, 1919–1939', *Planning Perspectives* 2, 169–200.

—— (2003), 'Building better communities: Social life on London's cottage council estates, 1919–1939', *Journal of Historical Geography* 3, 376–95.

Bazin, Hugues (1995), *La culture hip-hop*, Paris.

Bell, Donald (1984), 'Working-class culture and fascism in an Italian industrial town, 1918–1922', *Social History* 1, 1–24.

Bellasai, Sandro (2005), 'The masculine mystique: Antimodernism and virility in fascist Italy', *Journal of Modern Italian Studies* 3, 314–55.

Benenson, Harold (1993), 'Patriarchal constraints on women workers' mobilization: The Lancashire female cotton operatives, 1842–1919', *British Journal of Sociology* 4, 613–33.

Benninghaus, Christina (2000), 'Mothers' toil and daughters' leisure: Working-class girls and time in 1920s Germany', *History Workshop Journal* 50, 45–72.

Berger, Stefan (1994), *The British Labour Party and the German Social Democrats. 1900–1931*, Oxford.

—— (ed.) (1995), *The Force of Labour: The Western European labour movement and the working class in the twentieth century*, Oxford.

—— (2000), *Social Democracy and the Working Class in Nineteenth and Twentieth Century Germany*, London.

—— (2005), 'Herbert Morrison's London Labour Party in the interwar years and the SPD: Problems of transferring German socialist practices to Britain', *European Review of History* 2, 291–306.

Berliner, Brett (2002), *Ambivalent Desire: The exotic black other in jazz-age France*, London.

—— (2004), 'Mephistopheles and monkeys: Rejuvenation, race and sexuality in popular culture in interwar France', *Journal of the History of Sexuality* 3, 306–25.

Bernhardt, Christoph (2005), 'Planning urbanization and urban growth in the socialist period: The case of East German new towns, 1945–1989', *Journal of Urban History* 1, 104–19.

Berstein, Serge (1994), 'Le Retour de la culture républicaine', *Vingtième Siècle* 44, 113–20.

Bessel, Richard (2004), 'The Nazi capture of power', *Journal of Contemporary History* 2, 169–88.

Bidlack, Richard (2000), 'The political mood in Leningrad during the first year of the Soviet–German War', *Russian Review* 1, 96–113.

Bittner, Stephen (1998), 'Green cities and orderly streets: Space and culture in Moscow, 1928–1933', *Journal of Urban History* 1, 22–56.

Blackledge, Paul et al. (2002), *Historical Materialism and Social Evolution*, Basingstoke.

Blackwell, Kay (2001), 'Women on Red Clydeside: The invisible workforce debate', *Scottish Economic and Social History* 2, 140–62.

Blau, Eve (1999), *The Architecture of Red Vienna, 1919–1934*, London.

Blewett, Mary (2006), 'Diversities of class and gender experience and the shaping of Labour Politics: Yorkshire's Manningham Mills strike, 1890–91 and the Independent Labour Party', *Labor History* 4, 511–35.

Bliznikov, Mika (1976), 'Urban planning in the USSR: Integrative theories' in Michael Hamm (ed.), *The City in Russian History*, Lexington, KY, 243–56.

Bloom, Jack (2006), 'The Solidarity revolution in Poland, 1980–1981', *Oral History Review* 1, 33–64.

Blum, Cinzia (1990), 'Rhetorical strategies and gender in Marinetti's *Futurist Manifesto*', *Italica* 2, 196–211.

Boardman, John (2003), 'Soil erosion and flooding on the eastern South Downs, southern England, 1976–2001', *Transactions of the Institute of British Geographers* 2, 176–96.

Bock, Gisela (1989), 'Die Frauen und der Nationalsozialismus. Bemerkungen zu einem Buch von Claudia Koonz', *Geschichte und Gesellschaft* 4, 563–79.

—— (1993), 'Gleichheit und Differenz in der nationasozialistischen Rassenpolitik', *Geschichte und Gesellschaft* 3, 277–310.

Bogart, E. L. (1919), *Direct and Indirect Costs of the Great World War*, Oxford.

Bookchin, Murray (1998), *Spanish Anarchists: The heroic years, 1868–1936*, Edinburgh.

Bosma, Koos and Helma Hellinga (eds.) (1997), *Mastering the City: North-European city planning, 1900–2000*, Rotterdam.

Bosworth, R. J. B. (2006), *Mussolini's Italy: Life under the dictatorship*, London.

Bourke, Joanna (1996), 'The great male renunciation: Men's dress reform in inter war Britain', *Journal of Design History* 1, 23–33.

Bouscaren, Anthony Trawick (1949), 'The European Christian Democrats', *Western Political Quarterly* 1, 59–73.

Bowden, Sue and Avner Offer (1994), 'Household appliances and the use of time: The United States and Britain since the 1920s', *Economic History Review* 4, 725–48.

Bowlby, Chris (1986), '*Blutmai* 1929: Police, parties and proletarians in a Berlin confrontation', *Historical Journal* 1, 137–58.

Boyer, George and Timothy Hatton (2002), 'New estimates of British unemployment, 1870–1913', *Journal of Economic History* 3, 643–75.

Boyer, John (1974), 'Catholic priests in Lower Austria: Anti-liberalism, occupational anxiety, and radical political action in late nineteenth-century Vienna', *Proceedings of the American Philosophical Society* 4, 337–69.

—— (1995), *Culture and Political Crisis in Vienna: Christian Socialism in power, 1897–1918*, London.

Bracewell, Michael (1998), *England is Mine: Pop life in Albion from Wilde to Goldie*, London.

Bracke, Maud (2003), 'The 1968 Czechoslovak crisis: Reconsidering its history and politics', *Contemporary European History* 3, 373–83.

Brader, Chris (2005), '"A world on wings": Young female workers and cinema in WW1', *Women's History Review* 1, 99–117.

Brantlinger, Patrick (1985), 'Victorians and Africans: The Genealogy of the myth of the Dark Continent', *Critical Inquiry* 1, 166–203.

—— (2003), *Dark Vanishings: Discourse on the extinction of primitive races, 1800–1930*, London.

Braunstein, P. (1999), 'Disco', *American Heritage* 7, 43–57.

Brecht, Christine and Sybilla Nokolow (2000), 'Displaying the invisible: *Volkskrankheiten* on exhibition in imperial Germany', *Studies in History and Philosophy of Biomedical Sciences* 4, 511–30.

Bridenthal, Renate, Susan Stuart, and Merry Wiesner (eds.) (1998), *Becoming Visible: Women in European history*, Boston, MA.

Briggs, Asa (1995), *The History of Broadcasting in Britain: The golden age*, Oxford.

Brooke, Stephen (2006), 'Bodies, sexuality and the "modernisation" of the British working classes, 1920s–1960s', *International Labor and Working-Class History* 69, 104–22.

Brower, Daniel (1982), 'Labor violence in Russia in the late nineteenth century', *Slavic Review* 3, 417–31.

Brown, John and Gerhard Neumeier (2001), 'Job tenure and labour market dynamics during high industrialization: The case of Germany before World War I', *European Review of Economic History* 2, 189–217.

Brown, Timothy (2004), 'Subcultures, pop music and politics: Skinheads and "Nazi Rock" in England and Germany', *Journal of Social History* 1, 157–78.

Browne, Janet (2001), 'Darwin in caricature: A study in the popularisation and dissemination of evolution', *Proceedings of the American Philosophical Society* 4, 496–509.

Browning, Christopher (1986), 'Nazi ghettoisation policy in Poland, 1939–41', *Central European History* 4, 343–68.

Bruley, Sue (1997), '"A very happy crowd": Women in industry in London in World War Two', *History Workshop Journal* 44, 58–76.

—— (2003), 'A new perspective on women workers in the Second World War: The industrial diary of Kathleen Church-Bliss and Elsie Whiteman', *Labour History Review* 2, 217–34.

Bruns, Claudia (2005), 'The politics of masculinity in the (homo)-sexual discourse, 1890–1920', *German History* 3, 306–20.

Brym, Robert and Evel Economakis (1994), 'Peasant or proletarian? Militant Pskov workers in St Petersburg, 1913', *Slavic Review* 1, 120–39.

—— (1995), 'Marriage and militancy in a working-class district of St Petersburg, 1896–1913', *Journal of Family History* 1, 23–43.

Bucher, Greta (2006), *Women, Bureaucracy and Daily Life in Postwar Moscow, 1945–1953*, New York.

Bucholtz, Erika (2004), 'Die Zentralen des nationalsozialistichen SS- und Polizeistaats: Gebäudenutzung und Bauplanung in Berlin, 1933–45', *Zeitschrift für Geschichtswissenschaft* 12, 1106–25.

Buckley, Cherry and Hilary Fawcett (2002), *Fashioning the Feminine: Representation and women's fashion from the fin de siècle to the present*, London.

Bullock, Alan (1990), *Hitler: A study in tyranny*, London.

Bullock, Nicholas (2007), 'Developing proptotypes for France's mass housing programme, 1949–1953', *Planning Perspectives* 22, 5–28.

Burke, Peter (1972), *Culture and Society in Renaissance Italy, 1420–1540*, London.

Burrow, John (2000), *The Crisis of Reason in European Thought, 1848–1914*, London.

Bush, Julia (2002), 'British women's anti-suffragism and the forward policy, 1908–1914', *Women's History Review* 3, 431–54.

Butler, Judith (1990), *Gender Trouble: Feminism and the subversion of identity*, London.

Calder, Angus (1992), *Myth of the Blitz*, London.

Campbell, Margaret (1999), 'From cure chair to *chaise longue*: Medical treatment and the form of the modern recliner', *Journal of Design History* 4, 327–43.

—— (2005), 'What tuberculosis did for modernism: The influence of a curative environment on modernist design and architecture', *Medical History* 4, 463–88.

Canning, Kathleen (1992), 'Gender and the culture of work: Ideology and identity in the world behind the mill gate, 1890–1914' in L Jones et al. (eds.), *Elections, Mass Politics and Social Change in Modern Germany*, Cambridge, 175–99.

—— (1992), 'Gender and the politics of class formation: Rethinking German labor history', *American Historical Review*, 3, 736–68.

—— (1996), *Languages of Labor and Gender: Female factory work in Germany, 1850–1914*, Ann Arbor, MI.

Cannon, S. (1997), 'Panama city rapping: B-Boys in the banlieus and beyond' in A. Hargreaves et al. (eds), *Postcolonial Cultures in France*, London, 150–66.

Carleton, Gregory (2005), *Sexual Revolution in Bolshevik Russia*, Pittsburgh, PA.

Carnevali, Francesca (2000), 'State enterprise and Italy's "economic miracle": The Ente Nazionale Idrocarburi, 1945–1962', *Enterprise & Society* 1, 249–78.

Carr, C. and J. Whitehand (2001), *Twentieth-Century Suburbs: A morphological approach*, London.

Carsten, F. L. (1992), 'The Arbeiterbildungsvereine and the foundation of the Social Democratic Workers Party in 1869', *English Historical Review* 107, 361–77.

Carter, Erica (1997), *How German Is She? Postwar West German reconstruction and the consuming woman*, Ann Arbor, MI.

Carter, Julian (2005), 'Introduction: Theory, methods, praxis: The history of sexuality and the question of evidence', *Journal of the History of Sexuality* 1/2, 1–9.

Casey, Emma and Lydia Martens (eds.) (2007), *Gender and Consumption: Domestic cultures and the commercialisation of everyday life*, Aldershot.

Caws, Mary Ann (2001), *Manifesto: A century of isms*, Lincoln, NE.

Çelik, Zeynep, Diane Favro, and Richard Ingersoll (eds.) (1994), *Streets: Critical perspectives on public space*, London.

Certeau, Michel de (1988), *The Practice of Everyday Life*, London.

Chambers, Iain (1985), *Urban Rhythms: Pop music and urban culture*, Basingstoke.

Chaplain, Renaud (2003), 'Les exploitants des salles de cinéma lyonnaises. Dès origines à la second guerre mondiale', *Vingtième Siècle* 79, 19–35.

Chauncey, George (1994), *Gay New York: Gender, urban culture and the makings of the gay male world, 1890–1940*, New York.

Cherry, Gordon (1996), *Town Planning in Britain since 1900: the rise and fall of the planning ideal*, Oxford.

Chick, Martin (1998), *Industrial Policy in Britain, 1945–1951: Economic planning, nationalisation and the Labour governments*, Cambridge.

CIA, III-3: Comment on the East Berlin Uprising, 17 June 1953 (Mori No. 144301), 18.6.1953 at https://www.cia.gov/library/center-for-the-study-of-intelligence/csi-publications/books-and-monographs/on-the-front-lines-of-the-cold-war-documents-on-the-intelligence-war-in-berlin-1946-to-1961/3–3.pdf.

—— Closing of Berlin Borders, 18 June 1953 (Mori No. 144211), 18.6.1953, at https://www.cia.gov/library/center-for-the-study-of-intelligence/csi-publications/books-and-monographs/on-the-front-lines-of-the-cold-war-documents-on-the-intelligence-war-in-berlin-1946-to-1961/3–4.pdf.

City of Manchester (1945), *City of Manchester Plan*, Manchester.

Claeys, Gregory (2000), ' "Survival of the fittest" and the origins of Social Darwinism', *Journal of the History of Ideas* 2, pp. 223–40.

Clapson, Mark (1998), *Invincible Green Suburbs, Brave New Towns: Social change and urban dispersal in post-war England*, Manchester.

—— (1999), 'Working-class women's experiences of moving to new housing estates in England since 1919', *Twentieth-Century British History* 3, 345–65.

Clark, Linda (1981), 'Social Darwinism in France', *Journal of Modern History* 53, D1025–D1044.

Clements, Barbara Evans (1991), 'Later developments: Trends in Soviet women's history, 1930–present' in Barbara Evans Clements, Barbara Alpern Engel, and Christin Worobec (eds.), *Russia's Women: Accommodation, resistance, transformation*, London, 267–78.

Cocks, Harry (2003), *Nameless Offences: Homosexual desire in the nineteenth century*, London.

—— (2009), *Classified: The secret history of the personal column*, London.

Collins, Marcus (1999), 'The pornography of permissiveness: Men's sexuality and women's emancipation in mid-twentieth-century Britain', *History Workshop Journal* 47, 99–120.

Colton, Timothy (1996), *Moscow: Governing the Socialist Metropolis*, London.

Condrau, Flurin (2000), 'Behandlung ohne Heilung. Zur sozialen Konstruktion des Behandlungserfolgs bei Tuberkulose im frühen 20. Jahrhundert', *Medizin, Gesellschaft und Geschichte* 19, 71–94.

Conquest, Robert (1986), *Harvest of sorrow: Soviet collectivisation and the terror-famine*, Oxford.

Conway, Kelly (2004), *Chanteuse in the city: The realist singer in French film*, London.

Cook, Hera (2005a), 'The English sexual revolution: Technology and social change', *History Workshop Journal* 59, 109–28.

Cook, Hera (2005b), *The Long Sexual Revolution: English women, sex and contraception, 1800–1975*, London).

—— (2007), 'Sexuality and contraception in modern England: Doing the history of reproductive sexuality', *Journal of Social History* 4, 915–32.

Cook, Matt (2003a), '"A new city of friends": London and homosexuality in the 1890s', *History Workshop Journal* 56, 33–58.

—— (2003b), *London and the Culture of Homosexuality, 1885–1914*, Cambridge.

—— (ed.) (2007), *A Gay History of Britain: Love and sex between men since the Middle Ages*, Oxford.

Corbin, Alain (1990), *Women for Hire: Prostitution and sexuality in France after 1850*, London.

Cottle, Simon (1993), *TV News, Urban Conflict and the Inner City*, Leicester.

Council of Mortgage Lenders (2001), *Affordability: Housing finance*, no. 51.

Cowan, Ruth Schwarz (1983), *More Work for Mother: The ironies of household technology from the open hearth to the microwave* (n.p. [USA]).

Cromeen, Martha (2007), *June 17 1953: A fifty-year retrospective on a German cold war tragedy, 1953–2003*, unpublished MA Dissertation, Baylor University.

Curtis, Sarah (2002), 'Charitable ladies: Gender, class and religion in mid-nineteenth-century Paris', *Past and Present* 177, 121–56.

Czarnowksi, Gabreiele and Elisabeth Meyer-Renschhausen (1994), 'Geschlechterdualmismen in der Wohlfahrtspflege: "Soziale Mütterlichkeit" zwischenn Professionalisierung und Medikalisierung, Deutschland, 1890–1930', *Homme: Zeitschrift für feministische Geschichtswis senschaft* 2, 121–40.

Daniel, Ute (1997), *The War from Within: German working-class women in the First World War*, Oxford.

Dauncey, Hugh and Steve Cannon (eds.) (2003), *Popular Music in France from Chanson to Techno*, Aldershot.

David, Alison Matthews (2002), 'Elegant Amazons: Victorian riding habits and the fashionable horsewoman', *Victorian Literature and Culture* 1, 179–210.

Davidson, Arnold (2001), *The Emergence of Sexuality: Historical epistemology and the formation of concepts*, London.

Davidson, Denise (2001), 'De-centring twentieth-century women's movements', *Contemporary European History* 3, 503–12.

Davidson, John (1891), *In a Music-Hall: And other poems*, London.

Davies, Andrew (1992), *Leisure, Gender and Poverty: Working-class culture in Salford and Manchester, 1900–1939*, Milton Keynes.

Davis, Belinda (2000), *Home Fires Burning: Food, politics and everyday life in World War One Berlin*, Chapel Hill, NC.

Davray-Piekolek, Renée (1994), *Paris grand-écran: Splendeurs des salles obscures, 1895–1945*, Paris.

Dean, Carolyn (2000), *The Frail Social Body: Pornography, homosexuality and other fantasies in interwar France*, London.

Denby, Elizabeth (1938), *Europe Re-Housed*, Woking.

De Wit, C. T., H. Huisman, and R. Rabbinge (1987), 'Agriculture and its environment: Are there other ways?', *Agricultural Systems* 3, 211–36.

Dickinson, Edward Ross (2001), 'Reflections on feminism, monism and the Kaiserreich, 1900–1913', *Central European History* 2, 191–230.

—— (2007), 'Policing sex in Germany, 1882–1982: A preliminary statistical analysis', *Journal of the History of Sexuality* 2, 204–50.

Diefendorf, Jeffrey (1993), *In the Wake of War: The reconstruction of German cities after World War II*, Oxford.

Dikeç, Moustafa (2006), 'Badlands of the Republic? Revolts, the French state and the question of banlieus', *Environment and Planning: D* 2, 159–63.

Dinges, Martin (2008), 'Veränderungen der Männergesundheit als Krisenindikator? Deutschland, 1850–2006', *Homme: Zeitschrift für feministische Geschichtswissenschaft* 2, 107–23.

Dirke, Sabine von (2004), 'Hip hop made in Germany: From old school to the Kanaksta moment' in Agnes Müller, *German Popular Culture: How 'American' Is It?*, Ann Arbor, MI, 96–112.

Dobroszycki, Lucjan (1984), *The Chronicle of the Łódź Ghetto, 1941–1944*, London.

Dobrotvoskaja, Ekaterina (1992), 'Soviet teens of the 1970s: Rock generation, rock refusal, rock context', *Journal of Popular Culture* 3, 145–50.

Dong-Woon, Kim (1995), 'J. & P. Coats in Tsarist Russia, 1889–1917', *Business History Review* 4, 465–93.

Donzelot, Jacques (2006), *Quand la ville se défait. Quelle politique face à la crise des banlieues?*, Paris.

Doumanis, Nicholas (2001), *Italy: Inventing the nation*, London.

Downs, Laura Lee (1990), 'Rationalization and equal pay: The Bedaux strike at Rover Automobile Company', *Social History* 1.

Driver, Felix (2001), *Geography Militant: Cultures of exploration and empire*, Oxford.

Dunning, Eric, Patrick Murphy, and John Williams (1988), *The Roots of Football Hooliganism: An historical and sociological study*, London.

Dupâquier, Jacques (1979), 'Population' in Peter Burke (ed.), *The New Cambridge Modern History*, XIII, Cambridge.

Durham, Martin (1998), *Women and Fascism*, London.

Duwani, Osman (2002), 'Popular music in the German-speaking world' in Alison Phipps (ed.), *Contemporary German Cultural Studies*, London, 197–218.

Edelman, Robert (2002), 'A small way of saying "no": Moscow working men, Spartak soccer and the Communist Party, 1900–1945', *American Historical Review* 5, 1441–74.

Eliot, T. S. (2005), *The Annotated Waste Land with Eliot's Contemporary Prose*, ed. Lawrence Rainey, London.

Elliott, Dorice (2002), *The Angel out of the House: Philanthropy and gender in nineteenth-century England*, Charlottesville, VA.

Embacher, Helga (1988), 'Der Krieg hat die göttliche Ordnung zerstört! Konzepte und Familienmodelle zur Lösung von Alltasgsproblemen, Versuche zur Rettung der Moral, Familie und patriachalen Gesellschaft nach dem Ersten Weltkrieg', *Zeitgeschichte* 9/10, 347–63.

Engel, Barbara Alpern (1989), 'St. Petersburg prostitutes in the late nineteenth century: A personal and social profile', *Russian Review*, 1, 21–44.

—— (1993), 'Russian peasant views of city life, 1861–1914', *Slavic Review* 3, 446–59.

—— (1994), *Between the Fields and the City: Women, work and family in Russia, 1861–1914*, Cambridge.

—— (1997), 'Not by bread alone: Subsistence riots in Russia during World War I', *Journal of Modern History* 4, 696–721.

—— (2004), *Women in Russia, 1700–2000*, Cambridge.

Erber, Nancy and George Robb (eds.) (1999), *Disorder in the Court: Trials and sexual conflict at the turn of the century*, Basingstoke.

Evans, Janet (1981), 'The Communist Party of the Soviet Union and the women's question: The case of the 1936 decree "In Defence of Mother and Child"', *Journal of Contemporary History* 4, 757–75.

Evans, Jennifer (2003), 'Bahnhof boys: Policing male prostitution in post-Nazi Berlin', *Journal of the History of Sexuality* 4, 605–36.

Evans, Richard (1976), *The Feminist Movement in Germany, 1894–1933*, London.

—— (1989), *Kneipengespräche im Kaiserreich: Stimmungsberichte der Hamburger politischen Polizei, 1892–1914*, Reinbeck.

—— (1990), *Death in Hamburg: Society and politics in the cholera years, 1830–1910*, London.

—— (2004), *The Coming of the Third Reich: How the Nazis destroyed democracy and seized power in Germany*, London.

—— (2006), *The Third Reich in Power, 1933–1939: How the Nazis won over the hearts and minds of a nation*, London.

—— (2009), *The Third Reich at War: How the Nazis led Germany from conquest to disaster*, London.

Faraut, Martine (2003), 'Women resisting the vote: A case of anti-feminism?', *Women's History Review* 4, 605–21.

Fauché, Serge (2001), 'Le Médecin et la bicyclette. Le sport vélocipédique entre sciences et idéologies à la fin du 19ème siècle', *Stadion* 27, 201–12.

Faulk, Barry (2004), *Music Hall and Modernity: The late-Victorian discovery of popular culture*, Athens, Ohio.

Faure, Alain (2004), 'Paris: "Gouffre de l'espèce humaine"?', *French Historical Studies* 1, 49–86.

FDGB [Freier Deutscher Gewerkschaftbund Großberlin], Bericht vom Einsatz Stalin-Allee, 16.6.1953 Archiv der Bundeszentrale für politische Bildung, <http://www.17juni53.de> .

Feld, Werner (1979), 'Implementation of the European Community's Common Agricultural Policy: Expectations, fears, failures', *International Organization* 3, 335–63.

Fenemore, Mark (2009), 'The recent historiography of sexuality in twentieth-century Germany', *Historical Journal* 3, 763–79.

Ferguson, Eliza Earle (2005), 'Reciprocity and retribution: Negotiating gender and power in *fin de siècle* Paris', *Journal of Family History* 3, 287–303.

Ferguson, Niall (2009), *The Ascent of Money: A financial history of the world*, London.

Figes, Orlando (1997), *A People's Tragedy: The Russian Revolution, 1891–1924*, London.

Fijalkow, Yankel (1996), 'Territorialisation du risque sanitaire et statistique démographique: les "immeubles tuberculeux" de l'îlot insalubre Saint-Gervais (1894–1930)', *Annales de démographie historique*, 45–60.

—— (1998), 'Surpopulation ou insalubrité? Deux statistiques pour décrire l'habitat populaire', *Mouvement Social* 182, 79–96.

—— (1999), 'Hygiene, population sciences and population policy: A totalitarian menace?', *Contemporary European History* 3, 451–72.

Fishwick, Nicholas (1989), *English Football and Society, 1910–1950*, Manchester.

Fitzgerald, Robert (1989), 'Employers' labour strategies industrial welfare and the response to new unionism at Bryant and May, 1888–1930', *Business History* 2, 48–65.

Fitzpatrick, Sheila (1999), *Everyday Stalinism: Ordinary life in extraordinary times: Soviet Russia in the 1930s*, Oxford.

—— and Yuri Slezkine (eds.) (2000), *In the Shadow of Revolution: Life stories of Russian women from 1917 to the Second World War*, Princeton, NJ.

Flam, Gila (1992), *Singing for Survival: Songs of the Lodz ghetto, 1940–45*, Chicago.

Flonneau, Mathieu (2003), 'Nôtre Dame de Paris défiée par l'automobile: l'éspace cathédrale entre "sécularisation" et sanctuarisation', *Histoire Urbaine* 7, 163–88.

Foot, John (1999a), 'Mass cultures, popular cultures and the working class in Milan, 1950–70', *Social History* 2, 134–57.

—— (1999b), 'Television and the city: The impact of television in Milan, 1954–60', *Contemporary European History* 3, 379–94.

—— (2007), *Calcio: A history of Italian football*, London.

Ford, Larry (2000), *The Spaces Between Buildings*, London.

Foucault, Michel (1990), *The History of Sexuality*, I: *The Will to Knowledge*, London [Paris, 1976].

Fourcaut, Annie (2004), 'Les premiers grands ensembles en région parisienne: ne pas refaire la banlieue?', *French Historical Studies* 1, 195–218.

Fout, John (1992), 'Sexual politics in Wilhelmine Germany: The male gender crisis, moral purity and homophobia', *Journal of the History of Sexuality* 3, 388–421.

Frader, Laura (1998), 'Définir le droit au travail: rapports sociaux de sexe, famille et salaire en France aux XIXe at XXe siècles', *Le Mouvement social* 184, 5–22.

Freedman, Lawrence (2002), 'Berlin and the cold war' in John Gearson and Kori Schake (eds.), *The Berlin Wall Crisis: Perspectives on Cold War alliances*, London, 1–9.

Freeman, Henry (1999), 'Anti-Darwinism in France: Science and the myth of a nation', *Nineteenth-Century French Studies* 3–4, 290–304.

Freestone, Robert (ed.) (2000), *Urban Planning in a Changing World: The twentieth century experience*, London.

Friedrich, Jörg (2008), *The Fire: The bombing of Germany, 1940–45*, London.

Frith, Simon and Jon Savage (1998), 'Pearls and swine: Intellectuals and the mass media' in Steve Redhead (ed.), *The Clubcultures Reader: Readings in popular cultural studies*, Oxford, pp. 7–17.

Frohman, Larry (2006), 'Prevention, welfare, and citizenship: The war on tuberculosis and infant mortality in Germany, 1900–1930', *Central European History* 3, 431–81.

Gaines, Donna (1991), *Teenage Wasteland: Suburbia's dead end kids*, London.

Galera, Yann (2002), 'La garde républicaine mobile à l'épreuve de l'émeute du 6 février 1934', *Revue de la gendarmerie nationale*, hors série numéro 3.

Gaze, John (1988), *Figures in a Landscape: A history of the National Trust*, London.

Gearson, John (2002), 'Origins of the Berlin crisis of 1958–62' in John Gearson and Kori Schake (eds.), *The Berlin Wall Crisis: Perspectives on Cold War alliances*, London, 10–21.

Geary, Dick (2000), 'Beer and skittles? Workers and culture in early twentieth-century Germany', *Australian Journal of Politics and History* 3, 388–402.

Gebhardt, Hardtwig (2001), '"Halb kriminalistisch, halb erotisch": Presse für die niederen Instinkte' in Kaspar Maase and Wolfgang Kaschuba (eds.), *Schund und Schönheit: Populäre Kultur um 1900*, Cologne, 184–217.

Geehr, Richard (1990), *Karl Lueger: Mayor of fin-de-siècle Vienna*, Detroit.

Gehrmann, Siegfried (1989), 'Football in an industrial region: The example of Schalke 04 Football Club', *International Journal of the History of Sport* 3, 335–55.

Geldern, James von (1996), 'Life in-between: Migration and popular culture in late-imperial Russia', *Russian Review* 3, 365–83.

Giesbrecht-Schutte, Sabine (2001), 'Zum Stand der Unterhaltungsmusik um 1900' in Kaspar Maase and Wolfgang Kaschuba (eds.), *Schund und Schönheit: Populäre Kultur um 1900*, Cologne, 114–60.

Gilbert, Pamela (2000), '"Scarcely to be described": Urban extremes as real space and mythic places in the London cholera epidemic of 1854', *Nineteenth Century Studies* 14, 149–72.

Giles, Geoffrey (2005), 'Legislating homophobia in the Third Reich: The radicalisation of prosecution against homosexuality by the legal profession', *German History* 3.

Giles, Judy (1992), '"Playing hard to get": Working-class women, sexuality and respectability in Britain, 1918–1940', *Women's History Review* 2, 239–55.

—— (2002), 'Narratives of gender, class and modernity in women's memories of mid-twentieth-century Britain', *Gender and Cultural Memory* 1, 21–41.

—— (2004), *The Parlour and the Suburb: Domestic identities, class, femininity and modernity*, Oxford.

—— (2007), 'Class, gender and domestic consumption in Britain, 1920–1950' in Emma Casey et al. (eds.), *Gender and Consumption: Domestic cultures and the commercialisation of everyday life*, Aldershot, 15–31.

Glickman, Rose (1984), *Russian Factory Women: Workplace and society, 1880–1914*, Berkeley, CA.

Goldman, Wendy (2002), *Women at the Gates: Gender and industry in Stalin's Russia*, Cambridge.

Gordon, Mel (2000), *Voluptuous Panic: The erotic world of Weimar Berlin*, Los Angeles.

Gordon, Rae Beth (2001), *Why the French Love Jerry Lewis: From cabaret to early cinema*, Stanford, CA.

Gradmann, Christophe (2004), 'A harmony of illusions: Clinical and experimental testing of Robert Koch's tuberculin, 1890–1900', *Studies in History and Philosophy of Biological and Biomedical Sciences* 3, 465–81.

Graf, Rüdiger (2003), 'Die Mentalisierung des Nirgendwo und die Transformation der Gesellschaft. Der theoretische Utopiediskurs in Deutschland 1900–1933' in W. Hardtwig (ed.), *Utopie und politische Herrschaft im Europa der Zwischenkriegszeit*, Munich, 145–74.

Granville, Johanna (2002), 'From the archives of Warsaw and Budapest: A comparison of the events of 1956', *East European Politics and Societies* 2, 521–63.

Grayzel, Susan (1999), *Women's Identities at War: Gender, motherhood and politics in Britain and France during the First World War*, Chapel Hill, NC.

Grazia, Victoria de (1989), 'Mass culture and sovereignty: The American challenge to European cinemas, 1920–1960', *Journal of Modern History* 1, 53–87.

Green, Nancy (1997), *Ready-to-Wear, Ready-to-Work: A century of industry and immigrants in Paris and New York*, Durham, NC.

Gribaudi, Maurizio (1987), 'Espace ouvrier et éspaces sociaux: Turin dans la première moitié du siècle', *Annales* 2, 243–63.

Gronberg, Tag (1998), *Designs on Modernity: Exhibiting the city in 1920s Paris*, Manchester.

Gross, Natan (2003), 'Mordechai Gebirtig: The folk song and the cabaret song', *Polin: Studies in Polish Jewry* 16, 107–17.

Grotum, Thomas (1994), *Die Halbstarken. Zur Geschichte einer Jugendkultur der 50er Jahre*, Frankfurt am Main.

Gruber, Helmut (1991), *Red Vienna: Experiment in working-class culture, 1919–1934*, Oxford.

—— (1998), 'The "new woman": Realities and illusions of gender equality in Red Vienna' in H. Gruber and P. Graves (eds.) *Women and Socialism, Socialism and Women: Europe between the two world wars*, Oxford, 56–94.

—— and Pamela Graves (eds.) (1998), *Women and Socialism, Socialism and Women: Europe between the two world wars*, Oxford.

Guenther, Irene (2004), *Nazi Chic? Fashioning women in the Third Reich*, Oxford.

Gunning, Tom (2000), *The Films of Fritz Lang: Allegories of vision and modernity*, London.

Gunther, Scott (2004), 'Building a more stately closet: French gay movements since the early 1980s', *Journal of the History of Sexuality* 3, 326–47.

Gutzke, David (2006), *Pubs and Progressives: Reinventing the public house in England, 1896–1960*, DeKalb, IL.

Habermas, Jürgen (1989), *The Structural Transformation of the Public Sphere: An enquiry into a category of bourgeois society*, trans. Thomas Burger and Frederick Lawrence, Cambridge [Darmstadt, 1962].

Habermas, Rebekka (2000), *Frauen und Männer des Bürgertums: Eine Familiengeschichte, 1750–1850*, Göttingen.

Hague, Cliff (1984), *The Development of Planning Thought: A critical perspective*, London.

Haimson, Leopold (2000), '"The problem of political and social stability in urban Russia on the eve of war and revolution" revisited', *Slavic Review* 4, 848–75.

Haine, W. Scott (1996), *The World of the Paris Café: Sociability among the French working class, 1789–1914*, London.

Hall, Alex (1974), 'By other means: The legal struggle against the SPD in Wilhelmine Germany, 1890–1900', *Historical Journal* 2, 365–86.

—— (1976), 'The war of words: Anti-socialist offensives and counter-propaganda in Wilhelmine Germany, 1890–1914', *Journal of Contemporary History* 2/3, 11–42.

Hall, Lesley (1996), 'Impotent ghosts from no man's land, flappers' boyfriends, or crypto-patriarchs? Men, sex and social change in 1920s Britain', *Social History* 1, 54–70.

Hall, Peter (2002), *Cities of Tomorrow: An intellectual history of urban planning and design in the twentieth century*, Oxford.

Halperin, David (1989), 'Is there a history of sexuality?' *History and Theory* 3, 257–74.

Hamm, Michael (1976), 'The breakdown of urban modernisation: A prelude to the revolutions of 1917' in Michael Hamm (ed.), *The City in Russian History*, Lexington, KY, 182–200.

Hammond, Michael (2006), *British Cinema Culture in the Great War*, Exeter.

Hancock, Eleanor (1998), '"Only the real, the true, the masculine held its value": Ernst Röhm, masculinity and male homosexuality', *Journal of the History of Sexuality* 4, 616–41.

Harding, Colin and Brian Lewis (1993), *Talking Pictures: The popular experience of the cinema*, Bradford.

Hardy, Dennis (2000), *Utopian England: Community experiments*, London.

Hark, Ina Rae (2002), *Exhibition: The film reader*, London.

Harris, Richard and Peter Larkham (eds.) (1999), *Changing Suburbs: Foundation, form and function*, London.

Harris, Victoria (1994), 'In the absence of empire: Feminism, abolitionism and social work in Hamburg, 1900–1933', *Women's History Review* 2, 279–98.

—— (2010), *Selling Sex in the Reich: Prostitutes in German society, 1914–1945*, Oxford.

Harrison, Hope (2002), 'The German Democratic Republic, the Soviet Union and the Berlin Wall crisis' in John Gearson and Kori Schake (eds.), *The Berlin Wall Crisis: Perspectives on Cold War Alliances*, London, 96–125.

Harrison, Michael (1991), 'Thomas Coglan Horsfall and "the example of Germany"', *Planning Perspectives* 3, 297–314.

Harsch, Donna (1993), 'Public continuity and private change? Women's consciousness and activity in Frankfurt, 1945–55', *Journal of Social History* 1, 29–58.

Hartmann, Heidi (1976), 'Capitalism, patriarchy and job segregation by sex', *Signs* 1, 137–69.

—— (1981), 'The family as the locus of gender, class and political struggle: The example of housework', *Signs* 6, 366–70.

Harvey, Adrian (2001), '"An epoch in the annals of national sport": Football in Sheffield and the creation of modern soccer and rugby' *International Journal of the History of Sport* 4, 53–87.

Haynes, Michael (2003), 'Counting Soviet deaths in the Great Patriotic War: A note', *Europe-Asia Studies* 2, 303–9.

Healey, Dan (1997), 'Evgeniia/Evgenii: Queer case histories in the first years of Soviet power', *Gender and History* 1, 83–106.

—— (2001a), 'Masculine purity and "gentlemen's mischief": Sexual exchange and prostitution between Russian men, 1861–1941', *Slavic Review* 2, 233–65.

—— (2001b), *Homosexual Desire in Revolutionary Russia: The regulation of sexual and gender dissent*, London.

—— (2002), 'Homosexual existence and existing socialism: New light on the repression of male homosexuality in Stalin's Russia', *GLQ* 8, 349–78.

Healy, Maureen (2004), *Vienna and the Fall of the Habsburg Empire: Total war and everyday life in World War I*, Cambridge.

Heathcott, Joseph (2003), 'Urban space and working-class expressions across the Black Atlantic: Tracing the routes of ska', *Radical History Review* 87, 183–206.

Heathorn, Stephen (2000), 'An English paradise to regain? Ebenezer Howard, the Town Planning Association and English ruralism', *Rural History* 1, 113–28.

Heggie, Vanessa (2008), 'Lies, damn lies, and Manchester's recruiting statistics: Degeneration as an "urban legend" in Victorian and Edwardian Britain', *Journal of the History of Medicine and Allied Sciences* 2, 178–216.

Heimann, Eduard (1923), 'The family wage controversy in Germany', *Economic Journal* 132, 509–15.

Heineman, Elizabeth (1996), 'The hour of the women: Memories of Germany's "crisis years" and West German national identity', *American Historical Review* 2, 354–95.

Hekma, Gert (1991), 'Homosexual behaviour in the nineteenth-century Dutch army', *Journal of the History of Sexuality* 2, 266–88.

—— (2005), 'New histories of masculinity', *European History Quarterly* 2, 327–35.

Hekma, Gert (2005) 'The moral state: Men, mining and masculinity in the early GDR', *German History* 3, 355–70.

Herrlinger, Paige (2004), 'Raising Lazarus: Orthodoxy and the factory *Narod* in St Petersburg, 1905–1914', *Jahrbücher für Geschichte Osteuropas* 3, 341–54.

Herzog, Dagmar (2005), 'Sexual morality in 1960s West Germany', *German History* 3, 371–84.

—— (2006), 'Sexuality in the post-war West', *Journal of Modern History* 2, 78–105.

Hewitt, Kenneth (1994), '"When the great planes came and made ashes of our city…": Towards an oral geography of the disasters of war', *Antipode* 1, 1–34.

Higgins, Patrick (1996), *Heterosexual Dictatorship: Homosexuality in post-war Britain*, London.

Higonnet, Margaret et al. (1987), *Behind the Lines: Gender and the Two World Wars*, London.

Hilberg, Raul (1980), 'The ghetto as a form of government', *The Annals of the American Academy of Political and Social Science* 1, 98–112.

Hilbersheimer, Ludwig (1955), *The Nature of Cities: Origin, growth, and decline, pattern and form, planning problems*, Chicago.

Hildermeier, Manfred (2003), 'Liberales Milieu in russischer Provinz: Kommunales engagement, bürgerliche Vereine und Zivilgesellschaft, 1900–1917', *Zeitschrift für Geschichte Osteuropas* 4, 498–58.

Hill, Darryl (2005), 'Sexuality and gender in Hirschfeld's *Die Travestiten*: A case of the "elusive evidence of the ordinary"', *Journal of the History of Sexuality* 3, 316–32.

Hill, John (1991), 'Television and popular culture: The case of the 1950s' in John Conver (ed.), *Popular Television in Britain*, London, 90–107.

Hirsch, Jameson (2006), 'A review of the literature on rural suicide: Risk and protective factors incidence and prevention', *Crisis: The Journal of Crisis Intervention and Suicide Prevention* 4, 189–99.

Hirschfeld, Magnus (1905), *Berlins Drittes Geschlecht*, 18th edn in Hans Ostwald, *Großstadtdokumente*, XXIII, Berlin [1904].

Hoffmann, David (1991), 'Moving to Moscow: Patterns of Peasant in-migration during the first Five Year Plan', *Slavic Studies* 4, 847–57.

Höher, Dagmar (1986), 'The Composition of Music Hall Audiences' in Peter Bailey (ed.), *Music Hall: The business of pleasure*, Milton Keynes, pp. 73–92.

Höhn, Maria (1993), 'Frau im Haus und Girl im Spiegel: Discourse on women in the interregnum period of 1945–49 and the question of German identity', *Central European History* 1, 57–90.

Höpfner, Rosmarie and Volker Fischer (eds.) (1986), *Ernst May und das neue Frankfurt, 1925–1930*, Berlin.

Horrall, Andrew (2001), *Popular Culture in London, 1890–1918*, Manchester.

Horsfall, T. C. (1905), *The Improvement of the Dwellings and Surroundings of the People: The example of Germany*, Manchester.

Houlbrook, Matt (2002), '"Lady Austin's camp boys": Constituting the queer subject in 1930s London', *Gender and History* 1, 31–91.

—— (2003), 'Soldier heroes and rent boys: Homosex, masculinities and Britishness in the Brigade of Guards, circa 1900–1960', *Journal of British Studies* 42, 351–88.

—— (2005), *Queer London: Perils and pleasures in the sexual metropolis, 1918–1957*, London.

—— (2007), ' "The man with the powder puff" in interwar London', *Historical Journal* 1, 145–71.

—— and Chris Waters (2006), 'The heart in exile: Detachment and desire in 1950s London', *History Workshop Journal* 62, 142–65.

Howell, David (1983), *British Workers and the Independent Labour Party, 1888–1906*, Manchester.

Hubbard, Phil (1999), *Sex and the City: Geographies of prostitution in the urban West*, Aldershot.

—— (2001), 'Sex zones: Intimacy, citizenship and public space', *Sexualities* 1, 51–71.

—— Lucy Faire, and Keith Lilley (2002), 'Remembering post-war reconstruction: Modernism and city planning in Coventry, 1940–1962', *Planning History* 1, 7–20.

—— (2003), 'Contesting the modern city: Reconstruction and everyday life in post-war Coventry', *Planning Perspectives* 18, 377–97.

Hughes, Anne and Karen Hunt (1992), 'A culture transformed? Women's lives in Wythenshawe in the 1930s' in A. Davies and S. Fielding (eds.), *Workers Worlds: Cultures and communities in Manchester and Salford, 1880–1939*, Manchester, 74–101.

Hughes, Annmarie (2004), 'Representations and counter-representations of domestic violence on Clydeside between the two world Wars', *Labour History Review* 2.

Hughes, David (2004), 'Just a breath of fresh air in an industrial landscape? The Preston Open Air School in 1926: A school medical service in sight', *Social History of Medicine* 3, 443–61.

Hughes, Geraint (2004), 'British policy towards Eastern Europe and the impact of the "Prague Spring", 1964–68', *Cold War History* 2, 115–39.

Humphries, Jane (1977), 'The Working class family, women's liberation and class struggle: The case of nineteenth century British history', *Review of Radical Political Economics* 3, 25–41.

Hunt, Karen (2004), 'Strong minds, great hearts, true faith and ready hands? Exploring socialist masculinities before the First World War', *Labour History Review* 2, 201–17.

Huq, Rupa (2006), *Beyond Subculture: Pop, youth and identity in a postcolonial world*, London.

Hustwitt, Mark (1983), ' "Caught in a whirlpool of aching sound": The production of dance music in Britain in the 1920s', *Popular Music* 3, 7–31.

Hylton, Jack (1926), 'Dance music of to-day', *Musical Times* 1 Sep., 799–800.

International Labour Office (1924), *Studies and Reports, Series G (Housing & Welfare), no 1: European Housing Problems since the War, 1914–1924*, Geneva.

Irons, Jessica (2005), 'Staging reconciliation: Popular theatre and political Utopia in France in 1937', *Contemporary European History* 3, 279–94.

Jackson, Jeffrey (2000), 'Music halls and the assimilation of jazz in 1920s Paris', *Journal of Popular Culture* 2, 69–82.

—— (2002), 'Making Jazz French: The reception of jazz music in Paris, 1927–1934', *French Historical Studies* 1, 149–70.

—— (2003), *Making Jazz French: Music and modern life in interwar Paris*, Durham, NC.

Jahn, Hubertus (1990), 'The housing revolution in Petrograd, 1917–1920', *Jahrbücher für Geschichte Osteuropas* 2, 212–27.

—— (1995), *Patriotic Culture in Russia during World War One*, London.

James, Martin (2003), *French Connections: From discothèque to discovery*, London.

Janik, Elizabeth (2004), '"The golden hunger years": Music and superpower rivalry in occupied Berlin', *German History* 1, 76–100.

Jankowski, Paul (2002), *Stavisky: A confidence man in the republic of virtue*, London.

Jeffreys, Sheila (2009), *The Industrial Vagina: The political economy of the global sex trade*, London.

Jellicoe, Geoffrey (1961), *Motopia: A study in the evolution of urban landscapes*, London.

Jenkins, Brian (2006), 'The *Six Février* 1934 and the "survival" of the French Republic', *French History* 3, 333–51.

Jenkins, Stephen (ed.) (1981), *Fritz Lang: The image and the look*, London.

Jenks, Andrew (2000), 'A metro on the mount: The underground as a church of Soviet civilisation', *Technology and Culture* 4, 697–724.

Jerram, Leif (2006), 'Kitchen sink dramas: Women, modernity and space in Weimar Germany', *Cultural Geographies* 4, 538–56.

—— (2007a), 'Bureaucratic passions and colonies of modernity: An urban elite and city frontiers in Germany 1890–1920', *Urban History* 3.

—— (2007b), *Germany's Other Modernity: Munich and the making of metropolis, 1895–1930*, Manchester.

Jivani, Alkarim (1997), *It's Not Unusual: A History of lesbian and gay Britain in the twentieth century*, London.

Joannou, Maroula (2005), 'Mary Augusta Ward (Mrs Humphry) and the opposition to women's suffrage', *Women's History Review* 204, 561–80.

Johnes, Martin and Gavin Mellor (2006), 'The 1953 FA Cup Final: Modernity and tradition in British culture', *Contemporary British History* 2, 263–80.

Johnson, Linton Kwesi (2006), *Selected Poems*, London.

Johnson, Robert (1979), *Peasant and Proletarian: The working class of Moscow in the late nineteenth century*, Leicester.

Johnston, Ronnie and Arthur McIvor (2004), 'Dangerous work, hard men and broken bodies: Masculinity in the Clydeside heavy industries, 1930–1970', *Labour History Review* 2, 135–51.

Jones, D. Caradog and Colin Clark (1930), 'Housing in Liverpool: A survey by sample of present conditions', *Journal of the Royal Statistical Society* 4, 489–537.

Jones, Greta (1980), *Social Darwinism and English Thought: The interaction between biological and social theory*, Brighton.

Jones, Phil (2005), 'The suburban high flat in the post-war reconstruction of Birmingham', *Urban History* 2, 308–26.

Joyce, Patrick (1992), *Visions of the People: Industrial England and the question of class, 1840–1914*, Cambridge.

—— (2000), *The Rule of Freedom: Liberalism and the modern city*, London.

Kaes, Anton (2000), *M*, London.

Kaiser, Wolfram (2004), 'Review article: Christian Democracy in twentieth century Europe', *Journal of Contemporary History* 1, 127–35.

Kalyvas, Stathis (1996), *The Rise of Christian Democracy in Europe*, Ithaca, NY.

Kanatchikov, Semën (1986), *A Radical Worker in Tsarist Russia: The autobiography of Semën Ivanovich Kanatchikov*, Stanford, CA.

Kaplan, Morris (1999), 'Who's afraid of John Saul? Urban culture and the politics of desire in late Victorian London', *GLQ* 3, 267–14.

—— (2005), *Sodom on the Thames: Sex, love and scandal in Wilde times*, London.

Kaschuba, Wolfgang (1990), *Lebenswelt und Kultur der unterbürgerlichen Schichten im 19. Und 20. Jahrhundert*, Munich.

Kater, Michael (1992), *Different Drummers: Jazz in the culture of Nazi Germany*, Oxford.

—— (2006), 'New democracy and alternative culture: Jazz in West Germany after the Second World War', *Australian Journal of Politics and History* 2, 173–87.

Kaye, Howard (1986), *The Social Meaning of Modern Biology: From social Darwinism to social biology*, London.

Kennedy, David and Michael Collins (2006), 'Community politics in Liverpool and the governance of professional football in the late nineteenth century', *Historical Journal* 3, 761–88.

Kenney, Padraic (1999), 'The gender of resistance in communist Poland', *American Historical Review* 2, 399–425.

Kersbergen, Kees van (1995), *Social Capitalism: A study of Christian Democracy and the welfare state*, London.

Kershaw, Ian (1992), 'Improvised genocide? The emergence of the "Final Solution" in the "Warthegau"', *Transactions of the Royal Historical Society* 2, 51–78.

—— (2001), *Hitler, 1889–1936: Hubris*, London.

Kessel, Martina (2003), 'The "whole man": The longing for a masculine world in nineteenth-century Germany', *Gender and History* 1, 1–31.

Kettering, Karen (2000), 'An introduction to the design of the Moscow metro in the Stalin period: "The Happiness of Life Underground"', *Decorative Arts* 2, 2–20.

Kift, Dagmar (1996), *The Victorian Music Hall: Culture, class and conflict*, Cambridge.

Kish Sklar, Kathryn, Anja Schuler, and Susan Strasser (eds.) (1998), *Social Justice Feminists in the United States and Germany: A Dialogue in Documents, 1885–1933*, Ithaca, NY.

Klein, Joanne (2005), 'Irregular marriages: Unorthodox working-class domestic life in Liverpool, Birmingham and Manchester, 1900–1939', *Journal of Family History* 2, 210–29.

Knight, Amy (1993), *Beria: Stalin's first lieutenant*, London.

Koenker, Diane (1981), *Moscow Workers and the 1917 Revolution*, Princeton, NJ.

—— (1995), 'Men against women on the shop floor in early Soviet Russia: Gender and class in the socialist workplace', *American Historical Review* 5, 1438–64.

Koester, Ulrich and Malcolm Bale (1990), 'The Common Agricultural Policy: A review of its operation and effects on developing countries', *World Bank Research Observer* 1, 95–121.

Kooijman, Jaap (2005), 'Turn the beat around: Richard Dyer's "In Defence of Disco" revisited', *European Journal of Cultural Studies* 2, 257–66.

Koonz, Claudia (1976), 'Nazi women before 1933: Rebels against emancipation', *Social Science Quarterly* 4, 553–63.

—— (1988), *Mothers in the Fatherland: Women, the family and Nazi politics*, London.

Korczynski, Marek et al. (2005), ' "We sang ourselves through that war": Women, music and factory work in World War Two', *Labour History Review* 2, 185–214.

Korr, Charles (1978), 'West Ham United Football Club and the beginnings of football in east London, 1895–1914', *Journal of Contemporary History* 2, 211–32.

Koshar, Rudy (2000), *German Travel Cultures*, Oxford.

Kotkin, Stephen (1995), *Magnetic Mountain: Stalinism as a civilization*, London.

Koven, Seth (2006), *Slumming: Sexual and social politics in Victorian London*, London.

—— and Sonya Michel (1990), 'Womanly duties: Maternalist politics and the origins of welfare states in France, Germany, Great Britain and the United States, 1880–1920', *American Historical Review* 4, 1076–108.

Kramer, Mark (1998), 'The Czechoslovak crisis and the Brezhnev Doctrine' in Carole Fink, Philipp Gassert, and Detlef Junker (eds.), *1968: The world transformed*, Cambridge, 111–71.

—— (1999), 'The early post-Stalin succession struggle and upheavals in East-Central Europe: Internal-external linkages in Soviet policy making (Part 1)', *Journal of Cold War Studies* 1, 3–55.

—— (1999), 'The early post-Stalin succession struggle and upheavals in East-Central Europe: Internal-external linkages in Soviet policy making (Part 2)', *Journal of Cold War Studies* 2, 2–38.

—— (1999), 'The early post-Stalin succession struggle and upheavals in East-Central Europe: Internal-external linkages in soviet policy making (Part 3)', *Journal of Cold War Studies* 3, 3–66.

Krasner, David (1995), 'Parody and double consciousness in the language of early Black musical theatre', *African American Review* 2, 317–23.

Krylova, Anna (2004), 'Stalinist identity from the viewpoint of gender: Rearing a generation of professionally violent women-fighters in 1930s Stalinist Russia', *Gender & History* 3, 626–53.

Krypton, Constantine (1954), 'The siege of Leningrad', *Russian Review* 4, 255–65.

Kühn, Volker (1984), *Das Kabarett der frühen Jahre: Ein freches Musenkind macht erste Schritte*, Berlin.

Kühne, Thomas (1996), '"…aus diesem Krieg werden nicht nur harte Männer heimkehren." Kriegskamaradschaft und Männlichkeit im 20. Jahrhundert' in T. Kühne (ed.), *Männergeschichte-Geschlechtergeschichte: Männlichkeit im Wandel der Moderne*, Frankfurt.

Kushner, Anthony (1989), *The Persistence of Prejudice*, Manchester.

Land, Hilary (1980), 'The family wage', *Feminist Review* 6, 55–77.

Lange, Horst (1996), *Jazz in Deutschland: Die deutsche Jazz Chronik bis 1960*, Hildesheim.

Langewiesche, Dieter (1979), 'Arbeiterkultur in Österreich: Aspekte, Tendenzen, Thesen' in G. Ritter (ed.), *Arbeiterkultur*, Königstein, 40–57.

Langhamer, Claire (2000), *Women's Leisure in England, 1920–60*, Manchester.

—— (2003), '"A public house is for all classes, men and women alike": Women, leisure and drink in Second World War England', *Women's History Review* 3, 423–43.

—— (2005), 'The meanings of home in postwar Britain', *Journal of Contemporary History* 2, 341–62.

Laqueur, Thomas (2003), *Solitary Sex: A cultural history of masturbation*, New York.

Law, Cheryl (1997), *Suffrage and Power: The women's movement, 1918–1928*, London.

Lawrence, Jon, Martin Dean, and Jean-Louis Robert (1992), 'The outbreak of war and the urban economy: Paris, Berlin and London in 1914', *Economic History Review* 3, 564–93.

Lees, Andrew (2000), 'Deviant sexuality and other "sins": The views of Protestant conservatives in imperial Germany', *German Studies Review* 3, 453–76.

Lefcourt, Jenny (2004), 'Aller au cinéma, aller au peuple', *Révue d'histoire modèrne et contemporaine*, Oct.–Dec., 98–114.

Leffler, Melvyn (1999), 'The cold war: What do "we know now"?', *American Historical Review* 2, 501–24.

LeGates, Richard and Frederic Stout (2003), *The City Reader*, London.

Le Goff, Jean-Pierre (1998), *Mai 68: l'héritage impossible*, Paris.

Lekan, Thomas (2004), *Imagining the Nation in Nature: Landscape preservation and German identity, 1885–1945*, London.

Lenz, Britta (2006), 'Vereint im Verein? Städtische Freizeitkulture und die Integration von Polnischen und Masurischen Zuwanderern im Ruhrgebiet, 1900–1939', *Archiv für Sozialgeschichte* 46, 183–203.

Leo XIII (1891), *Encyclical Letter of Our Holy Father By Divine Providence Pope Leo XIII On the Condition of Labour (Rerum Novarum: Official Translation)*, London.

Lewis, Beth (1971), *George Grosz: Art and Politics in Weimar Berlin*, London.

Lewis, Brian (2005), 'The queer life and afterlife of Roger Casement', *Journal of the History of Sexuality* 4, 363–82.

Liddington, Jill (2005), 'Era of commemoration: Celebrating the suffrage centenary', *History Workshop Journal* 59, 194–218.

Lidtke, Vernon (1985), *The Alternative Culture: Socialist labour in imperial Germany*, Oxford.

Liedtke, Rainer (1998), *Jewish Welfare in Hamburg and Manchester, c.1850–1914*, Oxford.

Lipsitz, George (1994), *Dangerous Crossroads: Popular music, postmodernism and the poetics of place*, London.

Livers, Keith (2001), 'The soccer match as Stalinist ritual: Constructing the body social in Lev Kassil's *The Goalkeeper of the Republic*', *Russian Review* 60, 592–613.

Longhurst, Brian (1995), *Popular Music and Society*, Cambridge.

Lowe, Keith (2007), *Inferno: The devastation of Hamburg, 1943*, London.

Lübbren, Nina (2001), *Rural Artists' Colonies in Europe, 1870–1910*, Manchester.

Luft, David (2003), *Eros and Inwardness in Vienna: Weininger, Musil, Doderer*, Chicago.

Lupi, Tineke and Sako Musterd (2004), 'The suburban "community question"', paper given at ESF Conference 'Cohesive Neighbourhoods and Connected Citizens in European Societies', Bristol, 17–18 June.

Lury, Karen (2005), *Interpreting Television*, London.

Lynch, John (1998), *A Tale of Three Cities: Comparative studies in working-class life*, London.

Lyon, Margot (1967), 'Christian-Democratic parties and politics', *Journal of Contemporary History* 4, 69–87.

Maase, Kaspar and Wolfgang Kaschuba (eds.) (2001), *Schund und Schönheit: Populäre Kultur um 1900*, Cologne.

McCloskey, Barbara (1997), *George Grosz and the Communist Party: Art and radicalism in crisis, 1918 to 1936*, Princeton, NJ.

McCreedy, Kenneth (2001), 'Planning the peace: Operation Eclipse and the occupation of Germany', *Journal of Military History* 3, 713–39.

McElligott, Anthony (1997), *Contested City: Municipal politics and the rise of Nazism in Altona 1917–37*, Ann Arbor, MI.

Machcewicz, Pawel (1997), 'Intellectuals and mass movements: The study of political dissent in Poland in 1956', *Contemporary European History* 3, 361–82.

McIvor, Arthur (2001), *A History of Work in Britain, 1880–1950*, London.

McKenna, Madeline (1991), 'The suburbanization of the working-class population of Liverpool between the wars', *Social History* 2, 173–89.

McKibbin, Ross (1998), *Classes and Cultures: England, 1918–1951*, London.

McLaren, Angus (1977), 'Abortions in England, 1890–1914', *Victorian Studies* 4, 379–400.

—— (1999), *Twentieth-Century Sexuality: A history*, Oxford.

McMillan, James (1999), *France and Women, 1789–1914: Gender, society and politics*, London.

McRandle, James and James Quirk (2006), 'The blood test revisited: A new look at German casualty counts in World War I', *Journal of Military History* 3, 667–701.

Maddrell, Paul (2005), 'The scientist who came in from the cold: Heinz Barwich's flight from the GDR', *Intelligence and National Security* 4, 608–630.

—— (2006), 'The Western secret services, the East German Ministry of State Security and the building of the Berlin Wall', *Intelligence and National Security* 5, 829–47.

Maderthaner, Wolfgang and Lutz Musner (1999), *Die Anarchie der Vorstadt: Das andere Wien um 1900*, Frankfurt.

—— (2002), 'Textures of the modern: Viennese Contributions to cultural history and urban studies', *Cultural Studies* 6, 863–76.

—— (2003), 'Outcast Vienna: The politics of transgression', *International Labour and Working-Class History* 64, 25–37.

Maines, Rachel (1999), *The Technology of Orgasm: 'Hysteria,' the vibrator and women's sexual satisfaction*, Baltimore, MD.

Malbon, Ben (1999), *Clubbing: Dancing, ecstasy, vitality*, London.

Mallgrave, Harry (1993), *Otto Wagner: Reflections on the raiment of modernity*, Santa Monica, CA.

Malmstad, John (2000), 'Bathhouses, hustlers and a sex club: The reception of Mikhail Kusmin's *Wings*', *Journal of the History of Sexuality* 1/2, 85–140.

Malone, Carolyn (2002), 'Campaigning journalism: The *Clarion*, the *Daily Citizen* and the protection of women workers, 1898–1912', *Labour History Review* 3, 281–97.

Mandel, David (1983), *The Petrograd Workers and the Fall of the Old Regime: From the February Revolution to the July Days*, London.

—— (1984), *The Petrograd Workers and the Soviet Seizure of Power: From the July Days 1917 to July 1918*, London.

Marchand, Bernard and Joélle Salomon Cavin (2007), 'Anti-urban ideologies and planning in France and Switzerland: Jean-François Gravier and Armin Meili', *Planning Perspectives* 22, 29–53.

Marcus, Sharon (1999), *Apartment Stories: City and home in nineteenth-century Paris and London*, London.

Mark, James (2005), 'Remembering rape: Divided social memory and the Red Army in Hungary, 1944–1945', *Past & Present* 188, 133–61.

Marks, Lara (1990), '"Dear Old Mother Levy's": The Jewish Maternity Home and Sick Room Helps Society, 1895–1939', *Social History of Medicine* 1, 61–88.

Markevich, Andrei (2005), 'Soviet urban households and the road to universal employment, from the end of the 1930s to the end of the 1960s', *Continuity and Change* 3, 443–73.

Marschik, Matthias (1999), 'Between manipulation and resistance: Viennese football in the Nazi era', *Journal of Contemporary History* 2, 215–19.

Marsh, Jan (1982), *Back to the Land*, London.

Marx, Karl and Friedrich Engels (2002), *The Communist Manifesto*, Oxford [1848].

Mastny, Vojtech (2005), 'Was 1968 a strategic watershed of the cold war?', *Diplomatic History* 1, 149–77.

May, Ruth (2003), 'Planned city Stalinstadt: A manifesto of the early German Democratic Republic', *Planning Perspectives* 18, 1–47.

Mayne, Allan (1993), *The Imagined Slum: Newspaper representations in three cities, 1870–1914*, Leicester.

Mazower, Mark (1998), *Dark Continent: Europe's twentieth century*, London.

Meacham, Standish (1998), *Regaining Paradise: Englishness and the early Garden City movement*, London.

Meller, Helen (1997), *Towns, Plans and Society in Modern Britain*, Cambridge.

—— (2001), *European Cities, 1890–1930: History, culture and the built environment*, Chichester.

Merrick, Jeffrey and Bryant Ragan (eds.), *Homosexuality in Modern France*, Oxford.

Meyer, Esther da Costa (1995), 'La donna è mobile', *Assemblage* 28, 6–15.

Michel, Henri (1982), *Paris Résistant*, Paris.

Micheler, Stefan (2002), 'Homophobic propaganda and the denunciation of same-sex-desiring men under National Socialism', *Journal of the History of Sexuality* 1/2.

Middleton, Nicos et al. (2003), 'Urban-rural differences in suicide trends in young adults: England and Wales, 1981–1998', *Social Science and Medicine* 7, 1183–94.

Middleton, Richard (2003), 'Music, modernisation and popular identity' in H. Dauncey and S. Cannon (eds.), *Popular Music in France from Chanson to Techno*, Aldershot, 1–6.

Miller, Neil (2006), *Out of the Past: Gay and lesbian history from 1869 to the present*, London.

Millman, Richard (1993), 'Les Croix-de-Feu et l'antisémitisme', *Vingtième Siècle* 38, 47–61.

Mitchell, B. R. (1962), *Abstract of British Historical Statistics*, Cambridge.

—— (1978), *European Historical Statistics, 1750–1970*, London.

Moeller, Robert (1989), 'Reconstructing the family in Reconstruction Germany: Women and social policy in the Federal Republic, 1949–1955', *Feminist Studies* 1, 137–69.

Moggridge, Donald (1992), *Maynard Keynes: An economist's biography*, London.

Montefiore, Simon Sebag (2004), *Stalin: The court of the Red Tsar*, London.

—— (2008), *Young Stalin*, London.

Moore, Alison (2005), 'History, memory and trauma in photography of the *Tondues*: Visuality of the Vichy past through the silent image of women', *Gender and History* 3, 657–81.

—— and Peter Cryle (2010), 'Frigidity at the fin de siècle in France: A slippery and capacious concept', *Journal of the History of Sexuality* 2, 243–61.

Moore, James Robert (2001), 'Progressive pioneers: Manchester Liberalism, the Independent Labour Party, and local politics in the 1890s', *Historical Journal* 4, 989–1013.

Moreck, Curt (1931), *Führer durch das lasterhafte Berlin*, Leipzig.

Mort, Frank (1999), 'Mapping sexual London: The Wolfenden Committee on homo-sexual offences and prostitution', *New Formations* 37, 92–112.

—— (2000), *Dangerous Sexualities: Medico-moral politics in England since 1830*, London.

Mosse, George (1985), *Nationalism and Sexuality: Respectability and abnormal sexuality in modern Europe*, New York.

—— (1990), 'The political culture of Italian futurism: A general perspective', *Journal of Contemporary History* 2–3, 253–68.

—— (1996), *The Image of Man: The invention of modern masculinity*, Oxford.

Moutet, Aimeé (1987), 'Une rationalisation du travail dans l'industrie française des années trente', *Annales* 5, 1061–78.

Müller, Agnes (ed.) (2004), *German Popular Culture: How 'American' is it?*, Ann Arbor, MI.

Müller, Corrine (2001), 'Der frühe Film, das frühe Kino und seine Gegner und Befürworter' in Kaspar Maase and Wolfgang Kaschuba (eds.), *Schund und Schönheit: Populäre Kultur um 1900*, Cologne, 62–91.

Mulligan, Gordon and Jason Crampton (2005), 'Population growth in the world's largest cities', *Cities* 5, 365–80.

Mumford, Eric (2000), *The CIAM Discourse on Urbanism, 1928–1960*, London.

Murphy, D., S. Kondrashev and G. Bailey (1997), *Battleground Berlin: CIA vs. KGB in the cold war*, London.

Murphy, Kevin (2005), *Revolution and Counterrevolution: Class struggle in a Moscow metal factory*, Oxford.

Murray, Bill (1984), *The Old Firm: Sectarianism, sport and society in Scotland*, Edinburgh.

Myhill, Andy and Jonathon Allen (2002), *Rape and Sexual Assault of Women: Key findings from the British Crime Survey*, Home Office, London.

Naiman, Eric (1999), *Sex in Public: The incarnation of early Soviet ideology*, Princeton, NJ.

Nead, Linda (2000), *Victorian Babylon: People, streets and images in nineteenth-century London*, London.

Neary, Rebecca Balmas (1999), 'Mothering socialist society: The wife-activists' movement and the Soviet culture of daily life, 1934–41', *Russian Review* 58, 396–412.

Neutatz, Dietmar (2001), *Die Moskauer Metro: Von den ersten Projekten bis zur Großbaustelle des Stalinismus (1897–1935)*, Cologne.

—— (2003), '"Schmiede des neuen Menschen" und Kostprobe des Sozialismus: Utopien des Moskauer Metrobaus' in W. Hardtwig (ed.), *Utopie und politische Herrschaft im Europa der Zwischenkriegszeit*, Munich, 41–56.

Noakes, Jeremy and Geoffrey Pridham (1985), *Nazism 1919–1945: State, economy and Society, 1933–38. A documentary reader*, Exeter.

Noiriel, Gérard (1990), *Workers in French Society in the 19th and 20th Centuries*, Oxford.

Nolan, Mary (2005), 'Germans as victims during the Second World War', *Central European History* 1, 7–40.

Nott, James (2002), *Music for the People: Popular music and dance in inter-war Britain*, Oxford.

Numbers, Ronald and John Stenhouse (eds.) (1999), *Disseminating Darwinism: The Role of place, race, religion and gender*, Cambridge.

Office of National Statistics (2009a), *Conception Statistics, England and Wales: Conceptions to women aged under 18: Annual numbers and rates*, <http://www.statistics.gov.uk/hub/search/index.html?newquery=teenage+conceptions>, accessed 3.12.09.

—— (2009b), *Housebuilding: September quarter 2009, England*, <http://www.communities.gov.uk/publications/corporate/statistics/housebuildingq32009†accessed 11.12.09>.

Ogawa, Mariko (2000), 'Uneasy bedfellows: Science and politics in the refutation of Koch's bacterial theory of cholera', *Bulletin of the History of Medicine* 74, 671–707.

O'Hara, Patrick (1997), ' "The woman of to-day": The *fin de siècle* women of the *Music Hall and Theatre Review*', *Victorian Periodicals Review* 2, 141–56.

Olechnowicz, Andrzej (1997), *Working-Class Housing in England Between the Wars: The Becontree Estate*, Oxford.

Oliver, P., I. Davis, and I. Bentley (1981) *Dunroamin: The suburban semi and its enemies*, London.

O'Mahony, Mike (2003), 'Archaeological fantasies: Constructing history on the Moscow metro', *Modern Language Review* 1, 138–50.

Operativstab PdVP Berlin, 17.6.09. LAGEBERICHT NR. 168 DES OPERATIVSTABES PDVP vom 17./18.6.1953, von 06.00 bis .... Uhr. Archiv der Bundeszentrale für politische Bildung, <http://www.17juni53.de/chronik/530617/53-06-17_paup-stab.html>.

Ost, David (1996), 'Polish labour before and after Solidarity', *International Labor and Working-Class History* 1, 29–43.

Ostermann, Christian (1996), ' "Keeping the pot simmering": The United States and the East German uprising of 1953', *German Studies Review* 1, 61–89.

O'Sullivan, Tim (1991), 'Television memories and cultures of viewing' in John Conver (ed.), *Popular Television in Britain*, London, 159–81.

Otter, Christopher (2004), 'Cleansing and clarifying: Technology and perception in nineteenth-century London', *Journal of British Studies* 1, 40–64; 157–60.

Otto, Rainer (1977), *Kabarettgeschichte: Abriss des deutschsprachigen Kabaretts*, Berlin.

Ouimet, Matthew (2003), *The Rise and Fall of the Brezhnev Doctrine in Soviet Foreign Policy*, London.

Ozouf, Jacques (1966), '*L'Humanité* et les journées de Février 1934 (1945–64)', *Le Mouvement social* 54, 151–71.

Palmer, Bryan (1995), 'Bread and roses: Sheila Rowbotham—the political and the accessible in the writing of gender history', *Radical History Review* 63, 159–65.

Park, Roberta (2005), 'Muscles, symmetry and action: "Do you measure up?" Defining masculinity in Britain and America from the 1860s to the early 1900s', *International Journal of the History of Sport* 3, 365–95.

Parry, D. L. L. (1998), 'Articulating the Third Republic by conspiracy theory', *European History Quarterly* 2, 163–88.

Passmore, Kevin (1995), 'Boy scouting for grown-ups? Paramilitarism in the Croix de Feu and the Parti Social Français', *French Historical Studies* 2, 527–57.

—— (2005), 'The construction of crisis in interwar France' in Brian Jenkins (ed.), *France in the Era of Fascism: Essays on the French authoritarian right*, Oxford, 151–99.

Pedersen, Susan (1993), *Family, Dependence and the Origins of the Welfare State in Britain and France, 1914–1945*, Cambridge.

Peniston, William (1998), 'The police and the subculture: Same-sex sexuality as crime in Paris in the 1870s', *Proceedings of the Western Society for French History* 26, 104–11.

Pensley, Danielle (1998), 'The socialist city? A critical analysis of *Neubaugebiet Hellersdorf*', *Journal of Urban History* 5, 563–602.

Persak, Krzysztof (2006), 'The Polish–Soviet confrontation in 1956 and the attempted Soviet military intervention in Poland', *Europe-Asia Studies* 8, 1285–310.

Peterson, Brian (1977), 'The politics of working-class women in the Weimar Republic', *Central European History* 2, 87–111.

Petrov, Iu. A (2000), 'Revolutionary Moscow: December 1905—rehearsal for civil war', *Russian Studies in History* 2, 52–75.

Phipps, Alison (ed.) (2002), *Contemporary German Cultural Studies*, London.

Pick, Daniel (1989), *Faces of Degeneration: A European Disorder, c.1848–c.1918*, Cambridge.

Pickering, Michael (2008), *Blackface Minstrelsy in Britain*, Aldershot.

Picon-Lefèbvre, Virginie (2003), *Paris—ville moderne: Maine-Montparnasse et la Défense, 1950–1975*, Paris.

Pinder, David (2005), *Visions of the City*, Edinburgh.

Platt, Harold (2004), '"Clever microbes": Bacteriology and sanitary technology in Manchester and Chicago during the Progressive Age', *Osiris* 19, 149–66.

Poggi, Christine (2002), '"Folla/Follia": Futurism and the crowd', *Critical Inquiry* 3, 709–48.

Poiger, Ute (1996), 'Rock 'n' Roll, Female sexuality and the cold war battle over German identities', *Journal of Modern History* 3, 577–616.

Poplawska, Irena and Stefan Muthesius (1986), 'Poland's Manchester: 19th-century industrial and domestic architecture in Lodz', *Journal of the Society of Architectural Historians* 2, 148–60.

Porter, Brian (2001), *When Nationalism Began to Hate: Imagining modern politics in nineteenth-century Poland*, Oxford.

Power, Anne (1999), *Estates on the Edge: The social consequences of mass housing in Northern Europe*, London.

Poynting, Scott (2007), 'The resistible rise of Islamophobia', *Journal of Sociology* 1, 61–86.

Preston, Margaret (2004), *Charitable Words: Women, philanthropy, and the language of charity in nineteenth-century Dublin*, Westport, CT.

Pretzel, Andreas (2002), 'Aufbruch und Resignation: Zur Geschichte der Berliner "Gesellschaft für die Reform des Sexualrechts e.V.", 1948–196' in Andreas Pretzel (ed.), *NS-Opfer unter Vorbehalt: Homosexuelle Männer in Berlin nach 1945*, Hamburg, 287–338.

Pringle, Robert (2004), 'Modernization of terror: The transformation of Stalin's NKVD, 1934–1941', *International Journal of Intelligence and Counter Intelligence* 1, 113–23.

Purvis, June and Maureen Wright (2005), 'Writing suffrage history: the contending autobiographical narratives of the Pankhursts', *Women's History Review* 3–4, 405–33.

Rainer, Janos (1997), 'The development of Imre Nagy as a politician and a thinker', *Contemporary European History* 3, 263–77.

Rapp, Dean (2002), 'Sex in the cinema: War, moral panic, and the British film industry, 1906–1918', *Albion* 3, 422–51.

Rappaport, Erika (2000), *Shopping for Pleasure: Women in the making of London's West End*, London.

Ravetz, Alison (1974), *Model Estate: Planned Housing at Quarry Hill, Leeds*, London.

—— (1986), *The Government of Space: Town planning in modern society*, London.

—— (1995), *The Place of Home: English Domestic Environments, 1914–2000*, London.

—— (2001), *Council Housing and Culture: The history of social experiment*, London.

Read, Christopher (1996), *From Tsar to Soviets: The Russian people and their revolution, 1917–1921*, London.

Rearick, Charles (1985), *Pleasures of the* Belle Époque*: Entertainment and festivity in turn-of-the-century France*, London.

—— (1988), 'Song and society in turn-of-the-century France', *Journal of Social History* 1, 45–63.

—— (1997), *The French in Love and War: Popular culture and the era of the world wars*, London.

Recker, Marie-Luise (1981), *Die Großstadt als Wohn- und lebensbereich im Nationalsozialismus: zur Gründung der 'Stadt des KdF-Wagens'*, Frankfurt am Main.

Redhead, Steve (ed.) (1998), *The Clubcultures Reader: Readings in popular cultural studies*, Oxford.

Reed, Matt (2001), 'Historicising inversion: Or, how to make a homosexual', *History of the Human Sciences* 4, 1–29.

Reese, Dagmar (2006), *Growing Up Female in Nazi Germany*, Ann Arbor, MI.

Reid, Susan (2002), 'Cold war in the kitchen: Gender and the de-Stalinization of consumer taste in the Soviet Union under Khrushchev', *Slavic Review* 2, 211–52.

—— (2005), 'The Khrushchev kitchen: Domesticating the scientific-technological revolution', *Journal of Contemporary History* 2, 289–316.

Reynolds, David (2002), 'From World War to Cold War: The wartime alliance and post-war transitions, 1941–1947', *Historical Journal* 1, 211–27.

Richards, Jeffrey and Dorothy Sheridan (1987), *Mass-Observation at the Movies*, London.

Rider Haggard, Henry (1905), *The Poor and the Land*, London.

Ridgwell, Stephen (1995), 'South Wales and the cinema in the 1930s', *Welsh History Review* 4, 590–615.

Riedi, Eliza (2000), 'Options for an imperialist woman: The case of Violet Markham, 1899–1914', *Albion* 1, 59–84.

Rifkin, Adrian (1993), *Street Noises: Parisian pleasure, 1900–1940*, Manchester.

Riis, Thomas (1986), 'The experience and impact of Black entertainers in England, 1895–1920', *American Music* 1, 50–8.

Rioux, Lucien and René Backmann (1969), *L'Explosion de mai: 11 mai 1968—Histoire complète des événements*, Paris.

Ritter, Gerhard and Klaus Tenfelde (1992), *Arbeiter im deutschen Kaiserreich, 1871–1914*, Bonn.

Ritzel, Fred (1998), '"Was ist aus uns geworden? Ein Häufchen Sand am Meer: Emotions of post-war Germany as extracted from examples of popular music', *Popular Music* 3, 293–309.

—— (2001), 'Synkopen-Tänze: Über Importe populäre Musik aus Amerika in der Zeit vor dem Ersten Weltkrieg' in Kaspar Maase and Wolfgang Kaschuba (eds.), *Schund und Schönheit: Populäre Kultur um 1900*, Cologne, 161–83.

Roberts, Mary Louise (1994), *Civilization without Sexes: Reconstructing gender in postwar France, 1917–1927*, London.

Robinson, Robert and William Sutherland (2002), 'Post-war changes in arable farming and biodiversity in Great Britain', *Journal of Applied Ecology* 39, 157–76.

Rodger, Richard (2000), 'Slums and suburbs: The persistence of residential apartheid' in Philip Waller (ed.), *The English Urban Landscape*, Oxford, pp. 242–68.

Rosario, Vernon (1996), 'Pointy penises, fashion crimes and hysterical Mollies: The pederasts' inversions' in Jeffrey Merrick and Bryant Ragan (eds.), *Homosexuality in Modern France*, Oxford, 146–76.

Rose, Sonya (1998), 'Sex, citizenship and the nation in World War II Britain', *American Historical Review* 4, 1147–76.

Ross, Corey (2002), 'Before the Wall: East Germans, communist authority and the mass exodus to the West', *Historical Journal* 2, 459–80.

Rowe, Dorothy (2003), *Representing Berlin: Sexuality and the city in imperial and Weimar Germany*, Aldershot.

Rudolph, Nicole (2004), 'Domestic politics: The Cité experimentale at Noisy-le-Sec in Greater Paris', *Modern & Contemporary France* 4, 483–95.

Rupp, Leila (1997), *Worlds of Women: The making of an international women's movement*, Princeton, NJ.

Russell, Dave (1997), *Football and the English: A social history of Association Football in England*, Preston.

Rycroft, Simon (2002), 'The geographies of swinging London', *Journal of Historical Geography* 4, 566–88.

Ryklin, Mikhail (2003), '"The best in the world": The discourse of the Moscow metro in the 1930s' in E. Dobrenko and E. Naiman (eds.), *The Landscape of Stalinism: The art and ideology of Soviet Space*, London, 261–76.

Sadler, Simon (2003), 'The *Living City Survival Kit*: A portrait of the architect as a young man', *Art History* 4, 553–75.

Sampson, Gary and Alexander Yeats (1977), 'An evaluation of the Common Agricultural Policy as a barrier facing agricultural exports to the European Economic Community', *American Journal of Agricultural Economics* 59, 99–106.

Sandbrook, Dominic (2007), *Never Had it so Good: A history of Britain from Suez to the Beatles*, London.

—— (2008), *White Heat: 1964–1970—a history of Britain in the swinging sixties*, London.

Sandvoß, Hans-Rainer (2005), *Die 'andere' Reichshaupstadt: Widerstand aus der Arbeiterbewegung von 1933 bis 1945*, Berlin.

Sarasin, Philipp (2004), 'Die Visualisierung des Feindes: Über metaphorische Technologien der frühen Bakteriologie', *Geschichte und Gesellschaft* 2, 250–76.

Sassoon, Donald (2006), *The Culture of the Europeans from 1800 to the Present*, London.

Satre, Lowell (1982), 'After the match girls' strike: Bryant and May in the 1890s', *Victorian Studies* 1, 7–31.

Sauer, Bernhard (2005), 'Zur politischen Haltung der Berliner Sicherheitspolizei in der Weimarer Republik', *Zeitschrift für Geschichtswissenschaft* 1, 26–45.

Saunders, Thomas (1994), *Hollywood in Berlin: American cinema and Weimar Germany*, London.

Saurer, Edith (1997), 'Zur Säkularisierung des Sündenkonzepts: Die Genese des strafrechtlichen Konzepts der "Erregung der Öffentlichen Ärgernisses"', *Wiener Beiträge zur Geschichte der Neuzeit* 22, 200–19.

Savage, Jon (2001), *England's Dreaming: Sex Pistols and punk rock*, London.

Schake, Kori (2002), 'A broader range of choice? US policy in the 1958 and 1961 Berlin crises' in John Gearson and Kori Schake (eds.), *The Berlin Wall Crisis: Perspectives on cold war alliances*, London, 22–42.

Schivelbusch, Wolfgang (1998), *In a Cold Crater: Cultural and intellectual life in Berlin, 1945–1948*, London.

Schneider, Ulrich (1984), *Die Londoner Music Hall und ihre Songs, 1850–1920*, Tübingen.

Schofield, Michael (1965), *Sociological Aspects of Homosexuality: A comparative study of three types of homosexuals*, London.

Schulman, Seth (2000), *The Celebrity Culture of Modern Nightlife: Music hall, dance and jazz in interwar Paris, 1918–1930*, unpublished doctoral dissertation, Brown University.

Scott, James (1998), *Seeing Like a State: How certain schemes to improve the human condition have failed*, London.

Scott, Linda (2006), *Fresh Lipstick: Redressing fashion and feminism*, London.

Scrivano, Paolo (2005), 'Signs of Americanization in Italian domestic life: Italy's postwar conversion to consumerism', *Journal of Contemporary History* 2, 317–40.

Segel, Harold (1987), *Turn-of-the-Century Cabaret: Paris, Barcelona, Berlin, Munich, Vienna, Cracow, Moscow, St Petersburg, Zurich*, New York.

Seidman, Michael (2001), 'The pre-May 1968 sexual revolution', *Contemporary French Civilisation* 1, 20–41.

Sellars, A. (1998), 'The influence of dance music on the UK youth tourism market', *Tourism Management* 6, 611–25.

Sennett, Richard (1977), *The Fall of Public Man: The Forces eroding public life and burdening the psyche with roles it cannot perform*, London.

Service, Robert (2009), *Trotsky: A biography*, London.

Shack, William (2001), *Harlem in Montmartre: A Paris jazz story between the great wars*, London.

Shandley, Robert (2001), *Rubble Films: German cinema in the shadow of the Third Reich*, Philadelphia, PA.

—— (2004), 'The press and the system built developments of inner-city Manchester, 1960s–1980s', *Manchester Region History Review* Summer, 30–9.

—— (2006), 'Tenants arise! Consumerism, tenants and the challenge to council authority in Manchester, 1968–92', *Social History* 1, 60–78.

—— Duncan Tanner, and Andrew Walling (2004), 'Civic culture and housing policy in Manchester, 1945–79', *Twentieth Century British History* 4, 410–34.

Shapiro, Anne-Louise (1985), *Housing the Poor of Paris, 1850–1920*, London.

Sharp, Jane (1999), 'The Russian avant-garde and its audience: Moscow, 1913', *Modernism-Modernity*, 91–116.

Showalter, Elaine (1992), *Sexual Anarchy: Gender and culture at the fin-de-siècle*, London.

Silverstone, Roger (1984), *Television and Everyday Life*, London.

—— (ed.) (1997), *Visions of Suburbia*, London.

Simmonds, Alan (2001), 'Conservative governments and the new town housing question in the 1950s', *Urban History* 1, 65–83.

Simonelli, David (2002), 'Anarchy, pop and violence: Punk rock subculture and the rhetoric of class, 1976–78', *Contemporary British History* 2, 121–44.

Sinha, Mrinalini, Donna Guy, and Angela Wollacott (eds.) (1999), *Feminisms and Internationalism, Gender and History*, special issue, Oxford.

Skinner, Frederick (1976), 'Trends in planning practices: The building of Odessa, 1794–1917' in Michael Hamm (ed.), *The City in Russian History*, Lexington, KY, pp. 139–59.

Sladen, Chris (2005), 'Wartime holidays and the myth of the blitz', *Cultural and Social History* 2, 215–46.

Smith, Malcolm (2000), *Britain and 1940: History, myth and popular memory*, London.

Smith, S. A. (1985), *Red Petrograd: Revolution in the factories, 1917–1918*, Cambridge.

Smith, Timothy (2000), 'The plight of the able-bodied poor and unemployed in France, 1880–1914', *European History Quarterly* 2, 147–84.

Sohn, Anne-Marie (1995), 'The golden age of male adultery: The Third Republic', *Journal of Social History* 3, 469–90.

Soja, Ed (1989), *Postmodern Geographies: The reassertion of space in critical social theory*, London.

Solomon, Robert (1988), *Continental Philosophy since 1750: The rise and fall of the self*, Oxford.

Somerset, Richard (2000–1), 'Transformism, evolution and romanticism', *Nineteenth-Century French Studies* 1–2, 1–20.

Somerville, Siobhan (1994), 'Scientific racism and the emergence of the homosexual body', *Journal of the History of Sexuality* 2, 243–66.

Sonn, Richard (2005), '"Your body is yours": Anarchism, birth control and eugenics in interwar France', *Journal of the History of Sexuality* 4, 415–31.

Sonnessa, Antonio (2005), 'The 1922 Turin massacre: Working class resistance and conflicts within fascism', *Modern Italy* 2, 187–205.

Sosnovy, Timothy (1959), 'The Soviet housing situation today', *Europe-Asia Studies* 1, 1–21.

Soucy, Robert (1981), 'Centrist fascism: The Jeunesses Patriotes', *Journal of Contemporary History* 2, 349–68.

—— (1999), 'Functional hating: French fascist demonology between the wars', *Contemporary French Civilization* 2, 158–76.

—— (2005), 'Fascism in France: Problematising the immunity thesis' in Brian Jenkins (ed.), *France in the Era of Fascism: Essays on the French authoritarian right*, Oxford, 65–104.

Sparkle, Penny (1995), *As Long as It's Pink: The sexual politics of taste*, London.

Spector, Scott (2007), 'The wrath of "Countess Merviola": Tabloid exposé and the emergence of homosexual subjects in Vienna in 1907', *Contemporary Austrian Studies* 15, 31–47.

Spence, Jean (2004), 'Working for Jewish girls: Lily Montagu, girls' clubs and industrial reform, 1890–1914', *Women's History Review* 3, 491–509.

Stanley, Adam (2004), 'Hearth, home and steering wheel: Gender and modernity in France after the Great War', *The Historian* 2, 234–53.

Starr, S. Frederick (1976), 'The revival and schism of urban planning in twentieth century Russia' in Michael Hamm (ed.), *The City in Russian History*, Lexington, KY, 222–42.

Staub, Alexandra (2005), 'St Petersburg's double life: The planners' versus the people's city', *Journal of Urban History* 3, 334–54.

Steege, Paul (2005), 'Holding on in Berlin: March 1948 and SED efforts to control the Soviet zone', *Central European History* 3, 417–49.

Steinberg, Mark (1996), 'The urban landscape in workers' imagination', *Russian History* 1, 47–65.

Stenberg, Kim Yoonok (1998), 'Working-class women in London local politics, 1894–1914', *Twentieth Century British History* 3, 323–429.

Stevens, James (1953), 'A Berlin diary: Winter, 1953', *Tempo* 30, 22–7.

Stewart, Mary (2001), *For Health and Beauty: Physical culture for Frenchwomen, 1880s–1930s*, Baltimore, MD.

Stibbe, Matthew (2003), *Women in the Third Reich*, London.

Stieber, Nancy (1998), *Housing Design and Society in Amsterdam: Reconfiguring urban order and identity, 1900–1920*, London.

Stites, Richard (1984), 'Utopias of time, pace and life in the Russian Revolution', *Révue des études slaves* 1, 141–54.

Stovall, Tyler (1998), 'The colour line behind the lines: Racial violence in France during the Great War', *American Historical Review* 3, 737–69.

Strange, Lisa and Robert Brown (2002), 'The bicycle, women's rights, and Elizabeth Cady Stanton', *Women's Studies* 5, 609–26.

Stuart, Robert (1999), '"A 'De Profundis' for Christian Socialism": French Marxists and the critique of political Catholicism, 1882–1905', *French Historical Studies* 2, 241–61.

Studer, Brigitte (2000), 'Familialisierung und Individualisierung: Zur Struktur der Geschlechterordnung in der bürgerlichen Gesellschaft', *Homme* 1, 83–104.

Südekum, Albert (*c.*1909), *Großstädtisches Wohnungselend*, Berlin and Leipzig.

—— (1998a), *Reconstructing Women's Wartime Lives: Discourse and subjectivity in oral histories of the Second World War*, Manchester.

—— (1998b), '"They didn't want women back in that job": The Second World War and the construction of gendered work histories', *Labour History Review* 1, 83–103.

—— and Corinna Peniston-Bird (2000), 'Women in the firing line: The Home Guard and the defence of gender boundaries in Britain in the Second World War', *Women's History Review* 2, 231–54.

Sun, Raymond (2005), '"Hammer blows": Work, the workplace and the culture of masculinity among Catholic workers in the Weimar Republic', *Central European History* 2, 245–71.

Surh, Gerals (1981), 'Petersburg's first mass labour organisation: The Assembly of Russian Workers and Father Gapon', Pts. I and II, *Russian Review* 2/4.

Sweeney, Dennis (2003), 'Cultural practice and utopian desire in German Social Democracy: Reading Adolf Levenstein's *Arbeiterfrage* (1912)', *Social History* 2, 174–201.

Swenarton, Mark (1981), *Homes Fit for Heroes: The politics and architecture of early state housing in Britain*, London.

—— (2002), 'Tudor Walters and Tudorbethan: Reassessing Britain's inter-war suburbs', *Planning Perspectives* 3, 267–86.

Swett, Pamela (2004), *Neighbors and Enemies: The culture of radicalism in Berlin, 1929–1933*, Cambridge.

Szreter, Simon and Graham Mooney (1998), 'Urbanization, mortality and the standard of living debate: New estimates of the expectation of life at birth in nineteenth-century British cities', *Economic History Review* 1, 84–112.

—— Robert Nye, and Frans von Poppel (2003), 'Fertility and contraception during the demographic transition: Qualitative and quantitative approaches', *Journal of Interdisciplinary History* 2, 141–54.

Tartakowsky, Danielle (1986), 'Stratégies de la rue. 1934–1936', *Le Mouvement social* 135, 31–62.

Tatar, Maria (1996), *Lustmord: Sexual murder in Weimar Germany*, Chichester.

Taylor, Matthew (2005), *The Leaguers: The making of professional football in England, 1900–1939*, Liverpool.

Taylor, Richard (1983), 'A "cinema for the millions": Soviet socialist realism and the problem of film comedy', *Journal of Contemporary History* 3, 439–61.

Thébaud, Françoise (1994), *A History of Women in the West*, V: *Toward a Cultural Identity in the Twentieth Century*, London.

Theweleit, Klaus (1987), *Male Fantasies*, 2 vols., I: *Women, Floods, Bodies, History*, Cambridge (Minneapolis, MN, 1989).

—— (1989), *Male Fantasies*, 2 vols., II: *Psychoanalysing the White Terror*, Cambridge and Minneapolis, MN.

Thompson, Christopher and Fiona Ratkoff (2000), 'Un troisième sexe? Les bourgeoises et la bicyclette dans la France fin de siècle', *Mouvement Social* 192, 9–39.

Thompson, Victoria (2000), *The Virtuous Marketplace: Women and men, money and politics in Paris, 1830–1870*, Baltimore, MD.

Thumser, Regina (2000), ' "Ernst ist das Leben, Heiter is die Kunst": Kabarett im Österreich der Zwischenkriegszeit', *Zeitgeschichte* 6, 386–96.

Tilly, Louise (1979), 'The family wage economy of a French textile city: Roubaix, 1872–1906', *Journal of Family History* 4, 381–94.

—— (1992), *Politics and Class in Milan, 1880–1901*, Oxford.

—— (1995), 'Structure and action in the making of Milan's working class', *Social Science History* 2, 243–59.

Tilly, Louise and Joan Scott (1975), 'Women's work and the family in 19th-century Europe', *Comparative Studies in Society and History* 1, 36–64.

—— (1978), *Women, Work and Family*, London.

Timm, Annette (1998), 'The legacy of *Bevölkerungspolitik*: Venereal disease control and marriage counselling in post World War II Berlin', *Canadian Journal of History* 2, 173–214.

Tinkler, Penny (2003), 'Cause for concern: Young women and leisure, 1930–50', *Women's History Review* 2, 233–60.

Tiratsoo, Nick (ed.) (2002), *Urban Reconstruction in Britain and Japan, 1945–1955: Dreams, plans and realities*, Luton.

Todd, Selina (2003), ' "Boisterous workers": Young women, industrial rationalisation and workplace militancy in interwar England', *Labour History Review* 3, 294–310.

—— (2004), 'Poverty and aspiration: Young women's entry into the labour market in interwar England', *Twentieth Century British History* 2, 119–242.

—— (2005), 'Young women, work and leisure in interwar England', *Historical Journal* 3, 789–809.

Tomlinson, Richard (1985), 'The "disappearance" of France, 1896–1940: French politics and the birth rate', *Historical Journal* 2, 405–15.

Tosh, John (1994), 'What should historians do with masculinity? Reflections on nineteenth-century Britain', *History Workshop Journal* 38, 179–202.

—— (1999), *A Man's Place: Masculinity and the middle-class home in Victorian England*, London.

—— (2005a), *Manliness and Masculinities in Nineteenth-century Britain: Essays on gender, family and empire*, London.

—— (2005b), 'Masculinities in an industrialising society: Britain, 1800–1914', *Journal of British Studies* 2, 330–42.

Töteberg, Michael (1985), *Fritz Lang: Mit Selbstzeugnissen und Bilddokumenten*, Hamburg.

Tournès, Ludovic (1999), *New Orléans sur Seine: Histoire du jazz en France*, Paris.

Troitsky, Artemy (1988), *Back in the USSR: The true story of rock in Russia*, London.

Tsivian, Yuri (1998), *Early Cinema in Russia and its Cultural Reception*, Chicago, IL.

Tumbler, Howard (1982), *Television and the Riots*, London.

Tumblety, Joan (2003), 'Responses to women's enfranchisement in France, 1944–1945', *Women's Studies International Forum* 5, 483–97.

Turot, H. (1907), *Le surpeuplement et les habitations à bonmarché*, Paris.

Ugolini, Laura (2002), ' "We must stand by our own bairns": ILP men and suffrage militancy, 1905–1914', *Labour History Review* 2, 149–69.

United Nations (1957), *Report of the Special Committee of the United Nations on the Problem of Hungary*, General Assembly Official Records: Eleventh Session, Supplement No. 18 (A/3592), New York.

United Nations Department of Economic and Social Affairs, Population Division (2009), *World Urbanization Prospects: The 2009 revision*, New York.

Valli, Roberta Suzzi (2000), 'The myth of Squadrismo in the fascist regime', *Journal of Contemporary History* 2, 131–50.

Vallin, Jacques et al. (2002), 'A new estimate of Ukrainian population losses during the crises of the 1930s and 1940s', *Population Studies* 3, 249–64.

Veitch, Colin (1985), 'Play up! Play up! And Win the War! Football, the nation and the First World War, 1914–1915', *Journal of Contemporary History* 3, 363–78.

Vernon, James (1993), *Politics and the People: A study in English political culture, 1815–1867*, Cambridge.

Vining, Margaret and Barton Hacker (2001), 'From camp follower to lady in uniform: Women, Social class and military institutions before 1920', *Contemporary European History* 3, 353–573.

Virgili, Fabrice (2002), *Shorn Women: Gender and punishment in Liberation France*, Oxford.

Wacquant, Loïc (2006), *Parias Urbains: Ghettos—Banlieus—Etat*, Paris.

Waite, Robert (1998), 'Teenage sexuality in Nazi Germany', *Journal of the History of Sexuality* 3, 434–76.

Wakeman, Rosemary (2004), 'Nostalgic Modernism and the Invention of Paris in the Twentieth Century', *French Historical Studies* 1, 115–44.

Walkowitz, Judith (1982), 'Jack the Ripper and the myth of male violence', *Feminist Studies* 3, 541–74.

—— (1992), *City of Dreadful Delight: Narratives of sexual danger in late-Victorian London*, London.

—— (2003), 'The "Vision of Salome": Cosmopolitanism and erotic dancing in central London, 1908–1918', *American Historical Review* 2, 337–76.

Wall, Richard and Jay Winter (1988), *The Upheaval of War: Family, work and welfare in Europe, 1914–18*, Cambridge.

Wall, Tim (2006), 'Out on the floor: The politics of dancing on the Northern Soul scene', *Popular Music* 3, 431–45.

Ward, Stephen (1988), *The Geography of Interwar Britain: The state and uneven development*, London.

Ward, Stephen (2002), *Planning the Twentieth-Century City: The advanced capitalist world*, Chichester.

Warne, C. (1997), 'The mean(ing of the) streets: Reading urban cultures in contemporary France' in S Blowen et al. (eds.), *Recollections of France: Memories, identities and heritage*, Oxford, 226–45.

Weber, Eugen (1976), *Peasants into Frenchmen: The modernisation of rural France*, Stanford, CA.

Weihsmann, Helmut (1980), *Das Rote Wien: Kommunaler Wohnbau für Wiens Bevölkerung während der Sozialdemokratie, 1919–1934*, Vienna.

Weikart, Richard (2002), 'Darwinism and death: Devaluing human life in Germany, 1859–1920', *Journal of the History of Ideas* 63, 323–44.

—— (2006), *From Darwin to Hitler: Evolutionary ethics, eugenics and racism in Germany*, London.

Weiner, Susan (1999), 'Two modernities: From *Elle* to *Mademoiselle*: Women's magazines in post-war France', *Contemporary European History* 3, 395–409.

—— (2001), *Enfants Terribles: Youth and femininity in the mass media in France, 1945–1968*, Baltimore, MD.

Weinthal, Lois (2005), 'Postcard from the German Democratic Republic: A view of the domestic realm', *Space and Culture* 3, 325–31.

Wende, Waltraud (1999), *Großstadtlyrik*, Nitzingen.

Werrell, Kenneth (1986), 'The strategic bombing of Germany in World War II: Costs and accomplishments', *Journal of American History* 3, 702–13.

Westwood, Gordon [Michael Schofield] (1960), *A Minority: A report on the life of the male homosexual in Great Britain*, London.

Whisnant, Clayton (2006), 'Styles of masculinity in the West German gay scene, 1950–1965', *Central European History* 29, 359–93.

White, Jerry (1986), *The Worst Street in North London: Campbell Bunk, Islington, between the wars*, London.

Whitehand, Jeremy and Christine Carr (1999), 'Morphological periods, planning and reality: The case of England's inter-war suburbs', *Urban History* 2, 230–48.

—— (2001), *Twentieth-Century Suburbs: A morphological approach*, London.

Whitford, Frank (ed.) (1997), *The Berlin of Georg Grosz*, London.

Wilkinson, Glenn (1998), 'The blessings of war: Depictions of military force in Edwardian newspapers', *Journal of Contemporary History* 1, 97–115.

Williams, Charles (1998), *The Last Great Frenchman: A life of General de Gaulle*, London.

Williams, John Alexander (2001), 'Ecstasies of the young: Sexuality, the youth movement and moral panic in Germany on the eve of the First World War', *Central European History* 2, 163–89.

Williams, Kieran (1996), 'New sources on Soviet decision making during the 1968 Czechoslovak crisis', *Europe-Asia Studies* 3, 457–70.

Williams, Raymond (1958), *Culture and Society: 1780–1950*, London.

Williams, Richard (2004), *The Anxious City: English urbanism in the late twentieth century*, London.

Willmott, Peter and Michael Young (1957), *Family and Kinship in East London*, London.

Wilson, Elizabeth (1991), *The Sphinx and the City: Urban life, the control of disorder and women*, London.

Wishnia, Judith (1995), 'Natalisme et nationalisme pendant la Première Guerre Mondiale', *Vingtième Siècle* 45, 30–9.

Wistrich, Robert (1983), 'Karl Lueger and the ambiguities of Viennese anti-Semitism', *Jewish Social Studies* 3/4, 251–62.

Wollstonecraft, Mary (2007), *Vindication of the Rights of Woman*, Sioux Falls, SD [London, 1792].

Worpole, Ken (2000), *Here Comes the Sun: Architecture and public space in twentieth-century European culture*, London.

Wright, Anthony and Matt Carter (1997), *The People's Party: A history of the Labour Party*, London.

Publishers Acknowledgements

We are grateful to the following for permission to include extracts from song lyrics in this book.

Music Sales Ltd and Hal Leonard Corporation for The Jam: 'Down by the Tube Station at Midnight', words and music by Paul Weller, © copyright 1978 Careers and Stylist Music Ltd, Universal Music Publishing MGB Ltd, all rights in Germany administered by Musik Edition Discoton GmbH (a division of Universal Music Publishing Group). All rights reserved. International copyright secured.

Warner/Chappell Music Ltd for Marlene Dietrich: 'Allein in einer grossen Stadt', words by Max Colpet, music by Franz Waxman, © Siegal Ralph Maria Musik Edition Nachfolger KG (Germany). All rights administered by Warner/Chappell Music Ltd.

Photographic Acknowledgements

© akg-images: 2.2; © the Author: 4.3, 6.3; from Thomas Burke, *For your convenience: a learned dialogue instructive to all Londoners*, Routledge, 1937: 4.2; © Alain Nogues/Corbis Sygma: 2.6; from *Das Neue Frankfurt*: 5.2; courtesy of George Eastman House, International Museum of Photography and Film: 6.1; by permission of the French Ministry of Defence: 1.2; © Margaret Bourke-White/Time & Life Pictures/Getty Images: 5.3; © GAB Archives/Redferns/Getty Images: 5.9; © Hulton Archive/Getty Images: 1.1, 2.1; from Ebenezer Howard, *Garden Cities of Tomorrow: A Peaceful Path to Real Reform*: 5.1; © NYPL Performing Arts/Lebrecht Music & Arts: 3.3; Lewisham Local History Centre: 5.4; Local Studies Library, London Borough of Bromley: 5.5; Manchester Archives and Local Studies Unit: 3.1, 3.2; © The sun/nisyndication.com/John Frost Newspapers: 6.2; © 2010 BPK, Berlin/Scala, Florence: 2.3; © 2010 Christian Schad Stiftung Aschaffenburg/VG Bild-Kunst, Bonn, and DACS, London: 4.1; © NMPFT/Daily Herald Archive/Science & Society Picture Library: 3.5; © Roger-Viollet/TopFoto: 1.4, 2.4, 2.5, 3.4, 5.7, 5.8; © ullsteinbild/TopFoto: 1.3; © Dodge Color Inc./United States Holocaust Memorial Museum: 5.6

Index

Figures are indexed in bold.